Inside Case-based
Explanation

Artificial Intelligence Series

Inside Case-based Explanation

Roger C. Schank
Alex Kass
Christopher K. Riesbeck

The Institute for the Learning Sciences
Northwestern University

Ψ Psychology Press
Taylor & Francis Group

New York London

First Published by

Lawrence Erlbaum Associates, Inc., Publishers
365 Broadway
Hillsdale, New Jersey 07642

Transferred to Digital Printing 2009 by Psychology Press
270 Madison Ave, New York NY 10016
27 Church Road, Hove, East Sussex, BN3 2FA

Cover design by Kate Dusza

Library of Congress Cataloging-in-Publication Data

Schank, Roger C., 1946-
        Inside case-based explanation / Roger C. Schank, Alex Kass,
    Christopher K. Riesbeck.
            p.   cm.
        Includes bibliographical references and index.
        ISBN 0-8058-1028-5 (cloth). — ISBN 0-8058-1029-3 (pbk.)
        1. Case-based reasoning.   2. Explanation-based learning.
    I. Kass, Alex.   II. Riesbeck, Christopher K.   III. Title.
    Q338.8.S3   1994
    006.3—dc20   94-1638
                                                             CIP

Publisher's Note
The publisher has gone to great lengths to ensure the quality of this reprint
but points out that some imperfections in the original may be apparent.

Contents

List of Figures

List of Tables

Preface

This book is the third volume in a series that had its genesis more than 15 years ago. The purpose of the series is to provide a hands-on perspective on the evolving theories associated with Roger Schank and his students. That theoretical perspective has become known as the "Yale view of AI" (although none of the people associated with this view remain at Yale).

The *Inside* Series

Although Schank and his students have written many articles, theses, and books that present their theories in the normal academic form, we believe that the *Inside* series continues to serve a unique and important role. Most of the theses and articles that we and other artificial intelligence researchers write are intended to describe theoretical results to fellow researchers. At the other end of the spectrum, Schank has written several books that reach out to a popular audience whose interest in Yale AI is genuine but casual. The *Inside* books fill a gap left between the popular book and the academic article by aiming at the serious student of AI. That audience includes anyone who wants a more technical discussion than the lay reader, but who is not necessarily a fully trained AI researcher. In particular, we aim at graduate students in AI and professionals in other academic fields who seek the retraining necessary to join the AI effort, or at least understand it at the professional level.

We assume that the AI student may need more basic background than the mature researcher, but we also assume that the student will be willing and able to get down into the details of our work in a way that neither casual observers, nor active professionals generally have time to do. This is why we feel that the "micro programs" have been an important part of the *Inside* books. We believe in learning by doing. By providing miniature versions of the programs we describe, which the student can run, modify, and extend, we make it possible for the student to take a hands-on approach to understanding our theories. We have found that these miniatures have made *Inside Computer Under-*

standing and *Inside Case-based Reasoning* very valuable teaching tools, not only for advanced undergraduates and beginning graduate students in AI, but also for professional scientists, such as psychologists, educators, and even computer scientists trained outside the Schankian school, who wish to learn how to actually do the kind of work we do. We hope that *Inside Case-based Explanation* will continue this tradition by making some of our more recent work equally accessible.

Why Explanation?

The primary focus of this book is on constructing explanations. All of the chapters in some way relate to the problem of building computer programs that can develop hypotheses about what might have caused an observed event. This focus may surprise some followers of Schank's early work on language, particularly as represented in two earlier books, (Schank, 1975; Schank & Riesbeck, 1981); they may be wondering to themselves, "What does this new stuff have to do with natural language processing (NLP)?" But they shouldn't be surprised. The explanation process (in humans and machines) became a central focus of the Yale AI lab in the early to mid-1980s as an evolutionary consequence of our long-standing interest in human language understanding. Although Schank's initial focus was on the rather narrow problem of interpreting individual sentences, over the years we became more and more convinced that understanding a sentence required extensive use of rather high-level inference and memory processes. Eventually, this realization led us to spend much of our time studying inference, memory, and learning in their own right. Our original language-understanding goals never went away, but we came to believe that the hardest, most interesting obstacle to building computers that would understand language at human-like levels was not in any language-specific problems. The more we study the language-understanding process the more convinced we become that the key to building a computer that will understand language is building a computer that understands the world that language describes.

Understanding Interesting Stories

Because most researchers in natural language processing *don't* really want to work on inference, memory, and learning issues, most of their sample text fragments are chosen carefully to deemphasize the need for nontext-related reasoning. As a result, most

NLP programs have been fed a steady diet of very dull stories. When someone understands a boring story, most of his work is done once he has figured out what the words mean. But when someone understands an interesting story, the real work begins after the words have been parsed. Understanding interesting stories is not a language issue, per se, it's an explanation issue. The difficult part of understanding such stories is developing creative hypotheses about why the events that the story describes took place. For example, consider the following:

The Swale Story
Swale was a star 3-year-old racehorse.
Swale won the Belmont Stakes.
A few days later, he died.

This story is only three sentences long. There's nothing very tricky about the language in it. Nonetheless, it's the kind of story that an intelligent, curious reader may find quite interesting, because it may cause the reader to start wondering about what might have happened to Swale. (Note: If you don't find the question, "Why did Swale die?" interesting because you don't care about racehorses, perhaps you can substitute the question, "Why did the Space Shuttle, Challenger, explode?" or, "Why did the Soviet Union collapse?" The explanation process is qualitatively similar.) Such stories are difficult to really understand because understanding them fully means developing a hypothesis.

The ability to come up with hypotheses about what is really going on in a story is a hallmark of human intelligence. The biggest difference between truly intelligent readers and less intelligent ones (especially including less intelligent computer programs) is the extent to which the reader can go beyond merely understanding the explicit statements being communicated. It's not hard to build a computer program that can read The Swale Story and can then tell you who died, and what he did before he died. A program with a little inferential capability could also answer questions about how fast Swale probably was, what his life was probably like before he died, and so on. The ability to perform simple inference is often required to do text-level tasks, such as lexical disambiguation and resolving pronoun references. But the ability to perform text-level tasks does not constitute evidence of much human-level intelligence; in particular, there isn't much creativity involved. Smart readers do something that is actually rather creative when they read: They dig for explanations. This means more than just inferring those things that the author intended to communicate implicitly; even the author of The Swale Story might not know why Swale died. Achieving a creative level of understanding means developing hypotheses about questions for which there may be no conclusively correct answer at all. The focus of our lab, during the period documented in this book, was to work on getting a computer program to do that.

Why Case-based Explanation?

The first reaction that most computer scientists have when they consider the explanation–construction problem is that it is computationally intractable. They have a good point. Building a completely new explanation from scratch is a very time-consuming process. Explanations are essentially causal chains. Small chains are reasonably easy to build, but the number of possible chains gets very large as the length of the chains goes up. For explanations the size that humans routinely create, the search space that a system that built such explanations from scratch would have to serve is very large. If we had to build all (or even most) of our explanations from scratch, we'd never have any time to do anything else.

For this reason (and others, that are discussed throughout the book) we've adopted a case-based approach to the explanation-construction problem. Readers of *Inside Case-based Reasoning* will already be familiar with the case-based paradigm. When applied to the explanation-construction problem, the paradigm suggests that the main steps in the process of explaining a given anomaly are as follows:

- *Retrieve* an explanation that might be relevant to the anomaly.
- *Evaluate* whether the retrieved explanation makes sense when applied to the current anomaly.
- If the retrieved explanation doesn't fit the current anomaly perfectly, then *adapt* the explanation in an attempt to produce a new variant that fits better.

The retrieval, evaluation, and adaptation of explanations are the three main issues for a case-based theory of explanation. Each of these problems is the focus of some of the chapters of this book.

Overview of This Volume

This book is divided into three parts:
- Part I is based on book chapters and articles through which Schank shaped the basic direction of research on case-based explanation construction. Many researchers have since pursued research in this area, fleshing out Schank's ideas, and, of course, taking things in new and different directions.
- Part II describes some of this more detailed theoretical work that has been done within the case-based explanation framework. The chapters in Part II each summarize a doctoral dissertation of one of Schank's students who took up his call to investigate the explanation process. Three of these chapters, which draw from the dissertations of Owens, Leake, and Kass, respectively, describe components of the SWALE case-based explanation system. Owens dealt with retrieval issues, Leake dealt with evaluating explanations, and Kass dealt with adapting explanations. Of course, the SWALE project addressed only a few of the many questions raised by Schank in the work sampled in Part I. Some other takes on those problems, also drawn from dissertations done under Schank's direction, are described in three other chapters in Part II, based on the work of Domeshek, Ram, and Jones. Domeshek presented another approach to retrieval-related issues; Ram, a different approach to evaluation; and Jones focused on a different form of adaptation. Taken as a whole, the six dissertation-based chapters of this book provide a fairly intensive examination of the principal issues in case-based explanation.
- Part III brings our discussion to the level of implementation. It presents the Micro-Swale program, complete with microversions of all three SWALE modules—a retriever, an evaluator, and an adapter—written in Common Lisp. This implementation includes a retriever, and evaluator, and an adapter, so that it illustrates the principal issues involved with case-based explanation. By performing the exercises that extend the modules slightly and connect them together, the student can produce a simplified version of the SWALE program, which can produce variations on its stored explanations, and thereby explain new anomalies.

This three-level organization should make it easy for different readers to get the level of detail they need. Some readers may really just want to understand the high-level framework of explanation-based understanding. They may be happy knowing what the important questions are. For these readers, Schank's chapters in Part I should suffice. They will want to read this part in its entirety, perhaps just skim Part II, and skip Part III altogether.

Other readers, such as those serious students of AI who are not computer programmers, may wish to understand more theoretical details, without necessarily learning LISP. They may want to see the basic form of some answers to Schank's questions without getting into implementation. These readers will probably want to read Part I and Part II carefully, but not bother with Part III.

Finally, there will be some readers who want to know as much detail as possible. These may include researchers from allied fields who want to understand the theories all the way down to the tools of the AI trade, which are programs. They may also include AI students, who are preparing to extend this work themselves. These readers will want to complement the chapters in Parts I and II with the programming exercises in Part III.

Acknowledgments

We would like to thank the following people for helping to make this book possible: Heidi Levin spent a lot of time proofreading early drafts, greatly improving the clarity of the presentation. David Guralnick provided a round of more technical proofreading, helping us reduce inconsistencies between chapters. Many of the figures were improved by Ann Kolb's artistic ability. Kemi Jona helped unravel the mysteries of various word-processing programs. Will Fitzgerald created the indices and produced the camera-ready copy. To these people and others who helped out along the way, we are grateful.

—Roger C. Schank
—Alex Kass
—Christopher K. Riesbeck

Part I
The Framework

1. The Explanation Game

Why does the explanation process deserve special focus? The answer, in short, is that explanation is at the heart of intelligence. Explanation is the process by which we make sense of the world around us. Before we can even begin to form intelligent plans or make intelligent predictions, we must understand the causes of the things we observe. In this chapter, which is adapted from Schank's (1986) book on explanation patterns, the central role that the explanation process plays in human thinking is described.

When this chapter first appeared it was, among other things, Schank's charge to fellow researchers to take up the study of explanation. One way to read the chapters of this book that were contributed by Schank's students is as a description of what happened when they took up his charge.

1.1 The Turing Test

The question of whether machines can think is perhaps a bit tired at this point in the history of computing, but the question of what would be required in order to make machines think is just beginning to be explored. Of course, each question relates to the other, so, in order to begin the process of building a thinking machine, we must consider not only if such a project is possible, but also what elements of the human thinking process are inextricably bound up with our sense of what we mean when we talk about a thinking machine. To build a machine with artificial intelligence (AI), we must come to understand, in a profound way, what it means to have intelligence. For years, researchers in AI could content themselves with adding yet another cute feature to their programs, allowing machines to do new things, one by one. But, it is becoming increasingly clear that to really make intelligent machines, as opposed to machines that exhibit one or two aspects of intelligence, one must attack the basic issues of the nature of human thought and intelligence head-on.

There have, of course, been many discussions of machine thought, by far the most famous of these by the British mathematician, Alan Turing (1963), when computers were in their infancy. Turing proposed a test, which he called the Imitation Game, that has become a common, but often misunderstood, way of judging the ability of a machine to understand. Turing's major argument was that the question of whether a machine can think is meaningless. He suggested the following alternative: If a person failed to distinguish between a man imitating a woman (via teletype) and a computer imitating a man imitating a woman, then the machine succeeded in the Imitation Game. Turing argued that success in this game was, in the long run, inevitable.

What Turing actually said, and what has been made of it, has not always been the same thing. He did not say that machines would be thinking if they played the Imitation Game successfully. He merely said that successful imitation was the real issue for computer scientists. In the subsequent history of AI, two general lines of argument on this issue have developed. One is that machines will never duplicate human thought processes; the other is that no matter how well machines imitate human behavior, they cannot be said to truly understand in the same way as a human being. To put this another way, the claims made are first, that the Turing test will never be passed; and second, that even if it is passed, it does not prove that machines understand. Of course, Turing himself disagreed with the first claim; he regarded the second one as meaningless.

It is now more than thirty years since Turing's paper. With the exception of Kenneth Colby (1973), a psychiatrist who found that other psychiatrists could not tell his computer version of a paranoid from the real thing, no researcher has claimed to have created a program that would pass the Turing test. And, no matter how many times people have affirmed that Turing was correct in his assessment of the validity of the question, it has failed to go away. Further, there is little reason to believe that it will go away. No achievement in building intelligent software can dispel it because there are always those who believe that there is something more to the nature of intelligence than any amount of software displays.

Critics of artificial intelligence seem always to be able to "move the line" that must be crossed. "It would be intelligent if it did X" is nearly always followed by "No, that was wrong; it would be intelligent if it did Y," when X has been achieved. But the problem of the ultimate possibility of an intelligence that is different from our own and possibly even superior to our own, embodied in something not made of flesh and blood, will not be determined by critics with arbitrary standards. It is time to look again at the twin questions of the criteria for the ultimate thinking ability of computer programs and the nature of what is meant by understanding.

1.2 On Men and Women

One of the interesting, if not serendipitous, facets of Turing's Imitation Game is that, in its initial conception, the problem is to find the difference between a man and a woman via teletype. The seeming implicit assumption is that there are differences between men and women that are discernible by teletype. On the other hand, given that the problem is merely to get the computer to do as well at the Imitation Game as the man did, and assuming that there is no difference between men and women that would be recognizable via teletype, the task of the machine is to duplicate a human in its answers. Thus, Turing's test doesn't actually depend on men and women being discernibly different. But, the nature of what it means to understand may best be illustrated by that distinction.

To see what we mean, let us consider the question of whether men can really understand women (or alternatively, whether women can really understand men). It is common enough in everyday experience for men and women to both claim that they really do not understand their opposite number. What can they mean by this? And, most important, how is what they mean by it related to the problem of determining whether computers can understand?

When the claim is made that men and women are really quite different (mentally, not physically), what is presumably meant is that they have different beliefs, different methods of processing information, different styles of reasoning, different value systems, and so on. (It is not our point here to comment on the validity of these assertions. We are simply attempting to use the principle of these assertions in our argument. These same assertions might be made about different ethnic groups, cultures, nations, and so on; we are simply using Turing's domain.)

The claim that we assume is not being made by such assertions is that men and women have different physical instantiations of their mental processes. (Of course, it is possible that men and women do have brains that differ physically in important respects, but that would be irrelevant for this argument.) So, what is it that makes men and women feel they have difficulty understanding each other? Empathy. Understanding involves empathy. It is easier to understand someone who has had similar experiences—and who, because of those experiences, has developed similar values, beliefs, memory structures, rules-of-thumb, goals, and ideologies—than to understand someone with very different types of experiences.

Understanding consists of processing incoming experiences in terms of the cognitive apparatus one has available. This cognitive apparatus has a physical instantiation (the brain, or the hardware of the computer) and a mental instantiation (the mind, or the software of the computer). When an episode is being processed, a person brings to bear the totality of his or her cognitive apparatus to attempt to understand it. What this means in practice is that people understand things in terms of their particular memories and experiences. People who have different goals, beliefs, expectations and general life-styles will understand identical episodes quite differently.

Therefore, no two people understand in exactly the same way or with exactly the same result. The more different people are from one another, the more their perception of their experiences will differ. On the other hand, when people share certain dimensions of experience, they will tend to perceive similar experiences in similar ways. Thus, men tend to understand certain classes of experiences in ways that are different from women's.

It is unlikely that an experience that in no way bears upon one's sex will be understood differently by men and women. Recall that the assumption here is that the baseline cognitive apparatus is the same regardless of sex. Any experience that does relate to the sex of the observer in some way will be processed differently. This can involve obvious issues, such as the observance of an argument between a man and a woman. There, we would expect a man to observe the episode from the point of view of the man and a woman to observe it from the point of view of the woman. In addition, such identification with different characters in a situation can extend to observations of situations in which the feuding characters are of the same sex, but one displays attributes more traditionally male and the other displays traditional female behavior. Identification, and thus perception, can thus be altered by one's understanding of the goals, beliefs, or attitudes underlying, or perceived to underlie, the behavior of the characters in an episode that one is observing.

Thus, for example, one's perception of the validity and purpose behind a war can be altered by whether one is the mother of a son who is about to be drafted or whether one previously fought in a war and found it an ennobling experience. In general, one's sense of what is important in life affects every aspect of one's understanding of events.

The claim then is that men and women, as examples of one division of human beings, do not, and really cannot, understand each other. The same argument can be put forward, with more or less success, depending on the issue under consideration, with respect to Arabs and Israelis, or intellectuals and blue-collar workers. In each of these cases, differing values can cause differing perceptions of the world.

1.3 On Computers and People

Now let us return to the question of whether computers can understand. What exactly does it mean to claim that an entity—either a person or a machine—has understood? On the surface, it appears that there are two different kinds of understanding to which people commonly refer. We talk about understanding another human being, or animal, and we talk about understanding what someone has told us, or what we have seen or read. This suggests that there are actually two different issues to confront when we talk about computers understanding people. One is to determine whether computers will ever really understand people, in the deep sense of being able to identify with them, or empathize with them. The other is whether computers will be able to comprehend a news story, interact in a conversation, or process a visual scene. This latter sense of understanding comprises the arena in which AI researchers choose to do battle. Often the critics of AI (e.g., Dreyfuss, 1972; Weizenbaum, 1976) choose to do battle over the former.

In fact, these two seemingly disparate types of understanding are really not so different. They are both aspects of the same continuum. Examining both of them allows us to see what the ultimate difficulty in AI is likely to be and what problems AI researchers will have to solve in order to create machines that understand.

Weizenbaum (1976) claimed that a computer will never be able to understand a shy young man's desperate longing for love, expressed in his dinner invitation to the woman who is the potential object of his affection, because a computer lacks experience in human affairs of the heart. In some sense, this seems right. We cannot imagine that machines will ever achieve that sort of empathy, because we realize how difficult it is for people who have not been in a similar situation to achieve that level of understanding. In other words, Weizenbaum's statement is, in some sense, equivalent to saying that no person can understand another person without having experienced feelings and events similar to those one is attempting to understand. Where does this leave the poor computer? Where does this leave a child? Where does this leave a happily married man who met his wife when they were both small children and married her when they were graduated from high school, before he ever had to cope with asking her out to dinner?

Weizenbaum is correct as far as he goes, but he misses a key point. Understanding is not an all-or-none affair. People achieve degrees of understanding in different situations, depending upon their level of familiarity with those situations. Is it reasonable to expect a level of empathy from a machine that is greater than the level of empathy we expect from human beings?

The important question for researchers in AI, psychology, or philosophy, is not whether machines will ever equal humans in their understanding capabilities. The important scientific questions are about people, not computers. What processes does a person go through when he or she is attempting to understand? With regard to the Turing test, we therefore need to investigate how our recognition of that understanding involves empathy and the ability to relate, and then to draw upon common experiences. Looking at the question this way will help us to better understand the nature of mental processes.

1.4 The Nature of Understanding

The easiest way to understand the nature of understanding is to think of it in terms of a spectrum. At the far end of the spectrum we have what we call *Complete Empathy*. This is the kind of understanding that might obtain between twins, very close brothers, very old friends, and other such combinations of very similar people.

At the opposite end of the spectrum we have the most minimal form of understanding, which we call *Making Sense*. This is the point where events that occur in the world can be interpreted by the understander in terms of a coherent (although probably incomplete) picture of how those events came to pass.

Now let us step back for a moment. Before we complete this spectrum, it would be worthwhile to discuss both what the spectrum actually represents and what the relevance of current AI research is to this spectrum.

There is a point on this spectrum that describes how an understander copes with events outside his or her control. The end points of this spectrum can be loosely described as, on the one hand, the understander thinking, Yes, I see what is going on here, it makes some sense to me; and, on the other hand, thinking, Of course, that's exactly what I would have done, I know precisely how you feel.

In our research (e.g., Schank, 1982; Schank & Riesbeck 1981) we have been concerned with the nature of understanding because we are trying to get computers to read and process stories. In the course of that research, we have considered various human situations that we wished to model. We built various knowledge structures that attempt to characterize the knowledge people have of various situations. The restaurant script, for example (Schank & Abelson, 1977), was used in an attempt to understand restaurant stories, and it was that script that prompted Weizenbaum's criticism about understanding *love in a restaurant*. Since that earlier research, we have come to realize that these knowledge structures function best if they are dynamic. That is, they must be able to change as a result of new experiences. In other words, we expect that as knowledge is used, it changes. Or, to put this another way, as we undergo experiences we learn from them.

At the core of such an hypothesis is the notion that in attempting to understand, we are attempting to relate our new experiences to our prior experiences by utilizing knowledge structures that contain those previous experiences. Consider, for example, the following situation. Imagine that you are hungry and that someone suggests a marvelous restaurant to you called Burger King. You happily go to this restaurant, armed as you always are, with a set of expectations about what will happen there. Specifically, you expect that you will: ENTER; BE SEATED; GET & READ MENU; ORDER; BE SERVED; EAT; PAY; EXIT. The items written in bold face are called *scenes* and can be best understood as bundles of expectations themselves that concern the particulars of how those scenes will actually take place. The assertion put forth in Schank (1982) is that such scenes are derived from experience and are subject to constant change by experience.

You were told that you were going to a restaurant, so you brought out your Memory Organization Package (MOP) for restaurants (M-RESTAURANT) that told you what scenes to expect. What you find in Burger King, however, is a different sort of thing altogether. The order of scenes is: ENTER; ORDER (without a menu exactly); PAY; SERVE (but it doesn't look much like the other SERVE); BE SEATED (but on your own); EAT; LEAVE. So what is a processor to do?

The obvious thought is that you have been fooled. This is not a restaurant at all. Or maybe this is just a weird restaurant. Without other evidence, it is hard to know what to do. What a processor can do is mark the expectation failures. That is, we expected that scenes would come in a certain order, and we expected that scenes would proceed in a certain manner, but they didn't. What we do in this case is to index the exceptions so that we will be able to recognize them when they occur again.

Now suppose that after you complain to your friend about Burger King, he suggests that you try another restaurant called McDonald's, instead. You are confronted with a new situation that you must attempt to "understand". And it is reasonable to say that you have understood McDonald's if you recall the Burger King experience (in other words, are reminded of Burger King) and use it to help create expectations about what will happen next. The key point, however, is what happens to your memory as a result of these two experiences.

You have now encountered two exceptions to a MOP that were themselves quite similar. It is reasonable, therefore, to create a new MOP that has expectations in it that correspond to these new experiences. We might call that new MOP, M-FAST FOOD. We can index this MOP as an exception to M-RESTAURANT, so that it will be available to change and grow as new experiences relevant to it occur.

The important point here then is that when we are reminded of some event or experience in the course of undergoing a different experience, this reminding behavior is not random. We are reminded of this experience because the structures we are using to process this new experience are the same structures we are using to organize memory. Thus, we cannot help but pass through the old memories while processing a new input. There is an extremely large number of such high-level memory structures. Finding the right one of these (i.e., the one that is most specific to the experience at hand) is one of the things that we mean by understanding.

In other words, an important part of what we mean by understanding is the accessing of extant knowledge structures in which to place our new experiences. We feel that we have understood when we know where a new input belongs in memory. Sometimes understanding is more profound than that, however. The creation of new knowledge structures in memory is also part of understanding. Such structures are created in terms of old ones. The more these new structures differ from the old, the more complicated understanding can be.

In this view, then, understanding is finding the closest higher level structure available to explain an input and creating a new memory structure for that input that is in terms of the old, closely related, higher level structure. Understanding is a process that has its basis in memory then, particularly memory for closely related experiences accessible through reminding and expressible through analogy. Further, the depth of understanding will increase if there are many available relevant personal experiences, in terms of which inputs can be processed. Finally, understanding means finding some memory, any memory at all sometimes, that will help one cope with an experience that initially seems novel. We want to feel that we have understood, and we feel that way to the extent that we can believe that what we have just seen really is like something we have already seen.

With this definition of the nature of understanding then, let us now return to our understanding spectrum.

1.5 The Spectrum of Understanding

Complete Empathy exists when individuals have many shared experiences that have, in turn, created very similar memory structures. The consequence of this is that, given a set of similar goals and beliefs, new episodes would be processed in the same way. This caveat is very important. Similar experiences, but different goals and beliefs, would still result in differing perceptions of the events; or, to put it another way, in a lack of *Complete Empathy* in understanding of each other's actions.

The point to be made about the understanding spectrum then, is: The more that goals, beliefs, and prior experiences and memories are shared, the more complete the level of understanding that can take place. On the opposite end of the spectrum, *Making Sense* involves finding out what events took place and relating them to a perception of the world that may be quite different from that in the mind of the actor in those events.

Let us now consider what may well be a midpoint on the understanding spectrum. We discussed earlier the problem of men and women understanding each other, in general. The point was that despite a cognitive apparatus that was identical, something was preventing complete understanding. This midpoint we label, *Cognitive Understanding*. By this, we mean that although a man may be able to build an accurate model of a given woman, he may still not really understand what her motivations, fears, and needs are. That is, he lacks *Complete Empathy* with her, but he still understands a great deal about her. To claim that he doesn't understand her can only mean understanding in its deepest sense. Certainly, by any measure of understanding that is less than *Complete Empathy*, he could rightly claim to understand what she does and not be accused by Weizenbaum of failing the understanding test.

Thus, there are obviously many different kinds of understanding. Where do computers fit in? The claim is that, given a spectrum as we have described, with mere Making Sense at the low end, Cognitive Understanding in the middle, and Complete Empathy at the high end, today's work on computer understanding claims the low half of the spectrum as its proper domain.

Making Sense—Cognitive Understanding—Complete Empathy

A legitimate argument can be made that computers will never understand, if what is meant by that is that they would be unlikely to understand much at the high end of this spectrum. Computers are not likely to feel the same way as people do, are not likely to have the same goals as people do, and will never, in fact, be people. Given that most people fail to understand each other at points very high on this spectrum, it seems no great calamity to admit to the likely failure of computers to achieve this level of understanding. Computers are unlikely to do better than women at understanding men or any permutation of vice versa.

On the other hand, computers can, and will, share some experiences with people. They may be able to read newspapers and build models of behavior almost as well as people do. And, perhaps, most important (with respect to what follows in this book, in any case), computers should be capable of explaining unforeseen events in terms of their own experiences, even to the point of being creative in their interpretation of new events. In order for them to do this, we will have to learn a great deal more about what it means to understand.

It does not follow that I will understand, in reading a news story about terrorism, better than a computer just because the terrorist and I share the feature of being human (and even perhaps the same age and sex). I can safely claim to understand such stories better than a computer can, as of now at least, but this is simply due to my experience with such stories and my general level of interest in human affairs, both political and sociological. If a computer were to attain a similar level of background knowledge and interest, it too would be able to understand such stories.

The real question is: Is it possible, and if so, exactly how would one go about getting a machine to have such knowledge, cause the interaction of new knowledge with old knowledge to generate the need to know more, and use that need to know to guide its processing of news stories?

This is only one kind of processing, however, and is thus really an example of only one kind of understanding. Another kind of understanding is shown by what we have already done with respect to computers and newspapers. Cullingford (1978) in SAM, DeJong (1979) in FRUMP, Lebowitz (1980) in IPP, and Lytinen (1984) in MOPTRANS all demonstrated computer programs that could process news stories at various levels. SAM summarized, answered questions, and translated a variety of fairly simple news stories. FRUMP did a more superficial analysis of a wider range of stories, providing summaries of the key points. IPP did an in-depth analysis of stories in one domain (terrorism), attempting to modify its memory and make generalizations from what it read. MOPTRANS also processed terrorism stories with an eye toward translating them from any of three or four languages into any other of those languages.

Did these programs understand? Certainly they performed some tasks that humans perform when they are said to be understanding. At the level of understanding measured by unsophisticated language comprehension tests, they understood in the sense that they could answer the who, what, where, and when questions. Is this understanding? Or to really understand do we have to be much more sophisticated in our analysis of a story?

One things seems clear: Understanding is not a yes or no, all or none affair. Granting that there are many levels to understanding, the key question for AI is not whether the levels we have already achieved can be construed to be examples of understanding, but rather how we can achieve the levels of understanding that are still eluding us. *Making Sense* has been achieved by computers in certain domains. On the other side of the spectrum, it may well be the case that computers cannot, in principle, completely understand people, any more than men can completely understand women or vice versa. *Complete Empathy* is just an end point on the continuum. There is a lot of space in between the end points. The real issue is not whether computers can understand, but how to make them understand better. To do this, we must get a better picture of what it means to understand.

How different are these three points on the spectrum in terms of what processes would be necessary in order to construct machines that met those criteria? What does a machine do in order to achieve the ability to *Make Sense,* and what would it have to do in order to *Cognitively Understand* or show *Complete Empathy?*

1.6 The Revised Turing Test

Turing's Imitation Game has not left everyone in AI thrilled by the prospects of having to meet its criteria as a measure of success. Colby (1973) argued that his paranoid simulation program did, indeed, pass Turing's test. He found that psychiatrists who were presented with output from Colby's PARRY program and output in a similar form from an actual human patient were unable to effectively distinguish between them. This passing of the Turing test failed to convince AI people that Colby's program understood or thought, nor should it have done so. Despite whatever validity Colby's program might have as a model of paranoia, it would seem that the failure of experts to distinguish between imitations and the real thing should not be taken as much more than a statement of the competence of the experts. In fact, in the case of the psychiatrists, the Imitation Game was a particularly poor test because a psychiatrist's choices when facing a nonnormal patient are not that extensive. PARRY was not brain-damaged or schizophrenic, so paranoid was, given the presence of a few paranoid signs, a reasonable choice. What Colby seems to have done is effectively simulated various aspects of the output of a paranoid, which may or may not reflect accurate processes underlying the production of that output. The issue, then, is one of the distinction between good output and good simulation.

Ideally, the test of an effective understanding system, if we may use that word, is not the realism of the output it produces, as Turing would have it, but rather the validity of the method by which that output is produced. Unfortunately, we cannot create a test that depends upon the evaluation of methods. We cannot do this for two reasons, one practical and one philosophical. The practical reason is that it is difficult to cut open either the machine or the human to see what is going on inside. Examination of hardware doesn't tell us much anyway. From a software point of view, people are extremely hard to test in a controlled experiment, given the wide range of their possible experiences prior to that experiment. Programs, on the other hand, are hard to evaluate with respect to establishing exactly what claims they are making.

The philosophical point is that we do not examine the innards of people in order to establish that they are understanding. It might seem that we grant them an ability to understand based on their humanity. But, it often happens, in schools, offices, and other places where such evaluations are made, that we do assess a human's ability to understand. It seems sensible, therefore, that the methods that are good for the human are also good for the computer.

Consider the spectrum of understanding again. For the sake of argument, assume that it is possible, in theory, to produce a program that meets the output requirements of each of the three levels of understanding noted earlier. To make this argument more concrete, we list some possible outputs for each of these points on the spectrum. Here's an example of *Making Sense*:

> input: news from the UPI wire
>
> output: a summary of a newspaper story or a translation of a speech into another language

Here's an example of *Cognitive Understanding*:

> input: a set of stories about airplane crashes, complete with data about the airplanes and the circumstances
>
> output: a conclusion about what may have caused the crash derived from a theory of the physics involved and an understanding of the design of airplanes, used in conjunction with algorithms that can do creative explanation

Here are some examples of *Complete Empathy*:

> input: I was very upset by your actions last night.
>
> output: I thought you might have been; it was a lot like the way you treated me last week.
>
> input: But I meant you no harm.

> output: Do you remember the way your father used to treat you on holidays when he made you call all your relatives? He meant no harm either.
>
> input: I see what you mean.
>
> output: I thought you might; there's no friend like an old friend.

Assuming that these input/output pairs are not entirely fanciful, we would now like to draw some conclusions about them that are reflective of our view of what a reasonable test should comprise. Our conclusions are effectively summarized with the following words: *accuracy, surprise, emotion*.

The claim we are making is that to the extent that output is an effective way of characterizing degree of understanding (although that is to a very limited extent; indeed, it may well be our only choice), we can judge the significance of that output in terms of its place on the understanding spectrum with respect to the following features:

- The extent that the output accurately accomplishes a task that a competent human could do.
- The extent that the output characterizes an especially original or important result that most humans cannot easily accomplish.
- The extent that the output effectively seems to replicate a real live human being with whom someone is familiar.

The foregoing three standards reflect the essence of the three points on the understanding spectrum that we have been discussing.

Turing's Imitation Game, then, can be seen, as a result of further insights into AI since the time that Turing first concerned himself with these issues, to be somewhat outdated. Merely fooling people is not the true task in AI. Rather, in addressing fundamental questions about the nature of intelligence, we must devise a set of requirements that any intelligent entity ought to be able to meet. And, if we are talking about intelligent beings with linguistic capabilities, any test we devise can have an added level of complexity. That is, the true value of language in an intelligence-testing framework is that we can transcend the limitations of only being able to get solutions to problems or answers to questions. Linguistically equipped intelligent beings can explain their own actions.

1.7 The Explanation Test

In the end, any system, human or mechanical, is judged on its output. We do not take apart a human to look at his or her insides in an effort to establish that the understanding mechanisms are of the right sort. Nor is it clear what the right sort of mechanisms are. We are faced with a dilemma then. We cannot use output to tell us if a system really understands. On the other hand, output is all we can reasonably expect to get.

To resolve this dilemma, we must address the question of self-awareness. The issue of consciousness is a vast one, and we do not mean to address it here. Rather, we wish to claim that the fundamental difference between a system that can produce reasonable output and one that meets the criterion that is implicit in the term *understanding system* is that an understanding system should be able to explain its own actions.

One might ask: Explain its own actions to whom? There are two answers to this question, each of them quite important in its own way. The first answer is, of course: to those who inquire about how the system works. The second answer is: to itself. It is this latter answer that represents the essence of the understanding process; although, quite naturally, it is the latter answer that is also the most difficult to assess.

A system that not only does interesting things, but can explain why it did them, can be said to understand at any point on the understanding spectrum where that explanation is sufficient. In other words, being able to say what sequences of actions were followed in a chain of reasoning passes the explanation test at the level of *Making Sense*. SHRDLU (Winograd, 1972), MYCIN (Shortliffe et al, 1973) and other programs in AI therefore, can be said to understand at the level of *Making Sense* because they can explain why they did what they did, to the extent of being able to describe the steps that they went through in performing their respective tasks.

SHRDLU manipulated blocks in a blocks world by responding to English commands. One of the aspects of that program that was most impressive was that when asked why the program had performed any given action, the program could respond with a causal sequence of actions. It could say that it had done X in order to do Y in order to do Z, and so on. At the end of its chain of reasoning, it had only the initial command given by the user. In that case, it would respond, "I did that because you asked me to." This latter response became well known and was psychologically very appealing. (E.g., Restak 1979 used the phrase "Because you asked me to" as the title of a chapter in a popular book on the brain. That chapter was on various aspects of AI and only touched on Winograd's work.) Although it was not put this way at the time, one of the reasons that Winograd's program was much appreciated was because it understood at the *Making Sense* level on the understanding spectrum. It understood its world of blocks as well as a human would. Now, it would not have passed Turing's test, because it understood nothing but blocks. But, we claim, it should be recognized as having passed the Explanation Test at the level of *Making Sense*.

Each point on the understanding spectrum has essentially the same requirements in the Explanation Test. For *Cognitive Understanding*, the program must be able to explain why it came to the conclusions it did, what hypotheses it rejected and why, how previous experiences influenced it to come up with its hypotheses and so on. We do not let a human being come up with innovative ideas, generalizations, correlations and so on, unless he can explain himself. Creative scientists are supposed to be able to tell us what they do, not what they do while they are being creative, but what the reasoning is behind what they have discovered. We may not expect Einstein to know how he came up with his creative ideas, but we certainly expect him to be able to explain the physics behind them. We will put up with unexplained brilliance for a while, but eventually we object, we believe that we are somehow being fooled. We cannot put up with a scientist who says, "$E = MC^2$; I don't know what that means, but I am sure it is true." There is no reason why we should let a machine off more easily. The machine must be able to answer the question, "How do you know?" to the satisfaction of an examiner in a school who would expect no less from his or her students for a similar accomplishment in a similar domain.

The last point presented on our spectrum, that of *Complete Empathy*, has no easier test. Any system purporting to satisfy this level of understanding must satisfy its examiner in the same way that a human would satisfy the examiner in a similar situation. We claim that this is not likely in its fullest sense, and that this improbability is what all the uproar is about with respect to the assessment of the possibilities for AI by laypersons. No machine will have undergone enough experiences, and reacted to them in the same was as you did, to satisfy you that it really understands you. One is extremely lucky to meet one person in a lifetime who satisfies that criterion.

The second aspect of explanation is much more complex. What would it mean for a system to explain something to itself, and why does that matter? What is important about understanding is how it changes over time. A machine that understands at the level of *Making Sense* fails to convince us that it really has understood because it continues to understand in the same way every time. The computer programs we built at Yale during the 1970s all had the feature, as do most AI programs, of behaving exactly the same way every time.

But, people, especially intelligent people, do not behave this way. They adapt to new circumstances by changing their behavior. How do they do this? We claim that the method they use for this adaptation is also based upon explanation, but explanation to oneself. Explaining something to yourself means, in essence, attempting to correct an initial misunderstanding by finding relevant experiences in your memory that might account for the incomprehensible event. The result of such explanation can be a new understanding of old information as well. In other words, explanation, learning, and also creativity, are inextricably bound together.

To explain something to yourself at the *Making Sense* level, one need only find a relevant knowledge structure in which to place a new input. Seeing a new event as an instance of an old event constitutes understanding at a very simple level. But, trying to find the theory that explains a group of events—that can be a much more complicated and more profound type of understanding. Explaining a group of events to yourself can thus mean coming up with a theory of those events. Thus, *Cognitive Understanding* really requires a good grasp of what would constitute a reasonable explanation for something in general.

From the perspective of a test of a computer's understanding ability, then, this spectrum allows us to set some criteria that will allow us to examine whether an understanding system is understanding by looking at that system's powers of explanation. But more important is a system's ability of self explanation. That is, one cannot easily examine how a system changes itself as a result of its experiences; one can just observe it over time. The claim is, however, that the concept of explanation is key in both cases. Explaining the world to others and to oneself is, in essence, the heart of understanding.

1.8 Questions and Explanations

One way to make the distinction between passing the Explanation Test at each level is to use the example of a joke. A computer understander that simply understood the joke, in that it could explain what had happened, would be understanding at the level of *Making Sense*. A program that actually found the joke funny, to the extent that it could explain what expectations had been violated, what other jokes it knew that were like it that it was reminded of, and so on, would be understanding at the level of *Cognitive Understanding*. Finally, a program that belly-laughed because of how that joke related to its own particular experiences and really expressed a point of view about life that the program was only now realizing, would have understood at the level of *Complete Empathy*. In all of these cases, perhaps the most important aspect of understanding is left untestable. Was the program changed in some way by the joke? This is not an irrelevant question for a person, nor should it be for a machine. It might be a bit difficult to answer in either case, however.

What will it take to get a machine to the level at which it satisfies people whom it understands at the level of *Cognitive Understanding*? Or, to put this question another way, what is it that people do with each other that makes us believe that they are understanding at that level? The answer can, we believe, be reduced to two words: questions and explanations.

People generate questions about those things that they do not fully understand. Sometimes those questions cause people to find explanations, sometimes novel and sometimes mundane, for the odd or unexpected situations that they encounter. Sometimes those questions remain, to be answered at a later date, or to be combined with new explanations as the seeds of more creative explanations.

The research described in this book is concerned with what it would take to achieve *Cognitive Understanding*. But it is not philosophical work. We are interested in pushing the level of intelligence that computers have already achieved to the next step. We are also interested in exactly what it is that people must be doing when they do intelligent things.

Because of that, this book is about questions and explanations. It is a book about people and machines. It addresses the questions of how humans formulate questions and how humans formulate explanations. The idea here is that if we can find out what it is that humans do when they are thinking and learning, then maybe we can model our machines on them.

The real intent of AI, is, we claim, to find out what intelligence is all about. We tend to say that a person is intelligent, to the extent that he or she is insightful, creative, and, in general, able to relate apparently unrelated pieces of information in order to come up with a new way of looking at things. We tend to claim that a person is unintelligent to the extent that his or her behavior is thoroughly predictable with reference to what we know that person knows. Thus, when people do things the way they were told to do them, never questioning and thus never creating new methods, we tend to see them as unintelligent.

We mention this here because we see the Explanation Test as a kind of intelligence test. We are not asking the computer to simply replicate intelligent behavior, because we have no knowledge of which aspects of such behavior are more intelligent than others. Is composing a sonnet a more or less intelligent act than playing chess? There is no way to answer this objectively, because it isn't the acts themselves that are at issue here, but rather the quality of those acts. Turing could not differentiate between these feats, because he did not have the experience of trying to build programs to do each task. But now, as a result of years of AI research, such a question is easier to answer.

We can make a program write bad sonnets or play poor chess fairly easily. Neither of these feats seems much of a mark of intelligence. Indeed, working on either of them would not be considered AI anymore, although such work was done by AI researchers not so long ago. Today, work on computer poetry or computer chess falls within the domain of AI only to the extent that it mimics the complex cognitive processes associated with the creativity inherent in both acts. Thus, if the computer poetry program started with a set of feelings and was able, by relating such feelings to its personal experiences, to create poetry, particularly poetry of some new type, we would be legitimately impressed. Similarly, if our computer chess program was capable of improving its playing ability by inventing a new strategy, or employing an old one that it recalled having seen in a match it knew about, that would be an AI-type feat.

We have come to understand in AI that it isn't the tasks themselves that are interesting. What matters is how they are done. Thus, we claim, the only way to know if our machines are intelligent is to make them do what we would expect a human to do in a similar situation. We must expect them to be able to explain how they did it. Furthermore, those explanations should have some connection with how the task in question actually was performed. Often, this is a difficult task for people to perform. We do not always know where our creative powers come from or how they were employed in any given instance. But, we can attempt to give rational explanations. We should demand no less from machines.

1.9 How the Explanation Test Works

It should be clear that there is no passing or failing of the explanation test as such. The reason for this is that the test refers to a continuum of understanding; thus it is possible to pass the test at one point and fail it at a point immediately to its right.

The test itself is simple. It revolves around the completion of a specific task. A mental task is given to a machine on the one hand, and a person on the other, as in Turing's Imitation Game. The interviewer is asked to question the machine or person about how the person came up with the behavior that he or she did. If the interviewer judges one subject's answers to be more insightful and explanatory than the other's, then that subject is judged to have passed the Explanation Test. If that subject happens to be the machine, then the machine can be said to be understanding at the level of explanation that the task itself was rated. In other words, the degree of passing is related to the complexity of the task.

As long as people give better explanations than machines for given tasks, then we can say they understand better than machines. When machines outstrip people in their explanatory ability, however, machines will be safely claimed to be better understanders, and hence more intelligent, than people in that area of knowledge. To give a simple example, machines can already outcompute humans. What they cannot do is explain the computation processes that they use, because they do not understand them any better than a hand-held calculator can be said to understand its operations. Thus, while we might prefer to use a computer for our calculations, until we prefer to use a computer over a mathematician to explain the nature of the operations in mathematics, machines will not be able to pass the Explanation Test for mathematics. Here, too, however, the different points on the spectrum are operating. We may be able to enable the machine to accurately explain what it does mathematically and thus achieve the *Making*

Sense level of explanation in mathematics. But, we would have to get a machine to understand why it did what it did to come up with some new mathematical idea, in order to claim the *Cognitive Understanding* level.

The Explanation Test, then, is not really a question of imitation. Our question is not so much whether a person could fool us into believing that he or she is a machine or whether a machine could fool us into believing that it is a person. Rather, we are interested in finding out whether anybody or anything that we talk to can be coherent in its understanding and explanation; can be creative and self-referential in its understanding and explanation; can be truly insightful in its understanding and explanation; and can be thinking about things on its own.

To understand is to satisfy some basic desire to make sense of what one is processing, to learn from what has been processed, and to formulate new desires about what one wants to learn. Our question is how people do this and how machines might do this.

1.10 Changing Machines

The issue, then, is change. Intelligent beings change themselves as a result of experience. They accomplish this change through the process of attempting to explain what they do not understand. In other words, they change when a given change facilitates understanding. How can we get computers to change themselves over time? How can machines adapt to new experiences that they cannot initially understand? The answer provided in this book can be expressed in three words: explanation, questions, and creativity. The task is to get computers to explain things to themselves, to ask questions about their experiences so as to cause those explanations to be forthcoming, and to be creative in coming up with explanations that have not been previously available.

During the course of processing a new event, information from old events is called into play. We understand new events by using our prior experiences. We interpret the new in terms of the old. To do this, we must be able to retrieve old events by matching aspects of new events to indices that enable old events to be retrieved.

When this retrieval occurs successfully, we think nothing of it at all and simply go on with our processing. In those cases, we are understanding in terms of fairly standard and nonspecific old memories, ones that cause no particular notice because they are so ordinary.

On other occasions, we take immediate note of the old episode that we have suddenly found in our consciousness. We say that we have been "reminded" of this old event, and often we tell others about it if there is someone to tell, or we ponder the old event for a while. The difference between these two circumstances is representative of the difference between processing that enables learning and processing that does not. And, most important for our purposes here, the difference reflects when explanation is necessary and when it is not.

A key element in reminding is explanation. The most important thing we can find out about human memory is what the indices to specific memories are like. The basis from which those indices often seem to be constructed are explanations that have been developed to differentiate one experience from another. In other words, if indexing in memory is the key problem in AI, then explanation is an important part of the solution. When we explain things to ourselves, other things come to mind. Creative thought, to a large extent, depends upon our ability to explain things.

Let us illustrate the explanation/reminding problem with a true story:

> I was having dinner with a friend of mine who eats only kosher food. He ordered a pasta dish made with cream sauce and mushrooms on the grounds that even though he was not in a kosher restaurant, the ingredients were all kosher, so it would be all right to eat it. When the dish arrived, it had small red bits of things in it which looked suspiciously like meat. Because he could not eat meat if it were meat (and probably could not eat the entire dish because of the meat), I asked him if he wanted me to taste the red things to see what they were. He laughed, said no, and then told me a story of which he had just been reminded. He said he had a cousin who decided to become more orthodox in his religious practices. The more he studied, the more he found out about orthodox Jewish rules. These included the fact that it was only acceptable for a man to have sex with his wife during two weeks out of every month. At this point he stopped studying. He told my friend that there were some things he just didn't want to know. My friend said that this applied exactly to the current case. He just didn't want to find out that he couldn't eat the dish. He decided not to eat the red things, but to eat the rest, as he just didn't want to know.

The concept of memory organization that we are talking about here is very well illustrated by this example. Once one has concocted an explanation of an event (in this case, the friend explained his own behavior with "there are just some things I don't want to know"), memories get activated. Because explanations themselves are such strong indices, other memories, especially ones in similar contexts (in this case, Jewish religious prohibitions), become activated whenever an explanation is concocted. Their value? Well, sometimes it is to illustrate a point by telling a story. But they have a much more significant use. They allow for us to check the validity of the explanations themselves. And, they often force us to think of new explanations when old ones seem to no longer suffice.

If we constantly predict something will happen and it never does, or the opposite always happens, we feel inclined to change our predictions. We need to remember events that show our predictive rules to be in error. Now, this doesn't mean that we always do remember them. People are very good at forgetting bad things that happen to them, thus enabling them not to have to revise their expectation rules. But, when they feel that their expectations really were wrong, they attempt to recall past errors to help them formulate new expectations. In order to do this, it is necessary to explain what went wrong initially; and to do that, one needs evidence. Because prior evidence must be around for consideration when a new expectation is to be formed, it is important that events that did not conform to that expectation were stored in terms of the failed expectation. Thus, one kind of index is a failed expectation itself. Events are stored in terms of the expectations that they violated.

Because humans are intelligent enough to wonder about why something has gone wrong when it goes wrong, it is important for them to attempt an initial characterization of what exactly the problem was. Thus, they construct initial explanations. These explanations serve as indices as well. The reason is clear enough. If explanations were not available, they would be lost. That is, what we were trying to learn at any given point would be immediately lost as soon as we stopped considering it for a moment. To avoid this, memory keeps available tentative explanations. Where to store them? With the expectations that failed, naturally.

1.11 Explanation *is* Understanding

A first assumption in this book then (first stated in Schank, 1982) is that when our expectations are found to be in error, we must attempt to explain why. Failures lead to attempts to explain failures. We want to avoid making the same mistake twice. How? By understanding what principles underlie the expectations that we had in the first place. We must understand them so we can fix them.

In the remindings that we examined, one thing that we found (Schank, 1982) was that each pair of events that we connected by a reminding had in common not only an identical expectation failure, but an identical explanation of that failure as well.

Explanation is critical to the understanding process. As understanders, we want to know what others around us are doing and will do. Furthermore, we want to know why others do what they do. Thus, people are constantly seeking explanations for the behavior of others. One of the simplest kinds of explanations is a *script* (Schank & Abelson, 1977). We believe that we understand why a person is doing what he is doing if we can point to a script that he or she is following. Knowing that someone is doing a particular action because it is part of the behavior prescribed by a commonly adhered to set of rules makes us feel comfortable that we have explained the person's behavior. We can, of course, look for explanations that are more profound than saying "he is doing that because he (or someone in his situation) always does that." We usually feel that we have understood without going that deep, however. And, it is this script-type of understanding that we are referring to when we talk about *Making Sense*. But, when script-based understanding is not enough, when we really want to understand something in a deep way, the explanation process must come into play. It is the creation of new explanations that produces *Cognitive Understanding*.

At the root of our understanding ability is our ability to seek and create explanations. When we seek an explanation for an actor's behavior we are trying to find a set of beliefs that the actor could hold with which the actions that he took would be consistent. So, what is understanding then? In this view, understanding can be seen to be no more than, and no less than, explanation.

In AI, we have gotten used to speaking of *computer understanding*, meaning by that term that an input sentence had been combined with a memory structure of some sort. To put this graphically, we have believed that:

An input sentence
plus
A memory structure that indicates where to place that sentence
results in
An understood sentence.

In other words, the process of understanding for computers in the early stages of AI research, was embodied in the notion that understanding something means putting it in its proper context, or *Making Sense* of it.

The major problem with this point of view is that, on occasion, either the proper context does not previously exist or it is difficult to determine exactly what that context is. Graphically:

An input sentence
with
No memory structure prepared to accommodate that sentence
results in
A sentence that needs explanation.

What we are doing when we understand is explaining what we have heard. Most of the time those explanations are very mundane, so we don't feel as if we are explaining anything. Rather, we are simply placing the new information in a previously extant structure. In other words, we don't have to explain why someone is reading a menu in a restaurant because we know exactly when and where such actions take place. Explanations are necessary when an action fails to come in the way we expected, or cannot be placed into an existing structure. When this happens, we need to explain it.

But, the point is that we are always needing to explain every action we encounter. We feel that we are explaining when we are doing something other than accessing an everyday, run-of-the-mill structure, or when, while using such a structure, we have still found ourselves incapable of deciding exactly what to do. Thus, explaining and understanding are the same thing; one is just more conscious a process than the other. And, explanation must be a more conscious process, because it occurs when something has screwed up and needs to be fixed.

2. The Explanation Process: Explanation Questions and Explanation Patterns

The previous chapter identified the explanation process as the crucial focus of study and explained why. This chapter, which is also adapted from chapters 4 and 5 of *Explanation Patterns* (Schank 1982), outlines his model of the explanation process, emphasizing what he sees as the creative nature of that process, and the strong role played by the recollection of old experiences, and their adaptation to new situations.

One concept developed in this chapter deserves special attention because it has played a central role in the research on *Explanation Construction* that we describe in Part II, and it will be central to the later chapters of this book. That is the concept of an Explanation Pattern (XP) The Explanation Pattern is, in essence, a trite explanation, one that has been used before, and can be adapted during the process of explanation for use in new circumstances. This process of adaptation of old standard explanations for use in new areas allows for creativity. Schank's basic argument is that in order to create a new explanation, what is required is to find an applicable old pattern, determine to what extent it differs from the current situation and begin to adapt it to fit that situation.

2.1 Adaptation, Creativity, and Explanation

There is an oft-repeated joke about how mathematicians solve new problems by first solving an old problem and then adapting the solution to the new situation. In fact, this behavior is not confined to mathematicians. Computer programmers, for example, write programs by adapting old programs to the new problem. Writers and artists adapt the old into the new in their creative acts. Creativity is often an adaptation of the old into the new.

What has creativity to do with explanation? Everything. When we come up with a new explanation, we are being creative. The claim we want to make is that the creativity embodied in coming up with a new explanation is at once the essence of what it means to think, and the heart of what we mean by understanding. Such creativity is not magical; rather, it is mechanistic in principle, and possible for computers to replicate. Computers can begin to achieve Cognitive Understanding. To do so requires an understanding of how humans explain, question, and create.

The issue, in the end, is one of change. When a standard memory structure is used to understand something, the net effect of understanding, in terms of its impact on memory, is nothing. You may have understood what you needed to, but as long as all processing conformed to the expectations that were available, and the standard patterns were used, little will be learned from the experience. However, when a new explanation is concocted, even though it will often just be an adaptation of an old Explanation Pattern, something is learned. A new pattern will be added to memory. Planning, even what seems to be the creation of brand new plans, is really no more than the adaptation of old plans to new circumstances. Learning takes place by the adaptation of old structures in memory to new circumstances.

2.2 Explanation and Generalization

Our attempts to explain what we don't understand are attempts to make generalizations about various aspects of the world. We don't seek to only know why a given person does what he does, although we may accept an explanation that pertains only to him if that's the best we can do. We also want to know how this new rule that we have just learned can apply to other, similar situations. We seek to generalize the behavior of others in such a way as to create rules that will hold in circumstances other than those we have just encountered. If we are successful at a stock purchase, for example, we wish to know if our success was due to our keen insight, our broker, the day of the week, the industry our stock belongs to, the nature of the market, the weather, or whatever. If we want to replicate successful behavior, then, we must know what details of that behavior were critical to our success and which details were irrelevant. Behavior is so complex that just because the result was successful it doesn't follow that we can easily repeat what we did. We may have done a great many things, most of which were probably irrelevant. (For example, one of us has an uncle, who was a successful football coach, who always wore the same brown suit to his games. We assume that he knew, in some sense, that this suit was not the reason that he was successful, but he replicated everything that he could.) We need to know what aspects of an event are significant and which are relevant with respect to what we can learn from the event for the future.

If we wish to account for failures, then when we do fail, we must explain our failures in such a way as to be able to modify the aspect of our behavior that was in error. Finding just which aspect is most significant can be a serious problem, however. We must know how to generalize correctly. Thus, we must come up with explanations that correctly cover the range of behaviors that interest us. Our explanations must be inclusive and instructive. They must include more behavior than we just saw and they must instruct us on how to behave in future situations of a like kind. Establishing what kinds of situations constitute a "like kind" is one of the main problems of generalization. It thus is, in some sense, the purpose of explanation.

Not every explanation is instructive or inclusive. Sometimes we explain things to make sure that they are not of interest. This is one reason why the explanation process must be more critically examined than the reminding process. We do not get reminded every time we attempt to explain something. Not all explanations are so significant as to cause a reminding. But any explanation that is intended to be additive is intended to be additive at a level of generality higher than that of the original phenomenon to be explained. We would like to learn something significant from our efforts at explanation, if we can. Let's now consider the explanation process in detail. The details can be found in Table 2.1.

Clearly, there is a great deal to be explained about the steps in the Table 2.1. First, we must discuss the role of reminding. Next, we shall begin to look at what an explanation question might be and how to determine which explanation questions are active. Then we are ready to discuss Explanation Patterns and the tweaking of those patterns, in greater detail.

2.3 Reminding as Verification

It is clear from this list what the role of reminding is in the process of explanation. If reminding occurs, it is one method by which the generalization of an explanation can be justified and through which the new explanation can be used at a high level to reorganize some rules in memory.

Table 2.1 The Explanation Process.

Step	Action
1.	Find an *anomaly*.
2.	Establish *the explanation goal* that underlies the anomaly.
3.	Establish *the explanation question* that is active.
4.	Find *an Explanation Pattern* that relates to the question.
5.	Check *the causal coherence* of the pattern as applied to the anomaly: If it is coherent—then go to step 6. If it is incoherent—either find a new pattern or *tweak* current pattern.
6.	Take explanation and establish whether it can be generalized beyond the current case by *reminding*.
7.	If a reminding is found, find breadth of the *generalization* to be formed.
8.	*Reorganize memory* using new generalized rule.

As an example of this consider the following:

Example 1. I was walking along the beach in Puerto Rico and noticed signs saying that it is unsafe to swim, yet everyone was swimming and it was clearly safe.

I explained this to myself, after seeing a second sign of a different sort warning about the dangers of walking in a given place, by assuming that the hotel that put up these signs was just trying to cover itself legally in case of an accident. At this point, that is after the explanation, I was reminded of signs in Connecticut that say "road legally closed" when the road is in full use. I had previously explained these signs to myself in the same way.

Here we have an example of reminding as verification. First an anomaly is discovered. Next an explanation is concocted. When the reminding occurs, it serves to convince the mind that the explanation that was concocted is reliable. It also gives potential for scoping the generalization that will be formed from the explanation. Here we see that both a state (Connecticut) and an institution (a hotel) can make the same rules for the same reason. Thus our new rule has to be generalized high enough to cover institutions that could have liability under certain circumstances. The trick here is to not over-generalize. We learn from these examples that some signs should be ignored. But which signs and under what circumstances? We want to learn to ignore signs some of the time but not all of the time. Should we ignore stop signs, or signs asking us to register at a hotel? Clearly not.

Honing the rule so that it correctly applies is an important part of the explanation process. Rules are honed by comparing the intentions of the actors in both cases. Thus, when one is reminded of one sign by another, the issue at hand is exactly what the intent of the sign is. It is not always easy to discern intent from a sign. But, a second sign, presumably put up for a different reason, is likely to help one determine the intent of the organization that put up the sign. The claim is that the mind naturally analyzes signs and the like for intent, so that, in some sense, you have already answered this question subconsciously. What reminding does is bring to the conscious processing two examples that have been analyzed similarly but not consciously. Thus, we can make generalizations by looking at two experiences that have already been determined to have some important aspect in common.

The role of explanation-by-example is thus crucial in reminding. People learn better by the use of examples, that much is obvious. Reminding makes it clear that we construct our own examples to help in learning a new rule in memory. What seems obvious is that the rules we know are grounded in sets of examples.

2.4 Finding Anomalies

It seems clear that remindings will be available as verification in only a small percentage of the explanations that we attempt. In unverified cases (i.e., unverified by reminding), we may look for other types of verification, such as seeing if our explanation meets certain standards of coherency for explanation. In other words, without a reminding to help us, we are on our own, so to speak.

People have powerful models of the world. Through these models, which are based on the accumulated set of experiences that a person has had, new experiences are interpreted. When the new experiences that a person perceives fit nicely into the framework of expectations that have been derived from experience, an understander has little problem understanding. However, it is often the case that a new experience is anomalous in some way. It doesn't correspond to what we expect. In that case, we must reevaluate what is going on. We must attempt to explain why we were wrong in our expectations. We must do this, or we will fail to grow as a result of our experiences. Learning requires expectation failure and the explanation of expectation failure.

But, expectation failure is not a simple process. When we have only a few expectations, and they turn out to be incorrect, finding which one failed is not that complex a process. In the real world, however, at any given moment we have a tremendously large number of expectations. In fact, people are constantly questioning themselves and each other, in a quest to find out why someone has done what the person has done and what the consequences of that action are likely to be. Thus, in order to find out how we learn, we must find out how we know that we need to learn. In other words, we need to know how we discover anomalies. How do we know that something did not fit?

The premise here is that whenever an action takes place, in order to discover what might be anomalous about it, we have to have been asking ourselves a set of questions about the nature of that action. In other words, we are constantly, during the course of processing, asking certain questions about that event, in order to fully understand it. Anomalies occur when the answers to one or more of those questions is unknown. It is then that we seek to explain what was going on. It is then that we learn.

To get a handle on this process, we must attempt to sort out the kinds of anomalies that there are. Knowing the kinds of anomalies that there are gives us two advantages. In order for us to find something to be anomalous, we must have been unable to answer a question about some circumstance. So, first we must discover the questions that are routinely asked as a part of the understanding process. Second, in finding out what anomalies there are, we also have the basis for the kinds of explanations that are created to take care of those anomalies. Thus, we understand what can be learned.

Since we learn from everything, by the aforementioned reasoning, it follows that everything can be anomalous. But what is "everything"? The things we see are the types of events that there are in the world. For example, we observe the actions of others in the world around us. To find anomalies (or more directly, to understand what they are doing), we ask questions of ourselves about their actions. For actions by individuals, we propose the following set of questions, which are asked in some sense every time that an action is observed:

1. *Patterns:* Is this an action that this person ordinarily does? Have I seen him do it? If not, then…
2. *Reference to self:* Is this an action that I would do? If not, then…
3. *Results:* Is this an action that will yield a result that is clearly and directly beneficial to the actor? If not, then…
4. *Plans:* Is this action part of a plan that I know to be a plan of the actor's? If not, then, is this an action that is part of an overall plan that I was previously unaware of that will, in the long run be beneficial to the actor? If not, then…
5. *Goals:* Is this an action that might be determined to be effective in achieving a goal that I know this actor has? If not, then, is this action helpful in achieving a goal that I did not know he had but might plausible assume that he might have? If not, then…
6. *Beliefs:* Is there a belief that I know that the actor holds that explains this action? If not, then, is there a belief that I can assume he might hold that would explain this action?

The result of this process is either a new fact (a plan, goal, or belief that one did not know that a given actor had), or else the action is unexplainable.

Every time someone does something, an observer, in an attempt to interpret the action that being observed, checks to see if that action makes sense. But, actions do not make sense absolutely. That is, we cannot determine if actions make sense except by comparing them to other actions. In a world where everyone walks around with his thumb in his mouth it is not necessary to attempt to explain why a given individual has his thumb in his mouth. In a world where no one does this, we must explain why a given individual has his thumb in his mouth. Clearly, Making Sense, and, thus, the idea of an anomaly in general, is a relative thing.

Relative to what? Naturally the answer is, relative to events in memory that we have seen before. The additive explanations that we discussed earlier pertain to the kinds of norms that there are, namely, norms for intent behind actions, norms for patterns of actions, and the normal causal chains of events that allow us to make predictions about the world in general. These are *predictive explanation, intent explanation,* and *pattern explanation.*

We are satisfied, as observers of actions, when the action that we observe fits into a known pattern, has known consequences that we can determine to be beneficial to the actor, or is part of an overall plan or view of the world that we could have predicted that the actor would be part of. When we are trying to understand our thumb-sucking adult, therefore, we can explain the action by pointing at the advantages of thumb-sucking (intent); we can explain it by reference to the group to which he belongs that normally does this behavior, perhaps neurotics or Martians (predictive); or, we recognize the pattern that is functioning here; for example, maybe he has just gone through a Rolfing session, and one always thumb-sucks afterwards (patterns).

The claim in the aforementioned list is that there is an order to this process. The one I just used for thumb-sucking is not optimal, for example, because known patterns either come to mind immediately or not at all. When we see that someone has done something, we first try to find the pattern to which it belongs. Failing that, the consequences that will result become an issue. If those consequences are beneficial to the actor, then nothing needs to be explained because there is no anomaly. If those consequences are not obviously beneficial, then we need to find out why the action has been attempted in the first place. This requires ascertaining what goals an actor has, what plans he believes will effect those goals, or what beliefs he has from which a goal may have been generated.

People are not processing information with the intent of finding out whether something is anomalous and needs explaining. In fact, quite the opposite is the case. An understander is trying to determine the place for an observed action. To do this, the understander must find a place in memory that was expecting this new action. Of course, he or she may not find one, because not everything in life can be anticipated.

So, an understander asks the question, "What structure in my memory would have been expecting this action had I reason to believe that that structure was active?" It is at this point that the aforementioned issues arise. We are always asking ourselves why things have happened the way they have, but we usually know most of the rudiments of the answer because what we are observing is usually fairly ordinary. When things are unusual and must be explained, it is because some of our routine questions have elicited some strange answers.

2.5 Explanation Questions

To understand how to create an explanation for an event, one must know the kind of explanation that one is seeking, and that entails knowing what kinds of questions people ask that need explaining. In order to talk about how to establish what explanation questions are of interest, we must, of course, examine what an explanation question is.

Once it has been determined that something needs to be explained, we formulate a particular question, the answer to which, presumably, will constitute the explanation we were seeking, and this make us feel that we have understood what was previously impossible to understand. We call the question that starts the explanation process, an Explanation Question (EQ). The claim here is that there exists a set of standard EQs from which particular EQs are determined to be active at any given point. We do not really formulate wholly original questions each time we demand an explanation. In fact, we tend to know what we are looking for before we start to look. EQs are, in a sense, indices to memory. It is the role of the EQ, therefore, to provide its own answer.

To the extent that there exists a standard set of questions, there must also exist a standard set of answers to those questions. This notion is at the core of what we are saying in this book. The claim is that explanation, creativity, learning, and such seemingly complex notions have at their core a rather simple base. That base is a reference to what has gone before. That is, we are constantly using what we have previously done as a way of extending what we can do. One phenomenon that we have seen that exemplifies this process is reminding. Another is the adaptation of old, seemingly erroneous patterns to new situations where they seem not to apply. However, before we go into any more detail about that, we must first discuss how EQs are selected.

2.6 Finding an Active EQ

There exist a large set of standard EQs, as we shall see. These can be quite useful for determining an answer to a specific question by transforming that question into a more general standard one for which there already exist some standard answers. Faced with an anomaly, the entire range of possible EQs is available to us. The task of the explainer is to determine which EQs are active at any given point. One way to delimit the EQs, such that they become active or inactive, is by features that uniquely characterize them.

Features of the anomaly help determine the indices for the EQs. Any anomaly has many possible features. Hence, part of the variability in the explanation process comes from the great deal of choice we have in picking features to focus on or assume in the anomaly that will determine the EQs that are posed and that, in turn, will determine the Explanation Patterns that can be considered as the basis of possible answers.

Following is a set of examples of real explanations. The examples were collected over the course of a year by asking graduate students at Yale to send an electronic mail message any time that they had an experience in which they found themselves explaining something to themselves. For each of these examples, one important issue is, *What question was the explainer seeking to answer when he or she came up with an explanation?* Another issue is, *How might that question be more easily answered by seeing it as an instance of a more standard general question (an EQ)?*

These examples are categorized by the features that are involved in selecting EQs. EQs correspond to the combination of all these features. Thus, in principle, there are 3 x 3 x 7, or 63 possible EQs. We discuss only some of these, of course.

A: *Type of failure.* As we discussed earlier, an event can be anomalous in three ways: Either a prediction explanation is needed, an intent explanation is needed, or a pattern-based explanation is needed.

A1: *Wrong prediction.* We predicted some event and something else (or nothing at all) happened. Or, some event violates what we would have predicted. Here the question was formulated: *Why do the primaries drag on so long, when one would imagine that that is very costly for the parties involved?* This specific question is then more easily answered by transforming it into the general EQ: *How is this apparently ineffective plan in reality a good plan for some unseen goal?* for which their exist standard answers and strategies for applying those answers to specific situations.

> *Example 2* (Simultaneous Primaries). Jim questioned why the primaries dragged on so long, complaining about how they dominated the news, making it harder to find out what else was happening in the world. He advocated a much shorter primary season, suggesting that best of all would be if they were all the same day. My explanation: The primaries are under the control of each political party. It's in the interest of the political parties to drag this on as long as possible because it is a way of getting free press coverage. The candidates don't

have to pay for advertisement, just hold yet another debate, and the media will compete over who can cover it most.

A2: *Unpredicted* (events). Something happens where we hadn't expected anything to occur. The question in this story is *What's causing that strange noise?* That question is answered with the help of the EQ: *What are the underlying causes of this bad event?*

> *Example 3* (The Ice Storm). During the ice storm last night, Suzie and I were in my apartment. Neither of us had realized that the snow had turned to freezing rain. We heard a long series of crackles and whooshing sounds. I said that it sounded like trees falling. During the ice storm of '79 (my first real winter), I was nearly killed by a falling limb, and I suppose I am now sensitized to that noise. Suzie was sure it wasn't trees, because there were so many similar noises. When we awoke, it turned out to be dozens of fallen trees.

A3: *Lack of context* (reasons). Someone did something and we cannot figure out why, here: *Why would a Jew choose to be a reporter in Lebanon?* This corresponds to the more general EQ: *What caused the actor to behave this way?*

> *Example 4* (Reporter in Lebanon). This morning, as I was watching the Reuters newswire on TV, one of the headlines at the beginning read *American TV network reporter feared kidnapped in Beirut.* Immediately, Jerry Levin, CNN's reporter in Beirut, came to mind, not as a conscious prediction, but just sort of idly. When I first noticed that he had been posted as Beirut bureau chief for CNN, I remember thinking that it was a bit risky for a Jew to take that assignment. Sure enough, it turns out that it's Jerry Levin who is missing and believed kidnapped.

B: *Type of event.* An event can occur in one of several broad worlds or classes of events. In general, people have questions about the physical world they inhabit, the social world that is made up of various institutions with their rules and the personal world that concerns the individuals whom they know.

B1: *Physical world.* Inanimate objects and causations cause us to wonder about why things happen the way they do. We have a simple model of the physical world that consists of a set of predictions about what will happen and a set of standard explanations for why things fail to work on occasion. One EQ that occurs in the physical world is: *What factors caused this event and can they happen again?* The specific question here is: *Why did the gate keep moving?* in the following story:

> *Example 5* (The Parking Lot Gate). Yesterday, walking to my car, I approached the automatic gate to my parking lot. The gate is the type that you insert a plastic card in to get in, and the gate automatically opens when you approach in your car to get out.
>
> At a distance of about 50 feet, I noticed that the gate rose about halfway up and went back again. I also noticed that there were no cars moving in the vicinity. The spontaneous spasm of the gate was highly unusual. I have approached this same gate on foot countless times, and this never happened before.
>
> I tried to explain why the gate behaved in this way. The first thing I did was to check again that I did not miss a car that was approaching the gate. I saw no car, but I did see a government police car parked in the distance in a place where cars do not usually park. I then wondered if the police car had something to do with the gate's behavior. Did the police have some device that triggered the gate? Were they watching the gate? I decided that this was unlikely and that I was paranoid.
>
> I then wondered if I had not in some way triggered the gate in my approaching it. I was reminded of the times that I passed through airport metal detector gates and triggered the alarm, due to something I was carrying. This seemed to make more sense, so I pursued it further. Was the parking gate triggered by some sort of metal detector? This seemed plausible, but cars have a great deal of metal in them and I do not. Was I carrying something with metal in it? Yes, but no more than I usually carry, and the gate had never mysteriously moved before when I passed it. Furthermore, if a car were the distance I was from the gate, it would not have triggered the gate. I rejected the metal detection explanation as well.
>
> I decided that for the purposes of the moment the gate was acting unusually because it might be broken. I hoped that the gate would work when I tried to get my car out of the lot. Fortunately, the gate did work.
>
> I told my wife the story of the gate and she came up with two explanations that I hadn't thought of. One was that someone

left a card in the device that reads the cards and this was causing the aberrant behavior. The second was that it had been raining heavily that day and perhaps the rain caused some electrical problem in the gate.

B2: *Personal world.* On occasion, various people whom we know may do things that we would not have anticipated and cannot quite comprehend. This requires us to formulate specific questions, such as *Why were people walking without shoes?* in the following example. The general EQ is: *What previous behavioral change led to this event?*

> *Example 6* (Shoeless Student). Yesterday I walked into a graduate student office and saw David sitting down reading the paper with no shoes on. I chalked it up to idiosyncratic behavior. Ten minutes later, I was walking down the hall and saw Jonathan walking toward me barefoot. At that point I decided that there must an explanation. I realized that it had been raining very hard that day and that David and Jonathan must have gotten their shoes and socks soaked. They had then taken them off to let them dry. Jonathan confirmed my hypothesis.

B3: *Social world.* We also concern ourselves with the institutions that are part of our lives and seek to formulate accurate models of them. When they do something that violates our model, we ask what we have misunderstood. The specific question here is: *Why did Yale give up on its principles in a tenure case?* The general question is: *What are the policies of this institution?*

> *Example 7* (Yale and Tenure). At dinner last night, we were talking about the woman who was denied tenure at Yale (History Dept.) and sued the university. Yale settled out of court. The woman claimed that she was denied tenure because she is female, and that they gave her position to someone less qualified. For academic reasons, the woman did not deserve tenure (opinion of the history faculty). Her position was given to another woman. Courts cannot decide academic qualifications. One would have thought that Yale would have fought it out in court, defending principles. Why didn't they?

> Some explanations I thought of: (a) It's cheaper to settle out of court than to let the case drag through the courts; (b) Yale settled out of court precisely because courts can't decide aca-

demic qualifications, so Yale gets to say, implicitly, that the woman was a poor scholar, although they chose to pay her off.

C: *Goal of experience.* Anomalies are explained for a reason, and these reasons conform to the goals such as coherency, context, prediction of individual behavior, prediction of group behavior, copying strategies, adding facts, and the seeking of universal truths. Each of these goals spawns questions related to them.

C1: *Coherency.* To establish if the actor has something coherent in mind when all signs are to the contrary, we ask appropriate questions. One EQ here is: *What are the plans of this institution?* Here is an example:

> *Example 8* (Hairdressers and Credit Cards). Diane was trying to figure out why hairdressers won't take credit cards. She thought that maybe they had a poor clientele, but realized it was also true in Westport. She never found an answer.

C2: *Context.* To find the natural context for a given event in the belief–action chain, we often must formulate appropriate questions, for example, *Why don't TV commentators attempt to be more analytical in their presentations?* This is answered with respect to the EQ: *What are the goals of this institution?*

> *Example 9* (Campaign Predictions). I noticed with Hart all the news people yesterday were saying that *that's what he's been predicting for two years,* as though he had such a sage understanding in advance of how the campaign was going to work. That's how they explain the situation, or at least provide background.
>
> I got very annoyed as different news shows repeated this, and I wondered why none of them was swift enough to look at other predictions made by other candidates of how they would do and blow the whole notion away. To explain this anomaly, I posit that they just want something to say to fill up airtime and are too dumb to think about what is really going on.

C3: *Prediction of individual behavior.* To find new predictive rules for the behavior of a given individual, we must inquire as to why they do what they do. This can apply to why particular animals do what they do, as well as to why we ourselves do what we do. For example, the question below is: *Why did I talk to the dog like that?,* which relates to the EQ: *How is this action typical of this actor?*

Example 10 (Barking Dog). Walking home, I was deep in thought when I heard the sound of a dog barking fiercely and saw it coming at me. Without stopping to think, I slipped my hands into the pockets of my coat and, without breaking my stride, made eye contact with the dog and asked: *Just what do you think you're doing? Hunh? HUNH? Just WHAT do you think you're doing?!* Startled by the sound of my own voice, I suddenly felt quite foolish. What was I doing speaking out loud, asking silly questions, no less!, to strange, hostile dogs in public places? Discreetly glancing around, I was relieved not to detect any witnesses. Then I realized that it had worked—the dog had shut up, backed out of my way, and was looking totally cowed and confused.

C4: *Generalization for group prediction.* To find new predictive rules that hold for a group, so as to eliminate the sense that certain events are anomalous, we ask about anomalies that we find, for example, *Why do underdogs win in New Hampshire primaries?* and find answers by relating to the EQ: *How does this behavior fit in with a group of behaviors?* In this instance.

Example 11 (New Hampshire Primaries). Political postmorteming over the Gary Hart win in New Hampshire reminded me of McCarthy in 1968. In February in New Hampshire, not much is happening other than waiting for the sap to rise in the maples, so voters are receptive to the energy and youth of young campaign workers. Similarly for the weather. It was snowing, so the candidate with the most 4-wheel-drive-vehicle–owning supporters was likely to win.

C5: *Additive facts.* To add new facts to one's personal data base that will better enable one to be able to function in the future, we ask about whatever circumstances we cannot control, or understand. For example, the following question is: *Why won't the door close?* This is related to *What were the underlying causes of this bad event?*

Example 12 (Car Doors). I've been spending more time in Alex's little Honda these days, and I never seem to be able to close the door completely. Whenever I get in or out of the thing, the dome light stays on to tell me that I haven't managed to close the door tight. Alex, on the other hand, never seems to have this problem. Last week, for the first time, I slammed the door hard enough to close it, but Alex didn't close his all the way. It struck me then that the problem wasn't with me, but the second person to close a door can't do it. After pondering a moment, I decided that the problem must be air pressure—when the car is sealed save one door, the pressure in the car keeps that last door from closing all the way. When another door is opened, the air has another place to go.

C6: *Copying strategies*. One way to get new rules for operating in the world is by copying those of others that seem to work. To do this, we ask about the strategies of others: How does IBM manage to make money on computers by doing what seems to be odd? This question relates to an EQ we have seen before: How is this apparently ineffective plan, in reality, a good plan for some unseen goal?

> *Example 13* (IBM Policies). The conflict: IBM sells foreign-language versions of its word-processing software in foreign countries, but refuses to sell them in the United States. There are people in the United States who would buy the foreign-language programs. My explanation: Since IBM has a vast and sophisticated marketing department, it must have determined that it's not cost-effective to distribute the foreign-language software in the United States.

C7: *Truth seeking*. The goal is to find universal truths that hold across wide ranges of phenomena. Thus, we seek to understand, for its own sake, the anomaly, for example, *Why is my friend doing this odd behavior?* This question brings up the EQ: *Is this actor a member of any group that is known to do this anomalous behavior?*

> *Example 14* (Holding the Pillow). I was spending a quiet evening with Suzie, who is in the midst of an internship in midwifery. She had had a difficult day (delivered her first dead baby) and was finally relaxing a little. We were sitting on the bed, and she was hugging a pillow to her breast. It was not a focus of her attention, she was just holding it there as we talked. This reminded me of the fact that I had seen someone holding a pillow like that before; I didn't remember the particular scene, but I did remember that the other person had also been a woman. I asked her why women do that. She was surprised and said she hadn't even noticed she was holding it, but that it somehow made her more comfortable. The feeling was quite palpable and changed when the pillow was held differently. My explanation, which she agreed with, was that it affected the level of some hormone associated with nursing; that would make holding things in that position feel good. The

pillow is roughly baby sized, and the phenomenon only worked in a narrow range of positions. There should be some sort of biological mechanism for making nursing attractive. Suzie's might have been activated by her work (or always present in women of that age) and she could have been sensitized to the feeling by her stressed–out, emotional condition. We had no other explanation of why that sensation should be so strong, or why neither of us could think of a man in a similar position.

One point to be made from looking at the aforementioned examples is the difference between the question that was asked directly and the EQ from which it was derived. Questions can be fairly difficult to answer if they are posed in the wrong way. EQs serve to focus questions by pointing the way to answers. Thus, in Example 14, for example, just asking why Suzie is doing what she is doing may not be very helpful. But, considering what group that she is a part of which shares the behavior to be explained may help a great deal in coming up with an answer. The assumption here then is that the specific question is generated first, but that in answering it, one must make reference to some EQ. The general EQ, then, helps provide the answer by pointing to known answers stored with it. In general, the process of question transformation, that is, the deriving of more answerable questions from less answerable ones, is critical to explanation.

2.7 Some Questions

Perhaps one of the most important observations one can make from looking at these examples of explanation is how ubiquitous a phenomenon explanation is. People seem to be explaining all kinds of things to themselves all the time. These examples were gathered from a rather intelligent group of people over a fairly short period of time. And, of course, the examples shown here are only a small sample of what was collected. Do unintelligent people do as much explanation? It seems likely that they do, but it is our belief that intelligence and the need to make explanations are linked phenomena.

But, what to make of the fact that at least one group of people seems to be explaining things to themselves quite frequently? The answer, we think, is this: People have a large set of questions to which they do not know the answer. They do not concern themselves with the facts of their ignorance at every moment of the day, but, when an opportunity comes to find the answer to an extant question, they take it. Perhaps, of more interest, they seek to generate new questions as new phenomena appear. What is the significance of this? First, with respect to understanding anything—written text, other people's actions, whatever—one must be able to generate and answer large sets of questions. Second, it seems clear that learning is dependent upon the successful generation and answering of these questions. Explanation, therefore, can be seen as a phenomenon whose role is to answer questions that have been generated by an understanding system, in response to a lack of information about a given subject.

The next step after posing questions is to attempt to answer them, of course. But, our problem now, in terms of the problem of defining the process of explanation, is how exactly such questions were posed. Further, after posing a question, because many possible questions could be posed, one must determine which questions are sensible enough to pursue, and which should be abandoned. Consequently, we shall now discuss the issue of where questions such as these come from.

2.7.1 Generating an Explanation Question

Consider the following story:

In the summer of 1984, Swale, the best thoroughbred racehorse of that year, the one who had been winning the most important races for three-year-old horses, was found dead in his stall. Newspapers around the country concerned themselves with the issue of why Swale had died.

The problem here is not figuring out how Swale died. Most people, when confronted with a story or situation such as this, can figure out or invent a theory of what happened. That is, it is possible to explain Swale's death in many different ways. The issue for us here is how we come up with potential explanations. There is no right answer. It might seem that there is only one cause of death, and, therefore, there is only one explanation. But, for our purposes, there are as many right answers as there are coherent hypotheses. And, in fact, different explanations satisfy different questioners. Thus, the first issue is what different questions there might be from which different hypotheses could be derived. To examine the problem of answers, one must first look at the questions.

To see how the explanation process begins then, let's consider what standard Explanation Questions might exist from which specific questions could be generated. The list presented here is by no means exhaustive. As we noted earlier, theoretically there are 63 different types of EQs. Moreover, these types can be further and further specified. An EQ is, in principle, an old favorite type of question that has been useful in the past for helping one to find answers. Thus, we could expect that different individuals would have different idiosyncratic questions that they prefer to ask. There is no right set. Rather, EQs are useful to the extent that they can help transform specific questions for which no answer exists into general questions for which a standard answer exists. Thus, the EQs presented here are simply ones that relate to this example in some way. The intent is to give the flavor of how EQs function, the real test of that coming in how they are used to find Explanation Patterns.

2.7.2 Physical Explanation Questions

The first set of Explanation Questions that we shall discuss are all about physical causal sequences, involving both simple physical events and human behavior. The basic concept is that one event causes or enables another event. In contrast, the explanations in the two sections that follow are based on concepts such as *typical behavior for an individual, group, or institution.*

EQ1: *What caused an unexpected event?*

The goal is to UNDERSTAND an UNPREDICTED event. EQ1 includes the question applied in Example 3 (The Ice Storm), which is *What caused the loud noises during the storm?* In that case, the unpredicted event of loud noises has potentially harmful CONSEQUENCES, because whenever we hear loud noises we think that something dangerous might be happening.

EQ2: *What factors caused this event?* and *Can they happen again?*

The goal is to AVOID an UNPREDICTED event. EQ2 is relevant in the following example.

Example 15 (Light bulbs). The light bulb in the hall blew for the second time in a month. Diane said that we must have put in an old bulb. I decided that it was a 100–watt bulb in a closed container, and that heat blew it. I put in a 60–watter and decided to give more strength to my belief that light bulbs in a closed space cause too much heat to accumulate, which causes them to blow out.

This EQ is simple enough to explain. When something doesn't work the way we expected it would, we want to know why. One reason is that we want to correct the aberrant situation so that it doesn't happen again.

EQ3: *What theory of physical causes explains this event?*

The goal is to UNDERSTAND an UNPREDICTED event. The issue here is to differentiate EQ3 from EQ2. For example, when an object fails to function properly, we can ask either *How do I fix it so it works right the next time?* or *What principle is governing the continuing failure here?* The first is EQ2, in simple English. The second is EQ3.

EQ3 is common enough among technically oriented people. Example 12 (Car Doors) is an instance of it. The person posing the problem was worrying about why things tend to work the way they do. He found himself posing theories of the physical phenomena involved. In fact, in Example 12, both EQ2 and EQ3 are active. The problem was to get the car door to close properly as well as to understand why there had been trouble closing it. It was possible to learn a rule about why doors of Hondas don't close easily, or simply to learn that opening the window will fix the problem, without learning why. This difference reflects the difference between EQ2 and EQ3.

EQ3.1: *What were the underlying causes of this bad event?*

This is a special case of EQ3, wherein the event was bad or dangerous, and hence our goal in understanding is to be able to avoid it. It differs from EQ3, in that EQ3 is understanding for curiosity's sake, while EQ3.1 has a serious purpose. We might give up on EQ3 before we give up on EQ3.1. EQ3.1 differs from EQ4–EQ6, in that EQ3.1 does not begin with any assumption that the victim in the bad event was at fault. For example, if someone were mugged several times, it would be possible to explain why that individual tended to get mugged by creating a theory about the victims of a mugging. If the theory were constructed that only short people get mugged, maybe elevator shoes might be a good solution. This having been said, we will introduce the remaining physical EQs with minimal additional comment.

EQ4: *How did the victim enable this bad event?*

The goal is to AVOID by MODIFYING ONE'S OWN BEHAVIOR. This is the behavioral analog of EQ2. The observer wants to learn how to recognize the conditions of danger before they occur so that the danger can be avoided. Thus, for example, if one got hurt in icy conditions, as in Example 16 (Slipping on Snow), then deciding not to go out on a snowy day would work here.

Example 16 (Slipping on Snow). This morning, as I stepped out the door into the snow, I expected it to be slippery but found instead that the snow was nice and crunchy—with better than average traction. Walking to my bus stop, I became aware that it was a bit late and I had better hustle if I wanted to make the bus. I started to speed up to a jog and went into a skid, almost falling. I wondered what had happened to my nice crunchy traction. I thought that it might be that the weather was changing. This didn't seem likely, because it had only been 3 minutes. I then thought that maybe the snow on this block was different. I have noticed in the past surprising differences in this few block area of how early flowers bloom, how soon snow melts, etc. This reminded me of ice I had noticed in that part of my route on the previous day. Although most of the way was clear, I had detoured around a bad-looking patch. Then, I decided that the snow itself was still high-traction. What was slippery was the ice underneath. I was slipping on old ice, which I had easily avoided when I could see it, but which now looked the same as where there was concrete under the snow.

EQ5: *What did the victim do wrong in this bad event?*

The goal is to DECREASE EFFECTS by MODIFYING ONE'S OWN BEHAVIOR. In this case, the observer worries about how to cope with the same situation, if it occurs again. In the slipping on snow example, the observer would want to generate some rules about how to walk in snow.

EQ6: *What circumstances led to this event?*

Here the goal is to AVOID by REARRANGING CIRCUM-STANCES. If something you value were threatened, you might take steps to preserve it. Thus when trying to explain a robbery, there are many explanations one could construct. One of these exemplifies EQ6, namely the creation of a set of impediments for the robber. In this case, *there weren't enough good locks* might be all the explanation that was required, with respect to a robbery.

The point of EQs, in general, is to establish what kind of explanation is necessary so that an explanation can begin to be constructed. One cannot come up with elevator shoes as a hypothesis unless one has asked the question: *What can I do to change my be-*

havior that fits in with my theory of why I am in danger in this circum-stance?

This is, actually, a rather important point. Asking the right question is critical in science, as any scientist knows. It is also critical in daily life. One simply cannot come up with creative answers without creative questions. The premise here is that creativity is, in fact, guided by the EQs presented here. In other words, there exist standard methods of finding creative solutions to problems. These methods are embodied in the selection and use of EQs.

2.7.3 Social Explanation Questions

There are social explanation questions as well.

EQ7: *Why did this institution act this way?*

As we have said, we try to understand why the institutions that we interact with do what they do. Thus, we seek to understand corporate or institutional policies when they affect us. In EQ7, we are trying to understand what the social factors are that cause a given institution to act the way it does. In other words, we need to know about the environment that an institution operates within in order to appreciate why it has evolved into its present shape. This is specified more particularly in the following set of EQs:

EQ8: *What are the policies of this institution?*

The goal is to UNDERSTAND institutional behavior, focusing on its PROTOTYPIC policies. We are seeking to know how an institution makes its decisions. Examples 7, 8, and 13 include speculation about the policies at Yale, small businesses, and IBM. The need to explain institutional behavior can revolve around an attempt to understand the policies of that institution. Policies are prototypic, in that the explanations have the form *Institutions of this type always do such and so.*

EQ9: *What are the goals of this institution?*

The goal here is to UNDERSTAND institutional behavior, focusing on PREDICTIVE goal-based behavior. In general, we seek to understand the institutions we deal with. In this case, understanding means being able to explain past actions as well as being able to predict future actions. As we shall see, the aforementioned EQs, plus the others given at the end of this chapter, give one the opportunity to do that.

EQ10: *What plans was this institution carrying out?*

EQ11: *What did this institution decide was most important?*

EQ12: *What will this institution do next?*
These three EQs all relate to the treatment of an institution as if it were a human actor.

2.7.4 Personal Explanation Questions

We seek personal explanations as well. These include particular observations about particular individuals as well as an attempt to understand stereotypical groupings of individuals. A great deal of this type of explanation involves seeing the action that needs to be explained as prototypical of actors who are members of a particular group, and attempting to place the actor of this action into that group. An explanation that is already extant can then be used as the basis for constructing a new explanation. We shall see how this works shortly.

EQ13: *What caused the actor to behave this way?*
This is the basic question of behavior, focusing on the actor as an individual. The goal is to UNDERSTAND the event as a RE-ACTION to some prior event.

EQ14: *Is the actor a member of any group that is known to do this anomalous behavior?*
This is the basic question of behavior, focusing on the actor as a member of some group. The goal is to UNDERSTAND the event as typical of certain GROUP behavior, by finding the applicable group. If we can find a group, then the behavior is no longer anomalous. We can predict future actions of that individual by resorting to a standard pattern of actions associated with the group to which we have determined that our actor belongs.

EQ15: *Why would the group that this actor is a member of do this anomalous behavior?*
Of course, we may not have a set of predicted actions associated with every group. Thus, we can attempt to understand a particular group better by creating a hypothesis about the theory of that group. That is the role of EQ15. In essence, it begins the process of theory formation. The result of answering EQ15 leads to knowledge that can, in the future, answer EQ14.

EQ16: *What makes this particular group behave differently from other groups?*
In order to create a theory about a group, it is sometimes necessary to speculate about that group in comparison to other groups. Concluding that Group A is like Group B can be a way of explaining the actions of Group A if those of Group B are known.

EQ17: *How does this behavior fit in with a group of behaviors?*

Sometimes we need to find out if various actions are related, in that they have the same cause. Viewing an anomalous action together with other actions can render the general phenomenon more understandable. Knowing which actions to compare a given action to is the hard part here.

EQ18: *What plans does this group have?*

Knowing that an actor is a member of a group can help us to predict the plans that the actor will use if it is the case that the plans of the group are known. Understanding that someone is a pacifist, for example, will help to explain why he backed away from a particular fight.

EQ19: *Why does this group have the goals that it does?*

We may want to know how a particular group came to have a given goal. In the terms we used in Schank and Abelson, 1977, we need to know the *themes* that drive the goals. In general, any goal or plan-related EQ for an individual actor has a group equivalent, wherein the actor has that goal or plan by virtue of belonging to some group known to have that goal or plan. Thus, an individual actor can have many diverse, and possibly conflicting, sets of goals, coming not only from the actor's personal needs and experiences, but also from the needs and experiences of the groups to which the actor belongs.

Other EQs for personal behavior can be derived from the nature of goals and plans (Carbonell, 1979; Schank & Abelson, 1977).

EQ20: *What counterplan was the actor performing?*

Counterplans are actions done to block the plans of other actors with which this actor is known to be in conflict. Seeing that an action fits a standard set of counterplans may help to explain it. For example, two politicians in a debate will always claim to disagree on every answer, even though what they actually say may mean the same thing. This is because each politician has to block his opponent's plan of appearing to be right.

EQ21: *What previous behavioral change led to this event?*

Because we are relying here on standard patterns of behavior, we must also know about changes in patterns. When a pattern changes, we expect it to affect future events and behaviors.

EQ21.1: *What led to the change in behavior?*

If we interpret an event as a change in behavior, then we have different explanations from those we use to explain a single action.

EQ22: *How is this action typical for this actor?*

Just as we must know the actions of an individual, to the extent that they are explained by his membership in a group, we must also know when they are explained by his simply being who he is. *That's just the way John is* is not a very deep explanation, but recognizing a pattern in a set of actions does give some comfort.

EQ23 *How is this event a typical counterplan applied to this actor?*

Sometimes, a salient feature of an actor is not what that actor does, but what happens to that actor. In EQ23, it is assumed that some other actor has done a typical counterplan against this actor. For example, in the movies, at least, detectives are always being led into traps.

EQ24: *How is this apparently ineffective plan in reality a good plan for some unseen goal?*

Reclassification can be an effective method of explanation. Things seem odd on occasion because they were misclassified in the first place. EQ24 allows for looking at an action as effecting a positive outcome by reconsidering the goals that were assumed to be operating.

2.8 Establishing Potential EQs

EQs function in two seemingly distinct ways. First, as we have seen, it is possible to have a question come to mind about why one slips on snow or why a hairdresser takes credit cards, for example, and then use the EQ as an aid in answering that question. In that case, the role of an EQ is as an index to a standard answer that can then be adapted to the particular question at hand.

The second way that EQs function is more or less the reverse of the first. One can be curious about something in a general way, but not be able to answer the question that one has posed to oneself because it is too general. In that case, an EQ can be used as a way of transforming the general question into a more specific one. This seemingly has the opposite effect from what we had in the first case. In fact, these two seemingly distinct methods are basically the same; that is, both of these methods represent different aspects of the question-transformation process.

The idea behind question-transformation is that if one has a question to answer, it is possible that it has been posed in such a way as to not enable a match between that question and the indices that point to facts in memory that might be answers to that question. Thus, questions that are not easily answered are transformed into ones that are easier to answer.

The two different uses of the EQ represent two different types of question–transformation. In the first, we transform specific questions that are unanswerable into their prototype (the EQ) for which answers exist. In the second, we make multiple transformations between the specific question and the EQ. Then, we take the EQ and attempt to use it to create more specific questions that might be easier to answer. If this seems as if it might be a neverending process, that is how it should be. The premise is that one continues to transform questions until one finds answers with which one is satisfied. In the following examples, many of the new questions that are derived from an EQ are incredibly stupid. But, some are just different enough from the ordinary to be interesting. One transforms according to one's goals. In our earlier example, the goal was assumed to be to find a creative solution to the problem of Swale's death. With such a goal in mind, we can consider more possibilities than we ordinarily might. The point is, creative explanation derives from this kind of extraordinary question–transformation process.

We saw, for the numerous examples earlier, how the questions asked related to EQs. In the next chapter, we see how those EQs help to find answers. Now, let's look at what kinds of specific questions can be derived from EQs after the general question *Why did Swale die?* is transformed by each EQ, in turn.

In trying to ascertain why Swale died, the problem is determining which of the general types of EQs could possibly be relevant here. An EQ is relevant if it in any way relates to the problem at hand. To establish if an EQ is relevant in the Swale case, let's examine them one by one:

2.8.1 Possible Questions

Each EQ has goals associated with it. Explanations are goal-driven. The task at hand, in the process of explanation, is to determine whether the goal within an EQ is relevant to the goals of the understander. In other words, there is no correct explanation. Rather, we must decide the kind of explanation that we want and pursue it. Seen that way, the previous EQs yield questions that we can ask about the situation that we have failed to understand.

For example, EQ2 (*How can I keep an unexpected physical event from happening again?*) translates, in the particular context of the Swale situation, into the question: *How can I keep Swale from dying again?* This is a rather odd question. Thus, EQ2 is not an active EQ for this example. EQ3.1 (*What theory of physical causes explains this event?*) becomes, in this example, the actual question: *What were the underlying medical causes of Swale's death?*

Clearly, such a question could be active, in the sense that it makes sense to ask it. Of course, it might not make sense for any given individual to ask it. That issue, however, is taken care of in later steps of the explanation algorithm. Initially, we only want to know which EQs are active. Later, we seek to determine which EQs are of interest to us personally.

2.8.2 EQs — Good And Bad

Following are the EQs that make sense to think about with respect to Swale's death, in terms of the question that that EQ translates into in this case.

EQ1: *What caused Swale's death?* derived from *What caused an unexpected event?*

This is the basic question. It does not need to be active, because the more specific versions, such as EQ1.1, are active.

EQ1.1: *How will Swale's death benefit others?* derived from *How will an unexpected event benefit others?*

This is a reasonable question. We can, at this point, create some convoluted plan that might have resulted in Swale's death. The trick here is to arrive at the correct characterization of the event. Is it a *death,* a *horse death,* a *racehorse death,* or a *valuable object theft?* The point is each of these might be the index to a pattern. For example, there is a movie called *The Killing ,* about the killing of a racehorse as a subterfuge for a robbery at the racetrack. People have been reminded of that movie when discussing Swale, when the idea of *horse death for profit* comes up.

EQ2: *How might Swale's death happen again?* derived from *What factors caused this event and can they happen again?*

This is not a reasonable question, although it could be transformed into a different question, *How might the same thing happen to another racehorse?* that is reasonable. That happens following, with the institutional EQs.

EQ3.1: *What were the medical causes of Swale's death?* derived from *What were the underlying causes of this bad event?*

This is a reasonable question.

EQ4: *How did Swale cause his own death?* derived from *How did the victim enable this bad event?*

Because horses do not control what happens to them this is not a reasonable question.

EQ5: *How did Swale increase the effects of his death?* derived from *What did the victim do wrong in this bad event?*

Because we don't know how Swale died, it is not reasonable to ask how Swale made things worse.

EQ6: *What circumstances that Swale had control of led to his death?* derived from *What circumstances led to this event?*

As with EQ4, this is not a reasonable question.

The institutional EQs focus on Swale as part of the "racehorse" institution.

EQ7: *Is early death a typical event in the life of a racehorse?* derived from *Why did this institution act this way?* This is a reasonable question.

EQ8: *Is early death a policy for racehorses?* derived from *What are the policies of this institution?*

EQ9: *Is early death a goal for racehorses?* derived from *What are the goals of this institution?*

EQ10: *Is early death a plan for racehorses?* derived from *What plans was this institution carrying out?*

EQ11: *Is early death more important than other things for racehorses?* derived from *What did this institution decide was most important?*

EQ12: *What do racehorses do after death?* derived from *What will this institution do next?*

None of these questions is reasonable, if for no other reason than racehorses are not planners.

EQ13: *What made Swale decide to die?* derived from *What caused the actor to behave this way?*

Not a reasonable question.

The personal explanation questions based on groups would consider Swale as a racehorse, but treat "racehorse" as a kind of animal, rather than an institutional actor. Hence, these questions are more likely to be reasonable.

EQ14: *Is Swale a member of some group for whom early death is normal?* derived from *Is the actor a member of any group that is known to do this anomalous behavior?*

EQ15: *Why might racehorses die young?* derived from *Why would the group that this the actor is a member of do this anomalous behavior?*

EQ16: *Why might racehorses, as opposed to any other kind of animal, die young?* derived from *What makes this particular group behave differently from other groups?*

EQ17: *Is Swale's death related to Swale's other activities, for example, his winning all those races?* derived from *How does this behavior fit in with a group of behaviors?*

These are all reasonable questions.

EQ18: *Is Swale's death a common plan for racehorses?* derived from *What plans does this group have?*

EQ19: *Why do racehorses have the goal of dying young?* derived from *Why does this group have the goals that it does?*

EQ20: *Is Swale's death a counterplan of Swale's?* derived from *What counterplan was the actor performing?*

EQ21: *Is Swale's death part of a changing pattern of behavior for Swale?* derived from *What previous behavioral change led to this event?*

EQ22: *Is Swale's death something Swale does all the time?* derived from *How is this action typical for this actor?*

These are not reasonable questions, because they all assume a planner is involved.

EQ23: *Is Swale's death the result of Swale being the victim of some counterplan?* derived from *How is this event a typical counterplan applied to this actor?*

This is not only a reasonable question, but one that many people come up with after thinking about the problem a little.

EQ24: *Is Swale's death, which we naturally assume to be a bad thing for Swale, really a good thing for him in the end?* derived from *How is this apparently ineffective plan in reality a good plan for some unseen goal?*

Notice that in some cases, the bad EQs translate into questions that are absurd; in other cases, they may be impossible even to state, and in still others they are sensible questions, if you relax your definition of "sensible" a bit. In other words, crazy ideas can come from pursuing a bad EQ seriously. Sometimes, of course, crazy ideas aren't so crazy after all.

2.9 Restricting EQs to Those of Interest

The next step in the explanation process is to restrict the theoretically possible explanation questions to those that actually might produce a reasonable answer. Once the active EQs are determined, the question that that EQ generates has to be put into terms that reflect the goals of the explainer. Not all active EQs are equally interesting, especially not to every explainer.

Now let's consider the active EQs for this example. Consider, for instance, the question that would be derived from EQ1.1, namely: *How will Swale's death benefit others?* In this phase of the explanation process, we take the active EQ and determine where the interests of the explainer match the goals inherent in the EQ. Thus, for example, if you are a detective or an insurance investigator, the question generated by EQ1.1 is very relevant. EQ1.1, under this view, is quite common, and we will call it *the Foul Play hypothesis.*

This is a critical point. Each of the active EQs generate a hypothesis that can be eventually translated into an explanation. The Foul Play hypothesis is a fairly standard hypothesis that should be called up in some standard situations. It is what we call an *Explanation Pattern* (XP), about which we shall have more to say shortly. Explanation Patterns are indexed under EQs. In fact, one of the primary purposes of having standardized questions such as EQs is to enable the finding of standardized answers, derived from XPs. Thus, FOUL PLAY is indexed under EQ1.1. It is not the only pattern under EQ1.1, but it is the only one we shall consider right now.

In order to correctly match active EQs with the goal of the explainer, therefore, what is really needed is a goal-biased version of the EQ. In other words, if goals are part of the EQ, then they can be matched to goals that are part of the interests of the explainer.

Now, the task of determining the relevant EQs is really one of establishing how the goal-biases inherent in the active EQ relate to one's interests. So, the FOUL PLAY pattern would be activated by EQ1.1 because detectives and other investigators are, by definition, people interested in who benefits from some crime or event. A random explainer, who just had a curiosity about Swale, could, of course, adopt the perspective of such an investigator; which means, in this case, no more than a decision to keep EQ1.1 active.

The EQ3.1 perspective (*What were the medical causes of Swale's death?*) is goal-biased toward a theoretical explanation. Here again, there are people whose perspectives are inherently oriented toward an EQ3 point of view. For example, often these people are scientists. Or, in this case, a veterinarian might look for this kind of explanation. The point is that in an automatic explanation system, the bias of the explainer would be preset. That is, if we had the task of saying what kind of explanation a veterinarian might look for, we would have classified a veterinarian as someone whose goals included theoretical explanations, and would follow the line of EQ3.1 in that case.

2.10 Is It Really Exhaustive Search?

One might get the impression from what has preceded that we are suggesting that the way we determine which EQs are possible is by testing each one, in turn, to see if it makes sense. In some sense, this is a viable algorithm. It may well be that there are occasions in which considering each possibility in turn is beneficial. This is especially likely to be worthwhile when the payoff is large. That is, sometimes an issue is significant enough to warrant an exhaustive search of that type, testing every possibility in its turn. And, one would expect that computers might well employ such a technique when looking for especially important explanations and when time is of no consequence. However, there is little reason to suppose that humans employ such algorithms.

But, as in the old joke about the woman who agrees to sex for $1 million and then is offended with a suggestion that she do it for $5, we are still just arguing about price. The cost of search is the issue. One can devise numerous methods by which only some EQs will be considered. These methods would employ, presumably, various indexing schemes that would call some EQs to mind if various conditions were met. Such conditions would include, one would assume, some of the features that we mentioned earlier. But, it is important to understand that we are just arguing about price. The cost of search is high, but one is willing to pay that cost at various times. On other occasions, one is willing to consider one or two alternatives and then further search is not worth the effort. Determining how much to search and what to consider when is an interesting topic, but probably not one of great theoretical interest.

2.11 Explanation Patterns

The ultimate objective of asking explanation questions is to access Explanation Patterns from which a new explanation can be generated. Explanation Patterns are stored under Explanation Questions. When a good EQ has been generated, it is highly likely that it will point the way to a relevant XP.

2.11.1 Finding the XP Indexed Under the EQ

The major value of Explanation Questions is to use them to find Explanation Patterns which are stored under them. Once a standard question has been found, a standard answer will not be too far away. There is no correct path to follow in deciding which Explanation Questions to pursue. One follows the interests that one has. In any automatic explanation system, goal-biases would be useful for deciding how to create an explanation within a certain perspective. So, for example, to get a veterinarian's perspective one would follow the EQ that matched according to the goal-bias that would be part of such a system's definition of a veterinarian.

In what follows, we assume that we are interested in creating many possible explanations so that we can illustrate the apparatus of explanation. The key point in explanation is that in most cases there really is nothing new under the sun. Certainly, there are occasions in which a brand new explanation is created, but understanding relies upon preestablished reference points that are learned over a period of time and applied in novel ways as needed.

Scripts and other knowledge structures (Schank & Ableson, 1977) are useful for placing events that are not obviously casually related into preestablished causal chains. The point is that one does not have to compute everything as if it had been seen for the first time. Understanding relies on our ability to take shortcuts, assuming that what we have just seen is not that different from something with which we were already familiar. All we need do, in many cases, is say "A is just like B, so I will proceed as if it were B." Not all understanding is script-based, of course, but planning mechanisms also exhibit this reliance on past experiences that have been codified and fossilized.

The same is true of explanation. A great many of our explanations rely on other explanations that we have used previously. People are inherently lazy in this way; this laziness is of great advantage, as we shall see. Much of the point behind the work on memory in (Schank, 1982) was to show how people use past experiences to help them interpret new experiences. Reminding is one of the key methods by which this is accomplished. Seeing A as an instance of B is helpful in making generalizations and, thus ,in learning about both A and B. The fact that generalizations are often inaccurate does not stop us from making them and does not lessen their value. In explanation, a similar phenomenon occurs.

We rely on *Explanation Patterns* to create new explanations from old explanations. This at once makes the process of explanation easier and makes its precision considerably less than ideal. Nevertheless, it makes creativity possible, and that is the point.

2.11.2 What Explanation Patterns Are

An Explanation Pattern is a fossilized explanation. It functions in much the same way as a script does. When it is activated, it connects a to-be-explained event with an explanation that has been used at some time in the past to explain an event similar to the current event.

Explanation Patterns are stored under EQs. Once an EQ has been determined to be of interest, various indices associated with the event to be explained can be used to activate one or more Explanation Patterns that may apply.

The value of an EQ is best understood by analogy to the primitive actions in Conceptual Dependency Theory (.Schank, 1972). The real value or meaning of the primitive actions was the set of inferences that they fired off. ATRANS, one of the Conceptual Dependency primitives, has no inherent meaning to a computer. It means the sum of all its inferences. ATRANS is interesting, in that it is a convenient shorthand for grouping together a set of inferences that have a great deal in common. What they have in common mostly is that they fire off whenever ATRANS is present. Thus, ATRANS is a kind of index that relates words that refer to it, to events that are true when the right sense of those words is present. Thus, the real value of a primitive action is in reference to a set of other actions also likely to be present when ATRANS is present.

The same situation exists with EQs. An EQ's real value, or its meaning in some sense, is in the Explanation Patterns that are indexed under it and which are caused to fire as likely hypotheses under the right conditions. To put this another way, in the case of EQ 1.1 (*How will Swale's death benefit or hurt others*), various Explanation Patterns may "come to mind" to be used in the current case, if they are indexed correctly. For example, EQ1.1 has within it the concept of a BENEFICIARY of the action. Thus the index BENEFICIARY OF DEATH is useful, if there is an Explanation Pattern with that title. An Explanation Pattern is a standard stereotyped answer, with an explanation, to a question. In this case, the question is: *Who would benefit from a particular death?*

Most people have an Explanation Pattern for such a question. It is what we called FOUL PLAY earlier. FOUL PLAY essentially provides an answer, together with an explanation, to the previous question. It says, for example, that one beneficiary is someone who stands to inherit money from the death. It also says that another beneficiary of a death is someone who has an insurance policy made out to him or her on the life of the dead individual.

We can see that there are really two Explanation Patterns here (actually there are probably many more). One is FOUL PLAY; INHERITANCE, and the other is FOUL PLAY; INSURANCE. Each of these is proposed as a hypothesis as the result of finding the XP indexed under a plausible EQ. The next step in the explanation process, therefore, is the evaluation of the reasonableness of the hypothesis indexed under the EQ. Thus, an EQ is valuable for suggesting to us that FOUL PLAY;INHERITANCE should be considered. Whether or not this is a reasonable hypothesis, we want to have it suggested to us, as there is no way of knowing a priori if it is reasonable until we have considered it for a while. Thus EQs force us to consider their inherent hypotheses. We can always choose to abandon those hypotheses, of course.

2.11.3 The Structure of an Explanation Pattern

An Explanation Pattern (XP) consists of a number of parts. First, we have an index to the pattern. This index is made up of a combination of states and events. Second, we have a set of states of the world under which those indices can be expected to be active. When those states of the world are achieved, the indices fire. The next part is the scenario. The scenario is essentially a little story that is a carefully constructed causal chain of states and events that starts with the premise of achieving the combination of states and events in the index and presents a plan of action for achieving that combination. The fourth part is the resultant state that follows from the scenario. This state may also be used as an index initially (e.g., early death in the Swale case). Also, attached to an XP are explanations that have been previously compiled from that XP. In this way, one can be reminded of similar cases. Thus, XPs are themselves a means of traversing memory. Last, every XP has a reason attached to it that can both serve as an index and as the ultimate explanation behind the use of the explanation embodied in an XP. In other words, every explanation can cause us to demand an explanation at a higher level.

To make this simpler to understand, the EQ poses a question, and the Explanation Pattern answers that question. But, this is all in the most general of terms. The question is not about Swale's death, but about beneficiaries of death in general. The answer is not about Swale, but about prior experiences with the general phenomenon. It could not be any other way, of course. Memory cannot concern itself with storing specific patterns about Swale. Such patterns, once encountered, are not likely to be of use ever again. Rather, memory stores patterns in the most general terms, and thus we must access them in the most general terms. This is the value of the EQ. After having received our answer in general terms (the XP), we can begin to try and alter that answer so as to make it relate to the particulars at hand. The method is to take a specific question and generalize from it in order to find a general question under which is indexed a general answer. Then, take the general answer and particularize it to find the specific answer that you were after originally.

The next step then, is to match the particulars. We would reason in the Swale case, under FOUL PLAY;INHERITANCE, that horses don't usually inherit money, so that that hypothesis is a bit silly. But, this false XP might bring to mind that horse owners do have insurance policies on their horses so that this hypothesis might yet be viable. From bad hypotheses often come good ones. This is the ultimate value of the XP with respect to creativity.

2.11.4 Finding Additional Patterns

The key to inventing creative explanations lies in intelligently indexing the Explanation Patterns. It would be nice if everything we would ever want to explain about Swale were listed under horse death. But this is unlikely to be the case. One way to explain something unusual is by reference to something different, for which there exists an explanation. So, one way to find a candidate set of Explanation Patterns is by changing the event that is to be explained into one that is like the original event but is different enough to possibly bring up a new idea that is relevant. In this way, we have the possibility of finding additional Explanation Patterns that are not connected to the indices at hand, but might be relevant. Thus, for example, we might know of an XP that relates to cars or elephants. We might want to test it to see if it might relate to a horse as well. Therefore, we attempt to change the event that needs to be explained into another event that we can explain.

To do this, we use a set of rules that we call tweaking rules. Tweaking rules are very important for the process of the transformation and adaptation of XPs into answers that are relevant to specific questions. To get a feel for what these rules look like, let's consider three of them here:

Rule 1: *Transpose objects that are alike in function.*

The idea behind a tweaking rule is to change what we were looking at into something else that might give us new ideas. Since we are interested in horses, let's consider a different aspect of a horse from the obvious aspects that are relevant in Swale's case. For example, a horse is transportation, and so is a car. Thus, one thing to consider would be rules relating to the "death" of cars. We can try this in any of the EQs. For example, "death of cars" plus EQ2 (*What actors caused this event that might happen again'?*) would index Explanation Patterns that we might try to apply to horses.

Here's a possible answer to the specific question about cars that came to mind as one of us considered this EQ: It happens that in his car there is a hose that pops out fairly frequently. He don't know what this hose's function is, but he knows what to do when the car fails to go—put the hose back in place. This is his own personal Explanation Pattern for "car death." Notice that this particular XP doesn't explain too much. This is true of many XPs, as we shall see. This one does its job in helping fix the car however, and that is what matters. He was reminded of it while thinking about Swale and considered for a moment the idea that Swale's hose had disconnected and no one put it back in time. Such a hypothesis can then be checked for credibility, of course. And, naturally, it is quite silly. But many times this kind of application of an XP and subsequent tweaking is not so absurd.

Rule 2: *Transpose objects in similar environments.*

For example, if we consider Swale to be a person who chose to live the way he lives, that is, in a stall, then EQ6 (*What circumstances led to this event?*) becomes relevant, and we can consider what would happen if a person had had the experiences that Swale had. If he were a person and he lived in a stall, we would assume that these cruel conditions killed him. Thus, the hypothesis, *Living in a stall would kill anyone* can be generated by this rule.

Rule 3: *Transpose objects that are alike in behavior.*

Suppose that we consider racehorses to be like star performers, in that they both constantly exert great effort for short periods of time and can become extraordinarily rich and famous. This makes EQ14 (*Is the actor a member of any group that is known to do this anomalous behavior?*) relevant. We might be reminded of star performers who have died young, such as Janis Joplin and Jimi Hendrix. This reminding enables the proposal that *Swale died from overdosing on drugs taken to relieve the pressures and boredom of stardom and available because of wealth.*

There are many more rules than these, of course. The real problem here is finding suitable Explanation Patterns. Heuristics for bringing up likely candidates are, thus, an important part of the task of explanation.

2.11.5 Indexing Explanation Patterns

The major value of EQs, as we have said, is in their connection to XPs. XPs often have a trite and boring form, like that of clichés or proverbs. Normally, such frozen patterns might bear little relation to any creative process. But, taken out of context, they can often shed light on new domains of inquiry. That is the philosophy behind the misapplication of Explanation Patterns. When one applies patterns where they do not obviously belong, interesting things can result.

For example, let's consider EQ7 (*Is early death a typical action for racehorses?*). To be useful, EQ7 would have to be a pointer to relevant XPs that might help answer this question. In other words, what we require of EQ7 is that it somehow point us to Explanation Patterns that will tell us about early death, this time from the perspective of the societal factors involved. To put this another way, the question we really want to consider is what kinds of things normally cause early death. That is, we can ignore racehorses entirely. (This is another tweaking rule, which says that one can eliminate set membership constraints from consideration.) What we want to know is, what societal conditions cause early death? Then, after getting some XPs from that question, we can begin to consider if they might be relevant to Swale at all.

Since Explanation Patterns have a way of looking like clichés or proverbs, let's consider some cliché XPs that might relate here.

So, for example, here are some Explanation Patterns that are fairly standard which can be found under EQ7:

> *Early death comes from being malnourished as a youth.*
>
> *High living brings early death.*
>
> *An inactive mind can cause the body to suffer.*
>
> *High pressure jobs cause heart attacks.*

What we are arguing here is that once these Explanation Patterns are found, they can be adapted to serve as explanations of the event under consideration. Now, clearly, some of these Explanation Patterns sound pretty silly when applied to Swale. On the other hand, they are possibilities. Some of them represent humorous possibilities and some of them are bizarre hypotheses which might just have something to them. It is not unusual for weird ideas to start the creative juices flowing, and that is just what we are suggesting here. People, and computers, can get their weird ideas from playing with standard XPs in unorthodox ways, and this is how fossilized explanations, derived from Explanation Patterns, can serve as the beginning of the creative process.

Could Swale have felt the pressure of being Horse of the Year and have had this pressure contribute to a heart attack? Sounds silly, but who knows? The point, of course, is that we have just generated a hypothesis. We took an XP unrelated to Swale, found under the index EARLY DEATH, which EQ7 uses, and related it back to Swale's life. We can now consider the legitimacy of this hypothesis.

Was Swale taking one too many uppers? Was he living high? He was a "star," after all. And stars do live high. So the XP fits the case, at least superficially. Where would this hypothesis come from? The argument here is that one would want to be reminded of a rock star or a star athlete. Should Swale remind you of Janis Joplin? Maybe not immediately, but Explanation Patterns can cause that reminding to occur. The task is first to cause those remindings to occur, thus bringing to mind various hypotheses, which later may be discarded. First, they must be invented. This kind of reminding can be the source of real creativity.

We can see this kind of "creativity by reminding" with respect to EQ14. In a seminar on Explanation, one of our students was reminded, while discussing Swale's death, of Jim Fixx, the author of a book on the health benefits of jogging that was widely read and respected. The irony is that Jim Fixx died while jogging at a comparatively young age. This kind of reminding can be very valuable for its ability to bring to mind questions, in this instance of the possible health hazards imposed by excessive running. And it is from the formulation of such questions that creative thoughts can occur. Formulating new questions is as important as formulating new answers.

In EQ14 *(Is Swale a member of some group for whom early death is normal?)*, we are trying to learn something new that will both explain the event under consideration as well as tie together one or more unrelated facts into some kind of explanatory whole. Thus, for example, if it were the case that many 3-year-old racehorses die we would want to realize that and use that fact as an explanation of Swale's death. That would, of course, not be an interesting explanation, but it is one kind of explanation that XPs provide, namely, routine ones that match the conditions of the XP perfectly.

Thus, not only clichés or proverbs are indexed as Explanation Patterns. We would also expect, as a rather standard form of Explanation Patterns, general truths. That is, one thing that we do when we explain something is to create a new rule that we can use in the future to help us understand. Such new rules are also indexed under Explanation Patterns to be used in the understanding process. Thus, Swale's death is in no way anomalous if we have the rule that many 3-year-old race horses die young, regardless of whether we know a fact that explains that rule.

Similarly, if Swale is a member of a class of actors known to die young or to be subject to heart conditions, then Swale's death is explained in the sense of explanation that we are discussing. So, we might have a rule that says that finely tuned athletes suffer more physical problems than others. This rule would render Swale's death nonanomalous.

Alternatively, we would like to be able to construct such a rule as a way of explaining the anomaly. To do this requires us to find a class of actors for whom we have information that is connected to all death. The reminding about Jim Fixx is an instance of this kind of rule-search. In order to be reminded in this way, the student would have had to have created a class of actors into which he could place Swale and into which he had already previously placed Jim Fixx. Then, having indexed Jim Fixx in the same way that he indexed Swale, presumably with something like EARLY DEATH, he would be reminded. The value of the reminding is to start the process of creating a new rule incorporating both events.

EQ16 *(Why might a racehorse, as opposed to any other kind of animal, die young?)* is enough like EQ14 that we can avoid getting too
detailed in our discussion. We might like to understand why athletes who run have heart problems. Or, we might want to investigate the issue of whether these problems could have been predicted better. Thus, we might want to consider other athletes with
heart problems to see if taken all together they might all have
something in common that enabled a deeper understanding of the
general phenomenon. Is early death a factor in athletes in general,
or just runners, or just dark-haired athletes?

In EQ23 *(Is Swale's death the result of Swale being the victim of
some counterplan?)* the question is whether Swale was in some way
preventing the goals of someone else. Since Swale was entered in
races, obviously he was preventing the losers from winning.
Known counterplanning techniques, that is, the Explanation Patterns indexed under EQ23, include killing one's opponent in a
contest. Thus, we have another possible explanation.

2.11.6 Modifying Aspects Of The Hypotheses

The next step in the explanation process, after a hypothesis has
been derived from an XP, is to begin to modify aspects of the hypotheses. Thus, we must take the hypotheses created in the last
step and see if they make sense. The hypotheses recalled were
created by simply copying what seemed to be relevant Explanation Patterns. Now the task is to see if they really are relevant.
We must alter the parts of the Explanation Pattern that have nothing to do with the actual case.

The INHERITANCE idea doesn't seem viable because horses
don't have relatives who fight for inheritances. The INSURANCE
idea makes sense if, and only if, the beneficiary of the policy that
insured Swale stood to make more money from his death than
from his being alive. The evidence with respect to that issue is just
the opposite, so this hypothesis can be disregarded.

The MALNOURISHED hypothesis seems wrong given what
we know about how valuable racehorses are treated. However,
before totally discounting this or any other hypothesis, we should
recall that explainers can have different goals rendering various
more or less viable relative to those goals. So someone who
wanted to make up an interesting story might consider a
racehorse who died early to have died from an earlier maltreat-
ment for use as a possible story line. Creative hypotheses are useful for things other than detective work of course.

LIVED TOO HIGH might he viable. Again it depends on our goals. We cannot discount it as a real explanation without investigating exactly how Swale did live. But it is a good candidate for a joke explanation. Humorists find good material from such exaggeration, and this kind of humor often originates from the construction of explanations in this manner. The same is true of MIND INACTIVE; BODY SUFFERED.

HIGH PRESSURE JOB CAUSED HEART ATTACK seems viable if we change "job" to "situation" and assume that Swale "knew" about the pressure on him. Since this last assumption seems a little tenuous, we again have a candidate for a joke, although this explanation seems more plausible because one cannot really know what a horse knows.

RUNNING ATHLETES SUFFER PHYSICAL PROBLEMS allows us to speculate on whether there really are any similarities between Jim Fixx and Swale that ought to be looked into. Swale didn't die while running, neither did he write a book. Plenty of racehorses live to a ripe old age, as do plenty of runners. Nevertheless, it is possible to hold on to this hypothesis as viable.

DARK-HAIRED ACTORS ARE PRONE TO HEART ATTACKS is lighthearted and probably irrelevant. If it were true, we could speculate on the cause. But, presumably ,it would be because of something other than hair color.

The PLOT TO LET OPPONENT WIN is entirely viable, however. Here we can assume that the owner of the second-best horse in Swale's next race was a serious possibility as the murderer, if it was found that he was murdered (but he wasn't).

The end of this step in the explanation process, therefore, is the retaining of the few hypotheses that remain viable as possible explanations. The next task is to consider if any of these new, viable hypotheses ought to be retained as beliefs.

2.11.7 Testing the New Belief

There isn't anything particularly unique about the process of testing the new belief. We are left with viable hypotheses for which we can attempt to find counterexamples. Or, we can try to find other facts that correlate with each new hypothesis that serve to strengthen it. We can try to test the causalities involved. That is, if we have asserted that A caused B, we can try to find other things like A that have caused other things like B.

The most important part of this process is living with the new fact. Recall that what we are trying to do here is create an additive explanation; that is, we are trying to learn something. And, what we are trying to learn is a set of expectations that, had we had them in the first place, would have caused us to have never noticed the anomaly. An event is anomalous, after all, only by reference to what we already know about the world. An event that is anomalous to one person will not be anomalous to another, if the second person had the appropriate expectations for that event. So, we are looking to learn new facts that will resolve current anomalies. But, ideally, the new fact that we learn will do more than simply resolve the current anomaly. We want to be able to explain events that we may encounter in the future. Once an anomaly is resolved, it ought not to seem anomalous to us the next time we encounter it or anything like it. In other words, we want to be able to understand more than we were able to understand before confronting the current anomaly.

Thus, for example, we want to be able to use the explanation PLOT TO LET OWNERS WIN at some future time. Or, to put this another way, we want the Swale episode itself to become an Explanation Pattern, such that when a baseball player who was likely to have been selected as Most Valuable Player for the year suddenly gets injured in an unusual way, we might suspect his nearest rival for the award.

In order to do that, we would need to first have verified that this was the case with Swale (which there is no reason to believe, really, but just suppose it for a while). Then, we would have to correctly index the Swale case such that it was something to be reminded of when a debilitating circumstance took a prized competitor out of action. We would also want to find this episode only when the circumstances were in some way unusual. We certainly wouldn't want to think about Swale every time a star football player got injured.

A new explanation need never be verified in actuality. We can keep whatever Swale hypothesis we like, for as long as we like. The real issue is how often the explanation we have concocted is used to help us explain something else.

2.12 Creating New From Old

We can see, then, that the most interesting role of Explanation Patterns, ironically, is not in using them to explain exactly the kind of event they were intended for. XPs are fossilized reasoning. They represent our intention not to think very profoundly about a subject. When we use an XP in its intended role, we are deciding to forego complex reasoning of our own in favor of using a well-established reasoning chain that is in favor amongst a particular group of reasoners. Essentially, the normal use of an XP is of the following form:

1. Identify event sequence needing explanation.
2. Establish index that is likely to lead to an XP.
3. Find relevant XP attached to that index.
4. Substitute XP into event sequence.

This is the normal situation, as we have seen. But what is interesting about XPs is their abnormal use. That is, it is in the misapplication of an XP that possibilities for creativity arise. Misapplication is a bit of a misnomer here, since that misapplication is often quite intentional. This misapplication-based creative explanation process, which is the subject in Part II, occurs when we decide not to forgo complex reasoning, when we decide not to be satisfied by merely applying a stored XP. This generally happens because there is no XP in memory that fits the current situation to our satisfaction. In these situations, we can still make use of retrieved explanations, but they serve only as a starting point. This is when things really get interesting.

Part II
Detailed Investigations

3. An Overview of Case-based Explanation

The framework Schank developed in the work collected in Part I of this book places the explanation–construction process at the center of intelligence, and outlines how the process works. Part I brought together a sampling of the work that has been done by Schank's students, in which they built on that framework. Each chapter in Part II is an effort to fill in part of Schank's outline, to make the theory specific enough to be implemented on a computer.

In Schank's framework, an explanation builder is called into action whenever a mental process, such as planning or story understanding, detects an anomaly. The overarching question addressed in this part of the book is how to build a computer program that can propose explanations for such anomalies as they arise. Each of the chapters addresses some aspect of that question.

3.1 The SWALE Project: Understanding Stories That Require Explanation

The first effort to build such a program was called the SWALE (System with Automatic Learning and Explanation) project. SWALE implemented a case-based model of explanation (see Hammond, 1989; Schank & Riesbeck 1981 for a broader discussion of case-based reasoning), in which new explanations are constructed by retrieving and adapting explanation patterns stored in memory.

The three most important questions faced by the SWALE team were as follows: (a) how to retrieve explanation patterns from memory that may address the anomaly; (b) how to evaluate the retrieved explanations in the context of the detected requirements; and (c) how to adapt the retrieved explanation patterns to meet the current requirements.

The SWALE project thus naturally divided into three modules—a retriever, an evaluator, and an adapter. This tripartite division turned out to be convenient because there were three contributors to the SWALE project; each contributor adopted one module, and the theory behind each module grew into a doctoral dissertation. Three of the six chapters that follow this are excerpted from those SWALE-related dissertations. Chris Owens' work on retrieval gave rise to the ANON program, which is described in chapter 4. David Leake's work on evaluation, which was implemented in the Accepter program, is described in chapter 6, and Alex Kass' work on adaptation, which grew into the ABE program, is described in chapter 8.

Of course, the SWALE-related theses do not represent all of the work that has been done on case-based reasoning and explanation. (See Koton, 1988 and Simmons, 1988 for description of some of the case-based explanation work we do not have room to explore in this book.) Even within Schank's group, other students who began within the same framework have attacked the retrieval, evaluation, and adaptation problems differently from the SWALE authors. Therefore, in order to give a richer picture of the issues involved in addressing these problems, we have included two chapters on each of the three main issues; each chapter describing the solution to a problem taken by a SWALE author is followed by a chapter that comes at the same problem from a different angle. Owens' chapter on retrieval issues is followed by Eric Domeshek's, which describes retrieval in a different context, and focuses on different aspects of the problem. Leake's work on evaluation is followed by a chapter by Ashwin Ram. Ram's work is broad in scope, but a central aspect of it is related to evaluation. Kass's work on adaptation is followed by a chapter by Eric Jones, in which a different aspect of the adaptation problem is the main focus. Of course, the non-SWALE theses had focuses that did not always match the focus of the corresponding SWALE-related thesis. We have, however, attempted to edit the chapters in this book to make the parallels as clear as possible.

The purpose of this overview chapter is to put the rest of Part II into perspective by bridging the gap between Schank's very broad framework, and the much more specific, technical descriptions of individual component processes that make up the chapters that follow. Our method of doing so is to describe the organization of the SWALE project, and the case-based explanation process that it implements. This should establish a useful context for understanding, not just for the SWALE-related chapters, but also for the other chapters that present alternative approaches to retrieval, evaluation, and adaptation issues.

In this overview, we don't describe the internal algorithms the modules use; instead, we describe the way that the modules are organized with respect to one another, and we try to answer the following questions: What does a case-based explainer look like at the highest level? How is it similar to other systems, and how different? How are the modules of a case-based explainer organized, and what information must they pass back and forth between one another?

The SWALE program was conceived as an approach to understanding a class of stories that no previous story-understanding theory had been able to handle. Earlier theories of story-understanding had focused on the text-processing issues and "straightforward" inference issues required to understand stories that explicitly spell everything out. By straightforward, we do not mean that it is straightforward to get computers to perform that type of inference, but that it is straightforward for people to do so. Many interesting issues must be addressed in order to get computers to understand such stories, but none of those issues are at the heart of what happens when people read stories that raise what a human reader would call interesting questions, especially interesting "why" questions. When people read the newspaper the day after the Space Shuttle exploded, they wondered why it had happened. When one reads a novel, one guesses about motivations that might explain the characters' actions. Interesting stories typically *don't* spell everything out; they leave the reader to develop hypotheses. This is the aspect of story understanding that the SWALE project focused on: After the low-level text processing and inferencing have been done, how does a story–understander develop hypotheses to address the "why" questions that the story raises?

3.1.1 Schema Application and the Inference Problem

What approach did the SWALE project take to the explanation problem? The answer is that we adopted a case-based approach to the problem. Case-based explanation is a schema-based theory of inference. As such, it owes a great deal to the schema-based theories that came before it, particularly script/frame theory (see Minsky, 1975; Schank & Abelson, 1977). A brief review of the purpose, as well as the limitations of script/frame theory,[1] should help make it clear what that approach was and why we adopted it.

3.1.2 The Inference Problem

Understanding is hard because the data that an understander is presented with is usually full of gaps. Whether we are trying to understand a story or an event in the real world, we are only told explicitly, by the author, or by our senses, a small fraction of the relevant facts. Much is left to us to *infer*. Some of the inferences we must make are so straightforward that we never become aware of making them, except perhaps in the rare case when a straightforward inference turns out to be wrong. For instance, if a man brings a menu to us while we are dining in a restaurant, we infer that the man is a waiter, and that we are meant to choose a meal to order by reading the menu. If we see a coworker arrive at work with a set of car keys in hand, we might assume that she drove to work. If we discover that a character in a story is in high school, we automatically infer that the character is in his teens. We may later discover that we were wrong, but until we do, we make the inference without even thinking about it.

Not all the inferences we make are quite as straightforward. Although all inferences are hypotheses, some actually have the *feel* of hypotheses. For instance, if we hear that someone had a stroke we might hypothesize that he had a "type A" personality. Or we might suppose that he has a history of hypertension in his family. If we are considering an issue carefully, acting as detectives in mysteries do, we might consider multiple alternative hypotheses, look for evidence to rule each in or out, and settle on a particular inference only after much computation.

3.1.3 Inference Chaining

The simplest theory of inference is one in which a system has a large corpus of inference rules that it chains together to create explanations. There are many problems with this theory, but the most important is that it is too inefficient, particularly for the straightforward inferences we must constantly make, just to understand the most straightforward events. Inference-chainers must do a good deal of search to make an inference chain. Fur-

---

[1]Readers interested in obtaining a detailed understanding of script application might benefit from the chapter about SAM, and the Micro-SAM exercises (Schank & Riesbeck, 1981).

thermore, since they solve each problem from scratch, they must do the same amount of search the 100th time they process a kind of event as they do the first time. That's the real flaw. It is reasonable for a completely novel inference chain to take a long time to build; complete novelty is difficult for people. But the inference-chaining model treats every problem as if it were completely novel. Systems built on this model bog down quickly because the "obvious" inferences are not obvious to them. That's where scripts come in.

3.1.4 Scripts

Scripts are frozen inference chains stored in memory. The reason for them is to reduce the standard inferences to a matter of recalling the appropriate script and applying it. Scripts don't make thinking easier—they make thinking unnecessary. That's the wonderful thing about scripts. Causal reasoning is a lot of work, but if you know a script that applies to a situation, you don't have to do much causal reasoning. Scripts transform the inference problem from one of constructing a chain to one of retrieving and applying a prestored chain.

For example, if you have a suitable restaurant script, you don't need to think about why the waitress brings a menu every time a customer is seated in the restaurant. Thinking through routine events like that every time is a waste of cognitive resources. If we had to do this all the time, we'd never have the time to think any "real" important thoughts. By freezing expectations in a knowledge structure, the inferencing needed to understand a phenomenon the first time it was experienced can be avoided during subsequent iterations. When actions go as expected, all you need to do is follow the script. Events mentioned in the script, but not directly observed, can be inferred. All the script needs to specify is what to expect and when to expect it. It specifically doesn't need to know why.

Things get more interesting when unforeseen deviations from the script occur. What happens when you go to a new restaurant, and the waitress doesn't bring a menu? How do you adjust? Can you just skip over this line in the script as if it were just ceremonial, or is it crucial? Can another action substitute, and if so, what? The restaurant script (as formulated in Schank & Abelson, 1977, e.g.) supplies no clues because the restaurant script doesn't tell you why the menu-bringing line appeared in the script in the first place. Usually, you don't need to know, but when things don't go as expected, you do. The fact that scripts, as originally formulated, lack this kind of information makes them brittle knowledge structures that are not adaptable.

Script–appliers handle routine inference more efficiently than inference–chainers, but they run aground when presented with events that are not routine. One obvious approach would be to combine the script-application approach with an inference–chainer. The script–applier could handle events that exactly match an available script. If no script that exactly matches the event is available, the system could fall back on inference chaining. This approach has something to recommend it. The problem with it is that a great many experiences are neither completely novel, nor are they exact fits with any preexisting scripts. Many experiences are variations on preexisting patterns. A system that must ignore its schemas, unless it has one that matches a new input exactly, is going to miss out on much of the value of those schemas. Humans do not treat events as completely novel when they are actually variations on previous patterns. Instead, they adapt their patterns to accommodate the new event. People react, even to rather surprising events, by attempting to explain them in terms of their previous patterns. If the experience calls for it, they will attempt to build a new variation on the pattern. For instance, if you have a pattern built up to explain the early death of successful rock stars, and you are confronted with the death of a famous athlete, you are likely to make some use of the rock-star pattern in a slightly rearranged form. This adaptation process is more time consuming than simple script application, but more efficient than throwing out the entire schema and building a new one from scratch.

3.1.5 Adding Adaptation to Script/Frame Theory

Case-based explanation is an extension of script/frame theory for handling inputs that are neither completely novel, nor completely routine. The key to building that more flexible understander is to relax the assumption, which script theory relied on, that schemas will be retrieved and applied in situations that precisely match the situations that those schemas were built to describe. Instead, one must assume that schemas will often be retrieved in situations that are only *sort of* like those they were originally built to handle.

Broadening the range of situations in which a schema will be applied introduces the need to evaluate the newly produced explanations for problems, and to do some creative adaptation to fix any problems that are found. In an adaptation-based theory of explanation, much of the burden of producing an appropriate explanation is moved out of the schema-retrieval module into the adaptation module, which we call the tweaker. The emphasis is shifted from pulling a perfectly appropriate structure out of memory, to being able to work with whatever the best structure pulled out of memory happens to be. Because this adaptation process is more time consuming than simply applying structures straight out of the schema library, it makes sense to add a storage module as well, allowing the system to save and reuse the new variations of its structures that the adaptation module produces.

In the augmented theory, "retrieve and apply" evolves into "retrieve, apply, evaluate, adapt, and store." Actually, the application, evaluation and adaptation steps are contained in a loop; when a new variation is produced, that new variation is instantiated and evaluated again. If there are still problems with the explanation, it can be further adapted.[2] Pseudo-code in Table 2.1 depicts the high-level algorithm.

3.1.6 Knowledge Organization for Case-based Explanation

A principal difference that distinguished inference-chainers from structure-appliers was the type of knowledge base that they employed; script appliers required a structure library but no rule base, whereas inference-chainers required a rule-base, and had no use for a library of schemas.

The adaptation-based model must maintain both in order to maintain the efficiency of a structure-applier without giving up the flexibility of a rule-based system. The ability to reuse the pre-stored knowledge structures provides efficiency. The rule-base provides flexibility by allowing the system to evaluate and modify those stored explanations to fit new situations. For instance, suppose the system is trying to explain the death of the racehorse, Swale (recall the Swale story in the preface). If the system is reminded of an explanation of sudden death resulting from cardiac stress caused by recreational jogging, the rule base will allow the system to first reject the explanation in its original form—horses don't participate in recreational jogging—and then to build a

---

[2]This methodology has been applied to tasks other than explanation as well as (Kolodner, 1987) and (Hammond, 1986). Some other work that specifically focuses on adapting explanations includes (Koton, 1988 and Simmons, 1988).

Table 3.1. High-Level Description of Case-based Explanation
Algorithm

```
LOOP1
    RETRIEVE XP
    LOOP2
        APPLY XP
        EVALUATE EXPLANATION
        TWEAK XP
    END LOOP2
END LOOP1
STORE NEW XP
```

- The outer loop involves retrieving an XP from the system's library and then running the inner loop on that retrieved XP. This outer loop iterates until a satisfactory explanation has been produced, or until the retriever cannot find any more relevant XPs.
- The inner loop (i.e., the apply, evaluate, tweak cycle) iterates until the evaluator decides either that a satisfactory explanation has been produced, or that it isn't worth trying to further tweak the current XP.

modification, because racehorses do participate in other forms of strenuous exercise that could cause cardiac stress.

3.1.7 Explanation Patterns

Understanding stories that raise open-ended explanation questions requires knowledge structures that are specifically designed to encode causal explanations. In order to adapt an old knowledge structure to a new situation, rather than just applying it, the system has to have explanations for why the elements of the structure are as they are. The structures we designed to meet these needs were based on the Explanation Patterns described earlier in Part I.

XPs are structures that explicitly encode causal coherence. This causal annotation is what makes explanatory memory structures adaptable, whereas those that don't encode causal reasoning are brittle. SWALE's XPs contain variables so that they can be instantiated to explain new cases. In some ways, XPs are a lot like scripts and their more general successors, called Memory Organization Packages (MOPS; Schank, 1982). But XPs serve a different function from scripts and MOPs. The central organizing principle underlying scripts is a temporal sequence of scenes. MOPs add the abstraction and subpart hierarchies, but are still essentially temporally ordered expectations. XPs, on the other hand, are intended to help process surprising events by giving a causal explanation of the event. (We use the term *explanation* to refer to an XP that has been instantiated for a specific case.) The central organizing principle is the inference chain rather than temporal sequencing. The causal network leads from a set of explanatory premises through some intermediate beliefs to an explanatory conclusion, which is what the XP explains. The explanatory premises are those beliefs for which no further explanation is given within the XP, although there may be other XPs that can be used to explain them.

The XP library contains the explanatory structures that the system has put together in the past, as well as those that it was told directly. The XPs themselves are made up of facts and rules that combine in a causal network to lead from a set of premises toward a conclusion. The conclusion is the event that the XP explains.

For example, the JOPLIN XP explains the death of a famous young rock star in terms of a drug overdose. The essential idea of that XP is as follows:

- Success leads to both stress and wealth;
- being a rock star leads to having many drug-using friends; and
- having wealth and having drug-using friends leads to easy access to drugs.
- Stress leads to a desire for stress reduction;
- access to drugs combined with desire for stress reduction leads to drug use; and
- drug use leads to drug overdose; overdose leads to death.

Computer output of the JOPLIN XP, which more closely resembles the internal representation of that knowledge structure, appears in Table 3.2.

Table 3.2. Computer Output Describing the JOPLIN XP

```
Assumptions:
  ?X? was A ROCK STAR.
  ?X? was young.
Chain of reasoning:
  ?X? had a HIGH degree of WEALTH LEVEL BECAUSE
    ?X? was A ROCK STAR [SOCIAL-CAUSE].
  ?X? had a VERY HIGH degree of STRESS LEVEL BECAUSE
    ?X? was A ROCK STAR [SOCIAL-CAUSE].
  ?X? had a HIGH degree of INFLUENCEABILITY BECAUSE
    ?X? was young [SOCIAL-CAUSE].
  ?X? had access to RECREATIONAL-DRUGS BECAUSE
    ?X? had a HIGH degree of WEALTH LEVEL
      [PRECONDITION-SATISFACTION].
  ?X? desired that: ?X? was drugged out BECAUSE ?X?
    ?X? had a HIGH degree of INFLUENCEABILITY
      [SOCIAL-CAUSE] AND
    had a VERY HIGH degree of STRESS LEVEL [MENTAL-
      CAUSE].
  ?X? TOOK DRUGS BECAUSE
    ?X? desired that: ?X? was drugged out [GOAL-SAT]
      AND
    ?X? had access to RECREATIONAL-DRUGS
      [PRECONDITION-SATISFACTION].
  ?X? had a drug overdose BECAUSE
    ?X? TOOK DRUGS [PHYSICAL-CAUSE].
  ?X? died BECAUSE
    ?X? had a drug overdose [PHYSICAL-CAUSE].
```

Because XPs contain an explicit representation of the causal relationships between their components, they are very adaptable knowledge structures. If some component of an XP is inappropriate when the XP is applied in a new context, the system has a relatively easy time determining which parts of the XP must be fixed in order to repair the problem, and which other parts of the XP are affected by the potential repair. This makes it possible to know what questions to ask and how to search for answers.

3.2 A Closer Look at the SWALE Algorithm

The algorithm in Table 3.1 contains five main steps, each of which is described in slightly more detail here. Those descriptions are followed by a detailed flow-control description, which ends the chapter.

3.2.1 Retrieval and Application

The first two steps in developing an explanation are called *XP retrieval,* and *XP application.* They involve extracting an appropriate XP from the system's large library and instantiating it with the variable bindings generated by the current situation. These first two steps in the explanation process are analogous to the structure retrieval and application phases performed by script-based story understanders, such as SAM (Cullingford, 1978) and FRUMP (DeJong, 1977). The structures are different and the retrieval criteria are different, but otherwise, the XPs are treated like scripts during these initial two steps.

If the anomalous event is well explained by the retrieved XP, creative explanation isn't really required. In situations such as this, the explanation process is pretty much reduced to script application. But because the needs of a more flexible understanding system require that we assume that many experiences will not completely match any structure retrieved from memory, it is crucial that the explanation process include a postapplication step in which the system identifies any weakness that the explanation may have.

3.2.2 Evaluation

The process of *explanation evaluation* is a complex one. Explanations can fail in many different ways: they can be inconsistent; incomplete, based on invalid assumptions; or can simply contain the wrong type of knowledge for the system's current purposes. Leake (1990) discussed the process of evaluating explanations in great detail. For our purposes, merely assume that the process can be performed. Our only real concern with regard to evaluation is what the output of an evaluator would look like. It is the description of how the XP is inadequate which drives the XP adaptation phase.

3.2.3 Adaptation

XP adaptation (or *tweaking* for short) is where the real creativity comes in. The tweaker addresses the problems found during evaluation by producing a new variation on the retrieved XP that does not suffer from the problem that the evaluator identified. There are many different tweaking strategies, each appropriate to a particular class of XP failures. Each strategy corresponds to a different question that it may be useful to ask about the failed explanation. For any given failure, the tweaker may know a number of relevant questions, and it may have to try asking itself more than one question before producing a variation that satisfies the evaluator.

Actually, the interaction between the evaluator and the tweaker is an iterative one. When the tweaker is done performing an adaptation, the resulting XP must be reapplied and then reevaluated. The system must ensure that the problem that originally caused the evaluator to call for tweaking has been addressed satisfactorily, and to check that no other problems of importance to the evaluator have been introduced. After each step of tweaking the evaluator has three choices:

- It can decide that the new variation is satisfactory, and should be adopted;
- it can decide that the system should give up on building a variation on the retrieved XP that fits the current case; or
- it can request further tweaking.

3.2.4 Storage

Finally, when the tweaker succeeds in creating an acceptable explanation, a module responsible for *XP storage* is employed to index the new variant in memory so the results of the tweaker's labor will be available for building new explanations in the future. Script–appliers didn't need storage routines because they never changed their structures; but the existence of an adaptation step makes a storage step necessary as well.

3.2.5 Communication Among Modules

Figure 3.1 below depicts the modules discussed earlier and diagrams the interconnections between them. The thin-bordered, rectangular boxes represent the input, output, and knowledge sources, whereas the heavy-bordered boxes with rounded corners represent the program modules. The numbered arrows in the diagram represent flow of information; each numbered arrow is described by the corresponding numbered paragraph following.

1. *The initial input goes to the XP retriever:* The explanation process begins when an anomaly is detected. Typically, this occurs when a surprising event is encountered during story understanding, but an anomaly is any event that the system decides needs explaining. Of course, this raises the interesting question of how anomalies get noticed in the first place,

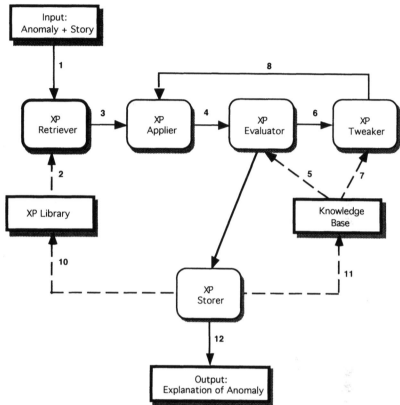

FIG 3.1. SWALE flow-control diagram.

which is beyond the scope of this chapter. We simply assume that a system that, in the course of understanding the
world around it (or understanding a story about that world),
at times becomes surprised by certain events and wants explanations of events in order to be better equipped to react
to those events. The machinery described here is responsible
for generating explanations that will help the system understand and react to the originally anomalous phenomenon.

2. *The XP retriever gets XPs from the XP library:* The XP retriever
extracts indices from the input anomaly and uses those indices to search the XP library for XPs that might serve as the
basis of a useful explanation.

3. *The XP retriever sends a candidate XP to the XP applier:* The retriever ranks the candidate XPs it retrieves and passes the
   most promising ones along to the XP applier, along with the
   story and the anomaly being processed. It holds the rest of
   the candidate XPs in reserve, in case the first choice doesn't
   work out. The applier then attempts to build an explanation
   based on the XP, binding the XP variables. Variable binding
   is achieved by unifying the variablized beliefs in the XP with
   the input anomaly and, if necessary, with the other facts in
   the story. Some of the variables in the XP may be left un-
   bound; this does not make the explanation useless, because
   even explanations that are not fully specified can provide
   useful information.

4. *The XP applier sends an instantiated explanation to the explanation evaluator:* The explanation evaluator has the job of determining whether the explanation is satisfactory. Many different criteria can be used to judge explanations, some relating to the plausibility of the various beliefs and inferences
   that make up the explanation, and some relating to the utility of the explanation for the particular tasks that the explainer is going to use the explanation for.

5. *The evaluator draws on the knowledge base:* The evaluator uses
   facts and inference rules in the system's knowledge base. For
   example, if a belief in the candidate explanation contradicts
   a fact in the knowledge base, the explanation will be rated
   less plausible then if it were confirmed by a fact in the
   knowledge base.

6. *The evaluator sends problematic explanations to the tweaker:* The
   evaluator can give up on an explanation if it decides that the
   explanation failed in ways that are too severe to be worth
   fixing. But explanations that are considered to be close
   matches, with some fixable problems, are fed to the tweaker,
   along with the anomaly and the story, and a characterization of the problem that the evaluator has found with the
   explanation. The tweaker then attempts to build a variation
   of the XP that will produce an explanation that is as much
   like the original as possible but does not suffer from the
   same explanation failure as the original explanation. For
   each type of explanation failure that the evaluator can produce, the tweaker knows one or more tweaking strategies.
   The tweaker determines which tweaking strategies are worth
   trying, and then ranks them and tries to run each in turn.

7. *The tweaker also draws on the knowledge base:* The tweaker knows general, domain-independent tweaking strategies. It gets the domain knowledge it needs to execute those tweaks from the knowledge base.

8. *The tweaker sends the new version of XP back to applier:* When one of the tweaking strategies produces a new XP, it is passed back to the XP applier, which will produce a new explanation based on that XP, which will be re-evaluated, and the cycle repeats.

9. *Satisfactory explanations are passed to XP storer:* When the evaluator determines that a newly generated explanation is satisfactory for current purposes, it passes it to the XP storer. The storer then does three things with the explanation to finish up the process; these are depicted in Arrows 10–12.

10. *The storer updates the XP library:* The process of explanation adaptation is a learning process. The storer completes the learning by recording the hypothesis that has been generated. The new XP is stored in the XP library so that it will be available for producing more explanations in the future, without having to go through the tweaking process again.

11. *The storer updates the knowledge base:* The storer also updates the knowledge base, adding any facts that were not previously in the knowledge base but are included in the XP.

12. *The storer produces the final explanation:* Although learning a new XP is an important side-effect of the explanation process, the more immediate point of the process is to make an explanation available to the processing routines which originally invoked the explainer so that they can use the explanation to react to the event.

3.3 Conclusion

In this overview we have attempted to motivate the case-based explanation problem in more computational terms than we offered in Part I, and to outline the approach to that problem taken by the SWALE system. The chapters that follow describe the details. Chapters that fill in portions of the SWALE outline will alternate with chapters that describe slightly different approaches to the relevant problems. The reader should emerge with a rich understanding of the issues that arise when one builds a case-based explainer.

4. Retriever and Anon: Retrieving Structures From Memory

Christopher C. Owens
Department of Computer Science
The University of Chicago

Editors' Introduction

This chapter, adapted from Chris Owens' thesis,[1] explores the mechanics of reminding—how does an intelligent system confronted with a new problem retrieve relevant solutions that it has stored in memory? The central question behind Owens' work is how a system can characterize a new problem in the right set of abstract terms, thus allowing it to match against an isomorphic problem in a different domain. This is very hard to do using traditional, bottom-up feature detectors, because most problems can be characterized in terms of many alternative sets of abstract features, most of which will not lead to useful remindings. The core idea behind Owens' solution to this problem is what he calls active memory: using the feature sets used to describe cases already in memory to provide top-down guidance to the feature extraction process.

This chapter includes descriptions of two different case-retrieval programs that implement aspects of Owens' theories of retrieval. The retriever from the SWALE program gets reminded of old explanations in an attempt to explain new situations, while the Anon program gets reminded of relevant advice-giving proverbs in the service of helping a system make critical planning decisions.

* * *

[1]Substantial portions of this work have appeared in the *Machine Learning Journal* (Owens, 1993).

4.1 Retrieval, Description, and Learning

For a case-based reasoner to make effective use of recalled prior experiences, it must be able to judge which of its cases are applicable to the current situation. Although the goal is to retrieve relevant knowledge structures or prior cases, the concept of relevance is poorly understood and not easily described in computational terms. A major goal in case-based reasoning is to redefine relevance in terms of better-understood and more computational algorithms and representational constructs, or at least to find some computable property that can be made to stand in for relevance.

Many case-based reasoning systems determine relevance on the basis of features shared between the current situation and prior cases in memory. A prior case sharing many features with the current situation is considered more likely to be relevant than a prior case sharing few features. Computationally, this means that a case-based reasoner needs:

- A *vocabulary* of features used to describe situations,
- A *case library* of data structures describing prior cases, each represented using features from the system's vocabulary,
- An *inference mechanism* for determining which features apply to newly encountered situations, and
- A *matcher* or a *lookup mechanism* for finding prior cases that share features with the current situation.

Case retrieval, under this view, is generally implemented as a process involving two discrete steps: First, the inference mechanism develops a sketchy description of the current situation, and, next, the matcher or lookup mechanism uses that description to search memory. Although this approach seems to reduce case retrieval to the computationally better-understood task of pattern matching or indexed data base retrieval, it suffers from an important shortcoming, a shortcoming that the work in this chapter attempts to address.

4.1.1 Underconstrained Description

In this chapter I argue against the disjoint, or describe-and-search view of case retrieval, and in favor of a model in which developing a description of the current situation is more closely integrated with searching for a relevant prior case. The main argument is that the disjoint model underspecifies the content of the vocabulary and the behavior of the inference mechanism; that the disjoint model ignores a valuable set of constraints, provided by the contents of memory and the process of memory search, which can be brought to bear on the choice of vocabulary and on the task of description.

Feature-based case retrieval is dependent upon the system's, or the system designer's, choice of a descriptive vocabulary being a good one, and on the inference mechanism's ability to generate good descriptions of the situations it encounters. But there is no external criterion by which the goodness or accuracy of a sketchy description can be judged. The goodness of a description is determined solely by the degree to which a pattern-matcher can use it to select cases from memory that are, in fact, relevant or useful; therefore, the appropriateness of a description depends not only on the current situation, but also on the contents of memory. A description that usefully describes a given situation, relative to a particular case library, (i.e., one that allows the system to discriminate among its cases and retrieve a relevant one) might not usefully describe the same situation, given a different case library.

For this reason, it is crucial for a case-retriever to be able to learn how to describe new situations in terms that will allow it to retrieve relevant cases. Because the disjoint model separates the task of describing the current situation from the task of searching for relevant prior situations, it leaves open a loop that, if closed, would provide a mechanism for two types of learning that are needed by case-retrievers: acquiring new descriptive features over the course of many experiences, and refining a particular description over the course of a single experience.

4.1.2 Learning: Acquiring Cases and Features

Over the course of reasoning about many situations, a case-based reasoner can learn not only by adding new cases to its memory, but also by adding new descriptive features to its representational vocabulary. The features that should be learned and added are those likely to lead to the appropriate retrieval of useful cases. This chapter presents a number of criteria that a system designer or learning system can use to identify such features. Many of the features depend upon the existing contents of memory, and, therefore, depend upon an integration of the feature acquisition mechanism with the case library itself.

Over the course of reasoning about a single situation, a case-based reasoner is attempting to build a description of the current situation using the features currently in its representational vocabulary. Because many of the features in a descriptive vocabulary are abstract, it is often costly to determine whether a feature applies to a given situation. Consequently, a case-based reasoner's inference mechanism must be selective in its use of descriptive features. It is important that the reasoner direct its inference toward determining the applicability of those descriptive features most likely to narrow its search to a small set of useful cases. This utility criterion is dependent on the current contents of the case library, and this chapter presents an algorithmic mechanism whereby the system can use the contents of memory to gain some control over its descriptive inference mechanism.

4.2 Retrieval and Labels

Labels, which are selected features whose presence or absence plays a primary role in determining the applicability of a prior case to a current situation, are central to a theory of retrieval. Labeling a case at the appropriate level of generality is not trivial. It is relatively easy to define a problem in concrete, domain-specific terms, but not as easy to define it in the abstract terms that would be needed to retrieve a thematically isomorphic case from a somewhat different domain. A system operating a chemical plant, for example, might know that the temperature and pressure in a particular reaction tank must be kept within certain limits and have specific procedures for dealing with exceptions. Because all situations in which Tank 17 has excessive pressure have something interesting in common, it follows that the system should represent the pressure in Tank 17 as one of its descriptive features and should use *overpressure in Tank 17* as one of its case labels. On the other hand, characterizations of critical planning situations can also be quite general and thematic. One can misprioritize one's goals, choose inappropriate tasks, or allocate resources inappropriately. The problem with recognizing an abstract characterization like *Too many cooks spoil the broth* , as opposed to a concrete characterization like *overpressure in Tank 17,* is that the features that characterize a *too many cooks* situation are themselves abstract, difficult to notice, and costly to infer. The knowledge structure characterizes situations in which MULTIPLE AGENTS are working on a COMPLEX, MULTISTEP PLAN. Determining whether MULTIPLE AGENTS and COMPLEX, MULTISTEP PLAN characterizes a new situation is inferentially costly.

XPs in general, and in particular, PFXPs (Plan-Failure Explanation Patterns; Owens, 1990) characterize plan failures abstractly. This is significant to the task of case retrieval, because abstract features are, in general, more costly to infer from initial situation descriptions than concrete ones.

A major problem for retrieval is that, if a case retriever has a large vocabulary of abstract features it can use to describe situations, its inference mechanism cannot be simply to examine all the features against the current situation and report which ones apply. As observed in Schank, 1986, "Real instances have indefinite numbers of features, some explicit, some inferred and many ignored." There are virtually an infinite number of facts about a situation, many of which would be irrelevant, or expensive to compute, or both.

In spite of the abstractness of these features and the concomitant costs of determining their applicability to a new situation, they are powerful cues to discriminate between *Too many cooks* and other potentially applicable knowledge structures in memory. The system can't do much about the inferential cost of determining whether these features apply to newly encountered situations, but it can do something about the cost of determining whether these features apply to cases. It can attach these features as labels to the cases, in effect caching the results of inference. From that point on, determining whether MULTIPLE AGENTS applies to a case in memory is simply a matter of checking the feature against the case's list of labels.

4.2.1 The Role of Labels

Labels can be concrete or abstract; they can be any feature that describes situations and cases. The fundamental choice in using labels is how complex and abstract the labels will be, and how much inference a system will perform before it begins to search memory. Two widely used approaches described later are *classical indexing*, which performs a great deal of inference to extract complex, thematic labels that are then used as indices into a data base of cases, and *retrieval as matching*, which uses larger numbers of shallower, less costly features as labels. Both of these approaches, however, suffer from the fundamental flaw of the disjoint model of case retrieval: They do not take advantage of knowledge about the population of cases in memory to determine how feature extraction and inference should proceed, and they ignore feedback that can be used for learning.

4.2.2 Labels and Classical Indexing

Classical indexing views a case library as a data base, indexed according to certain key features of the cases. The system retrieves a relevant knowledge structure by first characterizing the current situation in a functionally relevant way, and then using that characterization as a probe into a memory of knowledge structures. For example, a planner might care about situations in which a goal is blocked because of an inadequate supply of a resource.

In the classical indexing approach:

- A symbolic construct (for example BLOCKED GOAL - INSUFFICIENT RESOURCE)[2] is assigned as a label for situations of this type.

- The system has some mechanism for detecting a BLOCKED GOAL - INSUFFICIENT RESOURCE situation, and produces the appropriate symbolic construct accordingly.

- The retrieval mechanism allows the system to cluster together all knowledge structures indexed by this symbolic construct so that they are made available when memory is searched using this index.

In general, this approach performs relatively costly inference to extract highly thematic features from new situations, and it uses those features as the indices around which memory is organized. Examples of the use of indices to retrieve compound knowledge structures in schema-based or case-based reasoning are widespread; see, e.g., (Ashley, 1988; Charniak, 1981; Hammond,, 1989; Kolodner, 1984; Schank & Abelson, 1977).

4.2.3 Labels and Matching

The second broad category, *retrieval as matching*, attempts to use simpler features as labels, features that can be extracted from situations with less costly inference. The approach uses larger numbers of these simpler features to determine the applicability of an old case to a new situation. Labeling features, under this approach, tend to be either surface features, or features cheaply inferred from surface features via a preprocessing pass.

---

[2]Of course any unique symbol, such as FOO or the number 23, could be used. Throughout this discussion, bear in mind that the lexical form of any labeling construct has no semantics whatsoever. All semantics come from the particular set of knowledge structures indexed by that construct, and from the behavior of its detector (see following) for that construct.

Systems embodying this approach do not extract deep thematic descriptions of the current situation prior to searching for relevant knowledge structures. One instance of this approach is the Memory-Based Reasoning approach of Stanfill and Waltz (1986). This approach dynamically weights the importance of each feature based on how unusual it is vis-a-vis the contents of memory. Thagard and Holyoak (1989) argue for a connectionist mechanism for adjusting the weights of features in determining a match via constraint relaxation.

4.2.4 Intermediate Approaches

There is an intermediate approach taken by, among others, the PROTOS system of Bareiss (1989), that calls for features more abstract than surface features, but not as overarching or as thematic as the highly abstract features used in classical indexing. Other approaches, like CABARET (Rissland & Skalak, 1989) CASCADE (Simoudis, 1990), CASEY (Koton, 1988), and CLAVIER (Mark, 1989) deal more explicitly with the combined use of cheaply detected surface features and more expensive thematic features in case retrieval. Generally, these systems embody a fixed distinction between cheap and expensive features, with an explicit use of two passes at retrieval, one based on cheap features as indices, and the other based on more expensive thematic comparison of the candidate cases to the current situation. One goal of the work described herein is to integrate these two types of retrieval and comparison more closely.

4.2.5 Labels and Detectors

Both the classical indexing and the retrieval as matching approaches represent a commitment to at least some inference process to extract features from the world—shallow inference in the case of retrieval as matching, and deep inference in the case of indexed retrieval. Even systems that seem to match new situations against knowledge structures in memory on the basis of "all" of the features of the current situation must, in fact, do some kind of feature extraction, because "all" of the features of any real situation is an unlimited set. Kolodner and Thau (1988), for example, contrast their system PARADYME (see also Kolodner, 1989) with some other case memories, saying that indices are "not used to organize memory's hierarchies, nor to direct traversal at retrieval time." In other words, PARADYME's indices do not form the basis of static memory organization as they do, for example, in CYRUS (Kolodner, 1984) . Even though such systems do not use indices in the classical sense, they still must face the question of what abstract properties of situations to represent, which is the same question one must answer in choosing labels.

Computationally, labels require *detectors*—if cases in memory are labeled with some feature, then there must exist an inference mechanism to detect the presence of that feature in new situations. A detector is a piece of code that corresponds to a given label and has access both to the planner's inference capacity and to the system's sensors. The system gains its knowledge about the world by selectively running its detectors. Running a detector is like asking a question of the inference mechanism; the inference mechanism, in turn, has access to the system's sensors and working memory, which it uses to return an answer. [3]

Unfortunately for the two models of retrieval discussed above, the inferential cost of detectors can range from virtually free to extremely costly. And the value of the answer returned by a detector can be high or low, depending on the makeup of cases in memory and the degree to which the feature detected discriminates among those cases. Neither of the retrieval models can take advantage of this cost and benefit information; the following model I present addresses this concern.

4.3 Criteria for Labels

Some labels are more useful than others. Labels can be *syntactically* useful, which means that they discriminate among the cases in a particular system's memory, and they can be *semantically* useful, which means that similarly labeled cases are, in fact, similar from the system's functional point of view. Later we see how syntactic utility can be measured and taken into account at case-retrieval time. This section includes the criteria for semantic utility of labels in a planning system.

The problem of choosing labels is comparable with the task of organizing cases or abstractions into a set of meaningful categories, which is one of the general problems of machine learning. AI has used statistical approaches to category formation (e.g., Cheeseman, et al. 1988; Fisher, 1987; Quinlan, 1983; Stepp &

---

[3] In a simple variant on the essentially Boolean detector approach described here, detectors could return some numerical value that indicated *how strongly* the labeling term corresponding to the detector characterized the current situation, or *how confident* the detector is in its assessment.

Michalski, 1986) as well as the more knowledge-intensive methods of Explanation-Based learning, (e.g., DeJong & Mooney, 1986; Mitchell, Keller, & Kedar-Cabelli, 1986). A strong argument for a functional approach to category formation is presented in Schank, Collins, & Hunter (1986).

The work described herein is not about how categories ought to be learned, but about what kinds of categories a specific type of system needs. A theory of how categories are formed or how labels are learned is outside the scope of this work. Instead, this is a theory of what constitutes a useful label and how those labels can be used for indexing and retrieval of abstract knowledge structures.

4.3.1 Functional Criteria

It has long been observed (cf. Minsky, 1961) that functional terms define the categories a system should care about. For an example of functional relevance in the task of plan repair, consider the label SPREAD-TOO-THIN, that applies to situations corresponding to the following proverbs:

- *If you run after two hares, you will catch neither.*
- *Drive not too many ploughs at once; some will make foul work.*
- *He that hath many irons in the fire, some of them will cool.*

All situations labeled with SPREAD-TOO-THIN have something in common—an aspect of the agent's capacity is spread too thinly across a number of tasks. The aspect might be a physical resource; it might be a physical capacity of the agent, such as the amount of weight it can carry; or it might be the agent's capacity to monitor tasks. Although the applicable recovery strategies might differ depending on what resource is spread too thinly, the strategies are likely to involve behavior such as offloading subtasks, eliminating redundant steps, or increasing the effectiveness of the critical resource/capacity. Because of this common functionality, SPREAD-TOO-THIN is a good feature around which to organize a portion of memory and, consequently, a potentially good label for cases.

4.3.2 Types of Functional Relevance

A case-based or abstraction-based reasoning system seeks to retrieve cases or abstractions relevant to the current situation in which the system finds itself. But the specifics of functional relevance depend on the task in which the system is engaged:

- For case-based planners like CHEF (Hammond, 1989), CLAVIER (Barletta & Mark, 1988) , PLEXUS (Alterman, 1986) , or JULIA (Hinrichs, 1988; Kolodner, 1987), a case is relevant to the degree to which the plan constructed from that case satisfies the system's current goals.
- For a system whose goal is to build explanations, like SWALE (Kass, Leake, & Owens, 1986) or CASEY (Koton, 1988), a case is relevant to the degree to which the explanation derived from it subsumes the facts of the current situation and is plausible. (See Pearl, 1988, for a discussion of explanation plausibility.)
- For systems that explicitly critique, evaluate, and interpret cases, for example, a legal reasoner like HYPO (Ashley, 1988), the goal of retrieval is to find a case that is demonstrably similar to the current case along certain dimensions derived from a deep, domain-intensive analysis of the current situation and whose outcome supports the system's desired outcome for the current situation.
- For a categorization system like PROTOS (Bareiss, 1989) the goal is to find cases sharing certain predictive features with the currently-examined case, those features being either designed into the system or learned by causal or explanatory reference to a body of domain knowledge.

For labeling knowledge structures relevant to critical planning situations, four types of functional relevance are particularly significant:

- *Failure-related:* Failure-related labels capture some aspect of the central causality represented in the knowledge structure. A failure-related label clusters together knowledge structures in which a common element plays a role in the causal description of the failure. SPREAD-TOO-THIN is one example of a failure-related index. For another example, the *Too many cooks* knowledge structure can be labeled with MULTIPLE AGENTS, which also labels a number of other knowledge structures that deal with both desirable and undesirable aspects of multiple agent situations. It can also be labeled with COMPLEX TASK, which differentiates between situations in which multiple agents are desirable and those in which multiple agents create a problem. It can be labeled with domain-specific labels like MOVING, which identifies knowledge structures dealing with problems that occur when carrying objects.

- *Symptomatic:* Symptomatic labels relate an observable condition to the situation characterized by the knowledge structure. For example, RESOURCE CONTENTION between agents is symptomatic of a *Too many cooks* situation, even though at the level of representation of the knowledge structure, no explicit causal connection is made between the resource contention and the failure. (Imagine that you are working on a task with some helpers, and every time you reach for a tool someone else has it.) If the causal description contained within the knowledge structure were more detailed, then RESOURCE CONTENTION would be a failure-related label, and could have been acquired by the same explanatory mechanism. But because the connection between resource connection and the *Too many cooks* failure is beyond the representational power of the knowledge structure, the label can be learned only by statistical correlation. Symptomatic labels provide a place for the system to list observable features suspected to be causally implicated in the failure, but for which no causal connection has yet been inferred. A system that learns would transform symptomatic labels into failure-related labels by deepening the causal structure represented within a knowledge structure.

- *Recovery-related:* Recovery-related labels characterize an aspect of the recovery strategy contained within the knowledge structure. For example, there is a functionally useful difference between recoveries that require additional resources and those that do not. If REPAIR-REQUIRES-RESOURCES labels the former, then the system can, in a resource-constrained situation, search for cheap recovery strategies that are not so labeled. Note that recovery-related labels can be used to retrieve knowledge structures that relate to the current status of the planning system, rather than the current situation.

- *Direct:* Labels that exhibit direct functional relevance characterize the central causality in the failure, without being a subset of the symbolic constructs used in the representation of that causality. These labels define categories in which a certain overarching pattern of causality occurs, in cases where that pattern is not captured by any single symbolic construct within the representation. For example, if there are a number of knowledge structures that deal with situations in which a plan failed due to a low level of a resource, they can be clustered using a label, for example, INSUFFICIENT RESOURCE. The label does not appear within the description of any of the PFXPs to which it applies; its semantics derive from the common set of repair and recovery strategies that it labels.

Whereas these types of relevance guide the knowledge-intensive task of acquiring new features to add to the labeling vocabulary, a simpler, shorter term learning task is to obtain and exploit knowledge about the inferential costs and syntactic utility of features in order to control inference. The following section describes this task and a computational approach to it.

4.4 Balancing Inference and Search

The earlier arguments claim that the choice of labels should be based on functional criteria, but there is an equally important and often competing requirement: that labels be based on features that are observable. A feature that clusters together failure situations for which there is a common mode of repair is useful, but only to the extent that the system can encounter a new situation and determine whether that feature applies to it. If there is a detector for each label, some detectors will be more costly to run than others.

The more useful indices are characterized by relatively low complexity in extraction and therefore lower cost in processing resources. Features present in the input (i.e., low-level sensor readings), for example, are trivially easy to extract, as are error messages from the system's actuators, like ARM WEIGHT LIMIT EXCEEDED. On the other hand, more abstract labels can be costly for any combination of physical or computational reasons. There are costs associated with sensing, ranging from the simple "What's in front of me?" that merely requires the process requiring this information to wait in line to use the sensing apparatus, to the more costly "Go look around that corner and see what's there." that requires planning and carrying out a sequence of actions. Information may be computationally expensive if it requires a great deal of inference; for example: "Does this plan describe a task with independently executable subtasks?"

Unfortunately, the problem of feature extraction won't go away. In any given situation, there is always more information that can be gathered—more features that can be learned about the situation—by spending additional time sensing or making inferences. No description is ever complete, so any control structure that suggests first developing a description of the situation and then using that description either to extract abstract features or to select the existing features of the description, faces a difficult question: When is the description sufficiently complete that the system should stop enhancing the description and start using that description to extract indices?

4.4.1 Active and Passive Memory

The answer to the aforementioned question is that the entire model of retrieval on which it is predicated needs to be revised. There are two basic models of lookup applicable to the task of selecting a relevant knowledge structure. Under the classical indexing model, the view that has been implicitly described thus far, memory is passive. It is the responsibility of the problem-solving portion of the system to come up with a description of the knowledge structure that it wants—presumably to come up with a set of labels. On the basis of this description, memory can select a knowledge structure that best matches and can return it.

Accordingly, the features output by the describer must be functionally grounded in the conditions the system needs to recognize and the actions the system needs to perform. The applicability of a case in memory to the current situation is often predicated on some kind of abstract, thematic similarity (e.g., for a planner, *Both the current situation and the prior case involve a finite resource that is spread across too many tasks.*).

The task of description, as it stands apart from search, is underconstrained because there are many possible abstract descriptions that apply to any one situation, only some of which are likely to be useful in retrieving relevant prior cases. The utility of a description depends not only on its functional grounding in a system's recognition and action capabilities, but also on its relationship to the cases already in memory and the features used to describe those cases. A criterion for descriptions, ignored in the disjoint model, is that the descriptions enable the memory to discriminate reliably, and in a functionally relevant way, among the competing candidates for "best match" to the current situation. The process of description needs to know what is contained in memory and how it is described.

The problem with passive memory is that the process that extracts labels must know a great deal about what is in memory and how it is organized. It must know, for example, how the experiences or abstract knowledge structures in memory are described so that the description of the current experience will indicate the similarities and differences between the current experience and the experiences in memory. In effect, passive memory requires that the system fully understand a situation before it extracts labels from it. But, because the entire purpose of extracting labels is to retrieve knowledge structures that will help the system understand the current situation, it makes little sense to require understanding as a prerequisite to label extraction. Accordingly, passive memory is not an acceptable model.

Under the *active memory* model, on the other hand, the contents of memory have a more direct control over the process that extracts labels from the current situation. In one version of the active memory model, the abstractions are viewed as active agents, each competing with the others to characterize the current situation. Each abstraction demands the inferences it needs to make the mapping between itself and the particular facts associated with the current situation. Control of processing resources, under this model, constitutes resolving the competition between abstractions to have their questions answered, and deciding how many of those questions to answer. The questions, in this case, refer to requests to run a particular detector.

4.4.2 Incremental Retrieval

In active memory, the system performs incremental retrieval. When it begins processing a new situation, some information is available essentially for free—the kind of low-cost features described above. Using these features—analogous to presenting symptoms, as labels—the system may retrieve a large number of knowledge structures that match on the basis of those labels.

Given this pool of candidate knowledge structures, the system can examine them for labels with high discriminating power, which separate the pool into subpools. The more evenly balanced the sizes of the subpools, the higher the discriminating power of that label.

Labels with high discriminating power yield the highest benefit. Consider a pool of candidate knowledge structures, and imagine some label that happens to be present on all of those knowledge structures, or another that appears on none of them. Neither of these labels has great information content, because running the detector for these labels and determining whether either characterizes the current situation will not help to refine the choice of knowledge structures. If, on the other hand, a label is present on half of the candidate knowledge structures, then it is to the system's advantage to decide whether that label characterizes the current situation, because the label has a high information content. It is this benefit that must be balanced against the cost of feature acquisition discussed earlier.

As the system runs more and more of its detectors—as it infers more and more properties of the current situation—the number of knowledge structures in memory that match on the basis of those properties decreases. It is not necessary, however, to drive the number of matches all the way to one. If, for example, the system's goal is to recover from a failed plan, and if the known characteristics of the current situation specify 50 of the system's knowledge structures equally well, and if those 50 structures all suggest the same plan repair, then there is no reason to look for more information to help discriminate between those cases.[4] Recovery-related labels play an important role in retrieval.

On the other hand, often the same set of features label cases with different suggested courses of action. The MULTIPLE AGENTS label, for example, applies to the *Many hands make light work* class of situations in which a goal was accomplished more quickly due to the increased number of agents, as well as to the *Too many cooks spoil the broth* class of situations, in which the multiple agents resulted in a worse outcome. The system needs a label that is present on one PFXP and absent on the other, which allows it to discriminate between the cases. The feature COMPLEX HIERARCHICAL PLAN is such a discriminator; it applies to the situations in which too many agents get in each others' way, but not to the situations in which multiple agents improve the outcome.

4.5 Implementation: SWALE and Anon

This section discusses two programs, SWALE and Anon, each of which addresses memory organization, indexing, and retrieval. The SWALE program demonstrates the role of a thematically-organized memory in the context of a larger system; Anon explicitly embodies the principles discussed in the previous section.

---

[4]This condition does not, however, mean that the system should lump all of these cases together into one equivalence class. There may be other circumstances other than this particular retrieval instance under which the differences between the cases would be significant.

4.5.1 SWALE

As discussed early in the book, the task of SWALE is to build explanations of anomalous events. Given a description containing the facts of an episode, SWALE attempts to build a causally coherent framework that could tie those facts together. This causal framework, or explanation, becomes the abstraction under which the episode could then be labeled in memory. I wrote this program jointly with Alex Kass and David Leake. (An overview of the program can be found in Kass, et al., 1986. For further details see Kass, 1986; Leake, 1990; Leake & Owens, 1986; and Schank, 1986.)

4.5.2 *Indexing Strategies*

A system that reuses old explanations to understand new episodes must be able to store old explanations and find them when appropriate to help in understanding new situations. Moreover, this memory must fail gracefully: If it can't find an explanation exactly suited to the current episode, the near-misses must serve as departure points for new explanation creation. Memory, therefore, must support thematically based reminding with reasonable near-misses.

Continuing the Swale example, explanation patterns about death of racehorses would obviously be relevant, as would explanation patterns about deaths of athletes, about deaths of the young and famous, about destructions of important income-producing properties, and about other bad things that have happened to racehorses. How can a system find these explanation patterns so that they might be proposed as candidates?

The authors of SWALE believe strongly that all features of an episode are not used equally in a search for applicable structures. Our position is that an intelligent process must select the features to be used as indices into memory, and the search process must complement the processes by which explanation patterns have been labeled. We earlier used the term *indexing* to refer specifically to the process of deciding under which symbolic constructs to store an XP, as opposed to the process of choosing which features of the current situation to use as cues for retrieval which we called *feature extraction*, or as opposed to the actual mechanics of search and retrieval. Some of the indexing strategies we explored were:

Table 4.1. Retrieving Directly-Indexed XPs.

```
Processing INPUT-FACT.1805
    DEATH 176, which has
        ACTOR = SUCCESSFUL-RACEHORSE-174
        TIME = time of SWALE-DEATH

The fact SWALE's DEATH will be stored as the SWALE's
 DEATH line in
    SWALE's RACEHORSE-LIFE

Temporal anomaly detected:
 DEATH-177 occurs abnormally early in RACEHORSE-LIFE

Trying to pull up XPs indexed by the anomaly...
Seeing if one of these XPs is relevant:

    XP-EARLY-DEATH-FROM-RUN-OVER
    XP-EARLY-DEATH-FROM-ILLNESS
```

- *Index an XP via features participating in the anomaly that the XP is designed to resolve.* For example, Jim Fixx's death was surprising because his health seemed outstanding; the Jim Fixx XP described above can be indexed under the combination: DEATH + EXCELLENT PHYSICAL CONDITION.
- *Index an XP via a feature playing a role in the chain of causation contained within the explanation.* Using this strategy, the Jim Fixx XP could be indexed under: DEATH + HEART DEFECT or DEATH + JOGGING
- *Index an XP via any highly unusual feature of the episode that it originally explained, whether that feature played a causal role in the explanation.* If you get a flat tire during a blizzard, another instance of car problems in blizzards may remind you to get your tires retreaded.
- *Index an XP via features defining membership in a commonly stereotyped group.* (A group that has been previously defined for other purposes.) For example, one of the explanations we collected for Swale's death centered around other deaths of famous young star performers, with remindings of Jimi Hendrix and Janis Joplin. This explanation pattern is indexed under DEATH + SUCCESSFUL STAR PERFORMER.

4.5.3 Retrieval Strategies

Once XPs have been indexed using the aforementioned methods, complementary retrieval strategies can be applied to new episodes in order to find relevant XPs. SWALE embodied five retrieval strategies:

Directly-Indexed XPs. It is always possible that the system will be able to characterize the current situation in the same terms that were used to index one or more XPs. For example, if Swale's death is characterized simply as an EARLY DEATH, it is likely that there are a small number of explanation patterns that immediately address some aspect of the situation. For example, one version of SWALE's memory contained patterns that explained early animal deaths in terms of sickness or being hit by a car, each of which could be tested as a possible explanation for the current situation, as shown in Table 4.1.

The second strategy, *anomaly refinement*, suggests that when a proposed XP fails to apply to the input episode, then the features of the input episode that caused the XP not to fit are likely to redefine the anomaly in an important way. These features should therefore be used as indices for further search, as shown in Table 4.2.

Anomaly refinement, applied to the Swale story, yields a progressive redefinition of the anomaly from simply a death, to an early death, to an early death despite excellent physical condition. In this approach, whenever an XP fails to apply, the system looks at the features of the episode that caused the XP not to fit, and uses those features as indices for further search.

For example, as previously discussed, one of the system's XPs indexed under the initial characterization of DEATH was old age. But that XP failed to match the Swale situation because Swale was only 3 years old. Anomaly refinement says that this feature, YOUTH, caused the mismatch and is therefore interesting from an indexing point of view. Accordingly, the system, searching under DEATH + YOUTH can find the DEATH-FROM-ILLNESS XP. This XP, however, fails to apply because Swale, having recently won a horse race, would be inferred to be in excellent health. Anomaly refinement uses this failure to further specify the indices as DEATH + YOUTH + GOOD HEALTH. Certain foul play explanations might be indexed under these features, as well as sudden and unexpected types of illnesses such as heart attacks, for example the JIM FIXX XP.

Table 4.2. Anomaly Refinement in SWALE.

```
Checking #{EXPLANATION 180 EARLY-DEATH-FROM-ILLNESS}
as a possible explanation for
    [SCRIPT-LINE-ORDERING-FAILURE
        SCRIPT - #{TOKEN-NODE 179 - RACEHORSE-LIFE}
        FAILURE - PREMATURE-LINE
        LAST-NORMAL-LINE-NUMBER - 3
        MISORDERED-LINE-NUMBER - 4]

Found problem:
[XP-FAILURE
    PROBLEM-DESCRIPTION -
        [ATTRIBUTE-VALUE-CONTRADICTED
            ATTRIBUTE - HEALTH
            BELIEVED-VALUE - HIGH]
    BELIEF-LABEL - SICKNESS]

Found problem:
 [XP-FAILURE
    PROBLEM-DESCRIPTION -
        [ATTRIBUTE-VALUE-CONTRADICTED
            ATTRIBUTE - PHYSICAL-CONDITION
            BELIEVED-VALUE - HIGH]
    BELIEF-LABEL - BAD-CONDITION]
```

The transcript fragment in Table 4.2 shows SWALE identifying
GOOD HEALTH and GOOD PHYSICAL CONDITION as relevant.
Later, the program tries these features as indices to search for
XPs, in this case finding the JIM FIXX XP. This is shown in Table
4.3.

Table 4.3. Using the Refined Anomaly

```
found XP-182 indexed under DEATH
    with index: (PHYSICAL-CONDITION HIGH)
The explorer has returned #{EXPLANATION 183 FIXX-EP}
```

Anomaly refinement differs from specialization down a hierarchy
(e.g., that discussed in Kolodner, 1984 or Lytinen, 1984), which
provides a way to move from one memory structure to a more
specific memory structure based upon some attribute of the general memory structure being instantiated with a particular value.
Anomaly refinement, on the other hand, is a way to select the features of an episode that most closely characterize an anomaly.

The Jim Fixx XP, for example, is not indexed as a specialization of EARLY DEATH FROM SICKNESS, reachable if the sickness expectation is violated. Instead, it is indexed as an explanation to consider whenever the attention of the explainer is called to the juxtaposition of early death and excellent physical condition. Trying and failing to apply the early death from sickness XP is only one among many potential ways of focusing on that combination of features. It is entirely possible that failures of other XPs would also focus attention on the juxtaposition of death and excellent physical condition, thereby indexing the same Jim Fixx XP.

Anomaly shift. The third strategy, *anomaly shift*, suggests that when a proposed XP fails to apply to the input episode, any feature of the input episode should be challenged. The result might be a new anomaly.

Instead of refining the anomaly, anomaly shift uses the failure to shift the focus of explanation onto a different anomaly. Consider again the failure of the DEATH-FROM-SICKNESS XP: it failed because Swale, as noted earlier, was known to be in excellent health, inferred from his recent victory in a horse race. The feature causing the failure is Swale's good health. Anomaly shift challenges this feature. Preserving the XP's hypothesized belief that Swale was in fact sick and instead challenging the inference, the system could ask "How could a sick horse win a horse race?" This new anomalous combination of features could then lead to explanations such as latent illness, or illness masked by the use of drugs although not cured.

As a second and unimplemented example of these two retrieval strategies, consider the XP concerning *Death from being hit by a car*. This is an explanation of animal death that an explainer might have if it had processed stories about deaths of pets. This XP has the preconditions that the animal is small and that it is allowed to play unsupervised. If the system were to try to apply this to Swale's death, it would fail because Swale was large and, because he was an expensive race horse, was not allowed to play unsupervised.

Given this failure, under anomaly refinement, the retriever would consider each of the failure-causing features, namely largeness and careful supervision, as possible indices. The feature LARGE does not index any special kind of death in most people's memory, although one informal subject was reminded of a heart syndrome affecting particularly tall people. CAREFUL SU-

PERVISION might index the proverbial *Killed with kindness* XP that covers over-watered plants and over-fed tropical fish.

Applied to the same failures, anomaly shift suggests challenging the assumption that Swale was a large animal. Because large size is part of the basic definition of a horse, it is difficult to imagine how to challenge the inferences underlying it. But the strategy also suggests challenging the inferences leading to the conclusion that Swale was carefully supervised. It tells the system to look for explanations of how an expensive racehorse could be left unsupervised. (Maybe the trainer was unavailable, on strike, or deliberately distracted as part of a foul play scheme.) Although some of these proposed XPs look silly on the face, they might be candidates for adaptation. The goal of the retriever is, after all, to return creative, albeit wild, hypotheses that the other modules of the system would either rule out or use as a starting point for modification into something more plausible.

Unusual Feature Search. The fourth strategy suggests that any highly unusual or extreme feature of the current episode may index a relevant XP in memory. Swale, for example, had great monetary value compared with the normative instance of a racehorse. DEATH + GREAT MONETARY VALUE can index a variety of obvious XPs, such as being killed for the insurance money. See Table 4.4.

Table 4.4. Unusual Features Search.

```
a generalized RACEHORSE's MONETARY-VALUE is HIGH,
while a generalized HORSE's MONETARY-VALUE is UN-
KNOWN.

   Found XP-191 indexed under DEATH
      with index: (MONETARY-VALUE HIGH)
The explorer has returned
   #{EXPLANATION 192 INSURANCE-FRAUD-EP}
```

Unfortunately, this strategy is less causally grounded by the others, and depends for its success on an impoverished representation. Any realistically rich representation of the events involved in the Swale scenario is so detailed that it is difficult to identify any small set of features as "unusual" in any abstract sense. In a detailed representation of Swale, many features differ from the corresponding features of a generalized racehorse, and it is computationally costly to choose the interesting differences to pursue.

Causal Connection Search. The fifth search strategy allows the system to search for an XP given both a causal antecedent and a causal consequent, since knowing both sharply narrows the range of applicable XPs. This strategy is useful when the system acquires a new fact and tries to integrate that fact into a causal model of the situation. This might be in response to the system deciding that a new explanation is unacceptable because there is insufficient justification linking two steps (see Leake, 1992). In this example, the system looks for an XP to build a causal chain between poor emotional state and death (see Table 4.5), finding the suicide XP.

4.5.4 SWALE and Retrieval

The general task of a case retrieval algorithm is to find those cases in memory most similar to the current situation. Incremental retrieval, implemented in the anomaly refinement and the anomaly shift strategies, suggests new ways to deal with near misses. Under incremental retrieval, what the searcher finds useful about retrieved cases is not the ways in which they are similar to the current case, but the ways in which they are different. The features that cause matching and application to fail are interesting, because they can be used to direct further processing via the search heuristics described earlier.

Table 4.5. Searching for a Causal Connection.

```
Looking for an XP to connect:
?X?'s VERY-LOW EMOTIONAL-STATE with ?X?'s DEATH
found XP-193 indexed under DEATH
   with index: (EMOTIONAL-STATE VERY-LOW)

Found an XP to connect ?X?'s VERY-LOW EMOTIONAL-
   STATE to ?X?'s DEATH:

   XP is  #{EP 194 DISTRAUGHT-SUICIDE}
```

Although the strategy of using the mismatching features of near-miss candidate cases as search cues for further retrieval is powerful, it may be specific to the task of building explanations, as opposed to other case-based or memory-based reasoning tasks. The strategy of using differences as indices succeeds with knowledge structures whose purpose is to explain anomalies, because anomalies involve differences. The knowledge structures are labeled with features that characterize the anomalies they are designed to resolve, and because features that cause routine processing to fail are, by definition, anomalous.

4.5.5 Anon

The Anon program provides a mechanism for integrating feature extraction and memory search, and for explicitly reasoning about the costs and benefits of individual features. Anon's task is to maintain a library of abstract knowledge structures and match those knowledge structures against descriptions of planning situations. My goals in writing Anon were twofold. First, the program was to be a vehicle for experimenting with representational constructs, labeling vocabularies and retrieval mechanisms. Second, as argued in Owens (1989), it was to demonstrate a computationally feasible implementation of an active memory. In the Anon program, I focus on the concept of incremental retrieval and the tight integration of retrieval with other processing. Anon represents a framework in which to implement decision theoretic and other strategies relating to the choice of where to direct inference.

Anon exists to demonstrate the viability of the design in the context of a larger planning system. It does not stand alone, but rather makes assumptions about the structure and input/output behavior of the rest of the planning system.

In particular, the program assumes that there exist detectors of the kind previously described. The program further assumes that it knows something about the relative cost of running the various detectors. In its current implementation, Anon also assumes that detectors are independent and that they do not share partial results. Running one detector does not change the cost of running another.

Under Anon's model, memory has some control over the inference and sensing processes. The presence, or absence, of abstract features in the environment is determined in response to requests from memory, and those requests are based upon the need for information to discriminate among the available knowledge structures.

4.5.6 Top-Down and Bottom-Up Search

Allowing memory to gather information by requesting features suggests a very top-down view of search: Information from the environment would only be supplied upon request, and information would only be requested when needed to discriminate between competing knowledge structures.

Such an extreme top-down view of search and retrieval is typically implemented by placing all the system's knowledge structures in a discrimination net partitioned according to the system's labeling terms, for example as in Feigenbaum (1963). The system descends the discrimination net to find a knowledge structure that matches the current situation on the basis of all the features extracted in the course of descending the net.

Unfortunately, the discrimination net method exhibits certain problems:

- A system using a discrimination net must ask its questions in a relatively predetermined order and cannot ask the situationally cheaper questions first.

- A system using a discrimination net cannot exploit free information—information generated perhaps as a side effect of other processing that the system must do, regardless of whether it needs the information. Some of a planning system's detectors might be run by other than the memory search process—the answers they return should be usable immediately by the memory search process even if it has not yet descended to that particular branching point in the discrimination net.

- A system using a discrimination net would require a complex control structure to deal with having one of its questions answered "I don't know."

It is possible to take information utility into account when building a decision net. Quinlan's (1983) ID3 program provides one example of how this can be done; Fisher's (1987) COBWEB system and Cheeseman's (Cheeseman et al., 1988) AutoClass systems deal with the issues of learning the right features from which to construct clusters of similar knowledge structures. Static clusters and discrimination nets, however, do not support the kind of dynamic balancing of information cost against information utility at retrieval time, as described earlier. PARADYME(Kolodner, 1989), with its use of preference heuristics, takes information utility into account more dynamically, during the retrieval process, but it does not appear to provide a mechanism for merging information about feature acquisition cost with information about the discriminating power of features. Although PARADYME is also a fine-grained parallel retrieval scheme, it differs from Anon, in that PARADYME takes as input a description of the current situation and searches memory for a matching case, whereas Anon extracts a description incrementally as memory search proceeds. When a relevant knowledge structure is found, Anon's description of the current situation is only just exactly detailed enough to discriminate among the known cases in Anon's memory.

Another retrieval mechanism from which Anon differs is DMAP (Martin, 1990). DMAP searches memory by passing markers through a complex, richly indexed hierarchical knowledge representation. Anon, on the other hand, attempts to gain maximum utility from flat indexing relationships.

The other extreme is a completely bottom-up search, in which the system gathers as much information as it can about the current situation, and then uses that information as a template to match against knowledge structures in memory in a single pass. Using a bottom-up approach effectively says that the system should run all of its detectors first to yield a vector of features, and then use this vector of features as a retrieval probe. If the system has a rich and extensive labeling vocabulary, the cost of running a large number of detectors is likely to be prohibitive. Furthermore, only a small number of the detectors are likely to correspond to labeling terms with good discriminating power in the current situation. This approach precludes the efficiencies of incremental retrieval.

4.5.7 Incremental Retrieval in Anon

The Anon program uses an incremental approach combining some of the features of top-down and bottom-up search. This hybrid system tries to be intelligent about which of the features in its labeling vocabulary it will detect next, at each point in the retrieval process.

The code runs on the Connection Machine fine-grained SIMD parallel computer (Hillis, 1985). Although parallelism is not a particularly important theoretical aspect of the model, fine-grained parallelism provides an effective, natural mechanism for the dynamic calculation of feature utility, which is at the heart of the program. The dynamic calculation of feature utility is built on top of a basic retrieval mechanism, similar to that used in the document retrieval system described by Stanfill & Kahle (1986).

4.5.8 Memory Organization in Anon

Anon's memory contains approximately 1,000 knowledge structures, each corresponding to a very sketchy representation of a PFXP or critical planning situation. Each is labeled via an unstructured list chosen from the system's labeling vocabulary of about 80 terms. The indexing relationships are represented as doubly linked associations between label terms and knowledge structures, with one processor used for each two-way link.

Anon's memory does not explicitly maintain a hierarchy of categories—categories and hierarchy are implicit in the assignment of labels to knowledge structures.

Given any label term, the system can, essentially in constant time,[5] determine which of the knowledge structures in memory are labeled with that term. Similarly, given any knowledge structure, the system can determine which label terms are used to label it. As is shown later, these operations form the heart of a flexible, incremental retrieval system.

What has been described thus far is a flat data base with Boolean, atomic labels (or numerically weighted labels, depending on which type of detector the system is built around). Beyond this, Anon offers a mechanism for letting the content of memory inform the feature extraction process.

The goal of Anon's retrieval mechanism is to focus the system's feature extraction capabilities on the features that are likely to be most useful as retrieval labels, relative to the cost of acquiring information about those features. Accordingly, measuring the utility of a piece of labeling information is at the heart of Anon's incremental retrieval approach.

4.5.9 Anon's Basic Mechanisms

The feature utility determination and retrieval are accomplished using three basic operations:

Filter. Given a labeling term or a set of labeling terms, the system identifies the knowledge structures associated with that term. Anon uses Boolean features and ranks selections matching based on the number of features that match. The same approach is trivially extensible to employ numerical weights or feature salience metrics.

Filtering uses a scan/reduce model of computation. In addition to the processors representing the links between labeling terms and knowledge structures, there is a processor for each labeling term and one for each knowledge structure. When all the labeling

---

[5]Given, of course, that "constant time" on parallel hardware loses its theoretical significance. Once the number of indexing relationships exceeds the number of physical processors on the system, the complexity of the operations described later is essentially $n(\log n)$ in the number of indexing relationships.

terms to be selected during a given iteration of the retrieval process are selected, each labeling term broadcasts information to all processors representing links between itself and a knowledge structure. Each of those link processors then forwards information to the knowledge structure to which it points, so that each processor corresponding to a knowledge structure now has information about which of its labels were selected. The system then uses a parallel sort to rank the knowledge structures according to how closely their labeling terms match the labeling terms selected for the current iteration of the retrieval process.

To use numeric weights rather than Boolean values, the weights are applied to the link processors.

Typify. Once the system identifies a set of candidate knowledge structures, it can identify labeling terms that are highly representative of this set. Because these might not be the same labeling terms that were used for retrieval, these terms might be useful for learning new clusters and new labeling relationships. This process is easily accomplished by running the retrieval algorithm in reverse—forwarding information from the selected knowledge structures to the links, and from the links to the labeling terms to which they point.

This operation is essentially inductive syntactic generalization. If Anon has used a complicated conjunction of features to retrieve a given set of knowledge structures, it is possible that there is a single, previously unexamined feature that is highly representative of this set—which discriminates this set from the non-selected knowledge structures. This process will find such a feature.

Discriminate. Using the same calculation used to calculate typicality, the system can look for labeling terms that subdivide a specified set of knowledge structures. The closer the partitions are to equal sizes, the better the discrimination score for a particular label term. Just as terms that are highly typical of the retrieved set of knowledge structures are important, features that are present as labels for half of the current candidate knowledge structures and absent for the other half are also interesting—They have a high discriminating power and are likely to be the subject of a request from memory to the system's detectors.

This approach can also be used with weights to separate the knowledge structures into equally weighted subdivisions, rather than subdivisions of equal numbers of candidates, so that labels will be found that separate, for example, a large number of low-weighted knowledge structures from a small number of highly weighted ones.

The same computational technique can be used to identify features that correlate with each other across a candidate pool. For example, if the system is interested in a functionally significant but costly feature, it can use the discriminate operation to identify other features that correlate with it, with the expectation that some combination of these other features may be cheaper to acquire.

4.5.10 Basic Retrieval Operation

The steps that follow outlines the operation of Anon's incremental retrieval mechanism:

1. Acquire initial set of labels believed to characterize current situation.

2. Retrieve knowledge structures labeled with these labels, using *filter*.

3. Using *discriminate*, identify labeling terms with high discriminating power.

4. Select cheapest-to-acquire labels from previous step; run detectors to determine whether any apply to current situation.

5. Add those known to apply, to initial set of labels from Step 1.

6. Repeat from Step 2 until no further discrimination possible.

The system starts with an initial rough characterization of the current situation, consisting of a small number of labeling terms believed to apply. This initial characterization consists of information that was provided for free—such as information that becomes available as a side effect of other processing that the system was doing. For example, the fact that MULTIAGENT PLAN or RESOURCE-CONSTRAINED-SITUATION applies to the current situation might be known as a side-effect of planning decisions that the system needed to make.

Table 4.6. Anon's Initial Search.

```
Selecting: #<label SCAL: "Scaling of a resource.">
   Selecting: #<label BO: "Bad outcome">


I found 10 proverbs that each included all 2 of
those labels
#<proverb P3: "A pig that has two owners is sure to
die of hunger.">
#<proverb P331: "He who has one clock always knows
what time it is; he who has two is never sure">
#<proverb P150: "Double charge will rive a cannon.">
#<proverb P151: "Milk the cow but don't pull off the
udder.">
#<proverb P156: "Grasp all, lose all.">
#<proverb P157: "If you run after two hares, you
will catch neither.">
#<proverb P158: "If you buy meat cheap, when it
     boils you will smell what you have saved.">
#<proverb P161: "Too much spoileth.">
#<proverb P164: "Two captains sink the ship.">
#<proverb P329: "Too many cooks spoil the broth.">
```

In the case when few features are already known, the system can have a stock set of features it cares about—analogous to the stock questions that a detective asks upon encountering a crime scene— which questions are asked next depends on the answers to the first few questions.

First, the filter operation allows the system to retrieve a pool of knowledge structures labeled with the initial label set. Table 4.6 shows Anon's output of candidate knowledge structures, given an initial set of two labels.

Next, using the *discriminate* operation described in Table 4.7, the system identifies the labeling terms with the highest discriminating power vis-á-vis the current pool of candidate knowledge structures. Using this measurement of discriminating power and any of the aforementioned estimates of feature acquisition cost, identify the labels with the best cost/benefit ratio. These labeling terms go onto a list of terms, the presence or absence of which the system will try to detect in the current situation. Table 4.7 shows Anon's identification of the best discriminators among the 10 knowledge structures.

Table 4.7. Looking for Discriminators.

```
I found 9 proverbs that each included all 2 of those
labels.
Are any of the following 3 features present in the
  current problem?

    #<label ACT: "Action">
    #<label GOAL: "Managing goal priorities">
    #<label INSUF: "Insufficient resource">

Enter a feature or nil > insuf
  Selecting: #<label INSUF: "Insufficient resource">
```

As the system gains more information (i.e., if the program were connected to an actual planner, as it runs its detectors and determines which of the suggested labeling terms apply to the current situation), it returns to the filtering step, to further narrow the set of knowledge structures under consideration.

The system can continue to narrow the set of knowledge structures until either there is one knowledge structure remaining in the pool, or until there is no further discriminating information available. Table 4.8 shows two further iterations of the filtering and discriminating steps, employing the user as a detector. If multiple knowledge structures remain in the pool and no further discriminating information is available, some of the knowledge structures must be relabeled.

4.5.11 A Unified Control Structure

Note that this control structure allows the system to operate in either a top-down or bottom-up search mode, depending upon the availability of information. If a great deal of information is available about the current situation (i.e., if the situation is already represented using the same labeling terms used to organize memory), then memory does not need to assist in formulating a description of the current situation. The system can use those labeling terms as retrieval cues for a single iteration through memory search, looking for the knowledge structure that shares the largest number of labeling terms with the description of the current situation. If Anon starts with a large number of labeling terms in the initial set, then one pass through the process will suffice to uniquely specify one knowledge structure, which will be returned.

Table 4.8. Incremental Refinement.

```
I found 4 proverbs that each included all 3 of those
  labels
#<proverb P3: "A pig that has two owners is sure to
  die of hunger.">
#<proverb P156: "Grasp all, lose all.">
#<proverb P157: "If you run after two hares, you
  will catch neither.">

#<proverb P158: "If you buy meat cheap, when it
  boils you will smell what you have saved.">

Is the following feature present in the current
  problem?
     #<label STT: "Capabilities spread too thin">

Enter a feature or nil > stt
   Selecting: #<label STT: "Capabilities spread too
   thin">

I found 2 proverbs that each included all 4 of those
  labels.
   #<proverb P156: "Grasp all, lose all.">
   #<proverb P157: "If you run after two hares, you
   will catch neither.">
```

If, on the other hand, very little is known about the current situation, then memory should play a large role in developing a description. In this context discrimination net traversal is a useful mechanism, and Anon can exhibit the same behavior as a discrimination net traverser. If the system starts with an empty list of initial label terms and with no information about relative costs of feature acquisition (i.e., if all costs are set to unity), then the system works very much like a self-balancing discrimination tree. The first request for information would be for some feature, the presence or absence of which would split the system's knowledge structures into two equal-sized pools. The second request would be for some feature that would split the selected pool again into two equal-sized pools.

Given some initial description of the current situation and some information about the relative costs of acquiring knowledge about the current situation, the system operates in a way that is neither strictly top-down nor bottom-up. Anon maximizes the use of the *a priori* sketchy description of the current situation and, beyond that, uses its knowledge about the contents and organization of memory to direct its inference mechanism efficiently.

4.6 Memory and Idiosyncratic Questions

It is important to recognize that Anon's control structure causes the system to seek a great deal of information about the current situation if it is matching against an area of memory densely populated with knowledge structures, and to seek much less information if it is matching against a more sparsely populated area of memory. As a result, changing the knowledge structures in the system's memory changes the questions that the system asks in the process of developing a description of the current situation. There is no need to posit a separate "situation-describing" module that must be updated to reflect changes in the system's memory. Questions are asked as needed to discriminate among the knowledge structures in memory; changing memory changes the questions.

Consider again an explanation system faced with a task such as SWALE's (Kass, et al., 1986) goal of explaining the mysterious death of a star racehorse. Different individuals, each with idiosyncratic goals for an explanation, will build different explanations. An insurance examiner, for example, might be reminded of a valuable painting that mysteriously disappeared a year earlier in what turned out to be a fake burglary staged by the owner to collect the insurance money. A veterinarian might be reminded of the cow that died mysteriously the previous week and begin investigating whether the medical causes were the same. A racing examiner might be reminded of other cases of one competitor trying to disable another and might suspect the owners of Swale's competitors. A gambler might be reminded of other odds-on favorites suddenly being disabled or otherwise removed from competition. Each of these individuals retrieves different remindings from memory because each has described Swale's death in different terms. Each description is equally correct, but each leads to a different path of explanatory reasoning.

It is unreasonable to assume that veterinarians, insurance adjusters, and gamblers have totally different processes for extracting descriptions from situations. Moreover, it is difficult to account for these differences in retrieval with a system that separates feature extraction from the rest of memory. The differences might be accounted for by a process that maps retrieval goals to predictive features, as discussed by Stepp & Michalski (1986) or

Seifert (1988). This process could weight the importance of features depending on how relevant they were to the current set of retrieval goals. But this approach leaves unanswered the question of how retrieval goals and predictive features are linked together.

A model like Anon explains the individuals' different explanations of Swale's death as due to the fact that abstract feature extraction is driven by the case libraries of each individual. The veterinarian has a large case library of animal diseases and consequently describes the event in terms of features that can discriminate among these cases. Likewise, an insurance examiner discriminates among a second, different library of cases, and a gambler among a third. Each of these individuals extracts from the story the features necessary to discriminate among the cases in his or her own memory. Each individual can use the same kind of mechanism to extract abstract features from concrete descriptions of situations, but that mechanism is driven by a different case library in each case, and so results in a different set of features being extracted, a different case retrieved, and a different explanation generated.

4.7 Discussion

4.7.1 Retrieval and Feature Utility

An essential question in learning is *what to learn*: what category distinctions or descriptive features are worthwhile. This question arises more or less *statically* as "What terms should be included in the system's representation vocabulary?" and *dynamically* as "What features should the system try to extract now from this situation?" The main tradeoff in answering this question is to balance the expressive power of a descriptive feature against the computational and physical costs of determining whether that feature characterizes the current situation. This is the question that system designers address when they choose a reasonable set of primitives for a representation language, and it is the question that machine learning systems address when they make feature acquisition or categorization decisions.

The work described in this chapter represents an attempt to build a framework in which this tradeoff can be managed explicitly by a retrieval system. As such, it looks at two distinct means of describing the expressive power of a feature. *External functional utility* describes the utility of the feature to the system's external tasks: selecting actions, recovering from plan failures, and detecting opportunities or threats. *Internal functional utility* describes the utility of the feature to the system's internal task: choosing the prior case or abstract knowledge structure most relevant to the system's current situation. This decomposition makes evident that the internal task, involving judgments of similarity or relevance, only makes sense as it is grounded in the external task— choosing a relevant prior experience is only useful to the degree that the prior experience tells the system what to do, or what further information to gather.

The Anon program itself does not address what the system does with a knowledge structure once it is determined to be applicable. It is not a complete planning system, and therefore it doesn't make any statements about the external task. It does, however, illustrate a retrieval mechanism that can efficiently and dynamically calculate the internal utility of a feature, and thereby bring that utility measurement to bear on the question of what features to try to detect or extract next. It does so in a way that potentially allows external and internal utility to be expressed in comparable terms, and thereby to enter into the same calculation of which piece of detection or inference has the highest expected utility.

It achieves some of the same effect as algorithmic approaches to internal utility calculations, such as those found in systems like ID3, AutoClass, and COBWEB, in that it creates a hierarchy of feature salience, such that the features with the highest discriminating power are pursued first. It avoids, however, the problem of committing in advance to a static ordering of questions or a static hierarchy of feature importance. Anon's algorithm allows the information contained in the current candidates at any point in the retrieval process to direct the subsequent retrieval. The features of the candidates known in the candidates but untested in the input can be examined to decide which ones discriminate among the candidates. The system's memory of knowledge structures can be examined as a whole to decide which features carry a high information content with regard to the input.

Exclusively top-down search ignores such information as the system might have at its disposal, for example, features acquired as a side effect of other processing that the system needs to perform. Similarly, completely bottom-up search causes the system to waste its time detecting the presence or absence of features that do not discriminate among the knowledge structures that are currently under consideration. The balancing approach taken by

Anon is sensitive to and effectively uses available information, but it also allows the contents and organization of memory to drive the feature extraction process.

4.7.2 Criticalities and Future Directions

Because the point of this research is to enable systems to reason about the utility of feature acquisition, the major criticalities revolve around the system's measurements of utility. Anon shows how a system can measure discriminating power and use that measurement. The program itself, however, says nothing about external utility, beyond providing a mechanism whereby external and internal utility measurements can be combined to control inference. As a result, an important future direction is to say something about external utility and detection costs, beyond the obvious "They should be taken into account."

In particular, this suggests that content theories of repair and recovery should be extended to include detectability: the features to be included in a representation vocabulary are those that are functionally grounded not only in repair and recovery, but in detectability as well.

The issue here is to build a theory of feature detectors and their cost. Can anything be said about detectability at other than an ad hoc level? Are there significant different classes of features, relative to detectability? Can detection cost be predicted or estimated reliably? This is an issue not just for the system designer in choosing an initial representation vocabulary, but for the system as well as it acquires new descriptive features.

A key future direction is to apply the representation methodology suggested by this work, to a specific, concrete, real-world planning domain. Although the advice-giving proverbs that form the basis of Anon's knowledge structures provide a good cross-section of stereotypical plan failures, they are not themselves grounded in a specific planning task. The goal is to identify stereotypical recurring failures and corresponding recovery and repair strategies, to build feature detectors for the descriptive features that discriminate among those failures, and to use an Anon-like memory as a repository of the resulting knowledge structures. When such a system is built, it will enable us to determine whether the external and internal measurements of feature utility, as described earlier, can, in fact, be combined into a single mechanism for inference control.

4.7.3 Indexing: A Compromise

A theory of indexing and retrieval is inherently one of compromise. Given infinite computational resources, a system could choose the best knowledge structure from its memory by trying each in turn, simulating the results obtained from applying the advice contained in that knowledge structure to the current situation, and, after trying all the knowledge structures in its library, choosing the best. Or, a system with infinite computational and sensory resources could perform such a detailed analysis of the current situation that the resulting description of the problem would effectively embody the solution, making complicated matching of the current situation against prior experiences superfluous.

But computational resources are not infinite. A system cannot develop a rich, fleshed-out description of the current problem merely as a precursor to searching memory, nor can it devote a lot of computational resources to estimating the goodness of each of a large number of knowledge structures as a potential solution to the current problem. Furthermore, computing power is not the only limit on the search for the ideal knowledge structure to match against the current situation; information about the world comes at a price, too. An eye or camera, for example, can only look in one direction at a time. Often, gathering even low-level sensory information about the world involves costs in resources and time. A theory of indexing and retrieval is a theory of heuristic management of bounded resources.

The compromises inherent in a theory of indexing and retrieval manifest themselves in several places, most particularly the modularity of the system and the choice of an indexing or labeling vocabulary.

4.7.4 Modularity

The premise underlying most models of retrieval is that a system can solve problems by:

1. developing a sketchy description of the current situation,
2. comparing that description against the knowledge structures in its memory and selecting one or more knowledge structures that match it, and
3. adapting the retrieved knowledge structures to the problem at hand.

Within this framework, the tension lies in the balance between the sophistication of the "sketchy describer," the matcher, and the adapter. The more powerful the describer and the more extensive the memory, the less powerful the matcher and the adapter need to be. On the other hand, a strong, flexible, general adapter requires only a small memory and a weak matcher. In each case, the sophisticated module needs more access to the system's general inference mechanism. The modular approach remains a compromise because it cannot guarantee that the sketchy description captures anything essential about the current situation, nor can it guarantee that a knowledge structure matched on the basis of this sketchy description in fact contains useful advice.

Working around this modularity is an important part of the retrieval mechanisms already described. I presented a theory of indexing that tightly integrates the task of describing the current situation and the task of searching memory for relevant knowledge structures, both with each other and with the larger planning task. I developed Anon to demonstrate the ability of a memory, organized along functional lines, to drive a describer—an inference mechanism—and thus tailor descriptions to the needs of the memory search process. Such integration of feature extraction and retrieval results in retrieved knowledge structures that improve the capability of the system to implement repairs and recovery strategies.

4.7.5 Learning and Retrieval

Anon is not a learning algorithm. It is instead a framework for dealing with knowledge about the costs of feature acquisition that a system learns elsewhere.

The Anon program presents a novel approach to the mechanics of retrieval. As it is equally informed both by the contents of memory and the features of the current environment, it is neither top-down nor bottom-up in its approach to search. Although it exploits parallelism, it does so in a way that allows the system to search memory incrementally—interleaving the operation of the searcher with that of the inference mechanism that gathers information about the current situation. This approach allows the system to continually balance the cost of acquiring information against the value of that information. Although other systems, most notably ID3 (Quinlan, 1983), have attended to this balance, Anon manages it dynamically during the retrieval process.

With this algorithm I argue for a remodularization of memory-based systems. Memory should not be viewed as a passive information-retrieval system to be queried by an intelligent process elsewhere within a system. Memory implicitly contains much of the information necessary to direct inference and sensing; systems should make this information explicit and use it to direct incremental feature extraction and retrieval.

5. Abby: Exploring an Indexing Vocabulary for Social Advice

Eric A. Domeshek
College of Computing
Georgia Institute of Technology

Editors' Introduction

Indexing and retrieval are issues of broad scope. The same indexing issues that arise within the scope of a case-based explainer, such as SWALE arise within any case-retrieval program. Thus, although the Abby program does not do explanation, the case-retrieval issues it addresses are directly relevant to the endeavor of case-based explanation, such as that done by SWALE. We have included a chapter on Abby here because Domeshek's work addresses important issues in case retrieval, and because Domeshek's main focus is interestingly different from Owens'.

The two central subissues within indexing seem to be indexing strategy and indexing vocabulary. The strategy question is, basically, What algorithm should be employed to search for relevant cases? The vocabulary question is What description language can be used to label cases and retrieve them later? The two are obviously intertwined, but some indexing researchers focus more on one whereas others focus more on the other. Owens' chapter, for instance, is mostly about strategy issues; this chapter by Domeshek focuses on vocabulary.

Developing an appropriate representational vocabulary requires a penetrating analysis of the domain that the case-base is drawn from. Only by first determining what the crucial factors are in a domain can one determine which features should be included in storage labels and retrieval cues, and which features should be ignored as irrelevant. In this chapter Eric Domeshek describes his doctoral work on Abby, in which he examined the indexing-vocabulary problem in great depth within the domain of social relationships.

* * *

5.1 How Abby Works

Abby is a program that gives advice by telling stories about problematic social situations, often including an account of how those problems were resolved; such stories can serve as warnings of impending difficulties or proposals for resolution of existing problems. Abby's indexing vocabulary focuses on explaining happenings in the social world; these are happenings that tend to have both social consequences and social causes (and thus explanations that must make reference to social facts and conventions).

Consider the following sample stories from Abby's memory:

Story 1. I know a woman who was very much in love with her boyfriend. She decided to move to his town, even though that meant leaving behind all her old friends. She realized what she was getting into, and she put some effort into making sure things worked out. For one thing, she wasn't the stick-in-the-mud type, so it wasn't long before she was good friends with most of his friends, and, through her job, it wasn't much longer before she'd made a bunch of new friends of her own. She also made sure to keep in touch with her old friends by phone and letters. When it came time for vacation, she made sure that she got to spend some time in her old stomping grounds.

Story 2. I had a friend who started off his senior year of college getting dumped by his girlfriend. They'd been apart for the summer—he'd been out of town working while she stayed around school as a dorm supervisor for the summer school. He'd worked real hard at keeping things together: he called, wrote and visited. But she spent the summer having an affair with one of her summer school advisees. When he got back to school, she made it pretty clear that she thought things were over between them; at the very least she wanted the freedom to see other people.

Of course it was a major blow to him, but he managed to carry on; by the time you're a senior, you've got a good support network of friends to help pull you through. The interesting thing though is that in the months and even the years that followed—for at least 3 or 4 years—this woman would periodically call up my friend and try to rekindle the romance. She went so far as to try to seduce him even when she knew he was engaged. It seemed that in the end she was the one who was more hurt by the breakup.

Story 3. You know my life already. You know what the moral of my life is? "It's too late." I like to get around, I like pretty women and everything. But the only thing is, that after a while they know you're getting older.

I had a relationship years ago when I was young. A very pretty girl. But that ended. Now I see a nice girl, I kiss her, but that's all. It's forgotten. There's no relationship.

Each of these stories could carry a useful message for other individuals facing similar circumstances. A person considering relocating to be near a loved one might benefit from the example of the outgoing woman; someone suffering from a nasty unwanted breakup might find consolation in the second story; an older person dithering in indecision about relationships might see that they did not want to end up like the lonely old man of the final story. Abby's memory stores 500 stories like these describing more than 250 different problematic social situations. Abby's task is to retrieve appropriate stories from this corpus in response to descriptions of new problem situations.

Abby's task is a simplified version of a common human behavior: often, when we hear someone tell a story of personal problems, we respond, not with a solution ("dump him" or "marry her"), or with a rule ("if your spouse is jealous, then try not to do anything provocative"), but with an example drawn from our own life or vicarious experiences—such as one of the aforementioned stories. Giving advice on social problems by telling stories of other people's problems is an appropriate target task to model with case-based reasoning (CBR) techniques, particularly when the research goal is to focus on techniques for retrieval of past experiences. First of all, because this is the sort of task that people actually do quite frequently and quite well, we have reason to believe the task is not only possible, but also cognitively plausible. Second, social problems have the complexity and open-ended nature that characterize many real-world problems; these are exactly the properties that force more conventional rule-based systems to lose their way in huge search spaces as they string together small inferences into chains with unknown validity. Case-based systems can choose known past solutions even when there is insufficient knowledge available to derive such solutions or to prove that they will work.

From the point of view of CBR research, Abby's advice-selecting task has the nice property that it limits the system's processing responsibility. CBR systems are typically characterized as employing two major steps: (a) retrieve a case and (b) apply a case. Abby's task, as specified, allows us to focus on just the first step. The system simply chooses a story and tells it. It is up to a human user to read the story, interpret it in the light of the current situation, and decide how, or even whether, it offers applicable advice. Other systems described in this volume, such as Jones' Brainstormer, suggest ways in which a more complete system might make use of the stories Abby retrieves. Of course, such systems would require more complete representation of the content of the story and the generalizations of the domain in order to adapt and apply such remindings.

Leaving out the application phase allowed Abby to focus solely on the indexing problem. The "indexing problem" is a covering term for several related problems, but the most difficult, the one on which Abby was focused, and the one that is emphasized here, is the issue of *indexing vocabulary*: If retrieval of past experiences—in this case for use as advice—is to be based on a partial match between situation descriptions, what should be the content of those descriptions? Focusing on the indexing problem drove development of representational vocabulary for explanatory structures underlying story situations.

5.1.1 Explaining Social Events and States

It is traditional in AI representation theories to describe situations in terms of objects being in particular *states*. In blocks world, (Sussman,, 1975), for example, a BLOCK (an object) may be ON (a state) some other object; a BLOCK is either ON the TABLE, or it is ON another BLOCK, or it is being HELD (another state) in the block-manipulating robot's HAND. In conceptual dependency (CD) (Schank 1972), things such as PEOPLE were described in terms of physical states such as AT-LOC (e.g., (AT-LOC JOHN STORE) = "John was at the store") and social, mental, or emotional states (e.g., (AFFECT JOHN +8) = "John was happy").

Not surprisingly, describing situations in terms of states allows only a static view of those situations. CD, in fact, was far more concerned with the representation of *events* that accounted for state changes than with states themselves. More specifically, CD focused on the representation of actions—those events committed by agents, such as people, typically, in pursuit of some goals. Likewise, in systems intended for planning or problem solving (as represented by many blocks world systems), along with states came a set of operators defining the known ways of changing states; again, operators exist to be applied by agents trying to achieve goals.

Here, in the very definition of states and events, we already run into the first notions of explanation: Events are defined as happenings that cause state changes; agents often perform actions (a significant subset of all events) in the service of achieving goals. So if we want to explain a state, we can cite an event that brought the state into existence. If we want to explain an event, we can sometimes cite a goal held by an agent as the motivation for the event. AI has developed richer ways of describing the world and accounting for why aspects of those descriptions are as they are; research on natural language processing and on understanding people's everyday behavior helped lead to more elaborate representational and explanatory systems.

Schank and Abelson (1977) proposed two additional representational constructs to flesh out explanations of everyday events. Between goals and actions they interposed plans. Plan knowledge makes it easier to relate a goal to the great variety of specific actions that might be employed to achieve that goal; plans can also capture similarities among actions employed to achieve distinct but related goals. For instance, there is a large, but still fairly stereotyped set of ways to get others to do something for you—You can ask them, convince them, threaten them, force them, and so on; likewise, there are many larger purposes for which you might seek to get someone to come to your aid. Employing another agent to help you achieve your purposes is thus a useful plan.

To help answer the question "Where do goals come from?" Schank and Abelson proposed *themes*. Themes were explicitly an explanatory construct intended to quell what could otherwise be an endless sequence of "Why?" motivational questions. Mary had the goal of winning the big contract because she held a larger, longer term theme to BE-SUCCESSFUL; John wanted to take care of Billy because he was FATHER-OF this child. Although we could continue to ask "Why?"—Why did Mary want to be successful?

Why was John Billy's father?—such questions are rarely productive and thus are rarely asked. Either there is an obvious standard answer, or there is no reliable answer at all.

Later, Schank and Leake (1989) organized this collection of representational classes, proposing a simple standard package called the *intentional chain* as a canonical format for explanations of intentional behavior or states resulting from intentional behavior. The intentional chain offers an explanation of the following form: A state exists because an action was performed as part of a plan intended to advance a goal which derived from a theme. In Abby's domain of lovelorn problems, we could couch a standard explanation of how people come to be married as follows: By virtue of being an adult (a theme) a person comes to want to be married (a goal), and sets about finding a spouse (a plan), culminating in actually getting married (an action), with the result being that they are married (a state).

Table 5.1 shows, side-by-side the general template for an intentional chain and how that template might be filled out to represent this standard marriage explanation. In both diagrams, the left-hand column names the five pieces of the intentional chain: theme, goal, plan, action, and effect. In the diagram of the generic intentional chain, the right-hand column specifies the generic class of filler allowed for each slot (usually noting in parentheses a more general category to indicate commonalties). The right-hand column in the diagram of the marriage chain is filled with particular items of the appropriate classes.

Table 5.1. The Generic Intentional Chain and an Example.

Slot Names	Chain-Contents	Slot Names	Chain-Contents
Theme	theme (state)	*Theme*	be-adult
Goal	goal (state)	*Goal*	achieve-spouse-of
Plan	plan (event)	*Plan*	find-partner
Action	action (event)	*Action*	marry
Effect	state	*Effect*	x-spouse-of

The intentional chain, as a single straight-line explanatory mechanism, is a simplification incapable of expressing many richer causal patterns common in everyday reasoning. Nonetheless, this is a useful starting place, and the intentional chain is a useful building block. In the real world, agents seldom act under the influence of a single goal, but, rather, are constantly involved in making trade-offs or seizing on synergies. A couple wants children, but also wants time to build their careers; any choice of job and/or parenthood must be understood in terms of both of these goals. The couple's problem is typical of social situations in that it involves multiple agents with both common and divergent goals; one member of a couple may be willing to sacrifice the other's career for their joint goal of starting a family. In the next subsection, we build on the intentional chain to allow descriptions of these kinds of more complicated situations.

All explanations need not appeal to intentional causality; as pointed out by Leake (see chapter 6), the sort of explanation worth deriving depends on the purposes for which the explanation is being prepared. If you are an engineer examining the collapse of a bridge, it may be more important to focus on the physics of metal fatigue and calculations involving the sizing of critical supports than to consider the motives of agents who might have wanted to test out a novel design, save money on the bridge's construction, or drive across with an unusually heavy load. To date, less research effort has gone into designing and then exercising canonical forms for physical explanations than intentional and social explanations covered by the intentional chain and extensions built on it. Abby, with its focus on social issues, does not possess detailed representations for physical explanations.

5.1.2 Explanatory Representation and Indexing

What do representations of explanations for states and events in the social world have to do with the problem of indexing to stories containing advice? We want to retrieve stories from memory when they are appropriate. Common sense and prior research on indexing cases (Hammond, 1986) suggest that the best warrant for the relevance of an old experience's proposed course of action (or its warning against possible problems), is when the features that accounted for a desirable outcome (or for a problem) are shared by a new situation. The upshot is that it makes sense to index old cases according to their causally significant features, and to look for such features in new situations. The sorts of explanations we have been considering are essentially causal accounts of how states and actions came to occur; as such, these explanations identify causally significant features (at least according to the explanations' particular accounts of why things happened).

The woman who relocated to be with her lover was running the risk of losing contact with old friends and being isolated in her new home. An explanation for this situation might include that because she loved her boyfriend, she developed a desire to live in the same place as he, which caused her to relocate, resulting in her being near him (but not being near her old friends). This story might be relevant in other circumstances wherein one member of a couple was considering moving to be near another. It identifies potential problems (losing touch with old friends and being isolated) and proposes possible solutions (working to maintain contact, making sure to visit, being outgoing and making friends in the new town).

Abby indexes the woman's story by this explanation, but the explanation's straight-line causal chain is not the complete index. As an advice-giving program, it makes sense for Abby to choose its stories in response to common problems as well as common causes for those problems. Thus, one index to this story also includes the fact that the woman had some friends in her old neighborhood that she wanted to remain close to, and that her move had the regrettable effect of threatening those friendships. Including this problem specification in the story's index along with the original explanation helps increase the chance that this story will be retrieved at an appropriate time. After all, people move all the time, but losing touch with old friends and being isolated are not always paramount concerns; sometimes they have few contacts in the place they are leaving, sometimes they are moving somewhere where they already have a number of friends, and sometimes they are moving with a group (such as their family).

In Abby, the problems are in some sense the primary indices, with the explanations for those problems being included whenever they are available. Nonetheless, the problem descriptions borrow from the representational forms first developed to capture explanations. Abby generally describes the problems underlying its stories by casting them as slightly malformed intentional chains. What makes them malformed is that, although they may contain a theme, goal, plan, action, and effect, the normal causal linkages between those elements do not always hold. Somewhere in the chain there is a failure: the goal does not follow from the theme, the plan does not suit the goal, the action does not advance the plan, or the effect is not a normal consequence of the action.

In the example we have been considering, the problematic chain is constructed as follows: The woman has friends in her home town and, accordingly, has the goal to maintain those friendships, but for reasons accounted for in the original explanation, she moves to her lover's town, with the unfortunate effect that the old friendships are threatened. The break in this chain is that the move to a new town does not follow from any plan for her goal to maintain her old friendships; in fact, it runs directly counter to that goal. Packaging up these components into a mutant intentional chain helps to capture the nature of the problem, just as pairing the mutant chain with the normal explanatory chain that contains the same action helps to capture the cause of the problem. Laid out, side by side, these two chains depict a *tradeoff* faced by the woman in our story: she chose to be close to her lover at the expense of risking her old friendships.

Table 5.2. Chain Interaction for "Relocating Near Lover."

Theme	lover-of	*Theme*	friend-of
Goal	initiate-neighbor-of	*Goal*	maintain-friendship
Plan	act-as-partner	*Plan*	
Action	transfer	*Action*	
Effect	neighbor-of	*Effect*	ex-neighbor-of

In order to capture tradeoffs, we introduce the notion of a *chain interaction*: two intentional chains grouped together because they share a common action. Table 5.2 shows our analysis of this sample problem as a chain interaction. We adopt the convention that when, as often happens, a chain interaction contains one chain with a positive impact and another with a negative impact, we place the one with the positive impact (the normal intentional chain) in the left column.

Note that this chain interaction is only one of many possible descriptions of the problem in this situation. In our analysis, we also suggested that a possible problem here is that the woman might feel isolated in her new home. The story addresses that problem as well as the potential for losing touch with old friends. Abby can have several indices pointing to the same story (or to closely related stories recounting the same situation with slightly different slants). To let the system know that this story could also give advice about the problem of isolation in a new town, we would need a separate index specifying that problem.

Table 5.3. Index sketch for Second Example.

Theme	be-young-woman	*Theme*	lover-of
Goal	satisfy-sex	*Goal*	maintain-lover-of
Plan	dump-partner	*Plan*	
Action	have-sex (with other)	*Action*	
Effect	satisfied-sex	*Effect*	lover-of
Link: action-plan-sequence-action			
Theme	be-young-woman	*Theme*	lover-of
Goal	terminate-lover-of	*Goal*	maintain-lover-of
Plan	dump-partner	*Plan*	
Action	break-up	*Action*	
Effect	ex-lover-of	*Effect*	ex-lover-of

5.1.3 Abby's Index Frame

All indices in Abby are cast into a common format built from intentional chains and chain interactions. Abby's general *index frame* is designed to allow slightly longer and more detailed explanations of situations than would fit into a single intentional chain, or even into a chain interaction's pair of intentional chains with their common action. In order to allow an index to capture more of the history behind a problem, Abby's index frame has room for two chain interactions: the first one centers on an action that took place earlier in time than the second. These can be thought of as the *background chain interaction* and the *main problem chain interaction*. To tie these two chain interactions together, it also allows specification of a linkage between some fact in the background and some fact in the main problem.

The ability to specify a background to a main problem is quite often useful. For instance, many lovelorn situations can be described in terms of a problem created when one member of a couple breaks off a relationship although the other one wants it to continue. To discriminate among breakups, it helps if indices to such situations also encode information about what led up to the breakup. Such information might include what motivated the breakup, how the breakup was carried out, or what the course of the relationship had been. The second example story mentioned earlier can be described as a breakup initiated by the woman and unwanted by the man; but further, to justify the story's tone of "one who does you wrong will get his or her just desserts," it is

Table 5.4. Unexplained Failure of Old Bachelor to Marry.

Theme		*Theme*	be-man
Goal		*Goal*	achieve-husband-of
Plan		*Plan*	find-partner / defer
Action	not-marry	*Action*	
Effect		*Effect*	not-husband-of

important that the index also include the woman's infidelities leading up to the breakup. Table 5.3 sketches Abby's index for this story; it describes the woman following an extended plan to dump her old lover, finding other sexual partners in preparation for the ultimate break-up.

Abby's index frame has room for up to four intentional chains (two chain interactions) and all their parts, but it is not required that every index specify a filler for every available slot. The index for the story of the relocating lover sketched earlier is perfectly valid even though it only specifies the final chain interaction. The index for the third story, "The Lonely Old Bachelor," is sparser still. Table 5.4 sketches an index for that story which is notable because it does not really contain much of an explanation at all. All it says is that the old man wanted to marry, but never did, because he deferred carrying out the necessary plan to get married.

5.1.4 Representing the Connections in Intentional Chains

To say that explanations are going to constitute a significant part of a system's indices, and to say that explanations are going to be formed out of standard packages of themes, goals, plans, actions, and states is not to say very much. A serious attack on the indexing problem requires specifying exactly which items of any of these classes are useful, what features of each are relevant, and how items can combine into meaningful chains. Much of the work on Abby was devoted to generating hundreds of sample indices as a way of arriving at specific answers to these questions. To give a good feel for the results of this kind of research on indexing, it is useful to survey some of the generated representational vocabulary. Accordingly, following this brief introduction to Abby's task, domain, and the broad structure of its index representations, the balance of this chapter is devoted to presenting a suite of representations developed for, and used in Abby. Instead of focusing on the basic classes introduced earlier (THEME, GOAL, PLAN, ACTION, STATE), we examine smaller classes that describe the way those components are linked together into chains. These classes have the twin advantages of containing fewer members than the basic factual and motivational descriptors, and of constituting more clearly explanatory materials.

As a standard way of packaging THEMES, GOALS, PLANS, ACTIONS, and resulting STATES, the intentional chain works well as a building block for Abby's indices. But simply stringing items from these classes together in a line is not sufficient to describe how they relate to one another. Remember, while the original intentional chain presupposed that each component was in some sense caused by the one preceding it, Abby's version of the intentional chain is not restricted to describing normal successful goal pursuit. Abby coopts the intentional chain to describe goal pursuit failures as well. Abby's intentional chains may even describe fortuitous goal satisfaction or failure and would not naturally be characterized as records of goal pursuit at all.

Because an index frame's intentional chains can describe either success or failure, the linkages between chain components must be made explicit. There are three types of linkages worth recording. First, there are the normal CAUSAL linkages that give the chain its coherence: Theme causes goal causes plan causes action causes effect. But when an intentional chain records goal pursuit failure, we may also need linkages to describe *aberrations* of normal intentional causality. The next section presents Abby's vocabulary for intentional causation, including its ways of talking about aberrations in that causality.

Finally, Abby explicitly records relationships between the effect of an intentional chain and its three motivational components using components called IMPACTS. IMPACTS offer some answer to the question "So what?" So what that the woman is now near her lover? So what that her old friendships may become weaker than they were? These states matter because of, and can be interpreted in light of, a chain's theme, goal, or plan. Since Abby's intentional chains do not all record successes, impacts may be either positive or negative. The vocabulary of impacts is presented in the final section.

5.2 Causals and Aberrations

In a normal intentional chain, successive components are linked by causal relationships. This is one reason intentional chains make good index building blocks: A causal understanding of a mechanism provides a solid basis for modifying the mechanism (Hammond 1986). In this section I describe Abby's vocabulary for characterizing the causal links between elements of the intentional chain. The first four subsections describe the connections between THEMES and GOALS, GOALS and PLANS, PLANS and ACTIONS and ACTIONS and STATES. The last two subsections report a motley assortment of other causal linkages appearing only in the index frame's linkage slot: These include several different kinds of linkages between STATES and ACTIONS, as well as additional sources of GOALS.

5.2.1 Goal Causality

In order to understand the following discussion of linkages to goals, it is necessary to know a bit about how Abby describes goals. A goal describes a target state desired (or feared) by some agent (the holder). The target state can link two other items that may also be agents (the subject and object). Finally, the goal may include a specification of who should satisfy the goal (the actor). The justification for this last convention is that in the social world, the question of who acts to achieve a state is important; consider the difference between wanting to take care of your children and wanting your children to be taken care of by someone else. Abby's goals, then, may specify up to four involved agents, and the relationships between those agents are often important.

Under the rough heading of causality, there are four questions Abby is prepared to ask about a goal: the manner in which it derives from a theme, the sort of linkage between the theme's agents inherent in the goal, the context in which the goal was spawned by the theme, and the history of the goal. For any one goal, it would be unusual for all of these questions to have interesting answers. The four subsections that follow present the possible answers to these questions, together comprising Abby's vocabulary for goal causality.

This way of characterizing the linkage between theme and goal actually forms a natural extension to the overall goal taxonomy. It may seem odd to group the features covered here as causes of goals; some might seem like attributes of goals or context for goals. We separate these descriptors out from the characterization of the goal itself because they do not affect what states of affairs in the world would satisfy the goal. Instead, they characterize the conditions under which the goal arose, the goal's normal frequency and pattern of reoccurrence; they characterize the attitudes different agents have taken towards the goal, and, thus, what the consequences of success or failure might be. When the goal state itself suggests which plans might be relevant, this additional information suggests what sorts of plans are likely to succeed or fail.

Theme to Goal Pattern.

I know a woman who, in her later years, decided to spruce up her appearance. Well, actually, I think she was talked into it by her grown daughters. All those years she was raising the family, she had never taken much time for herself. So this was really a pretty big change for her. The thing was, her husband didn't take it well at all. He didn't seem to mind her dressing up more, but when she dyed her hair, he really blew his top. It's hard to say exactly why, but I suspect that whereas dressing well seemed like a simple exercise in self-respect, dying her hair seemed phony—sort of an admission that she didn't really like who she was.

Goals, like the desire to look more attractive, are not fixed and necessary consequences of themes; they may develop, wax, and wane over time. Abby considers goals to derive from themes in one of five ways. These suggest answers to questions like: How unique is this goal in the agent's experience? How persistent is the goal likely to be? The possible values are ONE-SHOT, EVOLUTION, PERMANENT, RECURRING, and PERIODIC.

The least constraining and one of the least common relationships between theme and goal is ONE-SHOT; this simply says that on one occasion, the agent developed this goal based on the theme. Saying a goal follows from a theme as a ONE-SHOT result simply means that something about the situation caused the goal to be active and that there is no other systematic relationship; it does not mean that the goal can only arise once, but it does suggest that the goal is rare and idiosyncratic. Examples of ONE-SHOT goals arising in Abby's stories include a young woman who wants to give an old man a good time in bed as a reward for his being lavish with her, a young man who wants to rescue a co-worker from a fire, and a person whose curiosity is aroused to ask why a couple has no children. There can also be one-shot fears like those felt by either of two young women almost driven to suicide, one by fear of depression, the other by fear of having lost her family's love.

A goal described as arising from a theme by EVOLUTION is more integral to the source theme than one whose connection is ONE-SHOT. EVOLUTION goals may only arise once from a theme, but they bear a deep relationship to the meaning of the theme—they are, in a sense, part of its course and fulfillment. The most common examples of EVOLUTION goals are goals to change the status of the thematic relationship itself, in either a positive or negative way. In many stories, lovers develop the goal to be married; in many others, lovers decide to break up. More subtle modifications of both personal and interpersonal themes often count as evolution goals. Older people may become more religious as time goes by, shifting their personal priorities; young people may become ambitious and work for greater status within existing relationships. Many states can appear as evolutionary goals and reflect the standing of the underlying theme; for instance couples may develop the goal to live in the same town or in the same household. Finally, some evolutionary goals aim at states that are not themes, components of themes or indicators of themes, but are simply desirable states at some phase of a theme: for instance, as they watch their grandchildren grow, it is not unusual for an old people to start thinking about what they can do to help the young ones financially.

Whereas goals derived from themes by EVOLUTION most often aim at some change—often initiation and termination of themes—goals that Abby describes as PERMANENT consequences of a theme tend to aim at state maintenance. That need not be maintenance of an entire theme or relationship, it might be maintenance of some specific state, like self-confidence or another agent's respect. Maintenance of thematic states can also take the negative form—a goal to keep a theme from coming into existence; one story tells of a young woman who did not want to get involved romantically with her professor. Alternately, permanent goals can describe policy-level commitments; like the people in a couple of stories described as wanting to start friendships, but without any potential partner being specified; this general friendliness can lead to specific instances of wanting to befriend certain individuals; that is they can specialize to other (possibly evolutionary or one-shot) goals.

In contrast to goals that arise at some stage in the history of a theme, or that persist throughout the life of a theme, many goals come up repeatedly in independent episodes. These are described as RECURRING goals. By far the most common RECURRING goal in Abby's corpus is the goal for low AROUSAL—the sex drive— that is described as deriving from the personal themes of most adults. Also common as recurring goals are the states COM-

PANIONSHIP and FREEDOM, but many other goals, too, can be satisfied intermittently including ENJOY, RESPECTFUL, EMPATHY, and CLEANLINESS. Recurring goals tend to be stated in absolute rather than comparative form: Someone wants sex or companionship on a particular occasion without reference to how he or she has felt in the past or will in the future (such concern for benchmarks is more befitting a maintenance or evolution goal). ONE-SHOT goals often share this focus on the immediate state.

The final sort of theme to goal relationship recognized in Abby is PERIODIC, which is used to describe goal states that not only recur, but that recur on a regular schedule. This applies to most of the physical functional states. The only cases of PERIODIC goals that actually occur in Abby are a couple of instances of the goal to have low FATIGUE. Note that AROUSAL is described simply as a RECURRING goal, because its cycle can be irregular. Goals that derive from themes in RECURRING and PERIODIC ways are largely coextensive with the *satisfaction goals* proposed by Schank and Abelson, and similar inferences apply.

Goal Agent Linkage

Couples' expectations sometimes get out of sync. I know one couple who ended up splitting because the woman thought it was her right to be supported by her boyfriend. He didn't see things that way, and was surprised when she started asking him for money all the time. He thought they were living in the modern 80s but she wanted to be kept in style just like her mother had been. Fortunately, this became apparent well before they had gotten so far as to be talking marriage. He just cut his losses and went on to look for a more independent woman whose expectations would be more in line with his own.

There can be several agents involved in a goal and they can be related in any number of ways. Beyond the normal given, that the holder of the goal is the holder of the generating theme, there are some common patterns that describe the way goals relate to the themes that spawn them. Several of these patterns have been picked out as goal–agent linkage patterns.

The simplest patterns are PERSONAL, PARTNER, and RECEIPT. PERSONAL goals stem from personal themes; lacking a partner, a personal theme cannot serve to link a goal to another agent. All the other goal–agent linkage forms discussed here depend on the goal being rooted in an interpersonal theme. PARTNER goals are those intended to benefit (or simply concerning) the theme partner; often the holder is committed to doing the work. RECEIPT goals are those in which the roles are reversed, and the holder is the beneficiary of the partner's actions. Different sorts of advice apply when problems arise in trying to achieve something for yourself, when what you want for someone else (or want to do for someone else) fails to work out, and when you want someone else to do something for you.

RECEIPT is just one of three linkage forms wherein the partner is expected to do something for the holder. There are two other positive versions of this sort that go beyond what would be obvious just by looking at which agents play which roles in the goal and its source interpersonal theme: MUTUAL goals and BALANCED goals. MUTUAL goals are those that cannot be achieved without the contribution of both the holder and partner. Prototypical mutual goals include initiating a new relationship or maintaining an old one, but many subgoals of relationships also fit this pattern, such as goals for companionship, which necessarily must involve both parties. Seifert (1987) offers an extensive analysis of planning strategies peculiar to mutual goals. BALANCED goals apply to states that need not hold simultaneously for both agents, but which are normally reciprocated; typical examples include APPROVE, LOVE, or RESPECTFUL. Although similar to MUTUAL goals, these are distinct because each version of the state in question is the responsibility of only one of the agents: If a husband respects his wife, she may still not respect him, but if either one of them fails to work toward mutual companionship, then neither of them can achieve satisfaction.

There are also three negative versions of linkage that describe situations wherein the holder has a goal requiring some action of the partner, but the partner does not want to play the part. These forms are UN-MUTUAL, UN-BALANCED, and NON-RECEIPT, and correspond to the positive forms after which they are named. The story given earlier, for instance, is a case wherein the woman expected to receive financial support from her boyfriend, but he did not expect to have to give it. These sorts of goals are problematic by their very nature; if you know that the partner has a negative attitude toward a MUTUAL, BALANCED, or RECEIPT goal, you have already gone a long way toward diagnosing the goal's failure and suggesting strategies for coping with it.

Goal Origination Context.

I know a couple whose young daughter developed cancer. They spent as much time as they could with the dying child. Of course,

*you can never spend enough; there just isn't enough time, and it is
so draining to hide your tears and go in to see your child with a
smile on your face. But at the same time you can spend too much.
While this couple was spending every free moment with their dying
child, their other children were feeling neglected. Sure it was selfish
of them, but sometimes you can't expect kids to understand these
things. Eventually they decided that for most visits, they would
split up and alternate which one would go to the hospital and
which would stay with the other kids. It was still very hard on everyone—both the parent handling the hospital visit alone and the
one prevented from visiting had a tough job—but I think it was the
best that could be made of a terrible situation.*

Abby considers only three options for the context in which a goal
originates from a theme: OPPORTUNITY, THREAT, and CRISIS.
CRISIS is meant to be equivalent to the category of the same name
in Schank and Abelson's classification. Aside from the extra levels distinguished in Abby's scheme, the main difference is that
these urgency distinctions in Abby are orthogonal to the other distinctions that contribute to classifying goals.

In Abby's corpus, OPPORTUNITY describes situations like a
woman who dislikes her daughter-in-law seeing her with another
man and spreading rumors that she's having an affair, a woman
getting divorced aiming for an especially large settlement by faking
a claim of spouse abuse, and a pair of housemates becoming interested in each other as lovers.

THREAT describes situations like that of the young woman
who tries to ignore the feeling that her advisor is sexually interested in her, the old man who wants companionship but whose
wife is ill, or the husband whose hopes that his wife will earn a
higher degree are threatened by her determination to have a baby.

CRISIS is reserved for pressing circumstances forcing major
action with respect to a goal; however, a social crisis is a relative
thing—it may not preempt all other goals and it may still allow
time for some planning (although emotions may not allow enough
rational clarity for much planning). An example of a prototypical
crisis goal appearing in Abby is the threat to life caused by a fire;
slightly less prototypical is a threat to life caused by extreme depression. Note that these crisis goals are the sorts of things that
turned up earlier as ONE-SHOT goals. A typical leisurely social
crisis is an unwanted pregnancy; it is emotionally absorbing and
demands action in some set amount of time, but it probably will
not supersede all other goals such as eating and sleeping.

Goal History.

If you don't tell people what you're feeling, you can't expect them to know. I know a woman who hated being bossed around by her mother-in-law. You might have thought she would mention it to her husband, especially because he seemed not to mind at all that his mother was always telling him what to do. You can't expect a mamma's boy to intuit that you're unhappy in your dealings with Mamma. Although her mother-in-law was a tyrant—bossing them around about everything—everything Mamma said was right and just fine with her husband.

I think she let things drift on this way too long. After 4 years of putting up with this, she tried to put her foot down and tell her husband that she wasn't going to take it any more. You know what he said? He said that his mother was his real family whereas his wife was just a business partner! Maybe he always felt that way, but you'd think she might have had more influence when they were first married, or at least she would have found out what kind of losing situations she was dealing with sooner.

Because social goals often are not dispatched neatly, once and for all, immediately upon arising, they can have interesting histories by the time they are encountered in the context of a particular story. This is especially true of RECURRING, and PERMANENT goals, but other goal types may accumulate histories as well. Abby describes a goal's history in one of eight ways. The simplest sort of history is NONEXISTENT, which means that there is no history for this goal; a goal that has never come up before may be more difficult to deal with, and you certainly cannot advise the agent to simply do what he or she did last time (or avoid doing what was done last time).

Four of the history classes assume that there has been some outcome for this goal in the past; that outcome may have been either positive or negative, and it may have been achieved with or without effort on the part of the agent. EFFORTLESS goals are those whose success in the past required no great effort; the goal of maintaining freedom as held by the stereotypic young man who has always avoided making a commitment to a relationship fits this description. LAPSED goals, on the other hand, are those that failed in the past for want of effort; the woman in the earlier story wanted her mother-in-law's respect but let things drift too long. If an agent has put effort into achieving a goal in the past, then it is described as either EFFORTFUL or TROUBLESOME, depending on whether it turned out positively or negatively. These are the sorts of situations in which you can expect agents to learn something specific from their past experiences. Effortless success or failure may require more specific coaching or may require a change of attitude, although, working hard at something that comes easily for others may also suggest that some attitude adjustment is needed.

There are three history types that describe situations where there is not really a past outcome: DROPPED, SUSPENDED, and SCHEDULED. Actually, for both DROPPED and for SUSPENDED goals, chances are there would be a negative outcome if the goal were still considered active. There are good and bad reasons for goals to become suspended: Distraction by a crisis is a good reason; laziness and indecision are generally bad reasons. There are standard strategies for reactivating threatened or failed suspended goals: You try to get back to them quickly —perhaps as soon as the distraction passes, perhaps on the next available cycle—and you devote extra effort to compensate for lost time. Stories about suspended goals include one of a woman who wanted to go to school but put it off to take care of her child, and one about a man who wanted to start a business, but was having trouble saving enough money while supporting his family. There are also conditions in which it makes sense to drop a goal in favor of other incompatible goals, and conditions under which it may or may not make sense to try and resurrect such goals. Abby knows a story of a man who, finding that his wife had remarried because she had thought him dead, dropped his intention to go back to living with her until years later; hearing that the other man had died, he tried to remarry her. SCHEDULED goals are ones that an agent fully intends to deal with, and not at some indefinite time in the future, but at some relatively specific time. Problems for scheduled goals generally either reflect failures of the planning process, or unfortunate circumstances. For instance, one story tells of a woman who was due to be married, but whose fiancé perished in a fire, leaving her grieving and unmarried for years.

Goal Current.

I had a friend whose husband was very sick. She divorced him with the consent of her children. She had a couple of good reasons. First of all, she's still young enough that she enjoys the company of other men. Second, by divorcing him, he can actually go on Medicaid much easier; the property that used to be in both their names is now in hers, so he is effectively a pauper.

> *California has passed a law that it is permissible for one to divorce a spouse who has Alzheimer's disease, and is in a state where he or she doesn't even know what time of day it is—even if the spouse has some lucid moments. They say its permissible to resume a normal life with male or female company. I would say there's nothing wrong with it because that person may be living, but in my opinion they are mentally dead. There's just nothing you can do about it.*

The final goal attribute that Abby tracks is the current status of a goal. This may be described in one of six ways intended to capture either the state of a goal with respect to pursuit, or, as in the aforementioned story, changes in a goal's status. The basic three states for a goal are SUSPENDED, ACTIVE, and PURSUING. As was the case with goal history, SUSPENDED indicates that a goal is being put off, and the reason for that may or may not be reasonable: Sometimes agents simply have to make value choices, as in stories in which one member of a couple relocates to be with their lover, sacrificing old friends, family ties, or a job; sometimes agents are afraid to pursue a goal, as in the story of the housemates who avoided starting a romantic relationship for fear of upsetting the status quo; sometimes they have pretty much given up, as was the case with the old bachelor of the chapter's introduction. ACTIVE on the other hand describes goals that an agent is still intending to pursue; the difference between ACTIVE and PURSUING is whether the action of the current intentional chain is actually part of a plan for achieving the goal.

The three less common current status descriptions are SPECIFY, VALUATE, and NONEXISTENT. SPECIFY and VALUATE are descriptions of a goal in flux. It is possible for the content of a goal to be more or less specific; often during the life of a goal, details of what exactly is wanted get fleshed out, and SPECIFY is available to describe such instances. For example, in some stories, people are described as having a general goal to make friends, and in specific situations, that goal is SPECIFIED so as to pick out particular people with whom to start friendships. Likewise, the agent's judgments of a goal's importance may shift over time, and particular episodes can be well described as instances wherein the value of the goal was judged to change; VALUATE is often used in describing changes in relationship; in several stories, it describes a person substituting one relationship for another; in one story, it describes a widow being convinced that a new relationship is worth having at all; in the aforementioned story, it describes a woman becoming convinced that it no longer makes sense to stay married. Finally, NONEXISTENT is used in the odd case wherein an agent does not hold a goal that the system has some reason to believe he or she might or ought to have held; the teenage girl who is ordered to stop seeing a particular boyfriend drops her goal to keep seeing him, but Abby can still describe the situation as a failure of her now NONEXISTENT goal.

5.2.2 Goal to Plan Linkages

It's not unusual for divorced couples to keep sleeping together. I knew a woman, who for over a year after her divorce, still relied on her ex for sex. She went out with other men, but could never bring herself to sleep with any of them. She realized she was being foolish, but couldn't stop herself. It turned out that a lot of her friends had the same problem. Finally, she figured out that the only way to stop was just to stop. She arranged that when she and her ex had to meet for business reasons, it was always in a public place, far from secluded couches or bedroom furniture. Having cut off that outlet, she found her interest in other men increasing. It wasn't too long before she was back in circulation, and it wasn't too much longer before she found another man to take as a serious lover.

The problem illustrated by this story is one in which the woman wants a relationship that will bring her sexual satisfaction, but settles on a plan that assures only the sexual release. The success of that one goal contributes to the failure of the larger goal, and part of what has gone wrong is the choice of an inappropriate plan. Abby's representation of goals is rather detailed, but its representation of plans, unfortunately, is not. Abby's situation descriptions make reference to just five very abstract plans (sometimes specialized a bit): ACT, FIND, MODIFY, SPUR, and RESPOND. The deemphasis of planning extends to the representations of linkages to and from plans. Because plans in Abby are very sketchy and abstract, when a plan link is characterized a particular way, it is often really the actions chosen to implement the plan that support the specific description. The point of these goal-to-plan links is to describe aspects of the planning process that may account for problems or offer likely opportunities for improvement.

Abby has six different ways of describing the relationship between a goal and a plan. The first two—the most commonly coded descriptions—are CHOSEN and DEFAULT. These apply when the plan is a reasonable choice for the goal; the difference between them is intended to reflect how much choice was really involved. DEFAULT is used to describe situations wherein the plan (or the action that fleshes it out) is tightly associated with the goal: it does not require much choice for a man seeking to end an affair to settle on the DUMP-PARTNER plan, dating teenagers seeking companionship ACT-IN-ROLE by socializing together. CHOSEN is used to describe situations such as a man dealing with his sex drive by choosing to CHEAT on his wife, or a woman trying to ensure her husband's loyalty by SPURring him to avoid looking at other women. Advising a shift away from a default plan may require more justification or instruction on the alternative.

When a plan is chosen, it is usually because of some specific qualities of the plan. The next two descriptions, EASIEST and EXTREME, comment on two such qualities. EASIEST describes plans that come ready to hand, requiring low effort either in their creation or execution. EXTREME describes plans that might be considered excessive, yet are chosen by agents intent on achieving their goals. Examples of plans chosen because they were EASIEST include the one described in the story above: divorced couples continue to sleep together when the loneliness gets to be too much; another example involves couples who fight over money matters rather than cooperate to save or earn more. EXTREME plans cover most types of compulsive behaviors, whether they be gambling, working, eating, or watching TV; often instances of the plan EXCEED-ROLE are classified as EXTREME as well. Obviously, the easiest plan is not always the best plan, and an extreme plan may be overkill incurring other excessive costs.

The last two goal-to-plan link types describe situations in which planning may not even be the best way to characterize the control of behavior. IMPROVISE describes situations in which no firm plan is adopted at all, and covers cases of opportunism and situational influence. For instance, stories of date rape, petty theft, and affairs with dorm or housemates all hinge on opportunistic goal pursuit; stories of drunken confessions or emotional outbursts of criticism or violence depend on unplanned situational factors. Finally, VACILLATE applies to situations in which an agent cannot settle on a plan, or returns to a previous plan after having abandoned it once or several times in the past. In Abby, VACILLATE describes the planning of people who make several suicide attempts, and couples who repeatedly break up and reform relationships. Having no plan at all, or not sticking to a plan, is a common bug.

5.2.3 Plan to Action Linkages

I think a lot of times men feel that marriage is something that women trap them into; they seem afraid of getting trapped before they are ready. Some of my women friends who are very serious about boyfriends know that the word marriage—they call it "the M word"—is something that's going to scare their boyfriends off. They just carry on without dealing with it or talking about it. Sometimes there just comes a point where they have to force the issue. Other women have more willpower, or are in a better situation.

I have a friend whose boyfriend had said things to her indicating that he couldn't imagine his life without her; so knowing that eventually it was going to happen, she waited for him to bring up marriage. She said that she wasn't ever going to ask him, that he was going to have to ask her. Happily he asked her before she got too restless; it was the waiting that worked. In this case, waiting made sense because he had the same vision of them together as she did, even if he couldn't talk about it using "the M word."

Patience is sometimes a virtue; other times, as with the regretful old bachelor, perpetual delay makes goal frustration permanent. DELAY is one of the five ways Abby has to describe the relationship between a plan and an action. Of those five, three describe actions that in some way are intended to contribute to the plan; the other two describe aberrations in which an action, or inaction, is not intended to advance the plan, instead serving to interfere with or to unravel the plan. The two aberrations help identify points of failure in goal pursuit and, thus, opportunities for advice.

The three positive linkages are PREPARE, EXECUTE, and ADJUST. PREPARE describes actions that would not normally be considered part of the plan per se; they may be part of the planning process. For instance, when you are going to ACT-IN-ROLE, often you first COMMIT to the action. When you want to break up with someone, you might refuse to advance the relationship beyond its current state, or you might fail to carry out some of the responsibilities of the relationship as a way of signaling the break up to come. EXECUTE is the most common linkage and describes any actions normally included in the plan. ADJUST describes actions that might not have originally been part of the plan, but are included at run time. For instance, Abby contains a story about a woman WOOing a potential husband deciding she has to tell him about a time in the past when she was gang raped.

The aberrant linkages are DEFER and ABORT. Whereas DEFER describes ongoing situations—a goal and a plan for satisfying it are held in abeyance possibly because other goals and plans are taking precedence—ABORT usually describes actions that indicate changes of mind—The aborted plan (and often its goal) are dismissed, often allowing other goals and plans to commence. The distinction between these two is the difference between procrastination and abdication or between disruption and termination. DEFER is used in one story to describe parents preoccupied with attending to a dying child, who have no time to spend with their other children. In a whole series of stories, it describes men and women waiting for romances to turn into marriages, or trying to put off the day when they have to make that kind of commitment. ABORT is used, for instance, to describe the decision of a woman who gives up her vow to forever honor her dead fiancé by agreeing to marry another man; it also characterized the decision of a woman to ask her mother's help caring for a new baby, thereby capitulating in a long struggle to build a life completely independent from her parents. From the perspective of the injured goals and what can be done to help them, the difference between these two links lies in the time gone by and the attitudes adopted, both of which affect the chances for successfully reinstating the plan and achieving the goal.

5.2.4 Action to Effect Linkages

It can be hard economically when your spouse dies. It's particularly common for an older widow to be left with very little when her husband dies. You have to be careful what you do in this kind of situation though. In one case I know of, a devoted son brought his mother to live with him, and she almost wrecked his marriage! His wife couldn't stand being bullied around by the old woman and threatened to leave if the mother stayed. None of the man's brothers or sisters could put up with the mother either, so the only thing he could do was rent her a room of her own and support her as she lived alone.

Compared to the linkages to and from plans just covered, Abby pays considerably more attention to the ways that actions produce their effects. The generic name for action-to-state linkages is

RESULTS, but this basic link type is specialized in many ways. Depending on the type of resulting state, Abby might describe the relationship as INITIATES, INDUCES, EVOKES, REALIZATION, or TIMING. If the state is graded and the result is a shift on the scale, then Abby might describe the linkage as AUGMENTS, MAINTAINS, or DRAINS; DRAINS, in turn, can be specialized as DIVIDES or DEBASES. When a shift on a state's scale results from a nonaction then it is described as DRIFT which might be GROWTH, STASIS, or DECAY.

INITIATES, INDUCES, EVOKES, REALIZATION and TIMING are defined as RESULTS whose consequents are, respectively, a GOAL, THEME, EMOTION, BELIEF, and INTERVAL. Compared to most distinctions in Abby's repertoire, noting these resulting state types in the link encodings adds little value, because the states themselves encode equivalent information. This redundancy originated with a decision to build on CD conventions describing causation of GOALS with the distinguished link INITIATES. Still, singling out the mental states makes a certain amount of sense, given their salience in Abby's world and the peculiarities of how mental states are caused. Beliefs, for instance, can arise any time an agent gets to observe an action, but the same action can often be performed without the agent's being allowed to observe it or its consequences. Emotional reactions can often be ameliorated by doing the same thing in a different manner, but you have to know enough to anticipate a possible emotional response. If nothing else, this redundancy makes indices a bit more comprehensible, by drawing attention to the nature of the resulting state.

Using specializations of the RESULTS linkage to encode shifts in state values is more obviously useful than encoding resulting state types, because it often saves us the trouble of explicitly encoding trends. Noting the difference between shifts caused by action and those caused by inaction may again be redundant, but it certainly says something significant about the sort of causing that is going on. For instance, STATUS is generally something you have to work at: One story tells of a young man bragging about his sexual exploits as a way of AUGMENTing his status among his friends; others tell of people transferring to new companies or working hard at jobs to gain status. AROUSAL, on the other hand, is something that increases of its own accord: Many stories describe the GROWTH of arousal over time when nothing is done to release it.

The different ways that an action can DRAIN a state are interesting because they say something about how to recover from problems caused by such drains. When a state is diminished because an action DIVIDES a resource, it may be possible to compensate by rebalancing priorities or by investing extra effort. For instance, when a young man spends too little time with his girlfriend because he is spending time with friends, he may be able to keep everyone happy by just making small adjustments. On the other hand, when a man goes off and starts an affair, he has DEBASED the loyalty he is supposed to show to his wife; no simple juggling can set things right again. Major changes like death and divorce also often DEBASE states subsumed by the lost relationship, as is the case in the story of the old widow.

Finally, there is one last type of RESULTS linkage that is a bit peculiar. FEEDBACK is used to describe situations wherein a state is both an enabling condition for the action and is reinforced by the action. Typical examples are attitudes that contribute to the agent's performing actions and which can be diagnosed based on those actions. One story tells of a man who married an older woman whose daughter had no respect for him because he was about her age and was being supported by her mother; he and the daughter were constantly fighting, which was both a sign of her lack of respect and a cause of continuing disrespect. Another story tells of a young woman who was so tied to her mother's apron strings that when a boyfriend first asked her to sleep with him, she went to her and asked permission; again, this was both a sign of her lack of independence and a contributing cause.

5.2.5 Other Action/State Linkages

A guy I know met a beautiful woman at a dance, took her out for an expensive day on the town, dinner at a fancy restaurant, and ended up at her place for the night. He really liked her, and before they parted, they agreed to meet the next weekend at a resort in the Catskills. So the next weekend, he made the long drive up there, but she never showed. As you might imagine, he was pretty ticked off by this, but he didn't let it spoil his weekend. He managed to have a good time at the resort anyway. Instead of brooding over his spoiled plans, he met some other new people. In the end, it turned out to be a blessing in disguise; during that weekend up at the resort, he ran into the woman he eventually married.

Indices allow room for two chain-interactions because the point of a story often depends on understanding some background to a problematic situation. The woman's failure to show up for the weekend only makes sense as a problem if you know that she had committed to meet him. In addition to the four classes of causal links out of which intentional chains are built, Abby allows several other sorts of links to describe connections between indices' background chain interactions and main problem chain interaction.

Beyond the action-to-state RESULTS links, Abby uses four other broad classes of links between actions and states. It is not surprising that the first three classes are state-to-action, state-to-state, and action-to-action links; the fourth class contains non-causal co-occurrence links that neither commit to causal mechanism nor require particular classes of concepts as arguments. The two state-to-action links are ENABLES and SUSTAINS; they simply distinguish between states that allow an action to commence and states that must be present throughout the duration of an action to allow it to continue. This is a basic distinction relevant to any sort of planning. There is just one state-to-state link, called LEADS-TO, and it provides no information about the nature of the relationship other than to claim that somehow the first state is causally implicated in leading to the second.

The taxonomy of action-to-action links is a bit more interesting because it includes a variety of intentional interpretations of action sequences. In particular, it distinguishes cases in which an action by one agent evokes a response by another, and cases in which two actions related to a plan are taken successively by a single agent. The first link type is called RESPONSE, the second PLAN-SEQUENCE. RESPONSE is used in indices wherein the problematic action is taken by one agent in response to some prodding by another agent, such as the story in which a shiftless niece asks for a loan and a man regrettably agrees to give her the money.

PLAN-SEQUENCE is used in indices in which the problematic action is a step in some larger plan that was initiated earlier. For instance, one story tells of a woman who stole some money and then set her husband up to take the blame; another story tells of a couple who had a common cemetery plot, and when the husband survived his wife and then remarried, his second wife was upset that he still insisted on spending eternity beside his first wife. Abby recognizes two variants of PLAN-SEQUENCE: FOLLOW-UP covers cases in which the second action is not strictly part of the original plan, but is nonetheless a consequence of the earlier plan; RENEGE covers cases in which the second action constitutes an abrogation of the earlier action's plan. An example of FOLLOW-UP is the responsibility to pay alimony following a divorce. Examples of RENEGE appear in stories like the one that opened this section, in which the woman made a date and then failed to show up. Problems produced by doing what another agent wants, problems produced by direct or indirect continuations of an initial plan commitment, and problems caused by failing to carry through on commitments, all these may call for different sorts of advice.

The noncausal links carry only temporal and identity information. The two basic types are AFTER and DURING. They are useful when it is inappropriate for an index to assert a causal relationship between two facts that are nonetheless worth relating. For instance, one index describes how a woman relocated to be near her boyfriend, and how AFTER she made this move they broke up; the story does not say whether the move in any way contributed to the break up, but the move was important background to the problem caused by the break up, which, in this case, was a lack of friends to help her through the rough times and to help pick up the slack in her social life. Another story tells of divorced parents getting into a fight DURING their daughter's wedding; again, while there might be some causal link between the wedding and the fight, what the story commits to, and what matters for the index, is only that the fight happened during the wedding and, thus, ruined the bride's day.

Two other co-occurrence links emphasize that a single fact can have multiple interpretations. EQUIVALENT says that two descriptions refer to the same thing: A man DOing something intended to save others from a fire may be EQUIVALENT to that man's getting himself killed. CONTINUATION says that two descriptions refer to the same thing, but allows descriptions to refer to different segments of a temporally extended action or state; for instance, a father who leaves his family and ignores his kids may continue behaving this way for a year, but different phases in the history of this neglect might suggest different consequences.

5.2.6 Other Linkages to Goals

It's a fact of life: Many husbands and wives cheat on their partners. What should you do if you find out your spouse is cheating? I know a woman who found a simple way to decide. She asked herself

the question: "Would my life be better with him or without him?"
She made her decision based on her answer to that question.

In her case, the answer was that life would be better with him. Her
husband got involved with a younger woman when they were both
in their 30s and had 3 young children. They were just starting to
get on their feet financially after struggling through hard times to-
gether. The bottom line was that they really still loved one another.
When she told him her decision to stick with him, he promised to
end his affair immediately. He kept his word, and they have had
more than 30 years together in a loving and trusting relationship.

A common sort of connection between the two chain-interactions of an index is for a resulting STATE in the background to lead to a GOAL in the main problem. The aforementioned story makes good advice when the choice of what to want in response to a problem is recognized as problematic in itself. In addition to the action/state links just described, Abby allows state-to-goal links and impact-to-goal links to tie the two halves of indices together. The links to be discussed here also supplement the theme-to-goal links described earlier; remember, even though goals are associated with themes, just because an agent holds a theme does not mean they hold or are pursuing a particular associated goal at any given moment. Goals are elicited by a combination of themes and circumstances. It is these circumstances that often can be summarized by the theme-to-goal origination context descriptions OPPORTUNITY, THREAT, and CRISIS. But sometimes a detailed description of those circumstances or of how those circumstances elicited the goal is important; in such cases, an explicit state representation and one of the state-to-goal or impact-to-goal links described here provides such a detailed description.

The most general state-to-goal link is called JUSTIFY; it simply asserts that the state was somehow responsible for the goal. There are many ways in which a state might JUSTIFY a goal: For instance, Abby includes stories in which people's ages contribute either to their desire to get married or to others' desire that they not marry; in one story, pregnancy raises concerns about health; in another, lack of confidence in a lover leads to a desire to put off marriage.

Three variants of JUSTIFY are distinguished: PURSUIT, DEVELOP, and CURIOSITY. PURSUIT describes cases in which the state responsible for the goal is itself a goal; this means that the link's consequent is either identical to the antecedent goal, or is a subgoal under some plan for that antecedent. An example of PURSUIT in Abby arises in the story of a man who wanted to make love to a woman, but being religious, decided to marry her first. Another common relationship between state and goal is when the object of the goal is some new state that is a normal development from the current state; for example, when people spend time together they may DEVELOP the goal to become lovers; when they are lovers, they may DEVELOP the goal to get married. Abby recognizes a special form of state-to-goal linkage in CURIOSITY; some states of the world prompt intelligent agents to ask questions—to develop goals for information. An example from Abby's repertoire is the childless couple who constantly had to fend off people asking them why they did not start a family.

COUNTER describes linkages wherein the object of the goal is to prevent a possible state or undo an actual state; for example, when one woman was propositioned by a friend of her husband, instead of being tempted into disloyalty, she acted on her desire to stay loyal and told her husband. If a negative state cannot be COUNTERed, then the state-to-goal linkage REPLACE can account for a goal to compensate by establishing an alternate state; one story tells of a woman who loses control of her newly married daughter and sets out to dominate her new son-in-law instead. States produced by others, either positive or negative, may lead agents to RECIPROCATE by adopting goals to establish a comparable state for the responsible agents; one story tells of a couple who complained that their neighbors were never helpful, but it turned out that they had never done anything particularly helpful for their neighbors either.

Impacts will be discussed at length later. In order to understand Abby's impact-to-goal links, all that is relevant is that these impacts are synopses of how states affect goals, and that there are two major classes of impact: positive and negative. Most of the impact-to-goal links are related to the state-to-goal links COUNTER, REPLACE, and RECIPROCATE just considered; the primary difference is that linking from impacts makes the positive or negative assessments explicit. For instance, the impact versions of RECIPROCATE are REWARD, PUNISH, and RECOURSE. REWARD describes the genesis of goals to do something nice for an agent that has produced a positive impact for you; PUNISH describes the genesis of goals to do something nasty to an agent that has produced a negative impact for you. RECOURSE describes the case in which the negative impact was a breach of a contract and the punishment is a legitimate response to the breach. An example of REWARD appears in a story of a young woman who sleeps with an older man because he spends money on her. An example of PUNISH appears in a story about a man who goes berserk, beating and sexually abusing a woman who announces that she is breaking up with him. RECOURSE usually describes stereotypic responses, such as a boss deciding to fire a worker who is not doing his job, or a woman wanting to divorce her husband when she finds out he is having an affair.

Two other impact-to-goal links, PREVENT and RESTORE, are similar to the state-to-goal links COUNTER and REPLACE. PREVENT describes goals spawned in reaction to threatened negative states, which may include the recurrence of actual negative states. RESTORE describes goals spawned to undo actual negative states. In one story PREVENT is used to account for the genesis of a goal to avoid getting married after a woman suffers the death of her first husband—the pain is so great that she does not want to live through it again. In another story, RESTORE is used to account for a goal to run out and get married again when a spouse dies. One last impact-to-goal link depends on situations wherein a new state is recognized as positive; CONSERVE describes the normal establishment of a new goal whose object is the maintenance of the positive state. An example of the CONSERVE linkage occurs in a story telling of how a woman, when she is widowed suddenly, finds herself free of all responsibilities and develops a goal to preserve this newfound freedom.

5.3 Impacts

Impacts describe the relationship between the final effect of an intentional chain and the chain's theme, goal, and plan. They give an intentional interpretation of the effect. Because Abby's chains are not always success stories, the impacts may describe ways in which the state constitutes a problem. Negative impacts are the problems about which Abby gives advice. In this section, Abby's taxonomy for each of the three types of impacts: plan impacts, goal impacts, and theme impacts is discussed.

5.3.1 Plan Impacts

I know a couple who just recently celebrated their 50th wedding anniversary. They had to celebrate it pretty much alone because none of their 5 children would attend—they all thought it was too phony to have anything to do with. This couple fought their way through their entire marriage, staying together only for the sake of the children. The children would rather they had split up.

The mother is a bitter and reclusive woman with a martyr complex. The father is an unpleasant alcoholic with a mean mouth and a rotten temper. All of the kids were messed up because they never learned how to develop positive relationships until they reached their 30s. They have all experienced failed marriages and had other troubles in their lives. They are each engaged in an ongoing struggle to forget the destructive and awful behavior they learned from their parents. It hasn't been easy. In their informed opinion, any couple who stay together just on account of the children is not doing them any favor, and ought to split up.

Plans can be chosen and executed, yet they do not always work out as intended; the aforementioned couple may have thought they were doing their best by the children, but they obviously did not carry it off very well. Abby uses six plan impacts, two positive and four negative. The positive impacts are COMPLETE and ADVANCE. COMPLETE applies when the state constitutes the final product of the plan, which generally means that the goal has been satisfied. ADVANCE applies when the state is a positive product of the plan but not its final goal-satisfying state. Despite Abby's focus on problems, there are many instances of these positive impacts in Abby's indices (and of positive goal and theme impacts as well) because problems are most often caused by actions performed for some positive reason. Advice intended to alleviate negative impacts may disrupt positive impacts, and we need to know the extent of such damage. Beyond that there is little more to say about these positive plan impacts.

The outcome of an action can affect a plan in either of two negative ways: it may make things worse or it may fail to make things better. These two impacts are described as CLOBBER and INSUFFICIENT. CLOBBER impacts can indicate faulty planning, bad luck in execution, or extraneous forces at work; which of these explanations holds can often be determined by examining other information encoded in the index frame, such as the plan-to-action linkage, the identity of the actor, and agents' assessments of the outcome (described in the next section). Consider two examples of CLOBBER impacts in Abby's indices: One young woman wanted to respect her new step-father and so tried to prod him into behaving more responsibly, but they just ended up fighting, which further undermined her respect for him. In another story, a woman's attempts at holiness included accusing others of devil worship—Abby considers those accusations more likely to get her into a mental hospital than into heaven. INSUFFICIENT impacts describe situations such as a couple who cannot get pregnant, a man who attempts but fails to rescue others from a fire, unsuccessful attempts at suicide, and efforts to hold a marriage together "for the children" that leave the children feeling miserable.

The last two plan impacts, FREEZE and ABANDON, often correspond to the plan-to-action linkages DEFER and ABORT; the difference is that the impacts describe the resulting states' interpretation, whereas the causal linkages describe the intents underlying the actions. Actions can result in the FREEZING of a plan even when the actor's intent was to carry out the plan. Similarly a resulting state can effectively mean that a plan has been ABANDONED even when the intent was not to ABORT the plan. For instance, some stories tell of people who wanted to marry, but whose partners blocked their plans; some describe possibly temporary delays, and others describe outright rejections. Another story tells of parents so poor they are unable to feed their children; in such circumstances, FREEZING the normal plan to care for the children does not imply that plan execution has been DEFERRED.

5.3.2 Goal Impacts

I know a woman who waited to marry until she was 34. It wasn't an easy marriage she got herself into, but she stuck with it. Her husband had been married previously, and 3 days before their wedding, his ex-wife tried to commit suicide—possibly to escape from her well-hidden cocaine habit. Her husband's 15-year-old daughter went to live with a grandmother, but the lazy, spoiled 13-year-old son moved in with them.

It's taken 2 years for things to become a little more normal. The kids' mother has been drug-free for 7 months. The resentful daughter has started talking to her new step-mother. The son has shaped up; he no longer spends all his time watching TV, and brings home decent grades from school. They are all working hard at keeping the lines of communication open.

When she looks back on it, she realizes that she could have called it quits after the first 2 months of marriage, but she decided to gut it out. She is glad they did, because she believes they are going to be stronger and happier as a result of what they have been through together.

The first class of impacts identified during Abby's development were goal impacts. Negative goal impacts were invented as a succinct way to describe problems, and most of the problems described by Abby's indices still center on such impacts. In this story, every member of the family seems to present some problem for the stoic newlywed. Abby uses four types of negative goal impacts and four positive impacts; each describes either the status of a pending goal or the outcome of goal pursuit. In addition, there are six other impacts describing changes in the value of a goal; these are harder to categorize as either positive or negative, but as used in Abby, they are usually negative.

The value modification impacts include two that describe increasing goal importance, two describing decreasing goal importance, and two describing goal dismissal. An increase in goal value may be described either by UPGRADE or CRISISIFY. An example of UPGRADE is the story of a man who broods over a lost love, making himself feel the loss more keenly. An example of CRISISIFY is a young man who becomes so aroused in making out with his girlfriend that he ends up raping her. CRISIS was introduced as a goal origination context earlier; CRISISIFY allows an index to identify a particular state that caused a goal to enter a crisis situation.

A decrease in goal value may be described either by DOWNGRADE or BACK BURNER. DOWNGRADE covers situations similar to straight goal tradeoffs, with one goal benefiting at another's expense; the difference lies in the agent's recognition of the conflict, and decision to de-emphasize the suffering goal. BACKBURNER describes situations where a goal is de-emphasized, not because of conflict with a more important goal, but because success on a related goal makes the goal seem less pressing. A case of a goal being DOWNGRADEd is an older widow, who has been fiercely independent, deciding to start dating again because she would rather have companionship than absolute freedom. A case of a goal being BACKBURNERed is the story cited earlier of the divorced woman avoiding the effort of starting new relationships with other men because she continues to have occasional sexual relations with her ex-husband.

The two impacts describing goal dismissal, SUSPEND and ABANDON, make the familiar distinction between temporary and permanent states of inaction; they are similar to the plan-to-action links DELAY and ABORT, and the plan impacts FREEZE and ABANDON. The difference, of course, is that dismissing a goal is a more sweeping decision than dismissing one of several possible plans for a goal. In many cases, the aftermath of an unsuccessful suicide attempt can be described as the a suicidal goal that was SUSPENDED. A teenager who obeys her father's order to stop seeing a particular boy can be described as ABANDONING the goal to be involved with that boy.

The four positive goal impacts include one describing goal *pursuit* and three describing different positive *outcomes*. When a state contributes to satisfaction of a goal, Abby uses the impact ADVANCE. When it comes to success, a state may either SATISFY, SATIATE, or SUBSUME a goal. SATISFY means that success has been achieved once and for all, as with goals to establish new relationships. SATIATE means that success has been achieved for a goal that is known to recur; for instance, a person may satiate his or her sex drive on one occasion, but they will feel a greater need later. SUBSUME means that continuing success has been arranged for a recurring goal, which in Abby usually means some long-term social relationship has been arranged; the difference between SATIATE and SUBSUME is the difference between having a one-night-stand and starting an affair. These distinctions derive from earlier NLP work (Schank & Ableson, 1977; Wilensky, 1978). As with the positive plan impacts, positive goal impacts are useful to Abby because advice for mitigating negative impacts may undermine positive impacts; the distinctions here help Abby notice whether any new problems introduced this way are likely to be chronic or not.

The four negative goal impacts include three describing problems in goal pursuit and one describing a negative outcome. It might seem strange that in a system whose whole purpose is to describe problems, the FAIL impact is the only way to describe negative outcomes for goals; in fact, the entire index frame exists to flesh out this vague description and the other negative impacts. The negative outcome impact FAIL contrasts with the negative status impact THREATEN. Some goals occasionally really do experience hard failures, such as final rejection of a proposal of marriage, or an instance of failing to have sexual relations. Instances of goals for states like COMPANIONSHIP that are general (in the sense of not specifying a particular object or referring to a particular occasion) may be negatively affected, but when do we declare that they have FAILed? For such goals, the difference between FAIL and THREATEN is a matter of timing and attitude. The dissolution of a relationship may fail the goal to maintain the relationship but only THREATEN the goals subsumed by that relationship.

THREATEN has two specializations, IMPEDE and BLOCK, the first describing situations where progress towards the goal is being slowed or made more difficult, the second applies when progress has been stopped or made impossible; again, the difference between BLOCK and FAIL is often simply a difference of attitude— whether the goal holder has given up or continues to work at achieving the goal. BLOCK often describes failures to act, either on the part of the goal's holder, actor, or some relevant co-actor. For instance, BLOCK is used to describe many situations where one agent wants to form a relationship with another, but the desired partner resists. IMPEDE applies when an agent wants to start a relationship but has not identified a particular partner, and rejects one potential partner. IMPEDE is also used to describe negative impacts such as those produced by distance on relationship goals like COMPANIONSHIP and EMPATHY.

5.3.3 Theme Impacts

There are a lot of lines married people use to justify their affairs. Sometimes I'm sure they can convince themselves that what they say is true. Sometimes they simply lie through their teeth. I know a man who told his mistress that his wife was a cripple confined to a wheelchair. He suffered because his wife could not offer him any kind of sex life. So the mistress saw herself as a humanitarian — helping the husband and taking nothing from the wife.

It was all hogwash. Imagine everyone's surprise when the wife happened to stop into a roadside motel to buy some pies just as her husband was checking in with his lover. The husband knew his game was up, the wife was just discovering there was a game, and the mistress finally figured out what the game was. Remember, you don't have to believe everything a salesperson tells you.

Theme impacts, the last of Abby's three impact classes, describe interpretations of states with respect to themes, as in this story where discovery of betrayal will lead directly to the termination of existing themes. These impacts fall into four broad groups: thread-existence, threadmovement, themestatus, and theme-support. *Threads* are sequences of related themes, as when a friendship blossoms into romance, followed by betrothal, and then marriage. Threadexistence impacts describe the initiation or termination of themes marking the beginning or end of threads. Thread-movement impacts, in contrast, describe the initiation or termination of themes interpretable as stages in an already existing thread. Theme-status impacts describe changes in the strength of an existing theme. Themesupport impacts apply when none of the previously mentioned theme changes have occurred, and simply mirror goal impacts for goals derived from a theme.

There are four thread existence theme impacts. INITIATE and TERMINATE, PRE-INITIATE and PRE-TERMINATE. These impacts should be relatively self-explanatory. Flirting with someone with whom you have no romantic relationship may make that person believe that you want such a relationship; this effect is described by the theme impact PRE-INITIATE. Going ahead and sleeping with this person, if construed as the beginning of an affair, would be described by INITIATE. PRE-TERMINATE likewise, describes a state that will lead to the termination of a theme (and the termination of an entire thread); this is the description used for the previous story. TERMINATE is reserved for actual breakups that mark the end of a thread.

There are five types of thread movement impacts. The two positive ones are ADVANCE and RESTORE. ADVANCE describes any theme transition that is part of the normal progression of a thread. RESTORE describes such a transition in the case where that stage of the thread had at one time been established but then was lost. For example, one story tells of a man who wanted to marry one woman so badly that he let himself be used by her repeatedly as a kind of waystation between her other unsuccessful romances. The two negative thread movement impacts, DERAIL and REGRESS, describe how a relationship could get into a situation where RESTORE might be necessary. DERAIL describes a transition to a theme that is off the normal course of the thread; for instance, in one story, a woman moves to a rural area to be with her lover, giving up her job and disrupting her career. REGRESS describes a transition to a theme that occurred earlier in the thread's development; breaking off an engagement could be a TERMINATE, but if the idea is just to buy more time before deciding to marry it might only count as a REGRESS. Finally, the last of the five thread movement impacts is FREEZE, which describes lack of change in a relationship; given Abby's emphasis on problems, this description is generally only used when change would be expected or desirable and thus is considered a negative impact.

The theme status impacts apply to states that bear directly on the health of a theme. Thus when states like LOVE, LOYALTY, and RESPECTFUL appear as effects, they can be interpreted as signs of theme status changes like STRENGTHEN and WEAKEN (or, again, taking history into account, RECOVER and RELAPSE). FREEZE, in addition to being a thread movement impact, is also used as a theme status impact. When a boy tries the classic line that he will love his girlfriend more if she will only sleep with him, he is playing on her belief that having sex will result in greater love and a STRENGTHENing of the relationship. When a married woman starts an affair with another man, the lack of loyalty can be interpreted as a WEAKENing of the marriage relationship. Where there has been a WEAKENing, there can be a RECOVERy; many stories that start with spouses going off to have affairs end with their coming back and being loyal from then on. On the other hand, in other stories, the once wandering spouse suffers a lust RELAPSE and strays into another affair.

The last group of theme impacts apply when there is no particular change to the theme itself, but the fate of some goal derived from the theme can be interpreted as having an indirect effect on the theme's status. The goal/impact distinctions reflected in these theme impacts are positive versus negative, and status versus outcome; in other words Abby uses theme impacts that parallel the goal impacts ADVANCE, SATISFY, THREATEN, and FAIL. These theme assessments need not be specified, but when the goal is an important enough part of the theme, it is worth noting that the theme too is affected by states that affect derived goals.

5.4 Conclusions

This chapter started with the big picture—CBR, indexing, representation, and an indexing framework for social situations—but much of the chapter dwelt on the details of one part of Abby's representations. Both extremes are important.

Developing representations is one of the central problems in AI. The work on Abby was a frontal assault on part of the representation problem for the domain of everyday social interactions. The work is interesting, in part, because it takes a somewhat different approach to generating and justifying representations than much work in the field. Starting from a CBR perspective and focusing on the indexing problem, this work takes support of reminding as its warrant for including features in a representational scheme; the requirement is simply that our representations must cover the similarities and differences among situations that would determine the relevance of remindings in support of the lovelorn advising task. Work on Abby, then, contrasts with more traditional approaches that justify representational vocabulary by appeal to explicit inference processes (often with much attention paid to the formal properties of the resulting system). The issue, in Abby, is simply adequacy of representational content to support the central cognitive process of reminding.

In this chapter, the detailed discussion of specific vocabulary items focused on those parts of Abby's vocabulary that describe causal and interpretive relationships; these linkages tie together the more basic descriptors covering the "facts" of a situation. Abby's representation of causal linkages rationalize and extend previous work. The explicit representation of impacts is a new addition to the literature. Both are important because the ability to link basic facts into a coherent explanatory interpretation is what leads our systems to attend more to certain features of a situation and less to others. Furthermore, the linkages themselves become features of the (interpretation of the) situation for the purposes of justifying remindings.

The bottom line is that work on indexing is an effective way to advance representation theories, and that building large indexed memories to support particular tasks forces specific representational commitments over a broad range of scales. Abby, then, is an exemplar of an approach to representation theorizing, and its representations constitute a data point sampled from the space of possible domains and tasks. The space is large, and the sampling goes on—one more method for expanding and better understanding AI's representational repertoire.

6. Accepter: Evaluating Explanations

David B. Leake
Department of Computer Science
Indiana University

Editors' Introduction

Once an explainer has been reminded of an old explanation, through the use of retrieval mechanisms such as those described in the previous two chapters, it is ready to apply that explanation to the anomaly that caused the reminding. However, the mere fact that a new situation reminds one of an old explanation does not guarantee that that explanation will make sense when applied to the new situation. We are often reminded of things that turn out to be irrelevant, or only partially relevant.

Therefore, after a case-based explainer retrieves an explanation, it needs to evaluate the suitability of that explanation for the problem at hand. The explainer must decide basic issues, such as whether there is enough evidence to make the explanation convincing, and whether there are inconsistencies between the explanation and facts of the current case. It must also check that the explanation supplies enough information to satisfy current goals.

In this chapter we examine the issues an explanation evaluator must consider and describe a program that evaluates explanations, called Accepter. The chapter is excerpted from the book, Evaluating Explanations: A Content Theory, David B. Leake (Lawrence Erlbaum Associates, 1992).

* * *

6.1 Evaluating Explanations

The success of explanation-based systems depends on their explanations. Learning or acting based on flawed explanations can have profound effects on performance: An investor who accepts the wrong explanation may go broke, a doctor who accepts the wrong explanation may harm his or her patient, and a police officer acting on the wrong explanation may pursue an innocent person and let the guilty one go free.

Everyday explanation construction often starts from incomplete and unreliable information, making it impossible to guarantee the quality of its results. In order to be assured of good explanations, explainers need to evaluate the quality of proposed explanations to decide which ones they should accept. In this chapter we describe a theory of explanation evaluation and the implementation of that theory in the computer program Accepter.

Accepter is a story understanding system that detects anomalies when its prior knowledge conflicts with new information. Those anomalies reveal gaps in its understanding and show the need for explanation to fill those gaps. Explanations are judged in terms of the system's information needs; its explanation evaluation tests whether candidate explanations resolve the anomaly and provide the information to accomplish new goals prompted by the anomalous situation. This theory of explanation evaluation contrasts sharply with other models of explanation evaluation that are neutral to changes in the knowledge and goals of the explanation system; Accepter's model depends crucially on context. In our view, goodness of explanations must be judged in terms of two things: what the explainer knows and what it needs to find out.

Our theory bases explanation evaluation on three factors: (a) the fit between the candidate explanation and the explainer's current beliefs and expectations (which determine the explanation's plausibility), (b) the anomaly that motivates the system to explain (which determines the initial focus of explanation), and (c) system goals beyond understanding (which determine additional information that the explanation must provide in order to be useful). Applying the theory in an AI system depends on developing practical mechanisms for reflecting each of these factors in the evaluation process.

Each factor raises difficult questions. First, the need to reconcile an explanation with current beliefs raises the classic problem of inference control. In principle, arbitrary amounts of inference can be necessary to find a relationship between any two pieces of information; identifying all confirming and contradictory information in memory would be an overwhelming task. Accepter addresses the inference problem by replacing inference with table lookup, comparing new hypotheses to standard patterns in order to find anomalies. The success of any table-based approach depends on the existence of a set of tables with sufficient coverage, and we substantiate the table-based method with a theory of pattern types that covers a wide range of everyday anomalies.

Second, evaluating whether explanations are relevant to particular anomalies requires a theory of what anomalies are and how they are explained. We address this with a taxonomy of anomaly types that Accepter uses to judge relevance of candidate explanations, and with a mechanism for deciding whether new explanations resolve anomalies.

Third, reflecting the influence of goals beyond routine understanding depends on analyzing the purposes that motivate explanation, and on developing heuristics for evaluation in light of those purposes. We have developed a categorization of purposes for explanation and the information they require; this model allows Accepter to identify useful information and to detect information deficiencies in the explanations it evaluates. Thus, Accepter implements a theory of the needs that motivate explanation and how those needs are reflected by the explanation evaluation process.

6.1.1 Evaluation in Case-Based Explanation

Any explanation system needs to be able to evaluate candidate explanations. However, three considerations make our model particularly important to case-based explanation.

First, case-based explanation is designed as a creative process. By using flexible retrieval and adaptation criteria, case-based explanation can extend knowledge into areas where it does not seem to apply (Kass, 1990; Schank & Leake, 1986; Schank & Leake, 1989). Sometimes this will lead to breakthroughs; other times it will lead to completely invalid hypotheses. Unlike explanation systems that function in neat domains with perfect knowledge, and can trust their explanation generation process to always build good explanations (e.g., Mitchell, Keller, & Kedar-Cabelli, 1986), creative explanation systems need ways to distinguish hypotheses that are inspired from those that are merely bizarre.

Second, the reuse of explanations in case-based explanation makes usefulness evaluation more important to case-based explanation than to conventional approaches. In explanation-based systems that build each explanation from scratch for a single purpose, the system can often rely on implicit constraints assuring that the explanation will be useful (e.g., the rule base of plan-recognition system may contain only rules about planful behavior, assuring that any explanation generated will be an explanation of the actor's plan). However, because a case-based explainer takes prior explanations as its starting point, in new situations it may sometimes use explanations constructed in very different contexts and for different overarching goals. Consequently, a case-based explainer cannot assume that the retrieved explanation was built for a similar task, requiring evaluation of the fit between information in the old explanation and the information needed for its current goals[1].

Third, because our model identifies specific deficiencies in candidate explanations, it can be used by a case-based explanation system to guide their repair. When Accepter detects problems, it characterizes them so that they can be used as indices for retrieving explanatory information–stored explanations, adaptation strategies, and general strategies to guide explanation–focusing explanation construction effort. Thus, in case-based explanation, the role of explanation evaluation goes beyond helping an explainer avoid bad explanations: It guides the transformation of bad explanations into good ones.

6.2 Explaining Anomalies

In our theory, explanation evaluation must reflect the explainer's reasons for explaining. Explanation-based understanding systems often explain each event for which they have no prestored schema (DeJong & Mooney, 1986; Mooney, 1990), simply in order to have schemas for each observed situation. However, as has been widely observed, not all explained situations lead to useful generalizations. In addition, in everyday situations, there are simply too many novel event sequences to explain each one. Real-

---

[1]Goal-based indexing (e.g., Hammond 1989; Kolodner 1987) alleviates this problem when stored explanations that reflect similar goals are available, but the explainer will still sometimes need to apply retrieved explanations in novel contexts.

world explanation cannot be indiscriminate: It must be aimed at filling system needs.

Focusing explanation requires answering a basic question: When does an understanding system need to explain? In predictive understanders, understanding is adequate as long as the world fits predictions. However, when anomalies arise they show that the understander's current world model is deficient and explanation is needed to repair the flawed beliefs (Schank, 1986). Our theory focuses on evaluating explanations prompted by anomalies during understanding.

6.2.1 What is an Anomaly?

In order to judge explanations of anomalies, we must first consider the nature of anomalies themselves. Intuitively, an anomaly is simply something surprising: When we ask people to say why an event is anomalous, they tell us which aspects of the event surprised them. Their response reflects the commonplace view that anomalousness is a property of the event itself. However, this view overlooks a key fact: No aspect of an event is anomalous unless it differs from what was previously expected or believed. Thus, anomalousness results from interactions between events and the understanding context.

For example, if a driver has a blowout on the highway, the driver's prior beliefs determine what, if anything, is anomalous about the blowout. If the blowout conflicts with the driver's expectation that tires last longer, the anomaly is their early failure; if the tires have been bald for months and were expected to fail long before, the anomaly is that the blowout happened so late; if the driver noticed broken glass on the road moments before the blowout and expected the tires to be punctured, the blowout might not be anomalous at all.

Anomalies are conflicts between new information and our active beliefs and expectations.

New anomalies may be triggered or old ones resolved by activating new knowledge. For example, the anomaly of the blowout might be resolved by the information that tires of the brand in question tend to fail early, but that information might prompt another anomaly: why a trusted mechanic put them on the car.

6.3 What Makes a Good Explanation?

6.3.1 Plausibility

Because explanations of anomalies are motivated by the failure to understand, a basic purpose of explanation is to demonstrate why the anomalous situation actually makes sense–why it follows from prior circumstances. In explanation-based learning (EBL) (DeJong & Mooney, 1986; Mitchell et al., 1986), explanations are deductive proofs that use prior knowledge and a correct domain theory to derive concept membership. Consequently, any explanation with the proper form is guaranteed to be valid; the plausibility of explanations is not an issue. However, plausibility is an issue in real-world explanation. Real-world explanation is abductive rather than deductive, with possible causes hypothesized to account for observed events. For any real-world event, it is possible to build countless explanations with appropriate structure, only some of which are plausible.

The extent of this problem is illustrated by the fact that, given any event to explain and any event as a candidate for its cause, a person can probably think of a way to derive the event from the candidate cause–even when the candidate cause is unlikely to actually be related. For example, despite the implausibility of any connection between a rise in the price of pork futures and an opera-goer getting a parking ticket, we can imagine many ways in which they could be connected, such as:

> When the price rose, a local investment club knew it would reap large profits, so its members decided to celebrate in a fine restaurant near the opera. Members took all free parking spaces, making area parking impossible to find. The opera-goer decided to park illegally rather than miss the curtain. As a result, the opera-goer got a parking ticket.

This explanation has a reasonable form but is not especially plausible, and we could imagine many alternative explanations as well.

Many explanations can be generated for any event, and only some of them are plausible.

In abductive explanation systems, the standard methods for estimating the likelihood of explanations involve content-independent structural criteria. These criteria are often based on Occam's razor, comparing explanations according to some syntactic minimality criterion (e.g., Charniak, 1986; Granger, 1980; Wilensky, 1983). For example, the explanations favored may be those involving the shortest derivations or involving the fewest assumptions. Other structural methods examine how beliefs in explanations are connected, favoring the explanations with the greatest structural coherence (Ng & Mooney, 1990; P.Thagard, 1989).

For everyday explanation evaluation, structural evaluation methods suffer from two serious problems. First, comparing explanations according to purely structural properties fails to capture the profound effect of their content. For example, comparing two explanations by the number of assumptions of each one neglects that it may be much more plausible to assume two common conditions than one unusual one. Second, even if syntactic criteria were sufficient to generate a comparative ranking of explanations, comparative ranking alone is not sufficient to guide everyday explanation. A system that can generate new explanations needs to be able to decide when to stop explaining: to decide not just whether a given explanation is the best candidate so far, but whether any of the explanations are adequate. Overcoming these problems depends on considering the content of explanations rather than only their form.

Accepter's model of plausibility evaluation is based not just on the structure of explanations, but on their content as well, given the explainer's prior knowledge.

6.3.2 Beyond Plausibility

In the understanding systems cited previously, the "best explanation" is equivalent to "the explanation believed most likely to be valid." We claim that it is impossible to select the best explanation without considering the overarching task: the best explanation is the one that best satisfies the explainer's needs. Need-based considerations are reflected in Accepter's two remaining criteria: relevance to the anomaly and usefulness for overarching goals.

Relevance to the Anomaly. In explanation-based schema acquisition systems (e.g., DeJong & Mooney, 1986; Mooney, 1990), explanation construction and evaluation are basically neutral to changes in surrounding context. Consequently, even when explanation is motivated by a conflict between a new situation and a prior schema, explanation is not guaranteed to focus on the aspects of the situation that were anomalous. We have already shown that the aspects of an anomalous event that need to be explained depend on what makes it anomalous: A tire blowout will be explained differently if what conflicts with expectations is the tire's early failure or the fact that it did not fail earlier.

*To be relevant to an anomaly, explanations must resolve the belief
conflict underlying the anomaly.*

To evaluate relevance of an explanation to the anomaly that prompts the explanation effort, Accepter's explanation evaluation process tests whether explanations both provide a derivation of the surprising event and also account for why expectations went wrong.

Usefulness for Overarching Goals. Anomalies reveal unexpected circumstances, and those circumstances may prompt new goals that require additional information from explanations. For example, if a tire fails a few weeks after being bought, an explanation such as "it was bought used and already had a lot of miles on it" might be sufficient to resolve the understanding problem. However, the failure of the tire might also prompt a new goal: to get a replacement. If the tire had a warranty that protected against purely internal failures but that gave no protection against damage involving road hazards, the goal of replacing the tire would motivate search for additional information: precisely what caused the tire to fail.

Good explanations must serve the explainer's overarching goals.

Goals are so important to explanation that in certain circumstances, validity of explanations takes second place. For example, consider the following scene from the movie *Breaking Away:*

> A used-car salesman is taking a prospective buyer out on a test drive. He stops suddenly to avoid a cyclist, and the car dies. He tries frantically to start it, but he can't. He explains to the buyer: "Damn. You know what I did? I think I put premium gas in this baby by mistake. It hates expensive gas."

The salesman does not believe the explanation, but it is excellent for his purposes. Not only does it divert blame from the car's mechanical condition, but it also introduces a new factor to sway the prospective buyer toward buying the car: that it is inexpensive to operate.

Thus, the fundamental criterion for goodness of explanations is simply whether the explainer can use them successfully. The role of explanation is not to enumerate plausible causes of an event: It is to provide the information that is needed for the explainer's goals. This is the guiding principle of Accepter's explanation evaluation.

6.4 The Accepter Program

Accepter is a story understanding program. As it understands, it monitors input information for anomalies. When it finds an anomaly, it characterizes the anomaly, retrieves explanations indexed under similar anomalies, and evaluates the goodness of the retrieved explanations—both according to their relevance to the anomaly and to their usefulness for overarching goals. Thus, Accepter explains in order to fill specific gaps in its knowledge and judges explanations in terms of goals to be served by the explanation effort.

6.4.1 The overarching framework

Accepter is designed to be embedded within a larger case-based explanation system. The system was originally developed as part of SWALE (Kass, 1986; Kass & Leake, 1987; Leake & Owens, 1986; Schank, 1986; Schank & Leake, 1989), in which its tasks included routine understanding, anomaly detection and characterization, search for explanations indexed under the anomaly characterizations, evaluation of the candidate explanations retrieved, updating memory to reflect accepted explanations, and generalization of adapted explanations. In SWALE, the Exploratory Searcher (by Chris Owens) performed additional explanation search when Accepter's routine retrieval failed, and the Tweaker (by Alex Kass) adapted explanations to repair the problems detected by Accepter. The current version of Accepter is a stand-alone system designed to exercise Accepter's anomaly detection and explanation evaluation.

6.4.2 Accepter's basic process

Figure 6.1 summarizes Accepter's processing. The program takes as input a story in which each fact is represented either in terms of conceptual primitives based on Conceptual Dependency

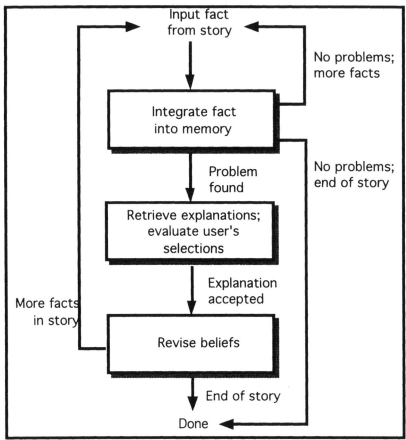

FIG. 6.1. Accepter's basic understanding process.

(CD) theory (Schank, 1972), or in terms of MOPs (Memory Organization Packages; Schank, 1982), which represent stereo-typed action sequences in terms of conceptual primitives and other MOPs. Accepter processes one fact of a story at a time, se-quentially building up expectations for succeeding events.

As Accepter integrates each fact of a story into memory, it checks for anomalies, given its prior expectations and beliefs. The anomalies it finds are presented to the user, along with candidate explanations retrieved from Accepter's library of explanations. Accepter's stored explanations are represented as explanation patterns (XPs) (Schank, 1986). Explanation patterns trace how the anomalous state or event (which we call the explanation's consequent) can plausibly be inferred from a set of assumptions (called the explanation's antecedents).[2] The user selects one of the retrieved XPs for Accepter to evaluate. The system judges its plausibility, relevance to the anomaly, and usefulness for a user-specified goal, as described in the following sections.

6.5 Judging Plausibility by Anomaly Detection

In order to judge an explanation's plausibility given explainer knowledge, an evaluator must judge the fit between that knowledge and the explanation. In a story understander, a natural method for detecting conflicts is to treat the explanation itself as a story to be understood and evaluated by the routine understanding process. Starting with the explanation's assumptions, each belief and rule can successively be integrated into memory, to determine whether the sequence of events traced by the explanation is reasonable or itself causes anomalies. Thus, anomaly detection is the heart of Accepter's plausibility evaluation.

6.5.1 Pattern-Based Anomaly Detection

Controlling inference cost is a fundamental problem for anomaly detection. In principle, anomaly detection may be arbitrarily expensive because anomalies can arise not only from direct conflicts between inputs and system knowledge but also from conflicts between their ramifications; noticing a particular anomaly may require building long inference chains tracing ramifications until a contradiction is found. In real-world domains, this chaining process is overwhelmingly expensive (Rieger, 1975). Consequently, practical anomaly detection depends on overcoming this potentially overwhelming inference cost.

When people have no specific knowledge about whether a given hypothesis is true, they estimate its likelihood by comparing the hypothesis to standard stereotypes. For example, Kahneman, Slovic and Tversky (1982) show that people use stereotypes to decide if it is reasonable for someone to have a given profession. If people in the profession normally fit a stereotype, people expect those who fit that stereotype to have the profession—no matter how uncommon the profession may be. This heuristic can cause

---

[2]For compactness, in the following examples we sometimes call a set of antecedents an "explanation" of an event, but we consider the actual explanation to be the entire dependency chain deriving the consequent from those antecedents.

errors, but is often useful, and can be applied with low cost since it relies on information likely to be accessible.

Accepter's approach to controlling anomaly detection cost is pattern-based. It replaces inference by table lookup of stereotyped patterns. Rather than building inference chains to trace the ramifications of an input, its method simply searches through a series of abstraction trees for relevant patterns. Information conflicting with those patterns is considered anomalous; facts that do not conflict are accepted. This table-based approach is a radical departure from traditional methods.

Accepter replaces inference chaining by table lookup through stereotyped patterns. This anomaly detection process is designed to efficiently provide basic verification.

To verify complex situations, Accepter simultaneously applies patterns to multiple aspects of a situation. By looking at an event from many perspectives, Accepter can identify many types of problems, giving a thorough evaluation and allowing its checks to reflect changing context.

The reasonableness of novel, complex events can be judged in terms of combinations of patterns.

Figure 6.2 sketches the anomaly detection process that Accepter uses to judge plausibility. Given an assumption on which an explanation depends, it begins by comparing that assumption to prior beliefs and expectations, searching for specific conflicts and confirmations. If neither is found, it compares the assumption to standard patterns. If no pattern conflicts are found, the fact in isolation is considered plausible, and the program attempts to activate a MOP to place it in context. If an appropriate MOP is found, Accepter recursively evaluates the instantiated MOP to establish its plausibility. If pattern conflicts are found, additional verification is done to confirm the problem and characterize it more precisely to facilitate retrieval of appropriate adaptation strategies[3]

---

[3]This process is also used to detect anomalies in inputs during Accepter's routine understanding process. There the characterizations of problems are used to guide retrieval of stored explanations.

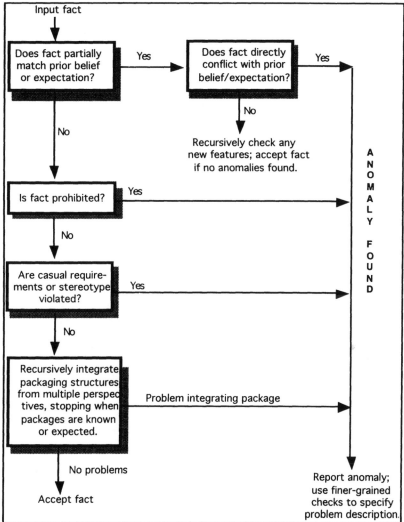

FIG. 6.2: Accepter's anomaly detection algorithm.

6.5.2 *Accepter's Patterns*

Overview of Pattern Types. The success of the pattern-based approach depends on a content theory: We need to establish what the types of patterns are and to establish that they cover a sufficient range of cases to account for the anomalies that people notice. We have identified and implemented the following patterns in Accepter:

- *Normative event sequences,* which include normal order of events and their normal temporal separations. For example, we know that we should be seated a few minutes after arriving in a restaurant.
- *Role-filler stereotypes,* which represent the usual types of actors or objects expected for each role of an action. Stereotypes for role-fillers are divided into two subtypes:
  - *Normative role-fillers,* which contain information on the standard types of objects that fill roles in an action. For example, we know that people who fly first class are usually business executives.
  - *Predisposing features,* which represent the attributes that make an object likely to fill a specific type of role. For example, we know that reckless drivers are likely to be involved in accidents.
- *Functional limitations,* which represent standard deficiencies of a class of actor or object for filling a functional role. For example, some microwave ovens are unusually low-powered.
- *Actors' behavior patterns,* which reflect the types of actions in which actors often participate. For example, some people like outdoor recreation or avoid exercise.

The following sections discuss Accepter's patterns in more detail, describing their organization in memory, the strategies used to retrieve them, and the information they contain. After developing the patterns, we discuss how well Accepter's checks satisfy the goal of basic anomaly detection.

Normative Event Sequences. Accepter uses MOPs to represent its information about standard event sequences and the timing between them. Based on its MOPs, Accepter generates expectations for standard separations between events, and it detects anomalies when those expectations are contradicted. For example, Swale died a few days after an important race. The fact of his death partially matches expectations, from the MOP characterizing a racehorse's life, that Swale would eventually die. However, it conflicts with the temporal prediction of the MOP, which is that the death will occur a few years after the horse's racing days are over. Accepter detects that the death is premature and consequently anomalous.

Table 6.1. Checking Explanation Believability.

```
Checking explanation's believability.
Integrating the antecedent SWALE'S M-JOG into mem-
ory.
Applying routine understanding process to
SWALE'S M-JOG . . .
Phase 1: Trying to recognize fact as known or
         expected.
         Checking if "SWALE'S M-JOG" is already known,
         or conflicts with facts in memory.

         Checking if "SWALE'S M-JOG" is expected from
         (or prohibited by) active MOPs.

Phase 2: Judging plausibility by comparing to
         patterns.

         Checking if the role-fillers of "SWALE'S
         M-JOG" are reasonable

         Checking if action/actor combination makes
         sense. . .
         Anomaly detected!
         ... SWALE AS ACTOR OF SWALE'S M-JOG has the
         problem NON-NORMATIVE-ROLE-FILLER.
```

MOPs are organized in Accepter's memory in an abstraction net, with MOP attributes, such as the events involved and their temporal separations, stored under the highest abstraction of the MOP to which they apply. Retrieval of the attributes is done by breadth-first search up the abstraction hierarchy, starting at the specific MOP in question.

6.5.3   Stereotypes for Actions' Role-Fillers.

Normative role-fillers: Normative role-fillers give information on the types of objects and subevents that usually play particular roles in a MOP. For example, joggers are normally human. As shown in Table 6.1, when Accepter evaluates the explanation of Swale's death by the XP built for Jim Fixx's death—that exertion from jogging overtaxed a hereditary heart defect—the normative role-filler conflict of a horse jogging makes Accepter consider the explanation implausible.

Normative role-filler information is stored in Accepter's memory under the MOPs and roles it describes. Information is stored under the most abstract MOP to which it applies, and property inheritance is used to make the information available to specifications of that MOP.

Normative role-filler patterns are represented in memory structures with four components: The packaging structure (MOP or conceptual primitive) to which the pattern applies, the role for which the pattern describes normative types of role-fillers, the usual category to which the role-fillers belong, and special features (with respect to other category members) that are expected for filling the role. For example, for a drug overdose to be believable, the drug taken must be a strong drug. Table 6.2 summarizes Accepter's representation for normative role-filler information for the drug taken in its MOP M-DRUG-OVERDOSE.

Table 6.2. Components of Normative Role-Filler Patterns.

Component	Example
Package	Drug overdose
Role	Drug taken
Usual filler type	Drug
Special filler features	High medicinal-strength

Normative role-filler information is useful for detecting role-fillers that are implausible. However, it gives no information about whether a plausible role-filler is particularly likely. The next type of pattern, predisposing feature patterns, complements normative role-filler information by supporting the likelihood of certain role-fillers.

Table 6.3. Is it Reasonable for Swale to Die of a Heart Attack?

```
Checking SWALE for features that make SWALE espe-
    cially likely to fill the role VICTIM of SWALE'S M-
    HEART-ATTACK
...SWALE AS VICTIM OF SWALE'S M-HEART-ATTACK CONFIRMS
    expectations from expectation for "HIGH
    EXCITABILITY is a predisposing feature for being
    VICTIM of M-HEART-ATTACK" from SWALE'S M-HEART-
    ATTACK.
```

Predisposing features for a role: Accepter considers that an object or event is likely to fill a role, instead of simply being possible, if it has certain features in addition to those associated with the normative role-filler type. For example, in Table 6.3, Accepter checks the reasonableness of Swale dying of a heart attack. The normative victim of heart attack is an animal—only animals have heart attacks, and any animal might be susceptible—but not all animals are actually likely to have them. If a particular animal is high-strung, however, the likelihood of heart attack is increased. Thus a predisposing feature for filling the victim role of a heart attack is being high-strung. Consequently, when the victim of a hypothesized heart attack is high-strung, Accepter considers the heart-attack to be likely.

To avoid excessive inferencing, Accepter's search for predisposing features is limited to features that are already explicitly known for the object, or that can be inherited from its abstractions. Predisposing feature information is indexed and inherited in the same way as normative role-filler information.

Accepter's representation of predisposing feature patterns includes the MOP, the role in that MOP, and a list of predisposing features for filling the role.[4] Table 6.4 shows the components of Accepter's predisposing feature pattern for heart attacks.

Functional limitations. Accepter's checks for normative role-fillers identify one potential source of problems: that roles are filled by unusual types of objects. However, the fact that a role is filled by the normal type of object does not assure that it will have the needed features to fulfill requirements for the role. For example, not all racehorses can reasonably be believed to run in races; a particular racehorse may be lame, causing it to be a much less likely competitor. Consequently, checks are needed for disabilities that arise from individual features. We call these functional limitation checks. Accepter's functional limitation checks rely on *functional limitation patterns* connecting features to disabilities. For example, we know that a school dropout is likely to have problems reading and an overweight person is likely to have problems doing physical exertion.

---

[4]It would be reasonable for predisposing feature patterns to include information about the types of objects likely to fill the role, as do normative role-filler patterns. However, this information is not included in Accepters representation of predisposing features.

Table 6.4. Components of a Predisposing Feature Pattern.

Component	Example
Package	Heart attack
Role	Victim
Predisposing features	High excitability

Any individual feature of a role-filler might cause it to have problems filling its role. But because most objects have countless features, it would be extremely expensive to check every feature for associated functional limitations. For example, racehorses have features such as lineage, monetary value, and press visibility, all of which are usually irrelevant to deciding whether it is reasonable for the horse to run in a particular race. Accepter restricts features to consider by only looking for functional limitation patterns associated with a subset of features: those that are unusual compared to the features of the normative type of role-filler.

Accepter's functional limitation patterns include the object, or category of objects with the deficiency, the MOP and role for which the deficiency arises, and a summary of the reason for the deficiency, which provides additional information for retrieving explanations from memory. Table 6.5 shows the limitation pattern for lame animals. The pattern represents the animals' likely difficulty moving their limbs.

Table 6.6 provides an example of anomaly detection using functional limitation patterns. The story the system is processing involves Last Chance Louie, a lame racehorse, participating in the Kentucky Derby. When evaluating Louie's racing, the program looks for unusual features of the horse compared to other race-

Table 6.5. Components of a Functional Limitation Pattern.

Component	Example
Object with limitation	Lame animal
Package the limitation affects	Move body part
Role	Actor
Problem description	Physical-disability

Table 6.6. Anomaly Detection Using Functional Limitation Patterns.

```
Checking if the role-fillers of "KENTUCKY-DERBY" are
   reasonable.

Checking if action/actor combination makes sense.

Searching up the abstraction net for limitations

LOUIE AS HORSE OF KENTUCKY-DERBY has the problem
   PHYSICAL-DISABILITY.

Anomaly detected!
PHYSICAL-DISABILITY problem: LOUIE AS HORSE OF
   KENTUCKY-DERBY CONFLICTS-WITH the prohibition of
   KENTUCKY-DERBY due to LAME-ANIMALs are unable to
   fill the role ACTOR of MOVE-BODY-PART.
```

horses, and identifies a problem because he is lame.

When Accepter finds that a role-filler feature causes problems in a MOP, it analyzes the importance of the problems by decomposing the MOP, to see how the feature affects each constituent part. The mechanism it uses is discussed in the following section on basic-action decomposition.

Actors' behavior patterns. An action may be anomalous even if the actor has sufficient ability to perform it: The actor may have special preferences that make him avoid that type of action. For example, Accepter's normative role-filler information about fast-food restaurants tells us that any human might eat in them, so it would not usually be anomalous to learn of anyone eating there. However, if the actor in question is a gourmet, our knowledge of gourmets makes us expect him to avoid fast-food restaurants if he can. Accepter represents this type of knowledge in *actors' behavior patterns*, which represent the actors' tendencies to favor participating in particular roles of an action or to avoid them.

Actors' behavior patterns are a generalized form of the expectations and prohibitions already described; they represent information about the classes of actions that an actor or actor class favors or avoids. Such information often comes from role themes, which represent stereotyped knowledge about the plans and goals associated with actors in certain societal roles (Schank & Abelson, 1977). For example, we expect that a police officer will direct traffic and investigate crimes. Sometimes role themes or individual experiences carry expectations for things that theme-driven actors

Table 6.7. Expectations and Prohibitions for the Basketball Draft.

```
Checking if a packaging MOP can be instantiated for
   "BIAS'S M-ATHLETIC-DRAFT".

Checking for packages focusing on the ATHLETE role
   of "BIAS'S M-ATHLETIC-DRAFT."

   A possible package for BIAS'S M-ATHLETIC-DRAFT is
   "There is a M-ACTIVE-PLAY with BIAS as its ACTOR".

   Verifying whether BIAS'S M-ACTIVE-PLAY is a reason-
   able package.

Doing routine understanding of the input . . .

Activating expectations/prohibitions from BIAS'S M-
   ACTIVE-PLAY.

Expectations:
   BIAS'S M-ATHLETIC-TRAINING.
   BIAS'S M-ATHLETIC-DRAFT.
   BIAS'S M-ATHLETIC-COMPETITION.

Prohibitions:
   BIAS'S M-RECREATIONAL-DRUGS.
```

will not do: for example, a police officer is expected to avoid drinking when on duty.

One of the role themes in Accepter's memory describes behavior of professional athletes, including prohibitions for breaking training. When Accepter is given the input that Len Bias is involved in the basketball draft, it packages the draft as part of an athlete's active career. The career carries with it expectations for competition, and a prohibition of drug use during active play, as shown in the output in Table 6.7.

Len Bias died the day after the basketball draft. When Accepter processes the news of his death, it detects the anomaly that the death is premature. It retrieves candidate explanations for that anomaly, one of which is the explanation for the death of Janis Joplin. Janis Joplin died of an accidental overdose of recreational drugs taken to escape the stress of stardom, which suggests the hypothesis that Bias too was taking drugs to ease the pressure of being a superstar, and died of an accidental overdose.

Table 6.8. Detecting an Implausible Belief.

```
Checking if "BIAS'S M-RECREATIONAL-DRUGS" is already
  known or conflicts with facts in memory.

No relevant belief found.

Checking if "BIAS'S M-RECREATIONAL-DRUGS" is ex-
  pected from (or prohibited by) active MOPs.

Problem detected installing "BIAS'S M-RECREATIONAL-
  DRUGS" in memory:
the prohibition of BIAS'S M-RECREATIONAL-DRUGS due
  to BIAS'S M-ACTIVE-PLAY.
```

When Accepter evaluates this hypothesis, it considers the hypothesis implausible because it expects Bias to avoid breaking training during his playing career, as shown in the output in Table 6.8.

Actors' behavior patterns are not limited to prohibiting generally unlikely actions: they can also be used to detect anomalies in which an action is surprising solely because it deviates from the specific actor's customary behavior. For example, if someone always goes to Burger King, we would be surprised to see him at McDonald's, even though going to McDonald's is something we would consider reasonable, based on general social patterns, and that does not conflict with any prohibitions.

Because preferences reflect the relationship of an actor to an action, when no behavior pattern is indexed directly under the action it may be necessary to abstract both the actor involved and the action performed in order to find an applicable pattern. Accepter first searches for patterns indexed under the specific action and actor. When no pattern is found, it searches under the specific action and increasing abstractions of the actor. If that fails, it repeats the process for increasingly abstract characterizations of the action.

Accepter's actor behavior patterns include three components: the actor, or class of actor, whose behavior the pattern describes; the type of action; and role in it that the actor often fills or avoids. Table 6.9 summarizes the components for person X's avoidance of eating in restaurant Y.

Table 6.9. Components of an Avoidance Pattern.

Component	Example
Package	M-restaurant at restaurant Y
Avoided role	Diner
Actor (or class of actor) avoiding role	Person X

6.5.4 Coverage of Accepter's Patterns

Accepter's initial set of anomaly categories was suggested by anomalies that arose in stories the system processed, and in the (sometimes fanciful) explanations offered to account for them. Thus, Accepter attempts to test both for anomalies that people might notice in the world (such as the death of Swale) and for anomalies that appear in wild hypotheses rather than real life (e.g., the idea that Swale might have been using drugs because he was overwhelmed by the pressure of being a star, and that he died of a self-inflicted drug overdose).

Although the categories were developed in response to very limited data, they span problems from many explanations that students hypothesized for Swale's death. After the categories were developed, we very informally tested their generality by collecting anomalies that people reported in real-world events, to see if the checks would also account for those anomalies. We collected a list of about 180 anomalies and explanations from students in the Yale AI lab (most of which are contained in Kass & Leake, 1987). The data were not gathered in a controlled way and may leave out some important anomaly classes, but they nevertheless provide an extensive range of anomalies that must be accounted for by any general purpose anomaly-detection system.

After a plausible context was hypothesized for each of the anomalies, they were grouped according to the problems they involved. The basic initial set of patterns spanned many of the anomalies, although the data suggested adding the category of functional limitations and finer grained motivational checks. The data also helped identify the limitations of the categories: For example, approximately 20% of the anomalies that people reported involved feature correlations (e.g., "Why are baseball pitchers lousy hitters?") and trends (e.g., "Why are insurance rates skyrocketing?"), which are beyond the scope of Accepter's anomaly-detection tests. However, conflicts with patterns account for a majority of the remaining anomalies.

Pattern-based checks can account for a significant proportion of our anomaly data.

Nevertheless, comparison with additional and more systematically collected data would be desirable to give further indications of the categories' coverage.

6.5.5 Finer Grained Checks

If pattern conflicts arise, the understander needs to account for the discrepancy by explaining them. However, pattern conflicts give little information about the focus needed for explanation: Pattern-based checks only identify unusual situations, rather than state why the unusual features might be surprising. Consequently, when pattern conflicts are detected, it can be useful to apply finer grained tests to generate a more specific problem characterization before explaining. The more specific characterization facilitates explanation construction by providing additional focus for explanation search.

For example, if someone tries to bake a casserole in a plastic dish, the type of dish is anomalous: People usually use ceramic ones. However, if the problem is described only as "using a plastic dish rather than ceramic," and that description is used to retrieve explanations, any reasons to favor plastic over ceramic might be retrieved, including reasons such as:

- Buying plastic is more affordable than buying ceramic.
- Plastic is unbreakable, so it's safer when there are small children around the house.
- Plastic containers are often made in brighter colors, so they're more cheerful to look at.

All these explanations fail to address the real issue in the anomaly, which is that using a plastic dish for a casserole is anomalous because of a bad effect: The dish will melt.

To suggest appropriate explanations, the anomaly description must state not only that plastic is unusual, but the more specific causal problem that it is unusual because it does not satisfy the requirement that casseroles be cooked in heat proof containers. After Accepter detects a conflict with patterns, it uses finer grained checks in an effort to analyze it in terms of specific causal problems, to guide the case-based explanation process more precisely.

Accepter supplements its pattern-based checks with three types of finer grained checks that recharacterize pattern conflicts. The checks are *basic action decomposition*, which evaluates a role-filler's suitability for a role, and two motivational checks: *examination of direct effects*, which is used to check whether an action is consistent with actor goals, and *plan choice checks*, which see if the actor's observed plan choice conflicts with the actor's decision making preferences (see Leake, 1992). This enables Accepter to provide precise guidance to the adaptation process.

6.6 Judging Relevance to the Anomaly

In order to resolve an anomaly, an explanation must account for what was surprising about the anomalous situation. For example, if we are surprised that a star dies young, both *early death from life in the fast lane* and *fatal overdose from increased strength of recreational drugs* account for the early death. However, which explanation is relevant to the anomaly depends on what made the death anomalous—why we were surprised. If the death was surprising because we did not think the star would consider using drugs, *early death from life in the fast lane* resolves the anomaly—it tells us how the star was driven to use them. If the death surprised us because we thought the star was too careful about dosages to risk overdose, *early death from life in the fast lane* is irrelevant, but *fatal overdose from change in strength of illegal drugs* resolves the anomaly because it shows why the star's carefulness could not prevent overdose. Thus for an understander to know which beliefs to revise, an explanation must provide information that shows why the false prior expectation failed to apply.

To resolve an anomaly, the information in an explanation must both account for the surprising features and show why prior reasoning went astray.

Accepter judges relevance to anomalies in two ways. First, during preliminary explanation search, it characterizes the current anomaly and uses that characterization to decide which of the explanations in its memory are likely to be relevant. This provides a preliminary filtering. After this filtering has been done, and after any needed adaptation of the retrieved explanation, the system does another check to assure that the revised explanation addresses the anomaly.

6.6.1 *Judging Relevance by Comparing Anomaly Characterizations*

The need to assure relevance to anomalies complicates explanation search, because explainers cannot simply look for any causes of the surprising event—they must find causes that also resolve the anomaly. To facilitate search for relevant explanatory information, we have developed a characterization scheme for anomalies. This characterization scheme establishes a vocabulary of anomaly types and a set of structures with slots for attributes relevant to that class of anomalies. Explanations in Accepter's XP library are indexed by their anomaly characterizations; when a new anomaly is encountered, the anomaly is characterized in the same vocabulary used to describe explanations, and Accepter searches its library for stored explanations with similar characterizations.

The principle behind this approach is simple: If problems are described in the right way, similar problems will have similar solutions. If anomaly characterizations capture the significant aspects of the situation to explain, anomalies with similar characterizations will have similar explanations, so explanatory knowledge can be organized by the anomalies it explains.

Anomaly characterizations both describe anomalies and organize their explanations.

For example, consider the event "Last Chance Louie finished fifth in the Belmont Stakes." This might be anomalous because the jockey had been sure he could make Louie win (making the result a PLAN-OUTCOME-FAILURE anomaly), or because Louie had been banned from racing (making the participation a BLOCKAGE-VIOLATION anomaly), or because we read a newspaper story saying that Louie would be withdrawn from the race (INFORMATION-FAILURE). Based on these characterizations, XPs for similar problems can be retrieved. For example, PLAN-OUTCOME-FAILURE might index the XP *muddy tracks can neutralize the favorite's advantages;* BLOCKAGE-VIOLATION might index the XP *powerful owners can have bans on their horses rescinded;* and INFORMATION-FAILURE might index the XP *newspaper listings can't reflect changes after press time.*

The previous examples again demonstrate the need for focusing explanation search on explaining the appropriate anomaly: Different anomalies may require very different explanations, so that it is unlikely an arbitrary explanation for the event would actually address the anomaly to be explained. By retrieving explanations indexed under the same anomaly type as the current problem, a case-based explainer can efficiently generate candidate explanations that are relevant to its needs for information. Table 6.10 summarizes our anomaly categories (for a more complete account and evaluation of their effectiveness, see Leake, 1991, 1992).

6.6.2 Judging Relevance by Identifying Flawed Beliefs

Although anomaly characterizations make it possible to retrieve explanations focusing on the right type of anomaly, explicit relevance evaluation is still needed. XPs that were relevant to a similar anomaly in the past will not always be relevant in the current context, and adaptation cannot be guaranteed to preserve a candidate explanation's relevance.

Explanations are relevant to an anomaly if they show why prior reasoning went astray—if the beliefs in the explanation either contradict a belief from which faulty prior expectations were derived, or show that prior expectations were based on insufficient information. To test relevance, Accepter first generates a subcontext in memory (McDermott & Sussman, 1973) that reflects only the previous information taken into account when generating its failed expectation. It then integrates the new explanation's beliefs into that subcontext by applying its routine understanding process. If anomaly detection finds conflicts between the subcontext of prior beliefs and the belief-support chain of the explanation, those conflicts show the expectation was based on false beliefs (assuming that the explanation itself is valid, which is judged by the plausibility evaluation process). If none of the beliefs in the explanation conflict but some are not expected in the subcontext, the new explanation takes precedence because it shows factors that previously were not taken into account, also resolving the anomaly.

The output shown in Table 6.11 traces Accepter's evaluation of whether the XP *exertion + heart defect causes fatal heart attack* is a relevant explanation for Swale's death. According to that explanation, Swale's death resulted from physical exertion, which overtaxed a heart defect, leading to heart attack and resultant death.

Table 6.10. Top Level Anomaly Categories.

Category	Sub-Category
Surprising-Plan-Choice	Irrelevant-Plan
	Redundant-Plan
	Preference-Failure
	Blocked-Plan
Surprising-Prop-Choice	
Plan-Execution-Failure	Prop-Substitution
	Plan-Delay
	Plan-Speedup
	Plan-Cancellation
	Plan-Outcome-Failure
Blockage-Violation	Inadequate-Role-Filler
	Bad-Actor-Ability
	Bad-Tool
	Unavailable-Role-Filler
Process-Execution-Failure	Process-Delay
	Process-Speedup
	Process-Outcome-Failure
Device-Failure	
Unusual-Feature	
Feature-Duration-Failure	

Swale's death is anomalous because it occurred earlier than is normally expected for a racehorse, so a relevant explanation must account both for why Swale died when he did (which is the surprising feature) and for why normal expectations for a racehorse's life span were superseded (why, in hindsight, the normal horse's life-span should not have been expected to apply to Swale). Table 6.11 traces Accepter's decision that the explanation *exertion + heart defect causes fatal heart attack* does both. In the first phase of the process, Accepter verifies that the explanation accounts for the surprising feature, since a heart attack prompted by current racing would cause immediate death. In the second phase, it verifies that the explanation also accounts for why expectations failed, because it shows a causally relevant factor (Swale's heart defect) that was not considered when forming the original expectation for Swale's life expectancy.

6.7 Judging Usefulness for Overarching Goals

Accepter's final set of tests judges whether explanations provide the information needed for current explainer tasks. Efforts to understand are often motivated by desire to accomplish particular goals, but understanding systems traditionally judge explanations in isolation from how the explanations will be used. EBL research has examined usefulness criteria in many different contexts (e.g., object recognition, planning, and problem solving) but for one class of task: efficient concept recognition (see Keller, 1988a for a survey). However, everyday explanation serves a much wider range of types of goals, and assumptions about usefulness evaluation from the recognition task do not necessarily apply to other purposes (Keller, 1988b; Leake, 1992) For example, the usefulness evaluation framework in EBL assumes only the antecedents of an explanation need to be considered when evaluating usefulness, not the rules used, and that all antecedents of an explanation must satisfy the same requirements (e.g., Mitchell, et al., 1986). Such assumptions do not apply to all tasks: for example, in order to use an explanation to find how to block an event, the explanation needs only to connect an event to a single necessary antecedent that can be blocked.

The following sections examine the range of goals served by explanation and discuss a model of explanation evaluation to reflect those goals.[5]

6.7.1 The Range of Explanation Purposes

As an example of the importance of goals in explanation and the types of information that different goals require, we consider the following story:

> Company X was beleaguered by high taxes, foreign competition, and outdated equipment, despite low labor costs due to being nonunion. Rumors of problems spread, and the company's stock plummeted, but its managers announced their deci-

---

[5]This section is adapted from the article "Goal-based Explanation Evaluation," *Cognitive Science*, Volume 15, Number 4, 1991. This material is reprinted with the permission of Ablex Publishing Corporation.

Table 6.11. Evaluation of an Explanation.

Part 1: Checking if explanation derives surprising
    event features.
Feature(s) important to the anomaly: TIME.
Checking if the explanation's consequent accounts
    for the problem that TIME of SWALE'S DEAD HEALTH
    conflicted with expectations.
Matching SWALE'S DEAD HEALTH and explanation's con-
    sequent . . .
The explanation accounts for the surprising fea-
    ture(s).
Part 2: Checking if explanation shows why the rea-
    soning underlying the expectation failed.
Checking whether explanation shows factors that are
    unusual compared to standard SWALE'S M-RACEHORSE-
    LIFE.
Using routine understanding to check whether SWALE'S
    PHYSICAL-EXERTION is standard in context of SWALE'S
    M-RACEHORSE-LIFE.
Building up new memory context with expectations
    from SWALE'S M-RACEHORSE-LIFE. Integrating SWALE'S
    PHYSICAL-EXERTION into that context.
SWALE'S PHYSICAL-EXERTION satisfies expectation for
    SWALE'S M-HORSERACE from SWALE'S M-RACEHORSE-LIFE,
    so it's routine.
Using routine understanding to check whether HEART-
    2169'S HEREDITARY-DEFECTIVE ORGANIC-STATE is stan-
    dard in context of SWALE'S M-RACEHORSE-LIFE.
Building up new memory context with expectations
    from SWALE'S M-RACEHORSE-LIFE. Integrating HEART-
    2169'S HEREDITARY-DEFECTIVE ORGANIC-STATE into that
    context.
HEART-2169'S HEREDITARY-DEFECTIVE ORGANIC-STATE
    isn't expected from SWALE'S M-RACEHORSE-LIFE, or
    from standard stereotypes, so it's distinctive.
EXERTION-HEART-ATTACK resolves the anomaly, by
    accounting both for why the surprising part of the
    situation happened, and why predictions went wrong.

sion not to have layoffs. The next week, it was rumored that they would lay off 20% of their work force.

Because the layoffs violate the managers' pledge, they are anomalous and might prompt explanation. However, different people involved in the layoffs would have different goals, which might make them want to account for the situation in different ways. This desire to highlight certain factors gives each explainer a different *explanation purpose* to guide explanation, as the following examples show:

1.   Someone who had believed the managers' pledge, and consequently expected that there would not be layoffs, would want to confirm that the layoffs would really occur. Here the explainer's goal is maintaining accurate beliefs, which prompts a plan to substantiate the layoffs. This prompts the explanation purpose of showing that the layoffs are confirmed by trusted information, which might be done by the explanation *a newspaper found a secret company memo from the company president, describing the timetable for the layoffs.*

2.   The same person might have the goal of avoiding future incorrect predictions in similar situations. One plan to achieve that goal is to explain why the current belief went wrong and repair the source of the problem. Here the purpose of explanation would be accounting for the bad prediction in terms of false prior beliefs. For example, if the explainer had trusted the managers, but the explainer could explain the conflict between reports by *the managers lied* ; that explanation would make it possible to avoid trusting their statements in the future.

3.   A worker who expected to be laid off might want to avoid being unemployed in the future, by finding a new job before being laid off next time. For this purpose, a suitable explanation might be *the layoffs were inevitable because of pressure to reduce costs to shore up the company's falling stock.* This explanation makes it possible to predict layoffs from changes in the stock price.

4.   A local politician might see the layoffs as bad for the area's economic health, prompting the goal of trying to have the workers recalled. To do this, the politician would have the explanation purpose of finding feasible repair points for the current situation. This would require building an explanation showing how the layoffs are caused or enabled by factors under government control, and whose removal will restore the desired situation. For example, the explanation the layoffs were forced by high taxes that reduced profitability suggests repairing the situation by lowering taxes in order to

make the factory profitable again, so the workers will be called back.

5. A worker who was still employed might worry about being laid off in the future, prompting the goal of preventing future layoffs. This would prompt the explanation purpose of finding causes of the layoffs that the worker can affect. An explanation might be *lack of unionization enabled the layoffs*, because the workers had a contract that gave employees no security. The worker could use this explanation to suggest what to do: to try to unionize.

6. The manager who ordered the layoffs might want to avoid negative publicity, and could decide to do so by deflecting blame. One explanation purpose for this goal would be to implicate other actors, perhaps by an explanation such as *an outside expert convinced management that the layoffs were essential*.

7. The owner of another factory might want to improve that factory's profitability. This goal might trigger the plan of analyzing other managers' decisions, to learn better management strategies. This could prompt the explanation purpose of deciding why the other managers chose to have layoffs, as opposed to alternative responses to the company's problems (e.g., increasing advertising to increase demand for products). A useful explanation might be *the managers chose layoffs instead of advertising because layoffs help win tax concessions from local government*.

8. A worker who wondered whether to look for a new job, or simply wait to be called back, would want to know how long the layoffs were likely to last. This would prompt the explanation purpose of clarifying the situation to help form predictions of the layoffs' duration. This might involve finding if the layoffs resulted primarily from long-term factors or short-term ones. A suitable explanation might be *the layoffs were caused by a decrease in demand because of temporary overstocks*.

9. A business consultant might want to develop a theory of how demographic trends force layoffs in different industries. A plan for that goal is to show how the theory accounts for particular episodes of layoffs, which would prompt the explanation purpose of finding causes of the current layoffs within the framework of that theory.

10.   A politician wanting to mitigate negative public opinion of the local economy, in order to be reelected, might want to show that the layoffs were an unavoidable side-effect of something desirable, perhaps through an explanation such as *layoffs are caused by American industry streamlining operations to become stronger*.

Even though all these explainers could have noticed the same anomaly when the rumor of layoffs began to circulate, each has different goals, prompting a different purpose for explanation. Although we can imagine single explanations that would be usable for multiple purposes, a given explanation's usefulness for multiple purposes is not assured. In the previous list, almost all the explanations given for one explainer are inapplicable to the others' purposes.

The wide range of explanations possible for the layoffs suggests how many factors can enter into the explanation of any situation, but our multiple explanations for the layoffs themselves leave out countless factors—generating a "complete" explanation of a real-world event is impossible. Good explanations must highlight a few important factors from the many that are involved: the factors that give the explainer the information it needs.

Explainer goals determine which of the countless possible factors an explanation must include, and how those factors must be connected to the event being explained.

In the preceding example, the explanations reflect 10 major explanation purposes triggered by anomalies:

1.   Connect situation to expected/believed conditions.
2.   Connect situation to previously unexpected conditions.
3.   Connect situation to factors from which it can be predicted.
4.   Connect undesirable state to possible repair points.
5.   Connect situation to causes that show how a given actor can control its occurrence.
6.   Connect situation to factors that suggest praise or blame for an actor.
7.   Connect an action to the actor's motivations.
8.   Connect situation to factors that discriminate between alternative responses.

9.   Connect situation to factors within a given theory.
10. Connect situation to types of factors that, when their influence is communicated to another agent, will cause a desired change in that agent's beliefs.

The first two purposes in this list are the purposes of an explainer seeking to resolve an anomaly, which we described in the previous section. The third through ninth purposes reflect needs arising primarily from a system's internal goal-based information requirements; this is the class of needs that we concentrate on here.

6.7.2 How Explanation Purposes Arise

Anomalies show flaws in system knowledge. When that knowledge is revised in response to the anomaly, the system may discover that its prior goals and plans need to be revised as well, in response to the system's new picture of the world. However, revising goals and plans depends on having appropriate information which may need to go beyond what is provided by the explanation that originally resolved the anomaly. When a system needs particular types of information from an explanation, its needs prompt explanation purposes that guide the explanation effort.

Explanation purposes are goals to build an explanation involving particular types of beliefs and links.

Explanation purposes determine the types of links and beliefs that an explanation must include; in Accepter, these are described in terms of basic evaluation dimensions. Accepter has individual heuristics for evaluating beliefs and links along each evaluation dimension, and it combines the heuristics as needed to build tests reflecting the multiple dimensions that may be important. Thus, in our model, goal-based evaluation decisions are determined by the following chain:

Anomaly
leads to
changes in world model
which lead to
explanation purposes
which lead to
groups of dimension checks
which lead to an
evaluation decision.

As a concrete example, we trace the beginning of this chain for an explanation of surprising layoffs. Suppose a worker is not laid off but is surprised, nevertheless, that the layoffs take place despite the managers' pledge. An explanation accounting for the failure of prior expectations might be *The managers lied*. That explanation shows the worker that management cannot be trusted to protect workers, which suggests that the worker's job could be threatened if hard times continue. This triggers a new goal for the worker: to protect his or her job.

To accomplish that goal, the worker might decide on the following plan: to punish those responsible for the layoffs, in order to deter anyone who might cause future layoffs. For example, if the person who made the decision was personally blamed in the press and by the laid-off workers, the negative publicity might provide an incentive for that person to try to avoid layoffs in similar future situations.

Carrying out the worker's plan depends on having certain information that may not be initially available: The worker needs to know who the perpetrator was. This gives rise to an explanation purpose: to connect the layoffs to factors that suggest blame for a particular actor. For other explainer goals, other explanation purposes apply; Table 6.12 sketches examples of how each of our explanation purposes can be triggered by a goal and plan.

Sometimes an anomaly will trigger more than one goal, or a goal will trigger multiple plans, causing multiple explanation purposes to be active simultaneously. However, even when multiple goals apply, limits on resources for information gathering may force a choice between them, in order to focus explanation effort on purposes serving the system's highest priority goals.

After an explanation purpose has been chosen, explanations must be evaluated to see if they fulfill that purpose. Although it would be possible to devise independent evaluation procedures for each purpose, parsimony suggests analyzing the purposes to find a set of simple component requirements that can be combined in different ways to describe multiple purposes.

Table 6.12: Examples of How Explanation Purposes Arise.

Goal	Plan	Explanation Purpose
Prevent bad effects that result from acting on false information.	1 Confirm reasonableness of new information.	Connect situation to expected/believed conditions.
	2. Find and correct flaws in prior knowledge.	Connect situation to unexpected conditions.
Minimize bad effects maximize good effects in similar future situations.	Predict similar situations in time to prepare.	Connect situation to predictive factors.
Use malfunctioning device.	Execute repair.	Connect undesirable state to repair points.
Re-achieve the good effects caused by anomalous event.	Re-cause event.	Connect to achievable causes.
Prevent recurrence of surprising bad state.	Punish current actors to deter future perpetrators.	Connect to factors suggesting blame.
Counter an adversary.	Predict and respond to adversary's actions.	Connect to adversary's motivations.
Protect current plans.	Deal with ramifications of new features.	Connect to factors that discriminate between alternative responses.
Refine/demonstrate a theory.	Use theory to account for unexpected data.	Connect to within-theory factors.
Have an action performed by another agent.	Convince other agent the action is desirable.	Connect situation to factors that will influence other agent.

Accepter's checks for explanation purposes are built from simple procedures for judging the role of antecedents along 10 evaluation dimensions: predictive power, timeliness, routineness, distinctiveness, knowability, causal force, repairability, independence, achievability/blockability, and desirability.[6] Some of these dimensions measure properties of individual beliefs, given the current context (e.g., knowability); others measure properties of how a belief is connected to an explanation's consequent (e.g., causal force). After an initial set of dimensions was defined for a few purposes, we found that needs for many of our other purposes could be described by simply using different combinations of dimensions from the initial set, and we believe that only a small set of additional dimensions would be needed for adding other purposes to the system.

6.7.3 How Goals Affect Accepter's Evaluation

In a planning system that used Accepter to maintain its world model, explanation purposes would be determined by needs of the overarching planner. In the current stand-alone version of Accepter, explanation purposes are selected by a human user. The user can choose among five explanation purposes: connecting the situation to factors that will help predict it, connecting it to factors that will help prevent it, connecting it to factors that can be repaired, and connecting it to factors that allow the assignment of blame or responsibility.

To evaluate whether an explanation is sufficient for a given purpose, Accepter tests the explanation's beliefs and links along relevant evaluation dimensions, beginning by applying dimension checks to the explanation's antecedents. If the original explanation does not have suitable antecedents, or its antecedents are not linked in suitable ways, Accepter next applies its tests to the antecedents of each subchain contained in the original belief-support chain. This process allows it to determine whether any part of the explanation provides the needed information. (In what follows, when we refer to the antecedents of an explanation we are referring to the antecedents of the subchain currently under consideration.)

If the original explanation or one of its subchains passes Accepter's tests, the program accepts it and outputs a description of the useful information it provides. If no subchain includes an adequate set of useful antecedents, Accepter outputs a description of any useful information found and summarizes the missing information to guide adaptation.

---

[6]Although the checks return yes/no decisions, the values for all dimensions actually fall along a continuum.

Accepter's heuristics for testing evaluation dimensions are generally very simple; a much richer model is needed. However, that issue is irrelevant to our main points, which are the explanation purposes themselves and the fact that the purposes can be described along a small set of dimensions.

Example: Explaining to Predict. When an understander's expectations fail, its knowledge needs to be updated to avoid future failures. To avoid failures, the understander needs to find out when in the future to predict the surprising situation rather than the one that it had mistakenly expected. To do this, it needs to find predictive features to look for next time—warning signs that the surprising feature or event will occur again. This prompts the explanation purpose *connect situation to events from which it can be predicted*. For example, when Challenger exploded, many people involved in the space program tried to explain the disaster, in order to predict potential future disasters and avoid them.

In order for a belief-support chain to be useful for prediction, it must satisfy four requirements, each tested by a test for a different evaluation dimension:

1. Occurrence of the chain's antecedents makes the event likely. This is tested by applying checks for the antecedents' *predictive power*.
2. The antecedents happen long enough in advance of the event for the prediction they trigger to be useful. This is tested by applying checks for the antecedents' *timeliness*.
3. One of the antecedents is unusual compared to the expected situation, so that it gives evidence for the surprising event occurring instead of the previously expected one. This is tested by applying checks for the antecedents' *distinctiveness*.
4. The antecedents are conditions the system is likely to be aware of in the future. This is tested by applying checks for the antecedents' *knowability*.

Note that the conditions do not specify that the explanation must be causal: Valid predictions are often based on noncausal reasoning. For example, a belief-support chain might enable prediction of the date of a shuttle launch by showing how the date can be predicted from scheduling patterns, even if those patterns are not accounted for in terms of their causes. For a more complete discussion of requirements for prediction and discussion of requirements for other purposes, see Leake, 1992.

6.7.4 Goal-Based Adaptation

The intent of our evaluation procedures is not to simply reject inadequate explanations: It is to identify any useful information they provide and to show what further elaboration is needed. In case-based explanation, the explanations that are retrieved simply give a head start to the explanation construction process. If the retrieved explanations are inadequate, the explanation construction process is continued by adapting the explanation to repair its flaws.

For example, suppose a driver is surprised that the car will not start and retrieves the explanation, *The gas is contaminated, clogging the fuel line.* This explanation leaves out information such as how the clogging occurred, which might be useful for repairing the clog; it also leaves out information about how the gas became contaminated, which might be useful to investigate if the driver suspects that someone sabotaged the car and wants to assign blame. These two different needs for information would suggest different adaptations of the explanation: Finding how the clogging occurs requires expanding on the internal structure of the explanation, to show how the contaminants caused the clog; accounting for the contamination of the gas requires augmenting the explanation to explain the contamination itself. After each incremental adaptation, a case-based explanation system reevaluates the resultant explanation to provide additional goal-based guidance for further adaptation. In this way, case-based explanation takes goals into account throughout the adaptation process.

6.7.5 Ramifications for Using Partial Explanations

EBL systems require complete deductive proofs as the starting point for their learning; they do not learn from situations in which, due to lack of information or other factors, only a partial derivation can be built. However, people learn from situations even if they cannot construct a definitive explanation. For example, suppose Mary notices that her car sometimes fails to start on cold days and decides that the cold is one of the factors contributing to the problem. She has not found necessary conditions for failure to start, because it probably fails to start under other circumstances as well; she has not found sufficient conditions, because the failure is intermittent, even in cold weather. Nevertheless, she can learn what she needs to know from her partial explanation. Because she knows that cold is one of the factors involved, she can prevent the problem by keeping her car in the garage on cold nights. Thus, by considering the goal that an explanation will serve, and requiring only that explanations provide the information needed for that goal, goal-based evaluation extends the applicability of explanation-based techniques: It enables an explanation-based system to judge whether it can base its processing on a partial explanation.

Sometimes an explanation must show sufficient conditions in order to account for the feature being explained; sometimes such thoroughness is unnecessary. Systems that treat explanations as being neutral to the overarching task must always apply the same criteria, which will necessarily be too strong for some tasks in order to be strong enough for all uses. Our goal-based evaluation criteria give a dynamic way to determine whether a partial explanation gives adequate information. The ability to use partial explanations allows systems to learn in complex situations that they cannot completely explain, extending the applicability of explanation-based approaches to complicated situations that are not well understood—in which explanation may be needed most.

6.8 Conclusion

Explanation-based approaches are powerful tools for guiding generalization, indexing, and repair of failures. However, they cannot give good results if applied to bad explanations that are invalid or that fail to provide the information the explainer needs. This chapter develops both a theory and a set of mechanisms for evaluating candidate explanations. The mechanisms allow explanation-based systems to identify problems, and case-based explainers to focus further processing to repair those problems.

To allow an understander to efficiently recognize the anomalies that reveal plausibility problems, we have developed a model of anomaly detection that replaces traditional inference chaining with pattern-based checks. The pattern-based approach allows low-cost verification of the fit between an explanation's assumptions and prior system knowledge.

To allow an understander to focus explanation on providing the information it needs for its tasks, we have also analyzed the goals that explanations can serve and the information needs triggered by those goals. Goal-based criteria are needed because no real-world explanation can include all the factors that are causally relevant to a situation: Explanations necessarily highlight a few factors. If the highlighted factors are irrelevant to the explainer's goals, the explanation will be useless, regardless of its plausibility; if the needed factors are included, the explanation is sufficient, regardless of how partially it describes the situation. By allowing use of partial explanations, this model provides a principled means of applying explanation-based methods to situations that cannot be completely explained.

Thus, the theory's evaluation criteria are dynamic: Context and overarching goals determine the information that explanations must provide. This theory, combined with the mechanisms that make it practical to apply, make it possible for a case-based explanation system to generate good explanations, even in domains that are complex and incompletely understood.

7. AQUA: Questions that Drive the Explanation Process

Ashwin Ram
College of Computing
Georgia Institute of Technology

Editors' Introduction

In the doctoral dissertation from which this chapter is drawn, Ashwin Ram presented an alternative perspective on the processes of story understanding, explanation, and learning. The issues that Ram explores in that dissertation are similar to those that are explored by the other authors in this book, but the angle that Ram takes on these issues is somewhat different. Ram's exploration of these processes is organized around the central theme of question asking. For Ram, understanding a story means identifying questions that the story raises and questions that it answers. Question asking also serves as a lens through which each of the subprocesses is viewed: The retrieval of stored explanations, for instance, is driven by a library of what Ram calls "XP retrieval questions"; likewise, evaluation is driven by another set of questions called "hypothesis verification questions."

To some extent, any program that builds explanations can be thought of as asking questions. In fact, any program that solves a problem and sets up goals and subgoals can be described as asking itself how a particular goal can be achieved. Ram's contribution is to make as many of the questions as possible explicit. By doing so, he helps his readers separate implementation details from important issues. It's the questions that the program asks that are important, not the details of how they get asked.

The AQUA program, which is Ram's implementation of this question-based theory of understanding, is a very complex system, probably the most complex among the programs described in this book. AQUA covers a great deal of ground; it implements the entire case-based explanation process in a question-based manner. This breadth poses a problem for this volume, because it isn't possible to cover all that ground in this chapter and have had to ignore many aspects of the program. We have focused on the high-level description of the questions the program asks, especially those it asks when constructing and evaluating explanations of volitional actions.

* * *

7.1 Introduction: Question-Driven Understanding

Story understanding is a goal-directed process. The memory of an understanding system is never quite complete: Knowledge structures may be missing, they may have "gaps" in them, or they may not be indexed correctly in memory. When one reads a story, these gaps give rise to questions about the input. The point of reading is to find answers to these questions, and to learn by filling in the gaps in one's world model. Questions represent the "knowledge goals" of the understander, things that the understander wants to learn about.

Most teachers have had the experience of thinking that their students understood some material because they were asking the "right questions." Children ask questions constantly in an attempt to understand and learn about the world around them. Even as adults, we express our curiosity in the form of questions, often to ourselves, as we wonder about novel situations, explore new hypotheses, and become interested in various issues. The ability to ask questions, it seems, is central to the processes of reasoning and learning.

This chapter presents a question-based theory of explanation, story understanding, and learning. Our main contribution to Schank's theory of explanation patterns is that the case-based explanation process in our model, although similar to that used by the SWALE program (Kass et al., 1986), is formulated in a question-based framework. Our emphasis is on the questions that underlie the creation, verification, and learning of explanations, and is complementary to the creative adaptation process modeled in SWALE. Furthermore, we focus on the use of possibly incomplete explanation patterns with questions attached to them, and the learning that occurs as these questions are answered. Finally, we propose a content theory of volitional explanations that is used for motivational analysis in story understanding.

We will discuss a computer program called AQUA (Asking Questions and Understanding Answers), that is based on our model of question-driven understanding and learning. The main point of the research is to create a model of a dynamic understander that is driven by its questions or goals to acquire knowledge. Rather than being "canned," the understander is always changing as its questions change. Such an understander reads similar stories differently and forms different interpretations as its questions and interests evolve. The intent is not to design a system that can acquire the "right" understanding of a topic, or form the "right" explanation for a story, but one that is able to wonder and to ask questions about the unusual aspects of its input. As it learns more about the domain, the system asks better and more detailed questions and creates better and more detailed explanations. This kind of questioning forms the origins of creativity; rather than being satisfied with available explanations, a creative person asks questions and explores the explanations in novel ways.

Question generation is the process of identifying what the reasoner needs to explain and learn about. Learning occurs incrementally as the reasoner's questions are answered through the creation and evaluation of explanations. Although the computer model is being used to explore cognitive issues such as the ones previously mentioned, there are also practical benefits of a system that can represent and reason explicitly about its own goals. Such a system can focus its limited resources on relevant aspects of its environment while paying less attention to irrelevant ones. This allows it to spend more time drawing inferences that are relevant and useful to its goals. This is important in reasoning situations in which the reasoner might draw a combinatorially large set of inferences, in learning situations in which it is impractical to focus attention on every aspect of a situation and remember every novel aspect, and in explanation situations in which it is difficult to evaluate the utility of a candidate explanation without reasoning about the goals that the explanation might support. The reasoning system needs a principled way to determine which inferences are worth drawing, which concepts are worth learning, or which explanations are worth pursuing. In order to ensure that the system does not spend its limited resources trying to infer everything it can, its knowledge goals are used to focus the inferencing, learning and explanation process on information that is useful to the goals of the system.

7.2 The Role of Questions in Explanation and Learning

The basic assumption of our theory is that asking questions is central to understanding. To illustrate what this means, consider the following story (*The New York Times*, April 14, 1985):

S-1: Boy Says Lebanese Recruited Him as Car Bomber.

> JERUSALEM, April 13—A 16-year-old Lebanese was captured by Israeli troops hours before he was supposed to get into an explosive-laden car and go on a suicide bombing mission to blow up the Israeli Army headquarters in Lebanon...What seems most striking about [Mohammed] Burro's account is that although he is a Shiite Moslem, he comes from a secular family background. He spent his free time not in prayer, he said, but riding his motorcycle and playing pinball. According to his account, he was not a fanatic who wanted to kill himself in the cause of Islam or anti-Zionism, but was recruited for the suicide mission through another means: blackmail. [p. A1]

If one wants to explain this story and learn more about the motivations of the terrorists in the Middle East, this story is interesting because it is anomalous. The usual stereotype of the Shiite religious fanatic does not hold here. Instead, this story raises many new questions. Some of the questions that were voiced by a class of graduate students when this story was read to them were:

1. Why would someone commit suicide if he was not depressed?
2. Did the kid think he was going to die?
3. Are car bombers motivated like the kamikaze?
4. Does pinball lead to terrorism?
5. Who blackmailed him?
6. With what fate worse than death did they threaten him?
7. Why are kids chosen for these missions?
8. Why do we hear about Lebanese car bombers and not about Israeli car bombers?
9. Why are they all named Mohammed?

10. How did the Israelis know where to make the raids?
11. How do Lebanese teenagers compare with American teenagers?

Some of these questions seem reasonable, (e.g., "Did the kid think he was going to die?"), but some are rather silly in retrospect (e.g., "Does pinball lead to terrorism?"). Some, although perfectly reasonable, are not central to the story but relate to other issues that a given student was reminded of, was wondering about, or was interested in (e.g., "Why do we hear about Lebanese car bombers and not about Israeli car bombers?").

The claim is that an understander has questions already extant in memory before it begins to read a story. These questions are left over from the understander's previous experiences. As the understander reads the story, it remembers these questions and thinks about them again in a new light. This raises further questions for the understander to think about. Many of these questions seek explanations, which are knowledge structures that allow the understander to answer its questions based on a causal understanding of the situation (e.g., "Kids are chosen because they are more gullible."). Explanations, in turn, can give rise to further questions (e.g., "Are Lebanese teenagers more gullible than American teenagers?").

Ultimately, the understander is left with several new questions that it may or may not have asked before. Certainly, after reading the blackmail story, one expects to have several questions representing issues one was wondering about that were not resolved by the story. For example, in this story it turns out that the boy was blackmailed into going on the bombing mission by a terrorist group that was threatening his parents. This makes one think about the question "What are family relations like in Lebanon?" This question remains in memory after reading the story. To the extent that one is interested in this question, one will read stories about the social life in Lebanon, and one will relate other stories to this one. To cite another example, one of the students in the class repeatedly related the story to his readings on the IRA, because he was interested in similar issues about Ireland.

Understanding is a process of relating what one reads to the questions that one already has. These questions represent the knowledge goals of the understander, that is, the things that the understander wants to learn (Dehn, 1989; Hunter, 1990; Leake & Ram, 1993; Ram, 1989, 1991, 1993; Ram & Hunter, 1992; Schank

& Ram, 1988). The purpose of building explanations is to find answers to these questions and, thus, to arrive at a more complete understanding of the issues one is interested in. However, while doing this, many new questions are often raised. These questions are stored in memory and, in turn, guide the understanding of future stories and affect the interpretations that are drawn. This process is shown in Fig. 7.1.

In contrast to the traditional view of understanding as a "story in, representation out" process, we view understanding as a "questions + story in, answered questions + new questions out" process. A theory of story understanding, therefore, must include a theory of memory, explanation, and learning in addition to a theory of parsing.

Although this type of reasoning may not be conscious, explanation and learning are motivated by a reasoner's goals and interests. When the reasoner encounters difficulties during understanding, planning, or any other task, it remembers the nature of these difficulties and learns in order to perform its tasks better in the future. The knowledge goals of the reasoner, which arise from these very difficulties, are used to focus the reasoning and learning process. Our model is very different from other approaches that rely on properties of the domain to determine what needs to be learned because it relies on the goals of the reasoner. For example, one might propose a rule, similar to that discussed by DeJong (1983), that the understander generalize a new schema whenever it reads a story in which a preservation goal (P-GOAL) is violated in a novel manner. But this should be so only if noticing violations of this P-GOAL is actually useful to the program. Any such rule must make a statement about the goals of the program, not just about the content of the domain. A similar argument can be made for the use of knowledge goals, or questions, to focus inference generation for understanding, explanation, or diagnosis (Ram, 1990b, 1991, 1993; Ram & Cox, 1993; Ram & Hunter, 1992; Ram & Leake, 1991). A goal-based model of explanation and learning is a plausible account of human behavior, and also has computational advantages for the design of learning programs.

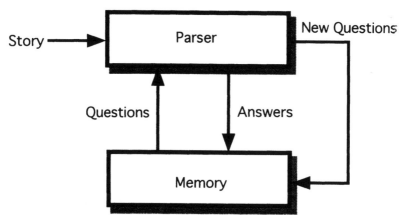

FIG. 7.1: Question-driven understanding.

Our theory of questions is based on a theory of understanding tasks. In addition to parser-level tasks such as noun group connection, pronoun reference, and so on, these tasks include higher-level tasks such as the integration of facts with what the understander already knows, the detection of anomalies in the text that identify deficiencies in the understander's model of the domain, the formulation of explanations to resolve those anomalies, the confirmation and refutation of potential explanations, and the learning of new explanations for use in understanding future situations. These are the basic tasks that an understander needs to be able to perform.

In order to carry out these tasks, the understander needs to integrate the text, which is often ambiguous, elliptic, and vague, with its world knowledge, which is often incomplete. In formulating an explanation, for example, the understander may need to know more about the situation than is explicitly stated. However, it is impossible to anticipate when a particular piece of knowledge will be available to the understander because the real world (in the case of a story-understanding program, the story) will not always provide exactly that piece of knowledge at exactly the time that the understander requires it. Thus, the understander must be able to suspend questions in memory and to reactivate them just when the information needed becomes available. In other words, the understander must be able to remember what knowledge is needed and why.

Furthermore, the system's understanding of any real world domain can never be quite complete. Conventional script-, frame-, or schema-based theories assume that understanding means finding an appropriate script, frame, or schema in memory and fitting it to the story. Schemas in memory are assumed to be "correct" in the sense that they are completely understood and constitute a correct model of the domain. If an applicable schema is found, an instance of the schema is created and applied to the story. The story is then assumed to be "understood." However, this model is inadequate because an understander's memory is always incomplete, especially in poorly understood domains. Some knowledge structures may be missing; others may have gaps in them. These gaps correspond to what the understander has not yet understood about the domain. Even if a schema appears to be correct, novel experiences or stories may reveal flaws in the schema or a mismatch with the real world. Furthermore, the schema may not be indexed correctly in memory.

Understanding tasks, therefore, generate information subgoals or questions, which represent what the understander needs to know to perform the current task, be it explanation, learning, or any other cognitive task. These questions constitute the specific knowledge goals of the understander. Learning is a process of seeking answers to these questions in the input, which in turn raises new questions while answering old ones.

For example, in order to understand the blackmail story S-1, the system must understand the motivations of the would-be suicide bomber (an explanation task). In other words, it must formulate the question "Why would the boy have done the suicide bombing?" The desired explanation for the suicide bomber's actions constitutes an answer to this question. The explanation task gives rise to further questions and subquestions: "Did the boy think he was going to die?", "Was the boy a religious fanatic?" Ultimately, the system finds an answer to a question in the input story, which enables it to complete its explanation task.

7.2.1 Types of Questions

A functional theory of questions must be based on a taxonomy of types of knowledge goals that arise from the underlying understanding tasks that the questions serve. To develop a taxonomy of these knowledge goals, we asked several subjects to voice the questions that occurred to them as stories were read out to them. We then analyzed those questions and grouped them according to the understanding task (e.g., hypothesis verification) that they were relevant to. The groupings were revised based on a functional analysis of the knowledge required for the subtasks in the computational theory of story understanding and explanation, the subtasks, in turn, being mutually refined based on our analysis of the question data.

It is interesting to note that, although our main taxonomic criteria were functional, the taxonomy fits the data well. Thus, we hypothesize that the theory, although intended as a computational model of an active reader, is also a plausible cognitive model. This is supported by the fact that the model is consistent with psychological data on question asking (e.g., Graesser, Person, & Huber, 1992; Scardamalia and Bereiter, 1991). The goal-based approach is also consistent with psychological data on goal orientation in learning (e.g., Barsalou, 1991; Ng & Bereiter, 1991; Wisniewski & Medin, 1991; see also Leake & Ram, 1993) and in focus of attention and inferencing (e.g., review by Zukier, 1986).

We propose the following taxonomy of knowledge goals for story understanding:

Text goals: Knowledge goals of a text analysis program, arising from text-level tasks. These are the questions that arise from basic syntactic and semantic analysis that needs to be done on the input text, such as noun group attachment or pronoun reference. An example text goal is to find the referent of a pronoun.

Memory goals: Knowledge goals of a dynamic memory program, arising from memory-level tasks. A dynamic memory must be able to notice similarities, match incoming concepts to stereotypes in memory, form generalizations, and so on. An example memory goal might be to look for an event predicted by stored knowledge of a stereotyped action, such as asking what the ransom will be when one hears about a kidnapping.

Explanation goals: Goals of an explainer that arise from explanation-level tasks, including the detection and resolution of anomalies, and the building of motivational and causal explanations for the events in the story in order to understand why the characters acted as they did or why certain events did or did not occur. An example explanation goal might be to figure out the motivation of a suicide truck bomber mentioned in a story.

Relevance goals: Goals of any intelligent system in the real world, concerning the identification of aspects of the current situation that are "interesting" or relevant to its general goals. An example is looking for the name of an airline in a hijacking story if the understander were contemplating traveling by air soon.

Each question focuses on a different aspect of a story. For example, explanation questions focus on different types of anomalies and on explanations for these anomalies. Asking an anomaly detection question is essential to detecting the corresponding anomaly. For example, asking the question "Does the actor want the outcome of this action?" is essential to the detection of a goal violation anomaly, in the sense that the program will not notice the anomaly if it does not focus on the goals of the agent, that is, if it does not think of asking the question.

To put this another way, the questions asked by the understander influence its final understanding. Thus, it is important for the understander to ask the "right" questions in order to achieve a detailed understanding of the situation. For the purpose of understanding stories involving motivations of people, we have developed a taxonomy of motivational questions that focus on those motivational aspects of stories that are needed to understand such stories.

In addition to their theoretical role in the model of story understanding, knowledge goals have also played an implementational role in the research by providing a uniform mechanism for the integration of various cognitive processes. For example, knowledge goals arising from, say, memory tasks are indexed in memory and used in the same way as knowledge goals arising from explanation tasks. A knowledge goal generated from one task may be suspended and satisfied opportunistically during the pursuit of some other task at a later stage or even during the processing of a different story. Implementational details of AQUA's opportunistic memory architecture may be found in Ram (1989). In the remainder of this chapter, we focus on questions arising from explanation goals, which are the basis for AQUA's explanation construction, verification, and learning methods.

7.3 AQUA's Explanation Patterns

When a new story or situation is processed, it is understood in terms of knowledge structures already in memory. As long as these structures provide expectations that allow the reasoner to function effectively in the new situation, there is no problem. However, if these expectations fail, the reasoner is faced with an anomaly. The world is different from its expectations. In order to learn from this experience and to continue processing the story, the reasoner must be able to explain what it does not understand. To do this, it needs to know why it had those expectations in the first place. It also needs to explain why the failure occurred, that is, to identify the knowledge structures that gave rise to the faulty expectations, and to understand why its domain model was violated in this situation. Finally, it must update its knowledge structures and store the new experience in memory for future use. Explanation is a central aspect of this process of understanding and learning.

The construction of explanations is also known as abduction, or inference to the best explanation. In AQUA, this is carried out through a case-based reasoning process in which previous explanation structures, represented as explanation patterns, are retrieved and applied to the anomaly at hand. This allows AQUA to understand the situation as well as to understand its own failure to model the situation correctly.

Explanation patterns (XPs) in AQUA have four components:

- *PRE-XP-NODES*: Nodes that represent what is known before the XP is applied. One of these nodes, the EXPLAINS node, represents the particular action being explained.
- *XP-ASSERTED-NODES*: Nodes asserted by the XP as the explanation for the EXPLAINS node. These comprise the premises of the explanation.
- *INTERNAL-XP-NODES*: Internal nodes asserted by the XP in order to link the XP-ASSERTED-NODES to the EXPLAINS node.
- *LINKS*: Causal links asserted by the XP. These taken together with the INTERNAL-XP-NODES are also called the internals of the XP.

An explanation pattern is a directed, acyclic graph of conceptual nodes connected with causal LINKS, which in turn could invoke further XPs at the next level of detail. The PRE-XP-NODES are the sink nodes (consequences) of the graph, and the XP-ASSERTED-NODES are the source nodes (antecedents or premises). The difference between XP-ASSERTED-NODES and INTERNAL-XP-NODES is that the former are merely asserted by the XP without further explanation, whereas the latter have causal antecedents within the XP itself. An XP applies when the EXPLAINS node matches the concept being explained and the PRE-XP-NODES are in the current set of beliefs. The resulting hypothesis is confirmed when all the XP-ASSERTED-NODES are verified.

Ultimately, the graph structure underlying an XP bottoms out in primitive inference rules of the type used by MARGIE (Rieger, 1975) or PAM (Wilensky, 1978). Schank (1986) describes XPs as the "scripts" of the explanation domain. Unlike scripts, however, XPs are flexible in the sense that their internal structure allows them to be useful in novel situations, while retaining the advantages of prestored structures in stereotypical situations. Access to an XP's causal internals is essential to the incremental question-based learning process in AQUA.

7.4 Explanation Types

Explanations can be divided into two broad categories, physical and volitional:

7.4.1 *Physical Explanations*

Physical explanations link events with the states that result from them and further events that they enable, using causal chains similar to those of Rieger (1975) and Schank and Abelson (1977). Physical explanations answer questions about the physical causality of the domain. For example, if the system had never read a story about a car bombing before, it might encounter an anomaly: "How can a car be used to blow up a building?" The answer to this question is a physical explanation:

1. A car is a physical object.
2. A car can contain explosives.
3. A car can be propelled by driving it.
4. Explosives can be blown up by the sudden impact of a car colliding with a building.
5. A building can be blown up by blowing up explosives in its immediate vicinity.

Thus, the explanation is that the bomber drove an explosive–laden car into the building, the impact caused the explosives to detonate, which caused the building to blow up.

7.4.2 *Volitional Explanations*

The particular content of the causal knowledge represented in explanation patterns depends, of course, on the domain of interest. AQUA deals with volitional explanations, which link actions that people perform to their goals and beliefs, yielding an understanding of the motivations of the characters. For example, consider the following story:

S-2: Suicide bomber strikes Israeli post in Lebanon.

SIDON, Lebanon, November 26—A teenage girl exploded a car bomb at a joint post of Israeli troops and pro-Israeli militiamen in southern Lebanon today, killing herself and causing a number of casualties, Lebanese security sources said...A statement by the pro-Syrian Arab Baath Part named the bomber as Hamida Mustafa al-Taher, born in Syria in 1968. The statement said she had detonated a car rigged with 660 points of explosives in a military base for 50 South Lebanon Army men and Israeli intelligence and their vehicles.

In the suicide bombing story S-2, the understander needs to explain why the girl performed an action that led to her own death. An explanation for this anomaly, such as the religious fanatic explanation, must provide a motivational analysis of the reasons for committing suicide.

AQUA has two broad categories of explanatory knowledge:

1. *Abstract explanation schemas* for why people do things. These are standard high-level explanations for actions, such as "Actor does action because the outcome of action satisfies a goal of the actor."
2. *Explanatory cases.* These are specific explanations for particular situations, such as "Shiite Moslem religious fanatic goes on suicide bombing mission."

For example, an explanation of Type 1 for Story S-2 might be "Because she wanted to destroy the Israeli base more than she wanted to stay alive." An explanation of Type 2 would be simply "Because she was a religious fanatic." The internal causal structure of the latter explanation could then be elaborated to provide a detailed motivational analysis in terms of explanations of the first type, if necessary.

Both types of explanatory knowledge are represented using volitional XPs with the internal structure discussed earlier. Volitional XPs relate the actions in which the characters in a story are involved to the outcomes that those actions had for them; the goals, beliefs, emotional states and social states of the characters as well as priorities or orderings among the goals; and the decision process that the characters go through in considering their goals, goal-orderings, and likely outcomes of the actions before deciding whether to perform those actions. A volitional explanation involving the planning decisions of a character is called a decision model (Ram, 1990a). The decision model has the following components:

The outcome of an action: Every action results in some set of states that may or may not be beneficial to the people involved in that action, depending on their goals at that time. The outcome of an action, therefore, must be modeled from the point of view of a particular volitional agent involved in that action (see also Carbonell 1979). The most common volitional participants are actor and planner, but any role involving a volitional agent must potentially be explained.

The decision process: Every agent involved in an action makes a decision about whether to participate in that particular volitional role (actor, planner, object, etc.) in the action. Such decisions represent the planning process that the agent underwent prior to the action. A complete model of this process requires a sophisticated vocabulary of goals, goal interactions, and plans, such as that of Wilensky (1983) or Hammond (1989). There are three basic kinds of decisions:

1. *Choice*: The agent chooses to participate or not to participate in a given volitional role in some action. The explanation must describe why the agent made this choice.
2. *Agency*: The agent is induced to participate, or not to participate, in a given volitional role in an action. This is similar to the previous case in that the agent "enters" the action of his or her own volition. The difference is that here the agent is acting under the agency of another agent. Thus, the reasoner must be able to model inter-agent interactions (Domeshek, 1992; Ram, 1984; Schank & Abelson, 1977; Wilensky, 1983).
3. *Coercion*: The agent is forced to participate, or not to participate, in a given volitional role in an action. This case arises when an agent is physically coerced into participation or non-participation.

Considerations in decisions: The system also needs to reason about what an agent was considering as the agent made a particular decision. Considerations model the goals and beliefs of an agent, along with orderings among these goals and expected outcome of the action being considered. Considerations are composed of three constituents: (1) goals considered by the agent while deciding whether or not to participate in an action, (2) goal-orderings, the agent's prioritization of these goals, and (3) the expected-out-come: the agent's beliefs about what the outcome of the action is likely to be. If the actual outcomes do not match with the agent's expectations and goals, the system can use these representations to reason about the failure of the agent's plans (see also Domeshek, 1992; Jones, 1992; Owens,1990).

Figure 7.2 depicts one of AQUA's volitional XPs, the religious fanatic explanation pattern. This pattern explains why an agent might perform a terrorist act that resulted in the agent's own death, as well as the destruction of something that belonged to an opposing religious group.

An explicit representation of the planning and decision-mak-ing process of the characters in the story allows AQUA to explain their actions in terms of their goals and beliefs. Each of these con-stituents may itself need to be explained further. For example, the system might question the social or mental (e.g., emotional) states that initiated a particular goal or goal-ordering in an agent, or how a particular belief about the outcome of an action came about. Explanations, therefore, may need to be elaborated according to the demands of the story and the goals of the system.

7.5 A Question-Based Model of Explanation

We now turn to the process implications of the model for the tasks of text interpretation and explanation in the context of story understanding and learning, and discuss the implementation of the model in the AQUA program. Methodologically, we used AQUA as a testbed for exploring issues of interpretation, learn-ing, explanation, and interestingness in an integrated framework.

AQUA's basic goal in reading is to answer its questions and to improve its understanding of the domain (terrorism). AQUA's output consists of answers to old questions about the domain plus, of course, new questions. AQUA is driven by its questions or knowledge goals. It is a dynamic program, and it reads similar stories differently and forms different interpretations as its ques-tions and interests evolve. AQUA would reread a story differ-ently from the way it first read the story because the questions and explanations generated during the first reading affect the questions raised on the second reading. Further details of the question-driven understanding process may be found in Ram (1989, 1991).

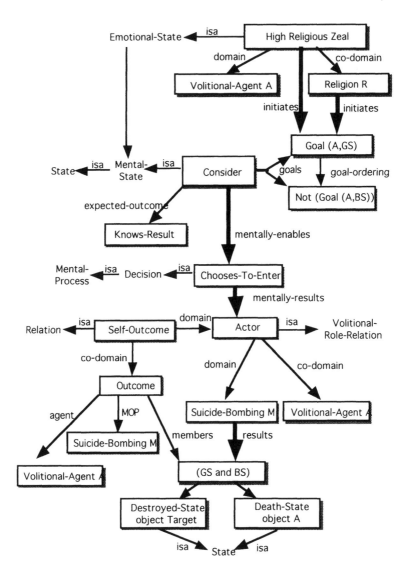

FIG. 7.2. Representation of XP-RELIGIOUS-FANATIC. A is the agent, R the agent's religion, M the action the agent chooses to do, and GS and BS the good and bad outcomes of that action.

Because questions represent the knowledge goals of the understander, they also provide the focus for learning. In addition to asking questions, therefore, AQUA can learn from answers to these questions. AQUA improves its explanatory knowledge of its domain by incremental refinement of this knowledge, using answers to questions that arise from the explanation process (Ram, 1993). AQUA retrieves past explanations from situations already represented in memory and uses them to build explanations to understand novel stories about terrorism. In doing so, the system refines its understanding of the domain by filling in gaps in these explanations, by elaborating the explanations, by learning new indices for the explanations, or by specializing abstract explanations to form new explanations for specific situations. This is a type of incremental learning because the system improves its explanatory knowledge of the domain in an incremental fashion rather than by learning complete new explanations from scratch.

The basic process of goal-based understanding involves the generation of knowledge goals seeking information required by various understanding tasks, the transformation of these knowledge goals into subgoals, and the matching of pending knowledge goals to information in the story. One might think of this as a process of question transformation, in which a reasoner generates questions that then trigger a parsing process, which can, in turn, generate more questions.

Each of AQUA's knowledge goals type is expressed as a question that focuses on a different aspect of the story. For example, explanation questions focus on different types of anomalies, and on explanations for these anomalies. Asking an anomaly detection question is essential to detecting the corresponding anomaly. Similarly, asking a hypothesis verification question is essential to verifying a proposed explanation for an anomaly, and to the learning that results. For the purpose of understanding stories involving motivations of people, we have developed a taxonomy of motivational questions that focus on those motivational aspects of stories that are needed to build volitional explanations based on the planning/decision model discussed earlier. This taxonomy is part of a larger taxonomy of questions based on the understanding tasks that AQUA needs to perform when it reads a story. Let us consider the explanation-related tasks in more detail.

7.6 The AQUA Processing Cycle

The performance task in AQUA is to "understand" human interest stories, that is, to construct explanations of the actions observed in the story that causally relate the actions to the goals, plans and beliefs of the actors and planners of the actions. Such an explanation is called a volitional explanation, and the process of constructing these explanations is called motivational analysis. In general, an explanation consists of several inference rules connected together into a graph structure with several antecedents and one or more consequents, as discussed earlier. Construction of such explanations is typically done by chaining together inference rules through a search process (e.g., Morris & O'Rorke, 1990; Rieger, 1975; Wilensky, 1981), through a weighted or cost-based search (e.g., Hobbs et al., 1990; Stickel, 1990), or through a case-based reasoning process in which previous explanations for similar situations are retrieved and adapted for the current situation (e.g., Kass et al. 1986; Ram, 1989, 1990a; Schank, 1986). The latter method, which is the basis for AQUA's approach to motivational analysis, is similar to the use of explanation schemas to build explanations (e.g., Mooney and DeJong, 1985) because it relies on the instantiation of "large" knowledge structures (cases or schemas) rather than the chaining together of "small" knowledge structures (inference rules). Rather than defend the case-based reasoning approach here, we will simply state the assumptions implicit in this approach (Ram, 1993):

Efficiency assumption: It is more efficient to retrieve and apply larger knowledge structures (here, XPs) than to construct them from scratch each time out of smaller knowledge structures or inference rules.

Content assumption: There are too many possible ways in which inference rules can be connected together, many of which will be irrelevant or meaningless. The content of the explanations produced through case-based reasoning is likely to be better than those produced through exhaustive search through inference rules, because cases (here, XPs) contain experiential knowledge about the ways in which the rules are actually connected together in real situations.

Typicality assumption: Situations encountered in the real world are typical of the kinds of situations that are likely to be encountered in the future because the world is reasonably stable and regular. Thus, it is worthwhile creating a new case (here, XP) to represent novel experiences because remembering this case will make it easier to process similar situations in the future.

The processing cycle in AQUA has three interacting steps: *Read, Explain,* and *Learn.* The interaction between these steps is managed through a question-based agenda system, in which tasks are *suspend*ed if there is insufficient information to run them, and *restart*ed when the questions seeking the missing information are answered:

- *Read* the story.
  Leaving aside the natural language aspects of the task, this is equivalent to processing a sequence of input facts representing the individual events in the story.
- *Explain* each action in the story.
  Build hypothesis trees representing possible explanations for the motivations of the actor, planner, and any other volitional agents involved in the action.
- *Suspend* the explanation task until one of the hypotheses in a hypothesis tree is confirmed.
- *Restart* the suspended task when this happens.
  Confirm or refute associated hypotheses, as appropriate.
- *Learn* when a hypothesis is confirmed.

7.6.1 The READ Step
In the *Read* step, AQUA reads a piece of text, guided by the questions in memory. It tries to answer these questions using the new piece of information.

Read some text, focusing attention on interesting input as determined later. Build minimal representations in memory.

Retrieve extant knowledge goals or questions indexed in memory that might be relevant, that is, whose concept specifications are satisfied by the new input. Use these questions as an interestingness measure to focus the aforementioned read.

Answer the questions retrieved in the previous step. Unify the answer with each question, and restart the suspended process represented by the task specification. That is, if the question is in service of hypothesis verification:

Answer question by either confirming or refuting it.

Propagate back to the hypothesis that the question originated from.

Confirm/refute hypotheses. If the verification questions of a hypothesis are confirmed, confirm the hypothesis and

refute its competitors. If any verification question of a
hypothesis is refuted, refute the corresponding hypothesis.

Explain the new input if necessary, i.e., if interesting and not already explained.

7.6.2 The EXPLAIN Step

The *Explain* step implements the basic explanation cycle in
AQUA. The outline of this step is as follows. Further details of
the explanation process are discussed in the next section.

Detect anomalies in input by asking anomaly detection questions

Formulate XP retrieval questions

Retrieve XPs that might help explain the anomaly

Apply XP to input:

If in applying the XP an anomaly is detected, characterize
the anomaly and explain it recursively.

If the XP is applicable to the input:

Construct hypothesis by instantiating the XP.

Construct verification questions to help verify or refute the
new hypothesis.

Index questions in memory to allow them to be found in
the next step.

Answer questions by reading further, focusing attention on input
concepts that trigger questions in memory.

Confirm/refute hypotheses when their verification questions are
answered, as appropriate.

7.6.3 The LEARN Step

Because questions represent the knowledge goals of the understander, they provide the focus for learning. AQUA can:

Generalize novel answers to its questions.

Index these answers in memory, so that the task that originally
generated the question would now find the information instead of failing.

As currently implemented, AQUA's memory consists of about 700
concepts represented as frames, including about 20 abstract XPs,
10 stereotypical XPs, 50 MOPs (most of which deal with the
kinds of actions encountered in suicide bombing stories), 250 relations (including causal and volitional relations), and 20 interestingness heuristics (most of which are represented procedurally).

The range of stories that AQUA can handle is limited only by the XPs in memory. We have focused mostly on the domain of newspaper stories about suicide bombing, such as stories about religious fanatics, depressed teenagers, kamikazes, and so on, although it would be straightforward to extend the program to other domains. This chapter focuses mainly on the Explain step, and on the corresponding knowledge goals for the task of learning from explanations and explanation failures.

7.7 A Closer Look at the EXPLAIN Step

The *Explain* step in the aforementioned understanding cycle implements the case-based explanation algorithm summarized below:

Input: R, a volitional-role-relation (actor, planner) between an action or MOP M and a volitional-agent A. By definition, A appears in the R slot of M.

Output: H, a hypothesis tree.

Algorithm:

- Invoke anomaly detection algorithm to determine whether R is anomalous.
- If so, create a root node for T and place the anomaly a at the root.
- Identify the set of anomaly category indices $\{I_a\}$ based on the anomaly a.
- Determine the set of situation indices $\{I_S\}$ by retrieving abstractions of M.
- Determine the set of character stereotype indices $\{I_C\}$ by matching A to known stereotypes.
- For each $\{I_a, J_S, I_C\}$ combination, retrieve any XP that is indexed by this combination (explanation pattern retrieval). This provides a set of potentially applicable explanation patterns $\{XP\}$.
- For each XP in this set $\{XP\}$, match the EXPLAINS node of XP to R. Retain the set of explanation patterns $\{XP\}$ for which this match succeeds.
- For each XP in this new set $\{XP\}$, create hypotheses H as follows (explanation pattern application):
  - instantiate XP
  - unify EXPLAINS node of XP with R
  - instantiate INTERNAL-XP-NODES and LINKS of XP

- instantiate pending questions attached to XP, if any
- create a new node in T to represent the hypothesis H and attach it as a child of the root node representing the anomaly a
- For each H in the set of hypotheses, verify H as follows (hypothesis verification):
  - instantiate the XP-ASSERTED-NODES n of the XP that was instantiated to form H
  - create a hypothesis verification question HVQ from each n that is not already known to be true in the story
  - create a new node in T for each HVQ of H and attach it as a child of the node representing H
  - invoke hypothesis evaluation algorithm to determine current best hypothesis
- When all the HVQs of any hypothesis H are verified (question answering), verify the hypothesis H and refute its competitors. Note that questions may be answered later while processing this or other stories.

The input to the algorithm is a volitional-role-relation, which is defined as a relation between an action or MOP (the domain of the relation) and a volitional-agent (the codomain of the relation). The relation represents the fact that the agent is the actor or planner of an action (the two types of facts that require motivational analysis). The output is a hypothesis tree, a structure that represents the multiple possible explanations for the relation. The algorithm has four basic parts: anomaly detection, XP retrieval, XP application, and hypothesis verification. Let us examine these parts in more detail.

7.7.1 Anomaly Detection

Anomaly detection refers to the process of identifying an unusual fact or situation description that needs explanation. The fact may be unusual, in the sense that it violates or contradicts some piece of information in memory. Alternatively, the fact may be unusual because, whereas there is no explicit contradiction, the reasoner fails to integrate the fact satisfactorily in its memory. Anomaly detection in AQUA is done through a series of anomaly detection questions based on the goals, goal-orderings, plans, beliefs, and decisions represented in AQUA's decision models (Ram, 1991; see also Leake, 1989). For example, the question "Did the actor want the outcome of his action?" allows AQUA to notice a goal-violation anomaly in which an agent performs an action that violates the agent's own goals. AQUA's taxonomy of anomaly detection questions is discussed later.

Each type of anomaly is associated with abstract explanation schemas that form the anomaly category indices for the XPs representing specific explanatory cases. For example, the anomaly GOAL-VIOLATION is associated with the abstract XPs XP-NOT-KNOW-OUTCOME and XP-GOAL-SACRIFICE. This is used in the XP retrieval step discussed later.

In addition to the reasoning about the actor of an action, AQUA also considers the planner's reasons for planning that action, if the actor and the planner are different. This involves building a similar decision model from the planner's point of view. AQUA builds separate explanations for the actor and planner of every event if they are different. If the actor and planner are the same person, group, or institution, the default explanation for the planner is simply that the planner planned the action because the planner wanted to carry it out successfully.

7.7.2 Explanation Pattern Retrieval

When faced with an anomalous situation, AQUA tries to retrieve one or more previously known explanatory cases or, if no cases are available, abstract explanation schemas that would explain the situation. An applicable XP is one whose PRE-XP-NODES can be unified with the current situation, with the EXPLAINS node being unified with the particular action being explained. Because it is computationally infeasible to match the PRE-XP-NODES of every XP with every action being explained, AQUA uses a set of indices as a heuristic to identify potentially relevant explanatory cases. Learning the right indices for an XP is therefore an important component of AQUA's learning process.

In general, XPs are indexed by stereotypical descriptions of their EXPLAINS nodes, and a description of the anomaly to be explained. For example, in order to explain an action performed by a volitional agent, AQUA uses three types of indices to retrieve potentially relevant XPs: (a) the anomaly category index, which identifies classes of XPs relevant to the given anomaly, (b) the situation index, which identifies XPs relevant to a particular situation (action or MOP), and (c) the character stereotype index, which identifies XPs relevant to a particular stereotype that the agent can be viewed as. XP retrieval is done through the generation of XP retrieval questions, which are described in more detail later.

7.7.3 Explanation Pattern Application

Once a set of potentially applicable XPs is retrieved, AQUA tries to use them to resolve the anomaly. This involves instantiating the INTERNAL-XP-NODES and LINKS of each XP, and filling in the details through elaboration and specification. The PRE-XP-NODES of the XP are merged with corresponding nodes in the story representation. The instantiated XP is called an explanatory hypothesis, or simply hypothesis. If there are gaps in the XP, represented as pending questions attached to the XP, the questions are instantiated and the story representation is checked to see if the questions can be answered.

7.7.4 Hypothesis Verification

The final step in the explanation process is the confirmation or refutation of possible explanations, or, if there is more than one hypothesis, discrimination between the alternatives. A hypothesis is a causal graph that connects the premises of the explanation to the conclusions via a set of intermediate assertions. The premises of the explanation are the XP-ASSERTED-NODES of the XP. XP-ASSERTED-NODES that assert facts that are not already known to be true in the story are turned into hypothesis verification questions (HVQs) for the hypothesis. If all the HVQs are confirmed, the hypothesis is confirmed (and its competitors refuted). If any HVQ is disconfirmed, the hypothesis is refuted.

The reasoner may use other methods for evaluating candidate hypotheses as well. Ram and Leake (1991) discuss several explanation evaluation methods, including those used by AQUA. As with the other steps in the explanation cycle, explanation evaluation is also implemented as a question-based process. At the end of this step, the reasoner is left with one or more alternative hypotheses. Partially confirmed hypotheses are maintained in a data dependency network called a hypothesis tree, along with questions representing what is required to verify these hypotheses.

7.7.5 Questions and Explanation

From the point of view of questions, the process model for the task of explanation can be formulated as follows:

Anomaly detection
- Ask anomaly detection questions based on the goals, goal-orderings, plans, beliefs, and decisions represented in decision models.

XP retrieval

- Ask XP retrieval questions based on the indices used by AQUA and attempt to match the current situation to the PRE-XP-NODES of an available XP.
- Retrieve specific XPs based on XP retrieval questions.
- Apply specific XPs or abstract XPs, if no specific XPs are found.

XP application
- Ask XP applicability questions based on the INTERNAL-XP-NODES and LINKS of the XP. Suspend XP application if necessary.
- At this point, the XP may be tweaked, as in the SWALE program (Kass et al., 1986).
- Instantiate nodes of the XP.
- Instantiate links of the XP.

Hypothesis verification
- Ask hypothesis verification questions (HVQs) based on the XP-ASSERTED-NODES of the XP.
- Suspend hypothesis verification, if necessary.
- Confirm/refute hypotheses later when HVQs are answered and select the best hypothesis based on hypothesis evaluation criteria.

7.8 A Taxonomy of Explanation Questions

The process model for question-driven explanation provides a functional basis for a taxonomy of questions that arise from the task of explanation. We now discuss the taxonomy of explanation questions in greater detail. This taxonomy is based on the explanation tasks that AQUA needs to perform when it reads a story. The categories will be illustrated using program transcripts showing examples of questions asked by AQUA as it reads a car bombing story.

7.8.1 Anomaly Detection Questions

Anomaly detection refers to the process of identifying an unusual fact that needs explanation. Anomalies fall into two categories:

1. *Physical anomalies*: Anomalies arising from reasoning about the physical causality behind the observed events. E.g., if this is the first suicide bombing story one has read, one might think about the question "How can a car be used as a bomb?"

2. *Volitional anomalies*: Anomalies arising from reasoning about
   why the characters in the story acted as they did. E.g.,
   "Why would someone commit suicide if they were not depressed?"

Questions that help the understander in this task are called
anomaly detection questions. These questions focus the understander on a particular aspect of the situation that might be
anomalous. Once an anomaly is detected, the understander uses
the anomaly characterization to retrieve potential explanations to
resolve the anomaly. Thus, the questions involved in the rest of
the explanation process can be thought of as anomaly resolution
questions.

Because the domain of AQUA focuses on human-interest stories, the program deals mainly with volitional anomalies.
Volitional anomalies can be categorized into two broad types:

1. *Contradictory knowledge:* Explicit contradiction of input or inferred information with knowledge or stereotypical information in memory. For example, the anomaly "Why do they
   choose kids for bombing missions?" arises if one expects
   that the terrorists would recruit well-trained military men for
   these difficult missions. (Note: AQUA uses a simple tem-
   plate-based natural language generator to describe concepts
   in memory. In the following transcripts, the generator output
   has been cleaned up to some extent for the sake of readability. Because AQUA actually uses the representation of
   questions in memory, not their printed output, the actual
   form of the output is not relevant to the operation of the
   program.)

  S-3: Terrorists recruit boy as car bomber.

```
Trying to explain
WHY DID THE TERRORIST GROUP RECRUIT THE BOY TO DO
     THE CAR BOMBING?

Anomaly! THE BOY is not a typical MILITARY AGENT.
```

2. *Missing knowledge:* Lack of explanatory knowledge in memory. These anomalies arise, not out of explicit contradictions, but out of the lack of some information that was expected to be present in memory. In other words, these
   anomalies arise out of the noticing of gaps in memory. For

example, the anomaly "Why would a person who was not a fanatic go on a suicide bombing mission?" arises when the understander realizes that its standard religious fanatic explanation is inapplicable, and it has no further explanations that apply to this situation. Similarly, in the following example, AQUA detects an anomaly for a novel action for which it has no explanations in memory:

S-4: *The terrorist group surrendered to the Israeli police.*

```
Trying to explain WHY DID THE TERRORIST GROUP
SURRENDER TO THE ISRAELI POLICE

Anomaly! THE SURRENDER violates THE GOAL OF THE
TERRORIST GROUP TO PRESERVE THE INDEPENDENCE OF THE
TERRORIST GROUP.

Characterized outcome as a BAD outcome for the ACTOR

Searching for stereotypical XPs

Anomaly! No XPs for why THE TERRORIST GROUP
SURRENDERED TO THE ISRAELI POLICE.
```

The first anomaly in this transcript arises from a contradiction, whereas the second one arises when AQUA encounters a gap in its memory. If AQUA did have an applicable XP to start with, or is able to fill this gap by learning a new XP that explains why terrorists surrender, the XP would be retrieved and applied to the story. This action would then be "explained" (and therefore not be anomalous) by virtue of the fact that it has been fitted into an XP that the program has.

Volitional anomalies are detected by asking a series of anomaly detection questions about the input. These questions arise by questioning different parts of the planning/decision models discussed earlier. For example, the understander could question the goals of the agent, or the agent's beliefs about the expected outcome of the action, or the agent's volition in choosing to perform the action. Each of these questions uncovers a different type of anomaly and proposes a different type of explanation for the anomaly. For example, questioning the goals of the agent allows the understander to detect goal violation anomalies, in which the agent performs an action that violates the agent's own goals.

In order to notice anomalies and build explanations based on the planning/decision model of volition, AQUA's questions must be generated from this model. This is done by walking over the representation of abstract XPs and questioning the applicability conditions of these XPs. For example, the abstract XP "Actor chooses to perform an action with a negative outcome because he did not know that the action would result in this outcome" relies on the beliefs of the actor about the outcome of the action. This is represented as one of the PRE-XP-NODES of the XP. This node gives rise to the question: Did the actor know that the action would have this negative outcome?

Before asking this question, however, AQUA must determine whether the outcomes of the action are indeed negative from the point of view of the actor. Thus, the XP "Actor chooses to perform an action because he wants the outcome of the action" must be tried first. This XP gives rise to the question: Does the actor want the outcome of the action? This question must be asked before the question about the actor's beliefs.

In principle, the understander could order its XPs at run-time by checking their applicability conditions to see which ones presuppose the others. Because AQUA does not learn new abstract XPs, abstract XPs are statically organized into a hierarchy that determines the order in which they will be checked. AQUA does learn new stereotypical XPs, which are specific versions of abstract XPs for particular situations; however, this does not require modification of the hierarchy of abstract XPs because new stereotypical XPs are indexed using existing abstract XPs as the category index. AQUA traverses down this hierarchy, generating questions based on the PRE-XP-NODES of each XP. These questions, therefore, can be viewed as comprising a discrimination net of volitional questions, in which each question raises further questions if its answer seems anomalous .

For example, if answered negatively, the question "Does the actor want the outcome of the action?", would signal an anomaly and raise further questions, such as "Did the actor know the outcome of the action?" and "Is there another result of this action, perhaps currently unknown, which the actor desired even at the expense of the outcome that he didn't want?" These questions are indexed in memory and used to determine the interesting aspects of the story. The above questions represent the fact that AQUA is interested in the beliefs of the boy, as well as further results of the suicide bombing mission. When these questions are answered later in the story, the corresponding explanation is reactivated, causing AQUA to focus on the inferences relevant to its questions. The theory of question-driven understanding, therefore, provides a principled method for determining interestingness and focusing attention.

Anomaly detection questions can be categorized as follows:

Decision questions: These questions focus on the decision that the actor took when he decided to do the action. Therefore, this is also a taxonomy of the planning decisions one would consider when deciding to do an action.

Personal goals:
- Does the actor want the outcome of this action?
- Does the actor want to avoid a negative outcome of not doing this action?
- Does the actor want a positive outcome of this action more than he wants to avoid a negative outcome of doing the same action?
- Does the actor enjoy doing this action?
- Does the actor habitually do this action?

Instrumentality:
- Is this action instrumental to another action that the actor wants to carry out?
- Is this action part of a larger plan that the actor is carrying out?

Interpersonal goals:
- Does the actor want a positive outcome of this action for someone he likes?
- Does the actor want to avoid a negative outcome of this action for someone he likes?
- Does the actor want a negative outcome of this action for someone he dislikes?
- Does the actor want a positive outcome of this action for a group that he belongs to?
- Does the actor want to avoid a negative outcome of this action for a group that he belongs to?

- Does the actor feel gratification in doing good for others?

Social control:
- Did someone with social control over the actor ask him to perform the action?
- Did someone with social control over the actor force him to perform that action?

Knowledge and beliefs:
- Did the actor know the probable outcomes of the action?
- Did the actor believe that the action would have a positive outcome for him?
- Did the actor know about the possible negative outcome of the action?

Interference questions: These questions focus on possible interference from external sources.
- Did someone want to block the actor's goal?
- Did someone want to prevent this state of the world? Would this state of the world violate this person's goals?
- Did someone want the actor to be involved in this action?
- Did the actor accidentally get involved in this action?

For example, consider the story S-4 again. These are the questions that lead to the anomaly being detected in this story:

S-4: The terrorist group surrendered to the Israeli police.

```
Trying to explain WHY DID THE TERRORIST GROUP
SURRENDER TO THE ISRAELI POLICE?

Did THE TERRORIST GROUP want the outcome of THE
SURRENDER?

Characterizing the outcome CAPTURED-STATE
        of THE SURRENDER
    from the point of view of THE TERRORIST GROUP (the
ACTOR)

DOES THE TERRORIST GROUP WANT TO ACHIEVE THE CAPTURED
STATE OF THE TERRORIST GROUP
```

```
Anomaly! THE SURRENDER violates THE GOAL OF THE
TERRORIST GROUP TO PRESERVE THE INDEPENDENCE OF THE
TERRORIST GROUP.

Characterized outcome as a BAD outcome for the ACTOR
```

In the foregoing output, only the questions that led to the anomaly are shown. To take a more complete example, consider the following abbreviated version of story S-1:

S-5: Terrorists recruit boy as car bomber.

A 16-year-old Lebanese got into an explosive-laden car and went on a suicide bombing mission to blow up the Israeli army headquarters in Lebanon...The teenager was a Shiite Moslem but not a religious fanatic. He was recruited for the mission through another means: blackmail.

When AQUA reads this story, it asks the following anomaly detection questions, which focus on the personal goals in the actor's decision model:

```
Trying to explain WHY DID THE TEENAGE LEBANESE BOY DO
     THE SUICIDE BOMBING?

Was THE SUICIDE BOMBING instrumental to another ac-
tion?

Does THE TEENAGE LEBANESE BOY typically do SUICIDE
BOMBINGs?

Did THE TEENAGE LEBANESE BOY want the outcome of THE
SUICIDE BOMBING?

Characterizing the outcomes DEATH-STATE and DESTROYED-
STATE of THE SUICIDE BOMBING from the point of view of
THE TEENAGE LEBANESE BOY (the ACTOR)

DOES THE TEENAGE LEBANESE BOY WANT TO ACHIEVE THE
DEATH OF THE TEENAGE LEBANESE BOY?

Anomaly! The SUICIDE BOMBING violates THE GOAL OF THE
BOY TO PRESERVE THE LIFE STATE OF THE BOY.

DOES THE TEENAGE LEBANESE BOY WANT TO ACHIEVE THE
DESTRUCTION OF ISRAELI ARMY HEADQUARTERS IN LEBANON?
```

```
No relevant GOALS found

Did THE TEENAGE LEBANESE BOY want to avoid a negative
outcome of not doing THE SUICIDE BOMBING?
No relevant OUTCOMES found
Did THE TEENAGE LEBANESE BOY enjoy doing the SUICIDE
BOMBING?
No relevant GOALS found

Did THE TEENAGE LEBANESE BOY habitually do SUICIDE
BOMBINGs?
No relevant ACTIVITIES found

Characterized outcome as a BAD outcome for the ACTOR
```

In addition to the foregoing questions, which focus on the actor's reasons for performing an action, AQUA also considers the planner's reasons for planning that action, if the actor and the planner are different. Many of the questions are similar to the previous questions. For example, AQUA would ask whether the planner wanted an outcome of the action, whether he knew the outcome of the action, etc. Thus, for the previous story, AQUA also asks the following questions:

```
Trying to explain WHY DID THE TERRORIST GROUP PLAN THE
SUICIDE BOMBING?

Did THE TERRORIST GROUP want the outcome of THE CAR
BOMBING?

Characterizing the outcomes DEATH-STATE and DAMAGED-
STATE of THE SUICIDE BOMBING from the point of view of
THE TERRORIST GROUP (the PLANNER)

DOES THE TERRORIST GROUP WANT TO ACHIEVE THE DEATH OF
THE TEENAGE LEBANESE BOY?
No relevant GOALS found

DOES THE TERRORIST GROUP WANT TO ACHIEVE THE
DESTRUCTION OF THE ISRAELI ARMY HEADQUARTERS IN
LEBANON?
Matches typical GOALS

Did THE TERRORIST GROUP typically do SUICIDE BOMBINGs?
Matches typical ACTIVITIES
```

`No anomaly detected`

In addition, AQUA also asks the following questions, which focus on the interaction between the planner and the actor:

Planner questions: Given an action that was planned and executed by different people or groups:

- Did the action result in a positive outcome for both the planner and the actor?
- Did the planner select the actor knowing that the action would result in a negative outcome for the actor?

For example, if one wonders why the planner gave the necessary resources to the actor and then realizes that one of the planner's goals was achieved by the action, one can hypothesize that a contract or exchange exists between the two.

When answered, anomaly detection questions either result in an anomaly being detected, in which case the anomaly needs to be resolved through explanation, or in no anomaly being detected, in which case an explanation has implicitly been found. For example, if the answer to "Did the action result in a positive outcome for the actor?" is yes, there is no anomaly; the explanation implicit in this question is the abstract one of "Actor does action to satisfy a goal." An explanation at this level is sufficient in many situations; a deeper explanation is required only when there is an anomaly at this level.

7.8.2 XP Retrieval Questions

When faced with an anomalous situation, AQUA tries to retrieve one or more XPs that would explain the situation. In order to do this, AQUA asks a series of XP retrieval questions about the situation. These questions are also called anomaly resolution questions, because their intent is to find explanations that help resolve anomalies. XP retrieval questions focus the understander's attention on a particular aspect of a situation, or allow it to view a situation in a particular way, with the intention of finding an explanation that might underlie it. These questions fall into two broad categories, corresponding to the taxonomy of motivational explanations:

1. *Abstract XP retrieval questions*: These questions focus the understander's attention on the goals, plans, and beliefs of the character. For example, the question "Did the boy want to kill himself?" focuses on the boy's goals with respect to this

particular outcome, the death of the boy. If the answer to this question is yes, an explanation might be that the boy actually did want to kill himself (a suicidal teenager perhaps), and suicide bombing was just a bizarre way of doing this. Another question of this type is "Did the boy know he was going to die?" This focuses on the boy's beliefs.

2. *Stereotypical XP retrieval questions*: These questions attempt to view the character as belonging to a particular stereotype. Their intent is to enable the understander to retrieve stereotypical XPs specific to the particular situation. For example, the question "Was the boy a zealous Shiite Moslem?" focuses on the religious beliefs of the boy. An affirmative answer to this question would cause AQUA to retrieve the "religious fanatic" XP, because this XP is indexed under a religious fanatic stereotype.

Although stereotypical explanations are not guaranteed to be correct, case-based explanation is based on the assumption that it is too inefficient to reason from scratch, starting from the general theory of motivations, in every situation. Stereotypical XPs provide a way to associate specific stereotypical causal rules with specific stereotypical situations and people. The features characterizing these stereotypes result in XP retrieval questions, which, in turn, allow the system to retrieve large explanation structures (XPs) directly. Applying these XPs results in explanatory hypotheses, which can then be evaluated. Thus, an XP retrieval question is a heuristic to find XPs that might be relevant without having to do the inferencing required to check if they are indeed relevant, which requires determining whether the causality underlying the situation matches that underlying the XP. If the question results in an XP being retrieved, the understander does the rest of the work to determine if the XP is indeed relevant.

XP retrieval questions at the abstract level of abstract XPs focus on the goals, goal priorities, beliefs, and decisions of the people involved, whereas those at the specific level of stereotypical XPs focus on particular stereotypes of people who are known to be associated with those kinds of actions. Thus, XP theory replaces general matching techniques for goals and plans with specific applicability conditions for stereotypical situations. The former are applicable to a greater range of situations but harder to determine; the latter are specific to particular situations but easier to match, infer, apply, and verify. This is the basic principle underlying case-based reasoning (and other methods of reasoning based on "large" knowledge structures such as scripts, frames and schemas).

The following taxonomy of XP retrieval questions provides a "content theory" of the knowledge needed to index and retrieve XPs. The taxonomy at the level of abstract XPs mirrors the taxonomy of anomaly detection questions. Because the particular XP retrieval questions at the level of stereotypical XPs depend on the stereotypes currently in memory, this category will be illustrated using examples, rather than a taxonomy.

Abstract XP retrieval questions:

Decision anomalies:

- Anomaly: *goal-violation*

   Situation: Actor does action that results in a negative outcome.

   Questions:

   - Did the actor actually want this outcome (*i.e.*, did we misperceive his goals?)
   - Did the action result in another outcome that the actor wanted even at the expense of the negative outcome?
   - Was the actor forced into doing this action?
   - Did the actor know that the action would have this negative outcome? ?
   - Did the actor have enough information about the environment?
   - Did the actor project the effects of the action correctly?

For example, because there is a goal-violation anomaly in this story, AQUA asks the following abstract XP retrieval questions:

```
Anomaly! The SUICIDE BOMBING violates THE GOAL OF THE
BOY TO PRESERVE THE LIFE STATE OF THE BOY.

Searching for abstract XPs

DID THE SUICIDE BOMBING RESULT IN A STATE?
and WAS THE GOAL OF THE BOY TO ACHIEVE THE STATE MORE
IMPORTANT THAN THE GOAL OF THE BOY TO PRESERVE THE
LIFE OF THE BOY?

No other RESULTS of THE SUICIDE BOMBING known.
Suspending explanation
```

```
DID THE BOY BELIEVE THAT THE SUICIDE BOMBING WOULD
RESULT IN THE DEATH STATE OF THE BOY?
No relevant BELIEFS found
Suspending explanation
```

These questions are indexed in memory and are used to determine the interesting aspects of the story. The questions represent the fact that AQUA is interested in the goals and beliefs of the boy, as well as further results of the suicide bombing mission. If a question is answered later in the story, the corresponding explanation is reactivated. For example, suppose that S-5 were to be continued as follows:

> S-5: ...*The boy was told that the car bombing would not cause him any harm.*

```
Answering question: DID THE BOY BELIEVE THAT THE
  SUICIDE BOMBING WOULD RESULT IN THE DEATH STATE OF
  THE BOY?
        with: THE BOY DID NOT BELIEVE THAT THE SUICIDE
BOMBING WOULD RESULT IN THE DEATH STATE OF THE BOY.

Restarting suspended explanation
   THE BOY DECIDED TO DO THE SUICIDE BOMBING DESPITE
THE VIOLATION OF THE GOAL OF THE BOY DO PRESERVE THE
LIFE STATE OF THE BOY    because THE BOY DID NOT KNOW
THAT THE SUICIDE BOMBING WOULD RESULT IN THE DEATH
STATE OF THE BOY.
```

Of course, this still does not explain why the boy did the suicide bombing, but the goal-violation anomaly is resolved. Once this explanation is confirmed, the other hypotheses are retracted.

Continuing with the taxonomy of abstract XP retrieval questions:

- Anomaly: *goal-violation* or *unusual-goal-ordering*
  Situation: Actor does action that results in a positive outcome and a negative outcome.
  Questions:
  – Does the actor prefer to achieve the positive outcome even at the expense of the negative outcome?
  – Does the actor actually want to avoid the negative outcome?

- Can the goal violated by the negative outcome be pursued later?

XPs:
- Goal priority elevation in particular contexts.
- Goal violated by negative outcome can be pursued later.
- Goal of positive outcome is temporarily urgent.
- Short term goals preferred to longer term goals.
- Personal goals preferred to group goals.
- Difficult goals postponed.
- New goals from wanting what others have.
- Actor's goal priorities were misperceived.
- Personal differences (individual, parental).
- Group differences.
- Cultural differences.

- Anomaly: *bad-plan-choice*
  Situation: Actor does action to achieve a goal even though another action looks better.
  Questions:
  - Did the second action have a negative side effect for the actor?
  - Did the actor know about the second action?
  - Was the actor capable of performing the second action?
  - Is the first action better in the long run? Is the cumulative effect of the first action better? Does the first action keep more options open?
  - Does the actor enjoy doing the first action?

- Anomaly: *failed-opportunity*
  Situation: Actor doesn't do action that would have resulted in a positive outcome for actor.
  Questions:
  - Did the actor actually want this outcome (i.e., did we misperceive his goals)?
  - Did the actor know that the action would result in the positive outcome?
  - Did the action also result in a negative outcome for the actor?

  – Was the actor capable of performing that action?

- Anomaly: *unmotivated-action*
  Situation: Actor does an action that doesn't satisfy any of his goals.
  Questions:
  – Did the actor think that the action would satisfy one of his goals?
  – Does the action actually satisfy a goal (i.e., did we misperceive the situation)?

Planner anomalies:
- Anomaly: *malicious-intent*
  Situation: Planner knowingly recruits actor for action that results in negative outcome for actor.
  Questions:
  – Was the planner's real intention to achieve a negative outcome for the actor?
  – Did the planner want some other outcome of the action, but also wanted to avoid the negative outcome from happening to himself?
  – Was the planner willing to sacrifice the actor's goal to achieve a goal of his own?
  – Did the planner want both the outcomes, i.e., was he killing two birds with one stone?
  – Was the planner in turn forced to make this decision?

In the story, for example, the *actor-planner* interaction gives rise to the following questions:

```
The PLANNER, THE TERRORIST GROUP, is not the same as
the ACTOR, THE BOY

Anomaly! The PLANNER, THE TERRORIST GROUP, planned an
action with a BAD outcome for the ACTOR, THE BOY.

Searching for abstract XPs
DID THE TERRORIST GROUP WANT TO ACHIEVE THE DEATH
STATE OF THE BOY?

DID THE TERRORIST GROUP WANT TO DESTROY THE ISRAELI
ARMY HEADQUARTERS?
```

and DID THE TERRORIST GROUP WANT TO AVOID THE DEATH
STATE OF THE TERRORIST GROUP?

WAS THE GOAL OF THE TERRORIST GROUP TO DESTROY THE
ISRAELI ARMY HEADQUARTERS MORE IMPORTANT THAN THE GOAL
OF THE TERRORIST GROUP TO PRESERVE THE LIFE STATE OF
THE BOY?

If any of these questions are answered, the corresponding XP is retrieved and applied to the story. If the explanation can be confirmed, the anomaly is resolved.

    Stereotypical XP retrieval questions:
- XP: Religious fanatic does suicide bombing.
  Questions:
  - Was the actor religious?
  - (If in the Middle East) Was the actor a Shiite Moslem?

- XP: Depressed teenager commits suicide.
  Questions:
  - Was the actor a stereotypical teenager?
  - Was the actor depressed?

In the current example, S-5, AQUA finds the boy's suicide bombing action anomalous. It tries to retrieve XPs to explain this action
and finds the religious fanatic XP indexed under the LEBANESE-
PERSON stereotype and the suicide-bombing MOP:

```
Searching for stereotypical XPs

Asking EQ: IS THE BOY A TYPICAL TEENAGER?
Asking EQ: WHY WOULD A TEENAGER DO A SUICIDE BOMBING?

   Situation index = SUICIDE-BOMBING
   Stereotype index = TEENAGER

No XPs found

Asking EQ: IS THE BOY A TYPICAL LEBANESE PERSON?
Asking EQ: WHY WOULD A LEBANESE PERSON DO A SUICIDE
BOMBING?

   Situation index = SUICIDE-BOMBING
   Stereotype index = LEBANESE-PERSON
```

```
Retrieved stereotypical XPs:
   XP-RELIGIOUS-FANATIC (category index = XP-
SACRIFICE)
```

AQUA also tries to retrieve abstract XPs to explain the anomaly. For example, because the anomaly is one in which the actor performs an action with a negative outcome for himself, AQUA asks the abstract XP retrieval questions that were described earlier. Abstract XPs are used only if no specific stereotypical XPs can be found. For example, consider the question:

```
IS THE GOAL OF THE TEENAGE LEBANESE BOY TO ACHIEVE THE
DESTRUCTION OF THE ISRAELI ARMY HEADQUARTERS IN
LEBANON MORE IMPORTANT THAN THE GOAL OF THE TEENAGE
LEBANESE BOY TO PRESERVE THE LIFE OF THE TEENAGE
LEBANESE BOY?
Not known
```

This question, when answered, would lead to xp-sacrifice, but because a stereotypical XP of this type has already been found (XP-RELIGIOUS-FANATIC), the abstract XP is not used to explain this anomaly.

7.8.3 XP Application Questions

Once a set of potentially applicable XPs is retrieved, the understander tries to use them to resolve the anomaly. This involves instantiating the XP, filling in the details through elaboration and specification, and checking the validity of the final explanation. Questions that help the understander elaborate explanations, or collect more information about the input, to help it construct a coherent understanding of the input are called XP elaboration questions and data collection questions, respectively.

When an XP is retrieved, it is instantiated to form a hypothesis. If this process raises any XP application questions, the explanation is suspended until answers to these questions become known. To illustrate this, consider the application of xp-religious-fanatic, retrieved in the previous step, to the current story. These questions correspond to the actual definition of xp-religious-fanatic shown earlier.

```
Applying XP-RELIGIOUS-FANATIC to WHY DID THE BOY DO
THE SUICIDE BOMBING.
```

```
THE BOY DID THE SUICIDE BOMBING
because THE BOY WAS A RELIGIOUS FANATIC.

Unifying EXPLAINS node

Installing NODES

Installing LINKS

    THE BOY IS A RELIGIOUS FANATIC because THE BOY IS A
SHIITE MOSLEM

    THE BOY WANTS TO ACHIEVE THE DESTRUCTION OF THE
ISRAELI ARMY   HEADQUARTERS
    because THE BOY IS A RELIGIOUS FANATIC

    THE GOAL OF THE BOY TO ACHIEVE THE DESTRUCTION OF
THE ISRAELI ARMY   HEADQUARTERS IS MORE IMPORTANT THAN
GOAL TO PRESERVE THE LIFE STATE OF THE BOY because THE
BOY IS A RELIGIOUS FANATIC

THE BOY DECIDED TO DO THE SUICIDE BOMBING because XP-
SACRIFICE
```

In this case, there are no XP application questions since the religious fanatic XP is applicable to the situation. However, the resulting hypothesis still needs to be verified.

7.8.4 Hypothesis Verification Questions

The final step in the explanation process is the confirmation or refutation of possible explanations, or, if there is more than one hypothesis, discrimination between the alternatives. Hypothesis verification questions (HVQs) are questions that arise from this task. For example, although there is no real difficulty in applying the religious fanatic explanation in story S-5, the explanation rests on certain assumptions. To verify the hypothesis, AQUA asks what the religion of the boy was, and whether he believed fanatically in that religion. When it reads that "the boy was a Shiite Moslem but not a religious fanatic," it answers these questions and refutes the hypothesis.

To generate the HVQs for a hypothesis, AQUA checks each of the XP-ASSERTED-NODES of the hypothesis. In the xp-religious-fanatic example, this raises the following hypothesis verification questions:

```
Installing HVQs to verify XP:

   WHAT IS THE RELIGION OF THE TEENAGE LEBANESE BOY?
   WHAT IS THE RELIGIOUS ZEAL OF THE TEENAGE LEBANESE
BOY?
```

This process is repeated for all the possible hypotheses. When this is done, AQUA is left with one or more alternative hypotheses, each with its own set of HVQs. This is represented using a hypothesis tree as described earlier. When new facts come in, AQUA checks to see if these facts would answer any questions in memory. If an HVQ is answered, AQUA reexamines the hypothesis to see whether it has been confirmed or refuted:

- If the HVQ is answered negatively, refute the hypothesis.
- If the HVQ is answered positively and this is the last HVQ for the hypothesis, confirm the hypothesis and refute its competitors.
- In each case, reevaluate belief in corresponding hypothesis.

Thus, when an HVQ is answered, AQUA knows what to do with the answer since the hypothesis structure represents the suspended explanation task that is waiting for the answer. In the current story, the xp-religious-fanatic hypothesis is eventually refuted when AQUA reads the sentence:

S-5: ...The teenager was a Shiite Moslem but not a religious fanatic.

```
Answering question: WHAT IS THE RELIGION OF THE BOY?
        with: THE BOY IS A SHIITE MOSLEM.

Answering question: WHAT IS THE RELIGIOUS ZEAL OF THE
BOY?
             with: THE BOY IS NOT VERY ZEALOUS ABOUT THE
SHIITE MOSLEM RELIGION.

Refuting hypothesis:
   THE BOY DID THE SUICIDE BOMBING
   because THE BOY WAS A RELIGIOUS FANATIC.
```

7.9 Evaluation Criteria

We have discussed how explanations are constructed through a case-based reasoning process, resulting in one or more abductive hypotheses. Regardless of how explanatory hypotheses are constructed, however, the evaluation of these hypotheses is a central and difficult problem. We categorize evaluation criteria into structural (or syntax-based) and utility-based (or goal-based) criteria (Ram & Leake, 1991).

7.9.1 Structural Criteria

Structural criteria use the structural or syntactic properties of the causal chain to evaluate hypotheses. A goodness measure for each hypothesis is computed based on the length of the causal chain, the number of abductive assumptions, or other such structural properties.

Most structural criteria appeal to Occam's razor by requiring minimality of hypotheses. Simply stated, a hypothesis that is "minimal" with respect to some criterion is preferred over one that is not (e.g., Charniak,1986; Kautz & Allen,1986). For example, Konolige (1990) argues that "closure + minimization implies abduction." To take another example, the TACITUS system for natural language interpretation merges redundancies as a way of getting a minimal interpretation, which is assumed to be a best interpretation (Hobbs et al., 1990). Minimality criteria include:

- *Length*: Causal chains with the shortest overall length are preferred.
- *Abductive assumptions*: Explanations requiring the fewest abductive assumptions are preferred.
- *Subsumption*: If two candidate hypotheses are found and one subsumes the other, the more general hypothesis is preferred.

Another approach focuses on the structural relationship of propositions in an explanation, rather than minimality:
- *Explanatory coherence*: The cohesion of an explanation is measured, based on the form of connections between an explanation's propositions, and the "best connected" explanation is favored (e.g., Ng & Mooney,1990; Thagard 1989).

Although structural criteria provide an easy way to evaluate the goodness of a hypothesis, they may not be sufficient to identify the best explanation in real situations. The shortest explanation, for example, may or may not provide enough information to understand how the details of a given story fit together. In general, explanations are not constructed in a vacuum; there is a real-world task that the reasoner is performing that requires the reasoner to seek an explanation in the first place. The reasoner may also need an explanation to help it with a piece of reasoning that it is trying of perform. Both these types to motivations for explanation influence evaluation criteria.

7.9.2 Utility-Based Criteria

A reasoner's motivation for explaining will often place additional requirements on candidate explanations, beyond their form. For example, explanations prompted by anomalies must provide particular information, in order to resolve the anomaly. For example, suppose that we expected team X to win over team Y because of the talent of X's star player, but we are told that team X actually lost. If someone explained the loss by "Y scored more points than X," the explanation would be inadequate. Although it is a correct explanation, it gives no information about why our expectation went wrong. The explanation "X's star was injured and couldn't play" does account for what was neglected in prior reasoning, and, consequently, is a better explanation. However, this explanation would not be preferred on structural grounds alone. The causal chain underlying that explanation is more complex, so it would not be favored by minimality criteria. Likewise, the explainer of the game has access to only one observation, the fact that team X lost, so coherence metrics that measure how an explanation relates pairs of observations, such as those described by Ng and Mooney (1990), give no grounds for preferring the second explanation.

To state our relevance criterion another way, an explanation must address the failure of the reasoner to model the situation correctly. In addition to resolving the incorrect predictions, it must also point to the erroneous aspect of the chain of reasoning that led to those predictions. An explanation is useful if it allows the reasoner to learn, or to accomplish current tasks. The claim here is that an explanation must be both causal and relevant in order to be useful.

An explanation of an anomaly, therefore, must answer two types of questions:

1. *Why did things occur as they did in the world?* This question focuses on understanding, and learning about, the causal structure of the domain.
2. *Why did I fail to predict this correctly?* This question focuses on understanding, and improving, the organization of the reasoner's own model of the domain.

The answer to the first question is called a *domain explanation* because it is a statement about the causality of the domain. The answer to the second question is called an *introspective* or *meta-explanation* because it is a statement about the reasoning processes of the system.

Each of the foregoing questions relates to a need to collect or organize the missing information that caused the anomaly, and that utility-based evaluation criteria must address. Let us consider the second question first.

7.9.3 Introspective Explanations

One of the questions an explanation must address is why the reasoner failed to make the correct prediction in a particular situation. In an XP-based system, this could happen in three ways:

1. *Novel situation*: The reasoner did not have the XPs to deal with the situation.
2. *Incorrect world model*: The XPs that the reasoner applied to the situation were incomplete or incorrect.
3. *Misindexed domain knowledge*: The reasoner did have the XPs to deal with the situation, but it was unable to retrieve them because they were not indexed under the cues that the situation provided.

When an explanation is built, the reasoner needs to be able to identify the kind of processing error that occurred and invoke the appropriate learning strategy to prevent recurrence of the error. For example, if an incomplete XP is applied to a situation, the knowledge activated by the resulting processing error must represent both the knowledge that is missing, and the fact that this piece of knowledge, when it comes in, should be used to fill in the gap in the original XP. Similarly, if an error arose due to a misindexed XP, the explanation, when available, should be used to reindex the XP appropriately. The learning algorithms used in AQUA are discussed in more detail in Ram (1993).

In general, a reasoner can encounter other kinds of difficulties as well (e.g., see Ram & Cox, 1993). Knowledge goals can be categorized by the types of gap or inadequacy in the reasoner's knowledge, by the types of failures or difficulties during processing, or by the types of learning that result. A hypothesis is evaluated from the point of view of knowledge organization goals by checking to see if it provides the information necessary for the type of learning that the reasoner is trying to perform. For example, suppose the reasoner reads a newspaper story about a Lebanese teenager who, it turns out, is blackmailed into going on a suicide bombing mission. Even if the reasoner already knows about terrorism, religious fanatics, and blackmail, the story may nevertheless be anomalous if the reasoner has never seen this particular scenario before. The difficulty arises from the fact that blackmail is not ordinarily something that comes to mind when one reads about suicide bombing. Here, the reasoner can learn a new connection between the knowledge structures describing suicide bombing and blackmail, respectively. In order to do this, the explanation must provide the information required to identify the conditions under which a suicide bombing is likely to be caused through blackmail.

This type of analysis is essential in determining whether an explanation is sufficient for the purposes of the reasoning task at hand. In this example, the reasoning task is to satisfy a knowledge organization goal, which is a question that represents a goal to learn by reorganizing existing knowledge in memory.

7.9.4 Domain Explanations

Another kind of knowledge goal is a knowledge acquisition goal, which is a question that seeks to acquire new causal knowledge about the domain. Such a question is answered using a domain explanation, which is a causal chain that demonstrates why the anomalous proposition might hold by introducing a set of premises that causally lead up to that proposition. If the reasoner believes or can verify the premises of an explanation, the conclusion is said to be explained. Explanations are often verbalized using their premises or abductive assumptions. However, the real explanation includes the premises, the causal chain, and any intermediate assertions that are part of the causal chain.

In order to be useful, a hypothesis must provide the information that is being sought by the knowledge acquisition goals of the reasoner. For example, if the reasoner has a goal to acquire knowledge about the biochemical properties of a particular virus, a description of a sick patient must provide the biochemical information in order to qualify as an explanation from the point of view of that goal. An alternative hypothesis that provides causal information suggesting how some drug might destroy the virus, although useful from the point of view of curing the patient, may not provide the required information.

AQUA uses the following criteria to evaluate hypotheses. Although AQUA uses a case-based approach using explanation patterns to construct explanations, the criteria listed here are also applicable to other kinds of explanation construction methods which rely on domain knowledge in the form of inference rules, cases, schemas, or other types of knowledge structures.

1. *Believability*: Do I believe the domain knowledge from which the hypothesis was derived? This is an issue for any learning program in a realistic domain for which a correct domain theory is not yet known.

2. *Applicability*: How well does the domain knowledge (the particular rules, cases or schemas) apply to this situation? Did it fit the situation without any modifications?

3. *Relevance*: Does the hypothesis address the underlying anomaly? Does it address the knowledge goals of the reasoner? In AQUA, the hypothesis is evaluated in the context of both knowledge acquisition and knowledge organization goals.

4. *Verification*: How definitely was the hypothesis confirmed or refuted in the current situation? Does the hypothesis spawn new knowledge goals (requiring further information to help verify the hypothesis)?

5. *Specificity*: Is the hypothesis abstract and very general, or is it detailed and specific? This is a structural criterion in the sense that it is based on the structure, and not the content, of the hypothesis. However, the structure of the hypothesis is evaluated in the context of the organization of causal memory.

Intuitively, a "good" explanation is not necessarily one that can be proven to be "true" (criterion 4), but also one that seems plausible (1 and 2), fits the situation well (2 and 5), and is relevant to the goals of the reasoner (criterion 3).

AQUA is a dynamic story-understanding program that is driven by its questions or goals to acquire knowledge. Rather than being "canned," the program is always changing as its questions change; it reads similar stories differently and forms different interpretations as its questions and interests evolve. AQUA judges the interestingness of the input with respect to its knowledge goals (Ram, 1990b), and learns about the domain by answering its questions (Ram, 1993). Both these processes are goal-based. Here, we are proposing that the evaluation of explanations be goal-based (or question-based) as well.

7.10 Using Questions to Guide Explanation

Questions in AQUA's memory represent gaps in AQUA's model of the domain. These questions serve as *knowledge goals*, the system's goals to acquire, reorganize, or reformulate knowledge in order to learn more about the domain. Some questions arise from unconfirmed hypotheses that the system is entertaining, or has entertained in a previous story. Other questions arise from other kinds of gaps in the system's knowledge or other kinds of difficulties during processing. Questions play a central role in reasoning and learning. In this chapter, we focus on the role of questions in explanation; other aspects of our theory of questions and knowledge goals are discussed in Ram (1989, 1991, 1993), Ram and Cox (1993), and Ram and Hunter (1992).

A program that uses its questions to guide explanation is an improvement over one that processes everything in equal detail, that is, one that is completely data-driven. For example, an understander that is completely text-driven would process everything in detail in the hope that it might turn out to be relevant. To avoid this, the understander should draw only those inferences that would help it find out what it needs to know. In other words, the understander should use its knowledge goals to focus its attention on the interesting aspects of the story, where "interesting" can be defined as "relating to something the understander wants to find out about."

It is useful to focus on questions because they arise from a "need to learn." There are two basic ways in which a fact can turn out to be worth processing in this sense:

> *Top-down*: A fact that helps achieve a knowledge goal or answers a pending question is worth focusing on because it allows the reasoning system to continue the reasoning task that required the knowledge in the first place.

> *Bottom-up*: A fact that gives rise to new knowledge goals or raises new questions is worth focusing on if the knowledge goals arise from a gap or inconsistency in the reasoning system's knowledge base, because the system may be able to improve its knowledge base by learning something new about the world.

The real issue here, of course, is how much inference should be done at the time the questions are generated, and how much should be done when the input comes in. The answer depends on six factors:

1. *Certainty of inference*: The probability of the inference rules used to find or infer answers to questions, or the likelihood that the conclusions will be true. In a logic system wherein an inference rule represents a deduction, this probability is 1.
2. *Cost of inference*: The cost of making inferences or of matching and applying inference rules. The cheaper the inference, the more it is worth the system's while to make it.
3. *Usefulness of question*: The usefulness of the conclusion that the question is seeking. Because questions are generated in service of reasoning tasks, this is the same as the importance of performing that task. If the task is very important, it is worth making the inference even if it is very expensive to do so.
4. *Likelihood of question being useful*: The likelihood that the question will be useful (i.e., the likelihood that the knowledge will actually turn out to be useful in performing the reasoning task). If questions are only generated from tasks that absolutely require that knowledge (as opposed to those that may be facilitated by that knowledge, if it were present), this likelihood is 1.
5. *Indexing cost*: The cost of keeping indexed questions in memory and matching to them. If there are too many questions in memory, it might be too expensive to find them or to match input to potentially relevant questions. This cost depends on the scheme used to maintain questions in memory, and is discussed later.
6. *Likelihood of question being satisfied*: These factors are "content-free" heuristics, in the sense that the reasoning system does not rely on knowledge of the content or types of questions that it is likely to generate, or on the content or types of inferences that the system is likely to make when given new input. In addition, one would like the system to generate the types of questions or knowledge goals that are likely to match the inferences normally made by the bottom-up processing that is always performed on incoming facts. The last criterion for inference control, therefore, is the likelihood of a question being satisfied, which depends on knowledge about the inferences that are likely to be made by the system's own inference processes.

These heuristics are not represented formally in the AQUA program. In other words, there are no explicit functions to compute each of these metrics and to make a decision based on them. However, the heuristics to determine the utility or interestingness of questions, and to index questions in memory, have been designed with these metrics in mind so that the process is efficient. More research is required to develop a theory of inference control based on heuristics that can be used by the reasoning system itself (as opposed to by the programmer) in making inference control decisions. The main concern in AQUA has been the formulation and indexing of questions, and their use in focusing AQUA's explanation, understanding, and learning processes.

7.10.1 Mechanisms for Question Management
Maintaining a collection of explicit knowledge goals, represented in AQUA as questions, introduces new issues into the design of AI programs. The goals themselves must be organized, applied, and disposed of when no longer useful. These management tasks were addressed by the following general mechanisms which were required in AQUA:

- *Question retrieval*: finding suspended questions that a new piece of knowledge might satisfy.
- *Question indexing*: storing questions in memory so that they are found only when they are relevant.
- *Process scheduling*: restarting suspended tasks that depend on questions when the questions are answered.
- *Hypothesis management*: deleting alternative questions and hypotheses when a question is answered, because their likelihood of being useful decreases if an alternative has been found.

7.10.2 Representation of Questions
Question representations have two parts:

1. *Concept specification*: the object of the question, i.e., the desired information. This is represented using a memory structure that specifies what would be minimally acceptable as an answer to the question. In general, a question may seek to acquire new knowledge or to reorganize or elaborate existing knowledge. A new piece of knowledge is an answer to a question if it matches the concept specification completely.

The answer could specify more than the question required, of course.

2. *Task specification*: what to do with the information once it comes in, which depends on why the question was generated. This may be represented either as a procedure to be run, or as a declarative specification of the suspended task. When the question is answered, because the program either pursued it actively, or opportunistically while it was processing something else, the suspended process that depends on that information is restarted.

In a sense, a question is similar to an open "slot" in a memory structure. AQUA's initial processing could be viewed as being similar to that of typical "script-based" understanders: Words in the input text are used to instantiate memory structures, and open slots in these memory structures are used as predictions for the rest of the story. However, there are three main differences (expressed here in a "slot-filling" terminology for comparison):

1. Typically, all open slots in newly instantiated structures are used as "requests" or "predictions" and cause the understander to look for fillers for those slots. AQUA, however, uses its interestingness heuristics to mark interesting slots to be used as predictions or questions. In addition, slots can be marked as being interesting by understanding tasks when their values are needed but not yet known.

2. Open slots arise not only from script like knowledge structures, but also from causal or explanatory structures.

3. Typically, the ultimate task of the understander is to fill in as many of these open slots as possible. However, the action of filling in a slot does not do anything more than provide a value for that slot. In AQUA, however, slots are not filled for their own sake, but rather for the sake of performing some kind of reasoning with that value (e.g., confirming a hypothesis), which may go beyond simple fact-gathering.

Thus AQUA subscribes to the basic slot-filling idea but extends this idea by selecting which slots are worth filling, by using different kinds of knowledge structures to provide slots, and by remembering why particular slots need to be filled so that it can use the filled values when they become known. The uniform representation of questions generated and used by different types of reasoning and learning processes allows us to design an integrated system in an easy and natural manner.

When a question is posed, AQUA searches its memory for a knowledge structure that matches the concept specification of the question. If one is found, the question is immediately answered; if not, the question is indexed in memory and the task is suspended until an answer is found. An answer to a question is a node that matches the concept specification of the question and provides all the information required by the concept specification. The answer node may be created to represent new information provided by the story, or internally generated through inference during other processing. When a question is answered, the answer node is merged with the concept specification, and the task associated with it is run.

7.10.3 Indexing Questions

Where should a question be placed in memory? Since a potential answer to a question may arrive at any time, particularly when the question may not even be "active," the question must be indexed in memory exactly where the answer would be placed when it does come in. This ensures that the question will be found without extensive searching through lists of questions. The issue of the amount of inference that should be done at this point was addressed earlier.

In AQUA, questions are indexed in memory on the basis of their concept specifications. For the task of story understanding, these questions are used to generate expectations that guide the system when the concepts to which they are attached are active.

7.10.4 Retrieving Questions

When a new fact becomes known, either because it is part of the input (e.g., it is read in the story), or because it is inferred for some other reason, the reasoner needs to retrieve questions in memory to which the fact could be relevant. The questions retrieved, in turn, determine how useful that fact is. AQUA's question retrieval strategies take advantage of the fact that questions are indexed on the basis of their concept specifications in an inheritance hierarchy. AQUA uses three question retrieval strategies:

> *Type retrieval:* When a new memory structure is activated, questions indexed off the types of the concept are retrieved. The new structure is matched against the concept specification of the question to see whether it provides the desired information. For example, if AQUA reads about a car, it retrieves

questions off the *car* concept to see if the car it read about could answer any of these questions.

Relation retrieval: AQUA uses a frame-based representational scheme in which slots and slot fillers specify relations between concepts. For example, the results slot specifies a causal relation of a particular kind between an action and a state. Similarly, the actor slot in an action frame specifies a participatory relation between the action and a volitional-agent. Relations are themselves represented as frames in memory (e.g., see Wilensky, 1986), allowing AQUA to reason about the relations themselves. Questions seeking relations between concepts are indexed in the appropriate slots in the frames representing these concepts. This allows AQUA to retrieve questions that seek relations between memory structures (e.g., the connection between a given terrorist attack and the destruction of some building).

Specialization retrieval: Finally, questions may be retrieved, given an input cue, by checking whether some specialization or refinement of that input might address questions. This allows the understanding process to be sensitive to the questions to which the system is currently seeking answers. Implementational details may be found in Ram (1989).

7.10.5 Question-Driven Learning

As argued by Hammond (1989) and others, a theory of case-based reasoning must include a theory of learning as well. Traditional case-based learning programs learn new cases by relying on existing cases that are "well understood," to guide them through novel experiences. AQUA extends this idea by not requiring that existing cases be well understood. When a story is understood, for example, AQUA may be left with several unanswered questions that are part of its representation of the story. Much of the learning in AQUA occurs through the answering of previous questions, which leads to the elaboration, modification, or reindexing of existing knowledge structures (in AQUA's case, XPs) to which these questions are attached. Details of the learning methods in AQUA may be found in Ram (1993). As AQUA reads, it asks better and more detailed questions about input stories, formulates knowledge goals to answer these questions, and learns when its knowledge goals are satisfied (perhaps in a later story). This results in a gradual improvement in AQUA's explanatory knowledge and, hence, in its ability to explain. Figure 7.3 shows an example of the question transformation process.

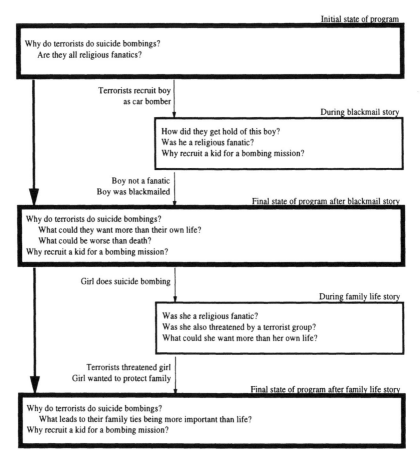

FIG. 7.3. Question-driven understanding is a process of asking questions and trying to answer them by reading a story. AQUA starts out with a set of questions. As it reads, some of these questions are answered and new questions are raised. After reading the story, AQUA is left with a set of new questions that are the starting point for reading future stories. Here, AQUA has read two stories, one about a boy being blackmailed into going on a suicide bombing mission in which no further details are given, and another about a girl being "persuaded" to commit a suicidal terrorist attack by a terrorist group who threatened her family.

7.11 Conclusions

The underlying theme of this research is a focus on the learning goals of the reasoner. In particular, we are developing a theory of knowledge goals, that represent the goals of a reasoner to learn by acquiring new knowledge or reorganizing existing knowledge by learning new indexing structures (Ram, 1991, 1993) or, in general, by reformulating its knowledge in other ways (Leake & Ram, 1993; Ram & Cox, 1993). Knowledge goals arise from gaps in the reasoner's knowledge that are identified when the reasoner encounters difficulties during processing. Because knowledge goals are often voiced out loud in the form of questions, we have used questions as a device to model goal–driven explanation, understanding, and learning processes.

This chapter focuses on the process of question-driven explanation, and on the questions that arise from, and support, the processes involved in explanation. In general, there are several types of knowledge goals that might arise out of difficulties during processing, and different types of learning that correspond to these knowledge goals. We are developing learning algorithms that deal with different types of processing failures, and investigating the extent to which these learning algorithms can be integrated into a single multistrategy learning system. We are currently implementing the Meta-AQUA system (Ram & Cox, 1993), an extension of AQUA that can use multiple explanation strategies to build explanations while reading a story and multiple learning algorithms to learn from the different types of problems and questions that arise during this process.

8. Tweaker: Adapting Old Explanations to New Situations

Alex Kass
The Institute for the Learning Sciences
Northwestern University

Editors' Introduction

This chapter, adapted from Kass' dissertation (Kass 1990b), addresses the third major question related to the SWALE program; it describes how an explanation-building program can make use of a retrieved XP that is a close, but not perfect match to the current problem. Kass addresses this question by describing a module that adapts the old explanation, producing a new variation that better fits the current problem.

The core of Kass' adaptation theory is a set of adaptation strategies that his program uses to build the variations. The process of adapting an XP comes down to selecting among the possible strategies, and then running the strategies collected. Although the strategy-selection problem is important and is given some attention in Kass' dissertation, it is less interesting and less important than the descriptions of the strategies themselves. Thus, we ignore the selection issues altogether in this chapter and concentrate on describing how the adaptation strategies work.

* * *

8.1 What Adaptation Strategies Need to Know

A good way to understand the approach to adaptation adopted by SWALE's tweaker is to compare its adaptation strategies to those employed by other systems. The idea of adapting an old explanation to fit a new situation is an application of the more general idea that underlies all case-based reasoning, which is to store solutions to problems in memory and then adapt them to new problems, rather than try to solve the new problems from scratch. Some of the issues relating to adapting explanations are specific to the explanation problem, but many of the important issues are general adaptation issues, that are also encountered in the context of other sorts of problems, such as planning and design. Therefore, it is worth comparing SWALE's explanation tweaker to a variety of adaptation systems, not just to the few that relate directly to the problem of adapting explanations.

When describing any theory of adaptation, whether it is a theory of adapting plans of action, designs, explanations, or any other knowledge structures, the most important question to answer is: What type of knowledge, and how much of it, should be built into the adaptation procedures? There is a spectrum of possibilities here, and there are important trade-offs involved with moving toward either end of the spectrum. At the extremes, the choice is between either a large number (hundreds, say) of very specific, domain-dependent adaptation strategies, or a very small number (four or five, perhaps) of very general, completely domain-independent strategies. Positions very near these extremes have been explored by earlier research. SWALE's adaptation strategies are best understood in light of the strengths and the weaknesses of these previous approaches to the adaptation problem.

8.1.1 Very General Adaptation Rules Are Too Weak

The most elegant option, at least superficially, is to have as few strategies as possible. A prominent example of the "neat" approach is Carbonell's (1983, 1986) work on what he calls the *transformational analogy* and *derivational analogy* approaches to problem solving.[1] His system attempts to solve new problems by adapting the solutions to old problems via a set of very general rewrite rules. A few typical rules, which Carbonell calls *T operators*, follow:

---

[1]The rules were originally described as part of the transformational analogy work. Derivational analogy is a more sophisticated form of the theory, but the transformation rules used are not the part that is more sophisticated.

- *Parameter substitution:* Substitute an object in the new problem specification for a corresponding object in the original problem sequence.

- *General insertion:* Add an operator to the solution sequence.

- *General deletion:* Remove an operator from the solution sequence.

Within the realm of adapting explanations, Phylis Koton's (1988) work on CASEY is also positioned rather far toward the general end of the spectrum. CASEY is a medical diagnosis system that attempts to build diagnoses of a new patient by finding similar cases in memory and adapting the associated diagnoses to fit the data pertaining to the new patient. CASEY's adaptation rules are of the following sort:

- *Add evidence:* Adds a piece of evidence to the causal explanation and links it to those states for which it is evidence.
- *Add measure:* Adds an abnormal feature to the explanation that CASEY cannot link causally.
- *Remove evidence:* Removes a feature that appears in the original explanation but does not apply to the current patient.

CASEY's rules are a good illustration of the kinds of trade-offs involved in designing adaptation strategies. As you can see, CASEY's rules are general in the sense that they incorporate no special, heart-disease knowledge. Thus, one might reasonably hope that applying CASEY to a new domain would involve little or nothing in the way of new adaptation strategies—a very desirable feature for a system to have. But the problem with CASEY's adaptation rules is how far they are from being operational. The adaptation rules are more on the order of what questions to ask then they are strategies for finding answers to those questions. Even as questions they are quite general. Equipping a system with adaptation rules that say things such as, "If the explanation doesn't contain enough evidence to support a particular conclusion, then find more evidence" is like telling someone who cannot afford to buy the expensive house he or she wants to remedy the situation by getting more money. The advice is valid and is applicable in a broad range of situations, but it isn't easy to put into practice. Figuring out that more money would solve the problem is the easy part; it's figuring out how to do that which is tricky. Of course, systems that employ very general strategies of this sort do know how to operationalize those strategies, but the method for doing so, which is really responsible for much of the work, is often outside the scope of the theory. The method for making the general heuristic operational is generally not nearly as elegant as the heuristics themselves. Furthermore, the method of operationalizing the strategies may change in a rather drastic manner from domain to domain, which undercuts the claim that it is easy to move the system from domain to domain.

8.1.2 Very Specific Rules Are Too Domain-Dependent

Systems that address the problem by shifting to a much larger, domain-dependent set of strategies have equally troublesome drawbacks. Such systems are a bit harder to find in the literature; researchers who use domain-dependent rules usually do not focus on that fact. However, Goel and Chandrasekeran (Goel & Chandra, 1989) report on a system that seems to have rules of the following form:

- *Cascading cooling-device rule:* If a cooling device does not cool sufficiently, try cascading multiple copies of the device.

The analog of such rules for an explanation-building system working with the sorts of explanations we have been talking about in this thesis—a domain-specific rule for adapting explanations—might look like the following:

- *A domain-specific rule for adapting explanations:* If an explanation doesn't specify an agent of an aircraft sabotage, and the aircraft is American, then assume that the agent is an Iranian terrorist.

These rules are directly operational; nothing further must be specified in order to implement them in specific cases. In fact, these rules specify all the domain knowledge needed to alter the explanation. No reference to the system's long-term memory is needed in order to carry out these adaptations. On the other hand, whereas building a lot of specific domain knowledge into each strategy addresses the efficiency issue when each strategy is looked at in isolation, it is not clear that the overall system that emerges will have desirable properties. Each rule may be very efficient in the narrow set of situations to which it applies, but that just shifts the burden from the search within a rule to the search the system must do in order to choose an appropriate rule. Furthermore, if the rules are all very specific and domain-depen-

dent, then there is little of the theory that carries over from domain to domain. One may create an interesting domain theory in
this way, but one is left without much of a general theory of adaptation at all. Clearly, a system must have very specific domain
knowledge in order to develop specific explanations. But that
knowledge seems to belong in a declaratively represented knowledge base where it can be updated easily and used for a wide
range of purposes. It doesn't seem right to hard-code it into the
strategies themselves.

8.1.3 Syntactic Heuristics Are Too Undirected

AM, a program that rediscovered mathematical theorems
(Lenat, 1980) made use of another kind of adaptation strategy
which is quite distinct from both the general and the domain-specific types described earlier. Lenat's strategies were exploratory
in nature; they weren't really intended to repair problems in a
knowledge structure, but rather were aimed at discovering new
concepts.

XP tweaking is a kind of learning by discovery like that
demonstrated by AM, although there are important differences between SWALE's tweaks and Lenat's heuristics. One important
difference is that Lenat's program was much less directed. Its
charge was simply to explore the space of mathematical concepts,
looking for "interesting" ones. Lenat was depending on an abstract characterization of what "interesting" meant, and where it
would be found, to guide the search. Learning interesting new
explanations is an important result of adaptation-based explanation, but it's not what the tweaker sets out to do. It sets out to
build an explanation to fit a specific story. Each tweak is invoked
to address a particular explanation failure. Exploration of the
space of explanations is guided by the specifics of the story being
processed. AM operated in a vacuum, attempting to dream up interesting new concepts. An adaptation-based explainer learns in
response to novel experiences, developing new hypotheses in response to a need.

A second important difference is that because Lenat was
working in a domain whose semantics happened to be well
matched to the syntax of the Lisp representations he was using to
represent his concepts, he was able to get away without having
the heuristics make use of an explicitly-represented domain theory. This made Lenat's theory very elegant, but also made it very
hard to extend the theory to different domains (as he points out in

Lenat and Brown, 1984). Tweaks are designed to operate on explanations in a broad range of domains involving human actions, where no such coincidence of syntax and semantics exists. For this reason, tweaking strategies need to rely on domain knowledge explicitly represented in a knowledge base.

8.1.4 SWALE's Strategies Balance Generality and Efficiency

It is relatively easy to formulate a small, elegant set of very general strategies, that apply to an extremely broad class of situations. But each of those strategies indicate very little about the specifics of how to accomplish the task that it needs to perform. Such strategies, therefore, must either employ inefficient general algorithms, such as undirected theorem proving, or they must rely on some hidden knowledge-dependent search strategies, in which case they are not as general or elegant as they first appeared; they actually rely on domain knowledge in a way that is not specified by the theory.

The difficult challenge is to develop a set of adaptation strategies that have enough knowledge to enable them to search intelligently without including the kind of knowledge that will make the strategies domain specific. This raises the following question: Is there any knowledge the system's rules could imply that is not specific domain knowledge? The answer is yes, and the knowledge that is needed is knowledge about how the system's general knowledge base is organized. Adaptation strategies don't need to know specific domain facts. They need to know how to find those facts in the system's knowledge base. This means that each strategy must know what sort of links in the knowledge base it should traverse in order to find the domain knowledge that it needs. An adaptation strategy is, thus, a heuristic for searching the knowledge base in a particular way in order to find a substitution, generalization, or specification that will repair a particular explanation failure.

To illustrate the kinds of strategies employed, and to distinguish them from both the general and the domain specific examples discussed earlier, consider a situation in which the program is equipped with a general terrorism XP, which it retrieves in order to explain the downing of Pan Am Flight 105 over Scotland. The resulting explanation basically claims that some (unspecified) terrorist exploded a bomb on the plane in order to strike at the United States. But suppose that the evaluator decides that a more specific explanation is needed—that the first explanation the system has come up with is too vague about who perpetrated the bombing. The evaluator wants the tweaker to refine the description to something more specific than the generic terrorism level. The tweaker's job is to search for a subcategory of terrorists, or possibly even a specific terrorist, which comprises a reasonable hypothesis. It would use rules of the following sort to do so:

- *A tweaking strategy for refining agent categories*: Search for a subcategory of the category mentioned in the original explanation, which is indexed as having a goal mentioned in the current context.
- *Another tweaking strategy for refining agent categories*: Search for a subcategory of the category mentioned in the original explanation, which is indexed as typically operating with the kind of tools mentioned in the current context.

To compare these rules with the general theorem-proving approach and with the domain-specific, rule-based approach, note that they contain knowledge that makes them more directed than general theorem proving, but that the knowledge is not domain-dependent. For instance, they encode that agent categories are indexed according to what goals those agents typically pursue and according to the tools those agents typically employ, but they don't encode anything specific about terrorism, airplanes, or explosives.

The very general rules, such as CASEY's rules, really correspond to classes of the tweaker's adaptation strategies, without making reference to how the memory is organized. At the level that I am proposing, new strategies must be added whenever the organization of the knowledge base is changed, but not—and this is important enough to bear repeating—when the content of the knowledge base is augmented. For example, when the knowledge base changes to reflect that some nation that used to be friendly to the United States had changed governments and is now unfriendly to it, no strategies need to be altered, as they would if strategies such as the specific aircraft sabotage rule discussed earlier were being used. Furthermore, strategies can be used across domains, as long as the same type of memory links are employed in the different domains. A new set of strategies is required only when a new set of memory organization links is required. In other words, because the strategies need to know about the structure, but not the content, of the knowledge, new strategies are not required

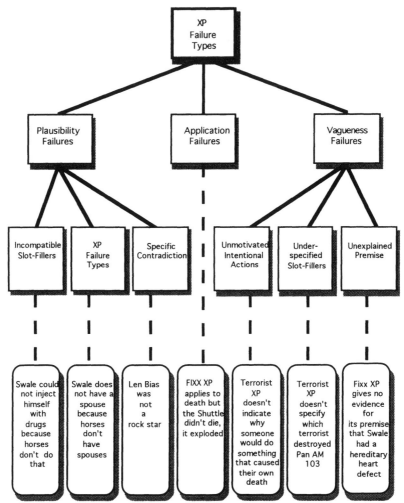

FIG 8.1. Taxonomy of XP failure types.

when it is merely the content of the knowledge base that is changing. They are required only when a new type of link is introduced.

8.2 Ways That Explanations Can Fail

A useful way to think about tweaking strategies is as analogy debuggers. When the explainer applies an old explanation to a new situation, it is essentially proposing an analogy: Perhaps this new situation is essentially like that old one. But real-life analogies are seldom as clean and complete as textbook analogies are. When one is reminded of an old explanation, it is not because the old explanation is about a perfectly analogous situation; the reminding process imposes much weaker constraints than that. Reminding occurs when there is a significant overlap between the situations at some level of abstraction, but there are often "bugs" in the analogy.

Of course, the reason an explainer needs a tweaker is that the seeds of a useful explanation are often contained within a buggy explanation. When that happens, an inexpensive tweak or two can be all that's required to turn the failed explanation into a useful one—if the system chooses the right tweaks to try. Because the space of possible explanations is large, an explanation system cannot afford to apply brute force search to the tweaking problem. Even with an almost-correct explanation as a starting point, unguided tweaking could waste a lot of time going in unhelpful directions before it stumbled on a helpful explanation. After being reminded of a possible explanation for a new situation, an explainer must be able to pinpoint the specific sense in which the analogy between the source case and the target either doesn't hold or doesn't provide the information needed to process the current target case. Then, each type of bug must have a small set of tweaking strategies associated with it. The system can then proceed by first classifying the problem (this is the problem addressed by Leake's chapter in this volume) and then trying only the strategies it knows to be applicable to the type of problem identified.

Of course, the reason an explainer needs a tweaker is that the seeds of a useful explanation are often contained within a buggy explanation. When that happens, an inexpensive tweak or two can be all that's required to turn the failed explanation into a useful one—if the system chooses the right tweaks to try. Because the space of possible explanations is large, an explanation system cannot afford to apply brute force search to the tweaking problem. Even with an almost-correct explanation as a starting point, unguided tweaking could waste a lot of time going in unhelpful directions before it stumbled on a helpful explanation. After being reminded of a possible explanation for a new situation, an explainer must be able to pinpoint the specific sense in which the analogy between the source case and the target either doesn't hold or doesn't provide the information needed to process the current target case. Then, each type of bug must have a small set of tweaking strategies associated with it. The system can then proceed by first classifying the problem (this is the problem addressed by Leake's chapter in this volume) and then trying only the strategies it knows to be applicable to the type of problem identified.

A taxonomy of failure types that the tweaker must address is therefore a crucial prerequisite for a theory of tweaking. XP failures fall into three broad classes, corresponding to the three basic ways an explanation can fail; the explanation tweaker knows tweaks for each of these classes. The taxonomy of XP failures is described in Fig. 8.1.

- *Plausibility failures* correspond to explanations that do not make sense because they contradict some aspects of the explainer's world-model.

  Subcategories within this group include the following:
  - Slot-filler incompatibilities: Two of the slot-fillers within one of the XP's beliefs are incompatible with each other. For instance, an agent might be incapable of performing one of the actions he is claimed to have performed. Slot-filler incompatibilities are the most common plausibility problem. The tweaker recognizes two severity levels of such problems: stereotype violations, which are less severe, and physical or mental inabilities, which are more severe. For example, an explanation that conjectures that a nun committed a bank robbery generates a stereotype violation; nuns don't usually commit robberies, although they could. On the other hand, an explanation which conjectures that a horse injected itself with recreational drugs suffers from a physical-inability failure. Horses can't inject themselves because (among other things) they don't have opposable thumbs.
  - References to nonexistent slots: The explanation makes an indirect reference to some object which doesn't exist. For instance, if the SPOUSE INSURANCE XP were applied to explain a racehorse's death, the resulting explanation would make reference to the racehorse's spouse, which doesn't exist. Similarly, if the FIXX XP were applied to explain the destruction of an inani-

mate object, the resulting explanation would make reference to the object's heart, which also doesn't exist.

- Specific contradictions with the knowledge base: The explanation contains a fact that may make sense with respect to the general rules that the system knows, but which contradicts a specific fact in its knowledge base. A common version of this problem involves explanations that claim that one of their slot-fillers falls into a category that the slot-filler from the current context isn't in. A good example would be an explanation that claimed that Len Bias was a rock star.

- *Vagueness failures* correspond to explanations that are not detailed enough, not sufficiently convincing, or do not contain the kind of information that suits the explainer's needs.

  Subcategories within this group include the following:

  - Unmotivated intentional actions: An agent is posited to have performed an action that seems to be against the agent's own interest.
  - Incomplete explanations: One of the premises in an explanation requires further explanation, or one of the inferences supported by the explanation is not supported by sufficiently strong inference rules.
  - Underspecified slot-fillers: The explanation gives only a vague description of one of the slot-fillers in the explanation about which the system needs more information.

- *Application failures* correspond to XPs that the system cannot even match to the anomaly, and thus cannot, without some tweaking, instantiate in the current situation. In such situations the XP needs tweaking before an explanation can even be generated for evaluation.

8.3 SWALE's Adaptation Strategies

The heart of the adapter is an arsenal of adaptation strategies that equip the system to turn failed explanations into useful ones. Each strategy is a small program that is designed to alter an explanation in response to the detection of a specific failure of the sort described earlier. The input to these programs is an anomaly, a failed explanation, and a description of the failure that was detected. The output is a variation on the explanation which does not suffer from the same failure.

The adaptation strategies discussed in this thesis fall into three major categories: substituters, generalizers, and specifiers. Each of these categories represents a broad description of the kind of modification that the strategies of that type can perform:

- *Substituters* fix plausibility problems by replacing the problematic component of an XP with a new component that makes more sense in the new context.
- *Generalizers* fix plausibility problems by producing a version of the explanation that applies to a broader class of situations at the cost of eliminating some of the detail from the explanation.
- *Specifiers* do the opposite of generalizers; they repair vagueness problems by adding useful detail to an explanation at the cost of narrowing the scope of situations in which the explanation can apply.

The top-level breakdown categorizes strategies strictly at the level of input/output behavior, without making reference to how the adaptation is accomplished at all. Within the top-level categories, the tweaks are further distinguished from each other by three main factors: (a) how local the changes made by the strategy are; (b) what sub-part of an explanation pattern the strategy is designed to work on; and (c). how the strategy extracts the knowledge it needs to perform a particular manipulation from the knowledge base.

As depicted in Figure 8.2, the generalizer and specifier categories each split into local and nonlocal sub-categories, making for a total of five main categories: substituters, local generalizers, nonlocal generalizers, local specifiers, and nonlocal specifiers. Throughout the rest of this chapter I refer to the local generalizers as *component generalizers*, and the nonlocal ones I call *XP simplifiers*, since they prune away portions of the XP. Local specifiers are referred to as *component specifiers* and nonlocal specifiers, which operate by grafting additional explanatory structure onto the original XP are, called *XP elaborators*.

Within each of the five categories, the most important distinction between strategies is which slot-filler type, or which belief type, the strategy is equipped to manipulate. For example, some substituters replace the filler of the object slot in an action description, and others, the filler of the action slot; some add new beliefs to the XP, whereas others work on augmenting the causal links between the beliefs that are already there. The second im-

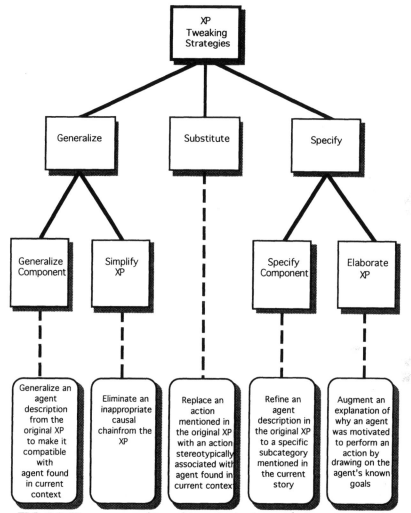

FIG. 8.2. Taxonomy of tweaking strategies with five examples.

portant dimension that distinguishes the strategies within each major category revolves around the algorithm that each tweak uses to search memory for the domain knowledge needed to make the desired change.

Two strategies may make the same broad type of change to an XP, but may differ according to how they search memory for the knowledge they need to make the change, which, of course, can have a large effect on the specifics of the actual change the strategy makes. For example, there are several strategies for attempting to find another agent that could have filled a particular role in an explanation. One substituter might search the knowledge base for replacements using agent-theme links whereas another uses causal-stereotype links. Although both strategies have the same goal—to find another plausible filler for the agent role part of a particular XP—they go about it different ways and are likely, depending on the idiosyncratic content of the system's memory, to come up with different candidates for filling that role. Much of the work involved in making a tweak to an XP is memory search—looking through memory for an appropriate substitution, generalization, supporting explanation, and so on.

If you think about what you do when you try to adapt an old solution to a new problem, you will realize that you are basically asking yourself a certain type of question and then struggling to come up with an answer. For instance, if you were reminded of the Janis Joplin explanation (star performer dies of overdose of recreational drugs taken to relieve stress associated with the star's life-style) when attempting to explain the death of a star racehorse, you will probably reject the explanation in its ready-made form because racehorses don't give themselves drugs. So, if you don't reject the explanation altogether, you will find that you are asking yourself the following question: *"Who else might have given Swale drugs?"* If you ponder this question long enough, you may come up with an interesting hypothesis. For instance, Swale's owner might have given him drugs to make him run faster.

In general, the process of adapting explanations can be thought of as asking oneself a hypothesis adaptation question, and then searching for an answer. The theory of adaptation must have at least two parts. First, it must specify the set of questions that should be asked. Then, for each question specified in part one of the theory, it must specify an algorithm that an adapter can use to come up with plausible answers.

Although the full theory should also specify how to choose between questions when more than one may be applicable, for the sake of simplicity, we ignore this question of strategy selection in this chapter and simply assume that if more than one strategy is applicable that they are tried in an arbitrary order until one succeeds. (See Kass, 1990b, for a preliminary discussion of strategy selection.) As long the number of strategies applicable to any situation is not too large, this is an acceptable solution.

The details of the theory reside in the strategies that answer each question. In my doctoral dissertation (Kass, 1990b), I propose 21 adaptation questions, and describe the algorithms required to ask them in great detail. The 21 hypothesis-adaptation questions follow:

1. What other actions are sort of like action Y?
2. What other actions does X (or agents like X) typically perform?
3. What other actions typically cause events like Z?
4. Who would have wanted to bring about one of the consequences of the action?
5. What types of agents typically perform this action?
6. Who could the agent who was originally proposed, have caused to perform the action on his behalf?
7. What implements are commonly used to perform this action?
8. What type of implements would this agent typically be expected to have available to him?
9. What implements are typically available in the location where the action took place?
10. Why would the negative effects of the action be particularly unimportant to the agent involved?
11. Why would the positive effects of the action be particularly important to the agent involved?
12. Which of the negative effects of his decision might the agent not have known about, and why?
13. Are there positive effects of the action that might have motivated the agent, but that were not mentioned by the original explanation?
14. Do I know an explanation that could provide a sub-explanation relevant to this premise? If not, can I build the sub-explanation on the fly?
15. Do I know an explanation that could explain how event A might have caused event B? If not, can I build the sub-explanation linking the two on the fly?
16. Is it possible that one of the beliefs in the knowledge base that led to contradiction with the XP might be inaccurate for some reason?

17. Which members of the original agent category would have desired one of the goal states achieved by the action in question?

18. Which members of the original action category typically involve an implement that is observable in the current situation, or that is related to the agent in question?

19. Can the constraint be generalized to make it compatible with the current slot-filler yet still maintain the causal coherence of the explanation?

20. What generalization of slot-filler A would be compatible with B yet still maintain the causal coherence of the explanation?

21. Can the problematic belief be removed yet still maintain the causal coherence of the explanation?

8.4 How Adaptation Strategies Answer Hypothesis Adaptation Questions

As you can see, some of the questions relate to explanations in which an action must be replaced, and others to explanations in which agents or implements must be replaced. Still others relate to explanations in which nothing needs to be replaced, but important subexplanations are missing, or elements are left unspecified. Each of the foregoing adaptation questions is associated with an adaptation strategy that the system employs to answer the question, and to develop the variation on the XP that will fit the current situation. There are four parts to the task that each strategy must perform in order to build a variation on an XP:

- First, the system must formulate the specific problem by isolating the part of the XP to be altered; then,
- it must search its knowledge base for possible answers to its question; next,
- it must check each potential answer to see if it makes sense in the context of the XP; and finally,
- if it succeeds in answering the question, it must build a new explanation based on the answer.

The algorithms employed by these strategies can be quite complex. (The reader who wishes to understand all those details should refer to Kass, 1990b) . We must be satisfied with conveying the general approach through brief descriptions of a few strategies in action, followed by a detailed examination of a trace of the program execution as it performs one sample adaptation.

8.5 Examples of XP Adaptation

We developed the adaptation-based theory of explanation by analyzing a set of sample anomalies and associated explanations. Most of the examples you see in this report revolve around unexpected deaths and disasters. We chose this domain principally because it often shows up in the news, so that it is easy to gather data. It also has the advantage that many of our informal subjects found death-and-destruction events sufficiently interesting and straightforward so that they could recall stored explanations and produce new ones.

In order to make the operation of the adaptation-based explanation process clear in a concrete way, we present here a high-level description of five sample adaptations that were performed by the ABE[2] program. Each example presented here consists of a story that the system attempts to process, an XP that is in some way relevant, a failure that occurs when applying the retrieved XP to the current story, and a variation of the XP that the adapter could produce.

8.5.1 Adaptation Example 1: Replacing an Action

One type of strategy quite commonly invoked involves replacing a single slot-filler within a belief in the XP with an alternate slot-filler. The replacement must be more appropriate to the given situation, and should also preserve most of the causal relationships that the original slot-filler participated in.

In the example that follows the tweaker is faced with a situation in which an agent is hypothesized to have performed an action that is not stereotypically associated with him. The tweaker addresses the situation by executing a strategy that replaces the original action with one that is stereotypically associated with the agent.

---

[2]ABE, was a descendent of the SWALE program. SWALE was developed by the Alex Kass, David Leake, and Christopher Owens. ABE was developed in order to further the development and testing of tweaking strategies by exercising SWALE's explanation tweaker independently of its elaborate retriever and evaluator. To do so, ABE was equipped with simplistic versions of the retriever and evaluator, which were intended simply to feed test examples to the tweaker.

Example Story:	The Len Bias Story. College basketball star Len Bias died 1 day after being drafted by the Boston Celtics. He was their first pick in the NBA draft.
An XP that might be relevant:	The Jim Fixx XP. Someone who regularly engages in recreational jogging also has a hereditary heart defect. The stress on the heart from exertion caused by jogging combines with the defect to cause that person to have a heart attack and die.
A failure that occurs when applying the XP to the story:	Len Bias wasn't known as a recreational jogger.
The type of failure this is:	An agent of some action in the explanation is not known to perform that action.
A question that is appropriate to that failure:	What other actions does the agent typically perform, that could have caused whatever the original action caused in the XP?
A result of asking that question about this example:	By substituting playing basketball for recreational jogging, the adapter can build an excellent explanation based on this XP that is appropriate for Bias. A defective heart ,combined with the exertion from playing basketball, caused a fatal heart attack in Len Bias.

8.5.2 Adaptation Example 2: Replacing an Agent

The following example is included to illustrate the point that just as it sometimes helps to replace the filler of an action slot, at other times the action should be kept as is, and instead it may help to replace the filler of the agent slot.

The SPOUSE INSURANCE XP doesn't quite make sense when applied to Swale since racehorses don't have spouses. But when a strategy is invoked which considers who it would make sense to conjecture in the role of killing a racehorse for the insurance money, a plausible explanation is the result.

Example Story:	The Swale Story. Swale was a star 3-year-old racehorse. Swale won the Belmont Stakes. A few days later, he died.
An XP that might be relevant:	Spouse insurance XP. Some agent is greedy and is married. The agent doesn't love his or her spouse. The spouse has a lot of life insurance. The agent is the beneficiary of the life insurance because spouses are generally the beneficiary of life insurance. Because the spouse has life insurance, the agent knows that he or she will get money if the spouse dies. Because of greed and lack of love, the agent kills the spouse.
A failure that occurs when applying the XP to the story:	Swale lacks a spouse.
The type of failure this is:	An object slot (spouse) referenced in the XP does not, in reality, exist.
A question that is appropriate to that failure:	Who would have wanted to bring about the effects of the action?
A result of asking that question about this example:	By searching for other agents with similar motivations, the adapter can build from this explanation the reasonable hypothesis that Swale's owner got greedy and killed him to collect the property insurance.

8.5.3 Adaptation Example 3: Loosening a Constraint

The previous example, in which the JIM FIXX XP was invoked to explain Len Bias' death, resulted in an explanation that would be plausible if it were not discovered that drugs were involved. But in light of that knowledge, another XP—the JANIS JOPLIN XP—seems more appropriate. Much of this explanation applies well to a famous basketball player, but it was originally encoded as applying to rock stars. A tweaking strategy that generalizes the rock star constraint to make the XP applicable to any star performer can be invoked to fix the situation, as shown in the following example.

Example Story:	The Len Bias Story. College basketball star Len Bias died 1 day after being drafted by the Boston Celtics. He was their first pick in the NBA draft.
An XP that might be relevant:	The Janis Joplin XP. A young rock star is very successful. Success leads to wealth and stress. Being a rock star leads to having lots of drug-using friends. Stress leads to a desire for lowering stress. Drug-using friends and wealth leads to access to drugs. Access to drugs and desire for lowering stress leads to taking drugs. Taking drugs leads to a drug overdose. Drug overdose leads to death.
A failure that occurs when applying the XP to the story:	Len Bias was not a rock star.
The type of failure this is:	A slot-filler does not fit one of the packaging descriptions (i.e. constraints) that the XP specifies.
A question that is appropriate to that failure:	What generalization of the original slot-filler might be more appropriate?
A result of asking that question about this example:	Generalize the Joplin XP to apply to any star performer. This example is included for two reasons: first, to emphasize the point that there is often more than one XP that can produce reasonable explanations for a given example; and second, to illustrate a case in which generalization is an appropriate course of action.

8.5.4 Adaptation Example 4: Making a Slot-Filler More Specific

Some adaptation strategies serve the function of making an explanation more specific. For instance, in the following example a generic terrorism XP is applied to explain a plane crash; the explanation that results, that a bomb set off by a terrorist caused the crash, is perfectly reasonable, but it doesn't say much about who the terrorist was. In some situations this might not matter, but in others it would (for instance, the *who* question is crucially important to those responsible for bringing the perpetrators to justice).

Developing variations of the stored explanation that can satisfy the system's need for a conjecture that is less vague requires a set of strategies whose job it is to turn vague slot-filler descriptions into more specific ones.

Example Story:	The Pan Am Story. Pan Am flight 103 exploded in mid air, killing all aboard. It was en route to New York City from Frankfurt, West Germany, via London, England.
An XP that might be relevant:	The Terrorist Bombing XP. Someone who is engaged in intense political conflict with the people of a particular nation may kill citizens of that nation by planting bombs in crowded areas in that nation.
A failure that occurs when applying the XP to the story:	Does not specify enough about who did the bombing. Note that this might not be a problem if the understander were a Pan Am engineer who just wants to know whether it was a design flaw that caused the crash, but it would be a problem if the understander were the government agency responsible for retaliating against the perpetrators.
The type of failure this is:	A slot-filler is insufficiently specified to satisfy the goals of the understander.
A question that is appropriate to that failure:	What members of the agent category specified in the original XP are known to have an effect of the action as a goal?
A result of asking that question about this example:	By searching for a more specific description of someone who might have had appropriate motivation to perform the action, the adapter can conjecture that perhaps an Iranian terrorist planted the bomb on the Pan Am jet in order to retaliate for America's destroying an Iranian airliner.

8.5.5 Adaptation Example 5: Extending an Explanation

The final example points out that sometimes a failed explanation doesn't have any contradiction that needs to be fixed, but instead is incomplete, and needs to be reinforced with sub-explanations. These sub-explanations can strengthen the explanation by providing causal support for a belief that was unexplained by the original XP.

Example Story:	A Suicide Bomber Story. A teenage girl exploded a car bomb at a joint post of Israeli troops and pro-Israeli militiamen in southern Lebanon. The bomber and a number of Israeli soldiers were killed by the blast.
An XP that might be relevant:	The Terrorist Bombing XP. Someone who is engaged in intense political conflict with the people of a particular nation may kill citizens of that nation by planting bombs in crowded areas in that nation.
A failure that occurs when applying the XP to the story:	This doesn't explain an important part of the anomaly: why someone would do something that resulted in her own death.
The type of failure this is:	An action that the explanation claims occurred is not sufficiently motivated by the XP. The explanation seems to claim that a more important goal was sacrificed in order to achieve a less important one.
A question that is appropriate to that failure:	Why might the negative side effects of the action be less important than expected to the agent involved?
A result of asking that question about this example:	By employing this strategy the adapter can hypothesize that besides having a political conflict motivation, the bomber was terminally ill and therefore did not value her own life as highly as most people would.

8.6 An Annotated Transcript of ABE in Action

This section presents an annotated transcript of the ABE computer program processing a particular story. The objective is to clarify, through example, some of the details of the adaptation process. Because the point of ABE is to exercise the hypothesis-adaptation questions and their associated strategies, other interesting issues, such as XP selection and evaluation of explanations, are glossed over. In fact, evaluation isn't performed by the program itself at all. Instead, the user is asked to evaluate the explanations that the program proposes.

The high-level outline of what happens in this run of ABE is as follows:

- The program is fed an anomaly to explain: in this case, it is asked to explain the unexpected death of college basketball star, Hank Gathers.
- It retrieves a set of XPs relevant to explaining deaths and disasters.
- It applies the highest ranking of the retrieved XPs to the particulars of the Gathers case.
- It presents the explanation to the human evaluator, who decides that the explanation requires tweaking.
- The program queries the human evaluator about just what is wrong with the explanation.
- The system then retrieves hypothesis-adaptation questions that might be applicable to the problem the user has identified.
- The retrieved questions are ranked, and the highest ranking question is asked. Its associated strategy is queued for execution.
- After the strategy is executed, the resulting explanation is resubmitted to the human evaluator. This version of the explanation is accepted by the evaluator.
- The system updates the knowledge base and adds the XP to the XP library.

(Note: In the transcript that follows the actual computer output is in fixed width font whereas the comments are in *italics*.)
To start the ABE program running, the user calls the EXPLAIN function, passing it the anomaly structure, which represents the anomaly for which the user wants an explanation:

```
-> (explain gathers-anom)

Explainer: Processing
> Hank Gathers was a star basketball player at the
Loyola Marymount
> University.
> He died suddenly while playing in an important col-
lege basketball game.
```

The anomaly being processed is:
    HANK GATHERS was in EXCELLENT physical condition.
    HANK GATHERS died.

*In this example the user requested an explanation of the predefined
anomaly, named the GATHERS-ANOM, about the sudden death of a
college basketball player. The anomaly itself is represented as two beliefs. The system prints out its paraphrases of those beliefs, along with
the text of the story associated with that anomaly. Internally, the beliefs
are represented in an abstract, conceptual representation from which the
program produces crude, English like paraphrases to help the user follow the system's progress and evaluate its explanations.*

*The first step the system performs is to see if it has explanation pat-
terns with indices that match any part of the anomaly. It then ranks
those that do match according to how many constants within the
anomaly description are specifically matched by the index pattern associated with each tweak.*

```
 XP-Retriever: Found 7 XPs to consider for this
anomaly:
    [5]    FIXX-XP
    [4]    JOPLIN-XP
    [4]    MAFIA-REVENGE-XP
    [4]    KAMIKAZE-XP
    [4]    KILL-FOR-INSURANCE-XP
    [4]    SEX-XP
    [4]    TERRORIST-BOMBING-XP
```

*In this case, the retriever extracts 7 XPs as potentially relevant. The
FIXX XP is ranked highest because it is a more specific match with the
anomaly. The other XPs are indexed as general explanations for death,
whereas the FIXX XP is indexed as an explanation for the death of
someone who appears to be in superior physical condition.*

*The next step after XP retrieval is to apply the highest ranking XP
to see what sort of explanation it produces in the context of the new*

anomaly. This involves instantiating the XP's variables by matching beliefs in the XP against beliefs in the anomaly and, if necessary, other beliefs culled from the story. Once an explanation is produced, it is displayed for the user to evaluate.

```
Applier: Attempting to apply FIXX-XP to GATHERS-ANOM
Found a match for:
               (from xp)     ?X? died
               (from story)  HANK GATHERS died

Evaluator: Evaluating explanation: FIXX-XP.EXPL-1

FIXX-XP.EXPL-1
Premise: HANK GATHERS DID RECREATIONAL JOGGING
Premise: THE HEART OF HANK GATHERS is in category
HEREDITARY DEFECTIVE HEARTS
THE HEART OF HANK GATHERS was weak BECAUSE
   THE HEART OF HANK GATHERS is in category HEREDITARY
DEFECTIVE HEARTS.
HANK GATHERS ran BECAUSE
   HANK GATHERS DID RECREATIONAL JOGGING.
HANK GATHERS had a heart-attack BECAUSE
   THE HEART OF HANK GATHERS was weak AND
   HANK GATHERS had a VERY HIGH degree of EXERTION
   LEVEL.
HANK GATHERS had a VERY HIGH degree of EXERTION LEVEL
   BECAUSE
   HANK GATHERS ran.
HANK GATHERS had a VERY HIGH degree of PHYSICAL
   CONDITIONING BECAUSE
   HANK GATHERS had a VERY HIGH degree of EXERTION
   LEVEL.
HANK GATHERS died BECAUSE
   HANK GATHERS had a heart-attack.
```

In this case, the FIXX XP has only one variable, which represents the deceased. This variable is bound by matching the variablized portion of the XP (which mentions a dying action) against the unvariablized portion of the anomaly (which mentions the same action).

Next, the user is allowed to evaluate the explanation that is generated by applying the system's chosen XP to the new situation. The user communicates an evaluation to the system through a series of menu choices.

```
— Please choose one of the following:
    1> Adopt this hypothesis.
       Install XP in memory + record entailed beliefs.
    2> Tweak this XP.
    3> Abandon this hypothesis for now.
    4> Abort the explainer.

Enter Choice -> 2
```

The user wants the system to try to tweak the XP. Therefore, the system presents a couple more menus that allow the user to identify the type of problem and to which of the beliefs within the XP the problem.

```
What failure type?
— Please choose one of the following:
    1> Agent-action-mismatch : physical-disability
    2> Agent-action-mismatch : stereotype-violation
    3> Agent-action-mismatch : mental-disability
    4> object-action-mismatch : physical-disability
    5> object-action-mismatch : stereotype-violation
    6> implement-action-mismatch : physical-disability
    7> implement-action-mismatch : stereotype-violation
    8> incomplete-explanation : covers-part-of-anomaly
    9> incomplete-explanation : unmotivated-action

Enter Choice -> 2

Identify the belief that is a problem
— Please choose one of the following:
    1> HANK GATHERS DID RECREATIONAL JOGGING
    2> THE HEART OF HANK GATHERS is in category
       HEREDITARY DEFECTIVE HEARTS
    3> HANK GATHERS died
    4> THE HEART OF HANK GATHERS was weak
    5> HANK GATHERS had a heart-attack
    6> HANK GATHERS had a VERY HIGH degree of EXERTION
       LEVEL
    7> HANK GATHERS had a VERY HIGH degree of PHYSICAL
       CONDITIONING
    8> HANK GATHERS ran

Enter Choice -> 1
```

The user indicates that the problem is a stereotype violation involving a mismatch between an agent and an action. In particular, the part of the explanation that proposes that HANK GATHERS did recreational jogging is objected to because Gathers was not known as a recreational jogger.

Once the problem is identified the tweaking process begins. The first step within the tweak process is to retrieve all the tweaks relevant to this type of stereotype violation.

```
Tweaker: Attempting to adapt FIXX-XP.EXPL-1
Tweaker: Failure is: XP Failure:
         Agent-action-mismatch : stereotype-violation
 Retriever: Retrieving XPs indexed under failure:
 Retriever: found - SUBSTITUTE-AGENT:MENTIONED-IN-XP
   DELETE-BELIEF
   SUBSTITUTE-AGENT:MENTIONED-IN-STORY
   SUBSTITUTE-AGENT:STEREOTYPICAL-AGENT
   SUBSTITUTE-ACTION:CAUSAL-INDEX
   SUBSTITUTE-ACTION:AGENT-THEME
   SUBSTITUTE-ACTION:RELATED-ACTION ; . . .
```

The system knows quite a few questions to ask about a stereotype violation involving a mismatch between an agent and an action. It should be noted that the names assigned to the questions by the program are slightly different than the names in this paper, but the mappings should be sufficiently clear.

After retrieval the next step is to filter out any strategies whose tweak input filters are not satisfied and then to rank the rest according to how specifically they match the failure that is the cause for tweaking. The specifics of the scoring method are beyond the scope of this paper. See Kass (1990) for details.

```
Filter: SUBSTITUTE-AGENT:MENTIONED-IN-XP is filtered
out because only one agent is mentioned in the xp.

  Ranker: Ranking remaining strategies.

  Current ranking priorities:
   CW = 1.0   HW = 1.0   SW = 1.0

TCE  THR  TMS
 0    0    3   Score: 3.0 - SUBSTITUTE-ACTION:
                           AGENT-THEME
 0    0    2   Score: 2.0 - SUBSTITUTE-ACTION:
                           RELATED-ACTION
 0    0    1   Score: 1.0 - DELETE-BELIEF
Choice point reached: 3 choices available.
```

```
Each choice involves: Trying another tweak on
FIXX-XP.EXPL-1
```

After the remaining questions are ranked, the highest ranking is exe-
cuted while the others are kept in reserve in case the first one doesn't pan
out. The program decides to begin by asking whether there is an action
that is typically associated with the agent that could have caused the
effects of the implausible action.

```
==== Running a tweak:
        Substitute a theme that is associated with
        the agent
        XP being tweaked:    FIXX-XP
        Anomaly to be explained:
            HANK GATHERS died
        Bindings: X is bound to HANK GATHERS.
        Explanation Failure being fixed: XP Failure:
            Agent-action-mismatch :
                stereotype-violation
====
Tweaker: Problem is with HANK GATHERS as the AGENT of
            DID RECREATIONAL JOGGING
```

The first step in executing this tweaking strategy is to collect the
arguments that the tweak's search-and-inference routine will need. In
this case, that means simply determining which agent node (the HANK
GATHERS node) will be the starting point for the search for stereotypi-
cally associated actions.

The next step is to search for actions associated with Gathers.

```
Tweaker: 5 actions associated with HANK GATHERS are
being considered:

  __

  Premise: HANK GATHERS had theme WON ATHLETIC AWARDS
  __

  HANK GATHERS PLAYED BASKETBALL BECAUSE
  HANK GATHERS is in category COLLEGE BASKETBALL STAR
  AND
  COLLEGE BASKETBALL STAR is in category BASKETBALL
  PLAYERS AND
  BASKETBALL PLAYERS had theme PLAYED BASKETBALL.
  Premise: HANK GATHERS is in category COLLEGE
            BASKETBALL STAR
```

```
Premise: COLLEGE BASKETBALL STAR is in category
         BASKETBALL PLAYERS
Premise: BASKETBALL PLAYERS had theme PLAYED
         BASKETBALL
  _
HANK GATHERS PRACTICED BASKETBALL SHOTS BECAUSE
 HANK GATHERS is in category COLLEGE BASKETBALL STAR
 AND
 COLLEGE BASKETBALL STAR is in category BASKETBALL
 PLAYERS AND
 BASKETBALL PLAYERS had theme PRACTICED BASKETBALL
 SHOTS.
Premise: HANK GATHERS is in category COLLEGE
         BASKETBALL STAR
Premise: COLLEGE BASKETBALL STAR is in category
         BASKETBALL PLAYERS
Premise: BASKETBALL PLAYERS had theme PRACTICED
         BASKETBALL SHOTS
  _
HANK GATHERS TOOK PERFORMANCE DRUGS BECAUSE  ; . . .
  _
HANK GATHERS LIFTED WEIGHTS BECAUSE   ; . .
```

The system comes up with five actions that it can associate with Gathers. One of these is directly indexed as associated with the GATHERS node (winning awards) whereas the others are the result of inference chains, involving the hierarchy of categories in which Gathers fits.

After the set of prospective replacement actions is collected, the system checks to see which might actually make appropriate substitutions by seeing whether any of the actions can form inference chains linking to aspects of the original XP to which the original action is linked.

```
Checking a candidate Replacement: HANK GATHERS WON
ATHLETIC AWARDS
 Trying to link up to: ("HANK GATHERS ran")
 Does NOT link up with the rest of the XP.
 Cannot create a tweaked explanation based on
     HANK GATHERS WON ATHLETIC AWARDS
Checking a candidate Replacement: HANK GATHERS PLAYED
     BASKETBALL
 Trying to link up to: ("HANK GATHERS ran")
 This chain DOES link up with the rest of the xp:
     Inference: HANK GATHERS PLAYED BASKETBALL ->
                HANK GATHERS ran
```

In this example, the relevant aspect of the original action, recreational jogging, is that it led to running, which led to exertion. The exertion combined with the heart defect led to a heart attack, which led to death. So the system checks to see if the replacements lead to any of these effects. Most of them don't. For example, winning awards does not cause running, physical exertion, heart attacks, or death; at least not by any short casual chain that the system could discover. However, playing basketball does, so it can form the basis of a tweak.

Once a suitable replacement action is found, the system builds a new variation on the FIXX XP in which playing basketball replaces recreational jogging.

```
Creating a new tweaked explanation.

Adding an index to FIXX-XP-1:
  ?X? PLAYED BASKETBALL
Adding: ?X? ran BECAUSE
         ?X? PLAYED BASKETBALL.
Adding: ?X? PLAYED BASKETBALL BECAUSE
         ?X? had theme PLAYED BASKETBALL.
Adding: ?X? had theme PLAYED BASKETBALL BECAUSE
         ?X? is in category COLLEGE BASKETBALL STAR
         AND
         COLLEGE BASKETBALL STAR had theme PLAYED
         BASKETBALL.
Adding: Premise: ?X? is in category COLLEGE
                 BASKETBALL STAR
Adding: COLLEGE BASKETBALL STAR had theme PLAYED
         BASKETBALL BECAUSE
         COLLEGE BASKETBALL STAR is in category
         BASKETBALL PLAYERS AND
         BASKETBALL PLAYERS had theme PLAYED
         BASKETBALL.
Adding: Premise: COLLEGE BASKETBALL STAR is in
                 category BASKETBALL PLAYERS
Adding: Premise: BASKETBALL PLAYERS had theme PLAYED
                 BASKETBALL

Deleting a belief: ?X? DID RECREATIONAL JOGGING
Deleting supporter inference:
 Premise: ?X? DID RECREATIONAL JOGGING
 Deleting supported inference:
 ?X? ran BECAUSE
  ?X? DID RECREATIONAL JOGGING.
Deleting orphaned beliefs.
```

Making the replacement involves (a) adding in the new belief, along with the inference chain that causes the system to believe it, (b) adding the inferences that link the new belief to its implications in the XP, and then, (c) deleting the old belief from the XP, along with any other beliefs that were around solely to support the belief being deleted.

Once the new XP is built, the next step is to repeat the evaluation procedure, allowing the user to see the new explanation and to decide whether it needs any more tweaking.

```
Evaluator: Evaluating explanation: FIXX-XP-1.EXPL-1


FIXX-XP-1.EXPL-1
Premise: HANK GATHERS is in category COLLEGE
         BASKETBALL STAR
Premise: THE HEART OF HANK GATHERS is in category
         HEREDITARY DEFECTIVE HEARTS
Premise: COLLEGE BASKETBALL STAR is in category
         BASKETBALL PLAYERS
HANK GATHERS had theme PLAYED BASKETBALL BECAUSE
 HANK GATHERS is in category COLLEGE BASKETBALL STAR
 AND
 COLLEGE BASKETBALL STAR had theme PLAYED BASKETBALL.
HANK GATHERS had theme PLAYED BASKETBALL BECAUSE
 COLLEGE BASKETBALL STAR is in category BASKETBALL
 PLAYERS AND
 BASKETBALL PLAYERS had theme PLAYED BASKETBALL.
HANK GATHERS PLAYED BASKETBALL BECAUSE
 HANK GATHERS had theme PLAYED BASKETBALL.
HANK GATHERS ran BECAUSE HANK GATHERS PLAYED
BASKETBALL.
THE HEART OF HANK GATHERS was weak BECAUSE
 THE HEART OF HANK GATHERS is in category HEREDITARY
 DEFECTIVE HEARTS.
HANK GATHERS had a heart-attack BECAUSE
 THE HEART OF HANK GATHERS was weak AND
 HANK GATHERS had a VERY HIGH degree of EXERTION
LEVEL.
HANK GATHERS had a VERY HIGH degree of EXERTION LEVEL
BECAUSE HANK GATHERS ran.
HANK GATHERS had a VERY HIGH degree of PHYSICAL
CONDITIONING BECAUSE
 HANK GATHERS had a VERY HIGH degree of EXERTION
 LEVEL.
HANK GATHERS died BECAUSE HANK GATHERS had
a heart-attack.
```

```
— Please choose one of the following:
    1> Adopt this hypothesis. Install XP in memory +
       record entailed beliefs.
    2> Tweak this XP.
    3> Abandon this hypothesis for now.
    4> Abort the explainer.

Enter Choice -> 1
```

*This time around, the user finds the explanation satisfactory and re-
quests that it be adopted. When an explanation is adopted, it is added
to the XP library. Because the distinction between the new variation
and the original was that the new one applies to people who play basketball, playing basketball is added as an index for the new XP. That
way, the next time a basketball player dies unexpectedly, this new variation will be preferred over the one that involves recreational jogging.
In addition, some new hypotheses are added to the knowledge base, such
as the belief that Gathers had a weak heart.*

```
Explainer: Explanation process successful. Storing
FIXX-XP-1.EXPL-1
 Adding #{XP 20 FIXX-XP-1} to the XP library.
 Indices:    ?X? PLAYED BASKETBALL -    ?AGENT? died
 Adding new hypotheses to the knowledge base:
 THE HEART OF HANK GATHERS is in category HEREDITARY
 DEFECTIVE HEARTS
 THE HEART OF HANK GATHERS was weak
 HANK GATHERS had a heart-attack
Explainer: Explanation process complete.
```

8.7 Conclusion

The tweakers in SWALE and ABE are able to adapt a stored explanation in order to build variations that can handle new situations, which differ slightly from situations that the program has
previously encountered. It has been clear for a long time that the
ability to understand the world efficiently depends on having
stored schemas available; it is simply too expensive to build anew
the full causal explanation of every event anew for each event
processed. What has not been clear until the theory of adaptation
began to emerge is how the knowledge stored in a schema could be
applied to a new problem that only partially matched a schema
stored in memory. Because only the most routine experiences will

match a stored schema completely, the lack of an adaptation theory has been a crippling limitation of schema-based systems.

9. Brainstormer: Refining Abstract Planning Advice

Eric K. Jones
Department of Computer Science
Victoria University of Wellington
New Zealand

Editors' Introduction

This chapter, adapted from Jones' dissertation, describes a system that adapts stored knowledge structures in order to make them fit new situations, just as the programs described in the previous chapter do. But the differences between Brainstormer and SWALE are as salient as the similarities. One surface-level difference is that whereas SWALE and ABE are programs that adapt explanations, Brainstormer adapts plans. A second, perhaps deeper difference is that whereas SWALE's tweaker takes specific previous cases, and tries to adapt them to specific new situations, the main idea behind Brainstormer is to adapt general knowledge, such as that which is encoded in proverbs (of the sort that the ANON program, described in Owens' chapter, is capable of retrieving) to a specific situation. Brainstormer can take the sort of vague advice a proverb offers and turn it into an operational plan. It can figure out how the proverb should be applied in a given situation.

* * *

9.1 Overview

When people lack sufficient domain-specific knowledge to solve a novel problem, they are often able to fall back on more abstract knowledge that is useful in a variety of domains. Much of this abstract knowledge is culturally shared: It is knowledge that most full-grown people in a given culture would consider "common sense." Having exhausted one's idiosyncratic or domain-specific expertise, shared general knowledge of one's culture is available to help. In order to make use of this general knowledge, people must be capable of building specific knowledge structures out of general ones—of adapting general knowledge to a specific context.

To study the application of abstract knowledge to novel problems, we have constructed the Brainstormer system. Brainstormer is a planner that operates in the domain of political and military policy as it relates to terrorism. Although Brainstormer knows something about terrorism, it is not an expert in this domain. Instead, Brainstormer's expertise lies in the more general domain of planning and social interaction. In this sense, all problems having to do with terrorism appear novel to Brainstormer. Just as people fall back on general knowledge to solve novel problems, Brainstormer uses abstract knowledge about planning and acting to resolve difficulties it encounters in attempting to plan to counter the actions of terrorists.

Brainstormer is not only a planner, it is a case-based reasoner (Hammond 1986; Kolodner et al. 1985): Its abstract knowledge about planning and acting is stored as a collection of culturally shared cases, consisting primarily of representations of proverbs. As a simplifying maneuver, we have sidestepped the problem of case retrieval and address only the problem of adapting abstract knowledge.[1] The system is handed a planning problem and a large set of culturally shared cases, and adapts these cases to help it plan. Brainstormer first tries to solve problems on its own, then considers its cases one by one in an attempt to resolve difficulties it has encountered.

We have focused on proverbs for two reasons. First, proverbs are a well-defined class of cases that encode useful culturally shared knowledge about the idiosyncrasies of human planning and social interaction (Owens 1988; Schank & Leake 1986; White 1987). *The grass is always greener on the other side of the fence*, for example, expresses a peculiarity of the human planning process: when comparing options, people tend to be biased in favor of the unfamiliar or the unpossessed. Second, representing a large number of proverbs has proved an effective strategy for developing and testing our representational vocabulary for abstract knowl-

---

[1]See chapters 4 and 5 in this volume, for a discussion of the issues involved in retrieving abstract knowledge.

edge. *The grass is always greener on the other side of the fence*, for example, not only encodes an important truth about human planning, but also points to the need for a conceptual vocabulary sufficient to encode the idea of choosing between options in terms of estimates of their utility. Brainstormer is capable of using a wide range of abstract knowledge expressed in its high-level, culturally shared vocabulary of planning concepts. Proverbs are just one useful class of expressions representable in this vocabulary.

The task of adapting abstract knowledge to assist planning divides into two subtasks: *transformation into the planner's operational vocabulary* and *problem reformulation*. In the next two sections, we describe these subtasks and explain why each plays an essential role.

9.2 Transformation into Operational Representations

In general, a culturally shared case relates to only a fragment of a planning task. Therefore, the result of adapting a culturally shared case is not a complete plan, but rather a representation that the planner can use to help it generate complete plans. To be useful, these representations must be encoded in a vocabulary that is *operational*, in the sense that Brainstormer's planning process can employ representations in this vocabulary without further modification (Mostow, 1983). The planner's operational vocabulary includes such things as rules for transforming goals and refining plans, and expressions that relate goals to sketchy plans that may accomplish them.

The need to transform abstract knowledge into the planner's operational vocabulary gives rise to a new challenge that most case-based reasoning systems do not have to face. Most of Brainstormer's cases can be transformed into concrete, operational representations in a number of different ways, each of which assists a different stage of the planning process. Brainstormer's adaptation process has to transform abstract knowledge into whatever operational representations happen to be useful to the planner in current problem solving.

Suppose, for example, that Brainstormer is presented with a representation of a terrorist attack and is asked to generate plans for preventing future terrorist attacks with similar causes. One of Brainstormer's cases is a representation of the proverb *An old poacher makes the best keeper*, which can be paraphrased as follows: "In a stereotyped attack-defense situation, a former attacker is a good choice for the actor of a plan of defense". There are a number of different ways this proverb can be adapted. Which one is appropriate depends on the stage of the planning process that the proverb assists. Three possible scenarios are:

1. The system is considering a plan of defense against terrorism, and is trying to decide between two plausible candidates for the actor of this plan. Then, An old poacher makes the best keeper should be adapted to suggest Pick the candidate with the most experience or expertise.
2. The system is considering a plan of defense, but is still casting around for candidates for the actor. Then, the proverb should be adapted to suggest Try an ex-terrorist.
3. Finally, suppose the system is stuck at the first stages of planning: It has no concept of how to proceed toward its goal of preventing terrorism. Then, the proverb could be adapted to suggest Try a plan of defense with an ex-terrorist actor.

These three results differ in both form and content because, in each case, the kind of information that the planner needs is different. In the first case, the system is trying to *choose between two options*, so the proverb should be adapted to suggest a preference to inform that choice. In the second case, the system is trying to *refine a plan*, so the proverb should be adapted to suggest a plan refinement rule. In the third case, the system is trying to *retrieve a plan for a goal*, so it is best to adapt the proverb to suggest a plan. In Brainstormer, preferences, plan refinement rules, and plans are distinct kinds of knowledge structures. Thus, the syntactic form of the result of adaptation is different in each case. There are important differences in content as well: For example, the concepts of *experience* and *expertise* that occur in the first case do not occur in the other two.

More generally, the adapter faces a problem of *mismatch in stage of planning process*. Cases the adapter is handed are often represented in a form that can be used fairly directly by one stage of the planning process, but must be substantially transformed in order to assist other stages of planning. If Brainstormer is to use its cases as flexibly as possible, it has to be able to carry out these transformations.

This transformation process turns out to involve reasoning with an abstract model of the planning process, which Brainstormer represents as a collection of Memory Organization

Packets or MOPs (Schank, 1982). The transformation process is described in detail in Jones (1992).

9.3 Problem Reformulation

To solve novel problems, transformation of cases into the planner's operational vocabulary must be coupled with a process of *problem reformulation,* in which a problem that appears difficult when represented one way is redescribed in a more perspicuous vocabulary.

Problem reformulation works in two stages. In the first stage, a seemingly novel planning problem is redescribed in an abstract vocabulary that matches the vocabulary of a particular culturally shared case. Having done this, several kinds of previously inaccessible knowledge may become available:

1. *Task reassessment.* The redescribed problem may contain new goals whose achievement would make progress on the goals of the original problem.
2. *Recommendation or analysis.* The redescribed problem may now match appropriateness conditions for applying the knowledge in the case. This knowledge either recommends a course of action (abstractly described), or makes an abstract causal analysis of the planner's situation.
3. *Indices.* Features of the new problem description may be able to serve as indices for retrieving relevant domain-specific information. This domain-specific information either helps confirm that the new description of the problem is appropriate, or suggests a more specific problem statement or solution.
4. *Elicitation templates.* If memory retrieval fails, these same indices can be used to elicit information from a user.

The second stage of problem reformulation exploits these new sources of knowledge. In this way, abstract knowledge can allow a planner to take a "fresh approach" to a seemingly intractable problem. Brainstormer uses problem reformulation to help it generate plans to counter terrorism. For example, we mentioned that Brainstormer can adapt the proverb *An old poacher makes the best keeper* to suggest *Try a plan of defense with an ex-terrorist actor* for the goal of preventing future terrorist attacks. Problem reformulation is an essential part of this process because the planning problem is to prevent future terrorist attacks, but the proverb talks of defending against attacks. Prevention and defense are different concepts, neither of which subsumes the other. On the one hand, there are many ways to prevent attacks other than defending. For example, one can bargain with an opponent to abandon the goal to attack, or threaten massive retaliation. Conversely, defending can be a plan for many goals other than prevention of attacks. For example, if an attack is inevitable, then defense may aim instead to minimize the anticipated damage.

It follows that adapting the proverb to fit the planning problem requires resolving this difference in vocabulary. Brainstormer accomplishes this by redescribing the problem of preventing terrorism using the vocabulary of defense. The redescribed problem includes a representation of a goal conflict between the terrorists and Brainstormer, in which the goal of the terrorists is to carry out attacks and the goal of Brainstormer is to defend against these attacks. Once the planning problem has been redescribed in this way, the following new knowledge becomes available to the planner:

1. *Task reassessment.* Brainstormer knows that its new goal of defending is a way of making progress on its original goal of preventing future terrorist attacks. Consequently, the system will attempt to find plans for this new goal.

2. *Recommendations.* Brainstormer can now apply the proverb's recommendation and suggest using a plan of defense with an ex-terrorist actor for the goal of defending against terrorist attacks. Moreover, because the terrorist attack has been redescribed as a goal conflict, the system can bring to bear any standard plans it has for resolving goal conflicts over and above the specific recommendations of the proverb.

3. *Indices.* The system now knows to look for specific standard plans of defense and for suitable ex-terrorists as actors of this defense plan.

4. *Elicitation Templates.* If Brainstormer fails to turn up any suitable candidates that match these indices, it uses these same indices to request assistance from the user.

In the next section, we describe the top-level structure of the Brainstormer system, and show how the tasks of transforming into the planner's operational vocabulary and problem reformulation arise within this framework.

9.4 The Architecture of Brainstormer

Brainstormer consists of two modules: the planner and the adapter. The planner attempts to solve planning problems posed to it by a user. The adapter assists the planner, by supplying appropriately adapted culturally shared cases whenever the planner runs into trouble.

Planning problems have two parts: a problematic situation and a set of goals, with respect to that situation for which the planner must generate plans. An example of a problematic situation is a particular past terrorist attack; typical goals include preventing future terrorist attacks with similar causes and retaliating against the agents responsible for the terrorist attack.

In the course of attempting to generate plans for these goals, the planner issues a stream of queries for knowledge structures it needs in the course of its planning. These queries correspond to difficulties it has encountered during planning. Queries are represented in the operational vocabulary of the planner. The adapter's job is to help the planner by finding answers to these queries. Conceptually, the input to the adapter is a set of culturally shared cases together with a list of queries that, if answered, could help the planner make progress in planning. The adapter's task is to transform its cases into answers to these queries.

This amounts to an expectation-driven architecture for adaptation: adaptation is driven by the need to match expectations in the form of queries issued by the planner. Early expectation-driven systems such as Cullingford's SAM (1978) simply maintained a list of active expectations that were exhaustively tested against inputs at each step of processing. In Brainstormer, however, the number of queries is too large for this approach to be practicable. Brainstormer's planner operates by pattern-directed retrieval of memory structures—rules for transforming goals, for example, or rules for refining plans. Every time the planner asks for a memory structure, Brainstormer's memory hands back any suitable candidates it retrieves and, at the same time, installs a query in memory requesting further memory structures that match the pattern of the planner's request. At any point in time, hundreds of queries may be active. Consequently, matching each query against a proverb is too expensive a proposition.

To overcome this difficulty, we employ an *opportunistic memory* (Birnbaum 1986; Dehn 1989; Hammond 1988; Hunter 1989; Ram 1989). Instead of storing queries in a global list, an opportunistic memory indexes queries in memory in terms of key features of their content, in such a way that potentially relevant queries can be retrieved whenever adaptation presents opportunities to satisfy them. Once retrieved, a query guides the adapter's search just like expectations in traditional expectation-based systems. In comparison to maintaining expectations in a flat list, however, an opportunistic memory has the important advantage that irrelevant queries—the great majority—are not checked at each step of processing. (See Fig. 9.1).

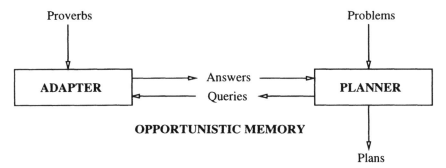

FIG. 9.1: The architecture of Brainstormer.

Queries have two parts: a pattern that potential answers must match, and a continuation procedure that says what to do with answers. A query's pattern is simply the request that gave rise to it, because these are the conditions that answers must satisfy. The continuation procedure takes answers to the query as input and uses them to continue planning.

Any answers that the opportunistic memory can retrieve immediately in response to a request from the planner are straightaway passed to the planner. But at the same time a query is also created and indexed in memory, so that if the adapter later comes up with any other relevant explanations on its own, these too will be passed to the planner and used in the same way. The planner, for its part, sees only a stream of answers to requests. From the planner's point of view, it makes no difference whether the answer arrives immediately or later as a result of adaptation: It will invoke the same planning routines in either case.

One issue that remains is how queries are to be indexed in memory so that they can be found when the adapter constructs answers to them. We have opted to store queries in terms of the kind of operational representation that they request. This has the effect of dividing the adaptation process neatly into two parts:

1. *Query finding*: A bottom-up phase in which cases are progressively transformed into the planner's operational vocabulary in a search for potentially relevant queries.

2. *Query fitting*: A top-down phase in which the planner's problem is reformulated under the joint guidance of the transformed case and a query. After problem reformulation, the case provides an answer to the query.

Although other approaches to query indexing are possible, our approach has the following important advantage. The combinatorics of adaptation turn out to be worst during problem reformulation. By indexing queries in terms of operational planner representations, problem reformulation is deferred until queries are retrieved. Consequently, queries help to focus inference throughout problem reformulation, where they are of greatest assistance to the adapter.

During query finding, certain components of cases are transformed into the operational vocabulary of the planner. The elements of this vocabulary are summarized in Table 9.1. After query finding, however, the remaining components of the case are still abstractly described. Next, during query fitting, the transformed case is matched against a query, triggering problem reformulation. Query fitting (and problem reformulation) is itself a two-step process. The first step is to redescribe some aspect of the planning problem in abstract terms; the second is to exploit the new knowledge that becomes available to the system once the problem is redescribed.

Table 9.1. Planner Data Structures in Brainstormer

Structure type	Interpretation and Use by the Planner
plan-for	Relates goals to sketchy plans that accomplish them
plan-refinement-rule	Rules used for plan refinement. Two subtypes: subgoal-refiners and role-refiners
goal-transformation-rule	Rules used in planning
explanation	Structures used in preventive counterplanning
prediction	Structures used in planning

To summarize, Brainstormer consists of two modules, the planner and the adapter. These modules communicate via queries, relying on an underlying opportunistic memory architecture to handle query creation and answer processing. The task of adaptation, thus, becomes a task of transforming culturally shared cases into answers to queries that can help the planner. This task, in turn, naturally divides into two subtasks: query finding and query fitting.

9.5 Redescription Inference

Underpinning both query finding and query fitting is a process called *redescription inference*. Redescription inference is a knowledge-intensive process that matches two representations in different vocabularies by transforming the first representation into the vocabulary of the second and then unifying the resulting representations with one another.

Redescription inference is necessary in Brainstormer because the user typically describes planning problems to Brainstormer in a domain-specific vocabulary very different from the abstract vocabulary of culturally shared cases. To bring the knowledge in culturally shared cases to bear on specific planning problems, this difference in vocabulary must be resolved. For example, there are many ways that a proverb might characterize a terrorist attack, including an act of frustration, an act of defiance, an act of revenge, an attack on civilians, a goal conflict, an illegal action, part of a propaganda campaign, and a political statement, among others.

Conversely, there are many ways in which any of the previous abstractions could be plausibly inferred from the planner's initial representation of a specific planning situation. For example, a goal conflict can be plausibly inferred by observing an action on the part of one person who violates a goal of someone else, or from the knowledge that two different people hold incompatible goals, or by noticing that someone is angry at someone else.

In short, adapting abstract knowledge to specific planning problems requires being able to reconcile descriptions of given objects expressed in incommensurate vocabularies. This is essentially a problem of bidirectional search. As the earlier examples indicate, this problem is potentially serious, because the branching factor is high in both directions. On the one hand, there are many possible abstractions of a given concrete situation; on the other, there are many ways to plausibly recognize an instance of any particular abstract concept in a concrete situation.

Redescription inference is used to relate different representations of a given object. Redescription inference in Brainstormer is used both during problem reformulation, and for transforming abstract knowledge into the operational vocabulary of the planner. Traces of redescription inference also turn out to be useful for representing proverbs.

There are two kinds of redescription inference: *part–whole inference* and *whole–whole inference*. Part–whole inference relates a part of some causal configuration to the whole configuration. For example, part–whole inference is needed to relate concepts like `terrorist-attack` and `goal-conflict`. A goal conflict in Brainstormer refers to a large causal configuration of goals and actions, whereas a terrorist attack is merely one way in which a goal conflict might manifest itself. In other words, a terrorist attack matches part of a set of conditions for plausibly inferring a goal conflict, but is not coreferential with the goal conflict. Similarly, part–whole inference can be used to relate a terrorist attack to a feud, a revenge scenario, or a war. Whole–whole inference, on the other hand, is useful in relating instances of concepts that plausibly corefer, such as an instance of a `terrorist-attack` and an instance of `illegal-action`. In the remainder of this section, we sketch redescription inference in Brainstormer.

9.5.1 Encoding the Results of Redescription

To motivate our discussion, we begin by outlining an example where redescription is required. As part of trying to come up with plans for preventing terrorism, Brainstormer issues a query for an explanation of a particular past terrorist attack. One of the system's cases is a representation of the proverb *No trouble but a priest is at the bottom of it,* which Brainstormer encodes as a causal connection between religious leaders and goal conflicts. Query finding transforms this initial representation into an explanation (of a goal conflict) and retrieves this query. Figure 9.2 depicts the query and the explanation used to retrieve it.[2]

---

[2]Brainstormer uses a frame-based representation system with a slot-filler notation:

```
<frame>
        <slot1> <filler1>
        <slot2> <filler2>
```

```
?explanation
    explained  terrorist-attack
                   actor  group
                              typical-elt  terrorist

causal-explanation
    explained  goal-conflict  =gc
    causals    (cause
                   cause   action
                              actor  religious-figure
                   caused  =gc)
```

FIG. 9.2. A query and a candidate answer, before query fitting.

The need for redescription arises during query fitting, at which point the system tries to match this explanation to the query. No difficulty is encountered until an attempt is made to match the terrorist-attack to the goal-conflict. At that point, the matcher complains that these are instances of incommensurate concepts and starts trying to redescribe the terrorist attack in terms of goal conflicts. Brainstormer's predefined concepts are arranged in an abstraction or type hierarchy; two frame instances are *commensurate* if, and only if, their type labels can be related in the type hierarchy. Redescription inference is always triggered by attempting to match two incommensurate concepts.

9.5.2 Vagueness and Dynamic Concept Formation

Before we can talk about how to efficiently redescribe a terrorist attack in terms of goal conflict, we have to make clear what we want the result to look like. What does a user really mean in using the proverb *No trouble but a priest is at the bottom of it* to explain a terrorist attack? Presumably, that the religious figure caused the terrorist attack as part of causing a goal conflict. Notice that the intended meaning is vague, in that it doesn't specify exactly how the religious figure is involved. The output of the adapter should be a representation of this information at the right level of ab-

---

Answers to queries are bindings to variables in the query of the form ?<type>. Each <type> is the name of one of Brainstormer's predefined concepts; bindings to the variable are restricted to instances of this concept. There is also a second kind of variable of the form =<symb>; these variables are used to enforce equality constraints between components of frames.

straction. What should this look like? We start with three inadequate answers to this question that point the way to a more acceptable one.

In Brainstormer's ontology, a goal conflict exists if two different agents hold incompatible goals, the pursuit of one of which negatively impacts the other. Here we can safely assume that the terrorists had the goal to carry out a terrorist attack, and that carrying out the attack violated goals of other agents: goals of people injured or killed in the attack, for example, and also Brainstormer's goal to prevent terrorism. Therefore, various goal conflicts obtain as a consequence of carrying out the terrorist attack.

A first attempt to represent the result of redescription might involve a four-step causal chain: A religious figure incites the terrorists to carry out the terrorist attack, causing the attack to occur, which violates a goal of someone else, thereby producing a goal conflict. Unfortunately, this representation is too specific, as it asserts that the religious figure actually causes the terrorists to have the goal to carry out the attack. The intent of the proverb is more vague. In particular, the religious figure may have been causally implicated in producing the terrorist attack in other ways as well; by facilitating its execution, for example, or by helping to ensure that its results are effective.

A second possibility is to represent the result of redescription using a one-step causal chain: the religious figure causes a goal conflict involving a terrorist attack. This representation, however, is too general. The output of adaptation is supposed to explain the terrorist attack, not the goal conflict. The proposed representation would also cover a situation in which a religious figure caused someone to have the goal to prevent the terrorist attack; although this may well give rise to a goal conflict once the terrorist attack occurs, it is hardly an explanation for the terrorist attack.

A third possibility is a disjunctive representation: List all of the ways that the religious figure could help the goal conflict come about that are also causally implicated in producing the terrorist attack, and represent the result of adaptation as the assertion that the religious figure interfered in one of these ways. Even assuming that an exhaustive list of disjuncts can be specified, this approach is still somewhat unsatisfying. Representing a vague piece of advice by cashing out all the ways it can be made more specific, although epistemologically adequate, is hardly concise or easy to reason with.

A truly satisfactory approach should allow us to represent the intended vague meaning of the proverb nondisjunctively, by creating a first-class object to represent "the thing that the religious figure caused, leading to the terrorist attack and the goal conflict." That way, the user's advice can be represented and reasoned about directly, without having to enumerate the various ways it can be specialized.

But what, in fact, does the proverb suggest that the religious figure caused? The answer, we believe, is an instance of a brand new concept: an instance of the class of actions that, like the terrorist attack, are performed intentionally and violate a goal of someone else, thereby signaling a goal conflict. In other words, we suggest that the advice asserts that a religious figure caused the terrorist attack under a new description built out of plausible recognition conditions for goal conflicts. Describing the terrorist attack in this way provides Brainstormer with an object that represents "the thing that the religious figure caused," whose internal structure suggests the various more specific ways that the religious figure could have been involved, without forcing a commitment to any one of them, and without enumerating all of them in a disjunction.

More generally, an important part of using abstract knowledge flexibly is being able to create and reason with novel concepts. Even if Brainstormer has never before been asked to describe a terrorist attack in terms of goal conflict, it should be able to do so if asked. This imposes new demands on our representation language. Many knowledge representation systems are incapable of representing new concepts on the fly. Usually, all possible concepts are hard-wired into an abstraction hierarchy that caches all subsumption relationships between these fixed concepts, and the system can only categorize inputs as instances of these concepts.

Brainstormer, in contrast, can dynamically extend its base set of concepts by the mechanism of lambda abstraction (Sowa 1984). A lambda abstraction, $\lambda(x)$(representations mentioning x), defines a new concept, whose instances are all of the x's that satisfy the conditions in the body of the lambda. In Brainstormer, we represent lambda-abstractions using the notation of *views*, which encode relationships between incommensurate representations of a single situation. Views are instances of lambda-abstractions. There are two kinds of views: *part–whole views* and *whole–whole views*, corresponding to the two kinds of redescription inference. Only part–whole views create new concepts dynamically; it is a

view of this type that is of interest here. Whole–whole views, in
contrast, construct instances of existing concepts.

```
causal-explanation
  explained part-whole-view =view
              source terrorist-attack =attack
                      actor group =terrorists
                            typical-elt
                              terrorist
              target goal-conflict =gc
                      actor1 =terrorists
                      actor2 brainstormer
                      goal1  achieve-goal
                             actor
                               =terrorists
                             state =attack
                      goal2  prevent-goal
                             actor
                               brainstormer
                             state =attack
  causals (cause
          cause  action
                 actor religious-Figure
          caused =view)
```

FIG. 9.3. The trace of redescription.

Figure 9.3 depicts the representation of the proverb after the
goal conflict has been redescribed to fit the planner's query. The
part-whole-view in this example encodes a part–whole redescription of the terrorist-attack as an instance of the
dynamically constructed abstract concept $\lambda(x)(x$ *is an intentional
action of some agent that violates a goal of someone else)*. As we discuss later, this new concept was built out of a configuration of
plausible recognition conditions for goal conflicts.

The part-whole-view in our example reifies "the thing the
religious figure caused" as an instance of a new class of action, so
that the system can reason about it without making any definite
commitment as to how the religious figure caused it. This representation of the proverb compactly encodes an answer to the
planner's original query, which Brainstormer can use to continue
planning. As we saw earler, the only way that Brainstormer could
represent this somewhat vague information without the benefit of
views is in terms of a clumsy disjunction of all the ways the advice might be made more specific.

By the way, from the planner's point of view, its problem has been reformulated using the vocabulary of goal conflict.

9.6 Memory Organization for Redescription

Now that we have specified the results we want from redescription, we show how Brainstormer's memory organization allows results like this to be efficiently computed. The task of redescription inference is to relate abstract and specific descriptions of the same situation. As we have seen, this involves bidirectional search, and, unfortunately, the branching factor is high in both directions. Therefore, neither backward chaining from a case nor forward chaining from a planning situation looks attractive.

One way to achieve greater efficiency is to make the abstract concept work together with the specific planning situation to guide inference. This suggests the following general strategy for organizing memory to support redescription inference: Create schemas for resolving differences in vocabulary and index these schemas in terms of the endpoints of the inference chains they help to construct. Search can then take place in a much smaller space of ways to instantiate these schemas.

```
gc-schema2
     lhs1 goal =goal1                    ;Someone has a goal
          actor agent =actor1            ;that an action
                                         ;   occur
          state action =act
     lhs2 cause =cs                      ;which causes the
          cause  =goal1                  ;action to occur.
          caused =act
     lhs3 action =act
          actor agent
     lhs4 violates-goal =v    ;The action violates a
          state =act          ;goal of someone else.
          goal  =goal2
     lhs5 goal =goal2
          actor agent =actor2
     rhs  goal-conflict
          actor1 =actor1
          actor2 =actor2
          goal1  =goal1
          goal2  =goal2
     abductively-infer (=goal1 =cs)
```

FIG 9.4. A viewing schema for goal conflicts.

We have followed this approach in Brainstormer. Associated with each of Brainstormer's hard-wired abstract concepts, such as goal conflict, are *viewing schemas*, which are special rules for inferring instances of that abstract concept. The antecedents of these rules are plausible recognition conditions for instances of the abstract concept; their consequents specify how the abstract concept should be instantiated.

A viewing schema that can relate the terrorist attack to the goal conflict is shown in Fig. 9.4. The `lhs` slots are the schema's antecedents, the `rhs` slot its consequent. The `abductively-infer` slot is described later.

Part–whole viewing schemas are indexed in memory in multiple ways, under every conjunction of the form (*concept, recog$_i$*) where *concept* is the concept that the schema infers, and the *recog$_i$* are components of the schema's recognition conditions whose presence is predictive of the schema's applicability. The schema shown in Figure 9.4, for example, is indexed in terms of (`goal-conflict, action`), (`goal-conflict, goal`), and (`goal-conflict, violates-goal`).

Whole–whole viewing schemas are very similar. Shown in Figure 9.5 is a viewing schema for relating `choose` and `design` frames. The schema encodes the knowledge that choosing a particular design specification can also be described as designing an artifact according to that specification. By convention, the `lhs1` and `rhs1` slots describe the two concepts to be related. The other preconditions and postconditions describe additional features of the memory structures associated with these concepts that are relevant to describing the relation between them. So, for example, the `lhs2` slot specifies that the result of the `choose` action must be a choice of a design specification, while the `rhs2` slot specifies that the corresponding `design` action must result in the chosen design specification.

Whole–whole schemas are indexed only in terms of the single conjunction of the types of the two objects to be related. The whole–whole viewing schema in Fig. 9.5, for example, is indexed in terms of the conjunction (`choose, design`).

9.6.1 The Redescription Inference Process

Brainstormer's memory of viewing schemas helps it to adapt cases to fit queries from the planner: Whenever the system tries to match pairs of incommensurate concepts, it uses viewing schemas

```
choose/design-1
     lhs1  choose  =ch          ;Choosing among a
     lhs2  results              ;list of options,
           cause   =ch
           caused  *choice      ;resulting in a choice
           object  *spec =spec  ;of a design
                                ;specification
     ;-->
     rhs1  design  =d           ;can be redescribed as
     rhs2  results              ;a design action that
           cause   =d           ;produces this
                                ;specification
           caused  =spec
```

FIG. 9.5. A whole–whole viewing schema.

to efficiently resolve its difficulty. Recall that two concepts are in-commensurate if they are unrelated in the abstraction hierarchy.

For example, we saw Brainstormer attempt to match an in-stance of a goal-conflict in a case it is handed to an instance of a terrorist-attack in a query. These two concepts are incommensurate, so Brainstormer retrieves all viewing schemas in-dexed in terms of these two concepts or generalizations of them. Action is a generalization of terrorist-attack in the ab-straction hierarchy, so the system retrieves gc-schema2, as shown earlier, using (goal-conflict, terrorist-attack) as an index. Next, the system matches the goal-conflict in the proverb to the consequent of the viewing schema, and matches the terrorist-attack to its lhs3 antecedent, then at-tempts to satisfy the schema's remaining antecedents.

Brainstormer tries to match all of these antecedents to existing memory representations, but is prepared to abductively infer some of them, if necessary. First, the system attempts to retrieve items from memory that satisfy the antecedents of the viewing schema. In this example, it retrieves its own goal to prevent terrorist at-tacks. Next, the system tries one-step backward chaining to sat-isfy the remaining antecedents. Limiting the system to one-step backward inference is somewhat arbitrary, but it has proved suf-ficient for our needs, while putting a hard limit on the adapter's computation. Finally, if some antecedents are still unsatisfied, then the system uses the abductively-infer slot of the viewing schema to determine if it is reasonable to abductively hypothesize them: abductive inference can proceed if the remaining antecedents are a subset of the filler of this slot (see Fig. 9.5).

If all antecedents of the viewing schema are now satisfied, the resulting variable bindings are then used to instantiate the schema's consequent, which is already bound to a component of the culturally shared case (here, the goal-conflict). Finally, a part-whole-view frame is built from this instantiated schema, as shown earlier in Fig. 9.3, and redescription inference is complete. Whole–whole inference proceeds in an identical fashion, except that this last step is skipped.

The process of matching antecedents of a viewing schema can recursively trigger further redescription inference. In the current example, the lhs3 recognition condition of the viewing schema requires that the actor of the action be of type agent. The actor of the terrorist-attack, however, is a group of terrorists, and groups are not agents. Brainstormer is, however, capable of redescribing a group of agents as a composite agent by retrieving and applying an appropriate viewing schema.

The possibility of recursive redescription inference means that Brainstormer's matching algorithm is actually a process of *means–ends analysis* (Fikes & Nilsson, 1971), in which the differences to be resolved are incommensurate type labels on concepts being matched, and the operators for resolving differences are viewing schemas.

It follows that in attempting to match two incommensurate items, Brainstormer can engage in a nontrivial amount of search. It is important to note, however, that this means–ends analysis approach is considerably more efficient than any obvious forward or backward chaining alternative, because search is much more tightly focused. Inference is only attempted if an important recognition condition of a concept is already known, and the system already wants to relate this condition to the concept. The foregoing figure sketches Brainstormer's algorithm for matching advice to queries.

As explained in Jones (1992), redescription inference derives ultimately from Merlin (Moore 1973) and is related to the idea of "views" in Jacob's (1987) ACE system.

(MATCH *case query***):**
IF the type labels of *case* and *query* match
THEN recursively MATCH corresponding slot fillers
of *case* and *query*
ELSE (REDESCRIBE *case query*).

(REDESCRIBE *case query***):**
1. Retrieve all viewing schemas indexed under *(case',query')*,
    where *case'* and *query'* are generalizations of the type labels of
    case and *query* in the abstraction hierarchy.
2. Until successful or no more viewing schemas, pick a viewing
    schema and do the following:
    a. MATCH *case* to the schema's consequent;
        MATCH *query* to the appropriate antecedent.
    b. Attempt to satisfy the other antecedents:
        i. Try memory retrieval.
        ii. Try one-step backward chaining.
        iii. Try abductive inference.
    c. IF all antecedents are satisfied
        THEN schema application is successful.
        IF the schema is a part–whole schema
        THEN construct an appropriate view frame as the
        binding associated with *case*

FIG 9.6. Matching and the redescription process.

9.6.2 Summary

Adaptation in Brainstormer involves redescribing specific planning situations to fit the abstract vocabulary of cases; we have seen that this can require being able to dynamically classify these situations as instances of abstract concepts. Existing representation systems are generally inadequate to this task. Like many frame-based representation systems, Brainstormer starts with a fixed set of base concepts arranged in a taxonomic hierarchy that encodes subsumption relations between the concepts. The system's representations of planning situations and abstract knowledge are initially encoded as instances of these concepts. In contrast to many other systems, however, the redescription process allows Brainstormer to flexibly and dynamically redescribe instances in terms of other concepts, thereby classifying them in new ways. Brainstormer can classify an instance in terms of base concepts that do not necessarily subsume it, and in terms of new concepts dynamically constructed from recognition conditions for other concepts.

9.7 A Detailed Example

In this section, we present an annotated transcript of part of a run of Brainstormer. For illustrative purposes, we give the system a memory of just one proverb—*He who has suffered more than is fitting will do more than is lawful*. User input is given in *italic*. Computer output is in typewriter font. The CAPITALIZED ENGLISH PARAPHRASES are all generated by Brainstormer from its internal representations using a simple template-driven, natural-language generator. The transcript has been trimmed and edited for readability.

A high-level outline of the example is as follows:

- *Input*: Brainstormer is asked to suggest plans for two goals—retaliating against a particular past terrorist attack by the P.L.O., and preventing similar attacks in the future.
- *Initial planning*: Brainstormer's planner transforms these initial goals in various ways, in a search for viable plans. Nothing turns up. In the process, Brainstormer's memory becomes studded with queries from the planner that, if satisfied, could allow it to make further progress.
- *Adaptation*: The proverb *He who has suffered more than is fitting will do more than is lawful* is adapted to answer an outstanding query from the planner for an explanation of the terrorist attack. First the initial representation of the proverb is transformed into an explanation, then it is matched to the query. Finally, evidence is found for unconfirmed premises of the explanation.
- *Final planning*: The explanation constructed by adaptation allows the planner to continue planning and eventually generate two concrete suggestions: *Improve living conditions in the refugee camps: try building a public housing project*, and *Get the Palestinians out of the refugee camps*.

The user begins by specifying the memory of proverbs that Brainstormer is to use, and the planning problem to be addressed. Recall that planning problems consist of a problematic situation—

here, a particular past terrorist attack—and a set of goals of Brainstormer that relate to this situation.

```
==> (set-case-memory '(suffer-pvb))
==> (set-problem plo-terrorist-attack)
==> (print-problem)
```

THE PROBLEMATIC SITUATION:
A TERRORIST ATTACK CARRIED OUT BY A GROUP OF
  TERRORISTS FROM THE P.L.O.

  Events:
      A GROUP OF PEOPLE WERE HELD HOSTAGE BY A GROUP
        OF TERRORISTS FROM THE P.L.O.
      A PERSON WAS KILLED BY A GROUP OF TERRORISTS
        FROM THE P.L.O.

GOALS OF BRAINSTORMER:
      * RETALIATE AGAINST AGENTS IMPLICATED IN CAUSING
        THE CONFINEMENT OF THE GROUP OF PEOPLE AND THE
        DEATH OF THE PERSON
      * PREVENT FUTURE INSTANCES OF CONFINEMENT
        OF A GROUP OF PEOPLE AND DEATH OF A PERSON
        THAT HAVE SIMILAR CAUSES

Next, the user starts the planner. Brainstormer's planner operates by progressively trying to transform its current goals into a form that may allow it to retrieve a relevant plan schema. In the interests of brevity, we only include one thread of the planner's transformation efforts.

```
   ==> (start-planner)
---Transforming goal
PREVENT FUTURE INSTANCES OF CONFINEMENT OF A GROUP OF
PEOPLE AND DEATH OF A PERSON THAT HAVE SIMILAR CAUSES
     into the new goals
PREVENT FUTURE INSTANCES OF CONFINEMENT OF A GROUP OF
  PEOPLE THAT HAVE SIMILAR CAUSES
PREVENT FUTURE INSTANCES OF DEATH OF A PERSON THAT
  HAVE SIMILAR CAUSES
---Attempting to retrieve a standard plan ... Failed.

---Transforming goal
PREVENT FUTURE INSTANCES OF DEATH OF A PERSON THAT
  HAVE SIMILAR CAUSES
     into the new goal
```

```
PREVENT FUTURE KILLINGS OF A PERSON THAT HAVE SIMILAR
   CAUSES
---Attempting to retrieve a standard plan ... Failed.

---Transforming goal
PREVENT FUTURE KILLINGS OF A PERSON THAT HAVE SIMILAR
   CAUSES
      into the new goal
PREVENT FUTURE TERRORIST ATTACKS CARRIED OUT BY GROUPS
   OF TERRORISTS FROM THE P.L.O. THAT HAVE SIMILAR
   CAUSES
---Attempting to retrieve a standard plan ... Failed.
```

When the planner can make no further progress, the user starts the adapter. The adapter's task is to transform a proverb in memory to meet a current query or information requirement of the planner. These queries were generated as a side effect of earlier planning. A large number of these queries were posted—on the order of 20 in the previous fragment—falling into three categories: requests for standard plans to satisfy a top-level goal, requests for counter-planning rules to transform those goals, and requests for descriptions of causal antecedents of the undesirable effects of the terrorist attack. It is a query of this third kind that our proverb ends up addressing; specifically, a query for an explanation of the terrorist attack.

The adapter begins by picking a proverb to adapt and then printing its representation. We set up our test run so that there is only one possible candidate, the proverb *He who has suffered more than is fitting will do more than is lawful*. The adapter prints the representation of the proverb in two different ways: first as a natural-language paraphrase, then using a slot-filler notation. The concept of *suffering* is represented as *a violation of a goal of the planner to maintain a condition*. Frames prefixed with an asterisk have not yet acquired real-world referents; all other frames stand for objects in the world of the planner's beliefs.

```
==> (start-adapter)
Attempting to adapt the following proverb:
   He who has suffered more than is fitting will do
more than is lawful

Initial representation of the proverb is as follows:
      "A VIOLATION OF A MAINTENANCE GOAL
      --ENABLES-->
```

```
AN ILLEGAL ACTION"

*enables.285
  cause  *violates.286
              goal  *maintenance-goal.287
                        actor *agent.288
      caused *illegal-action.289
              actor *agent.288
```

The adapter operates by progressively trying to transform the proverb into the operational vocabulary of the planner, in an attempt to generate representations that match a query in memory. One strategy for transforming the proverb is MOP-based reasoning with a model of the planning process. This strategy is attempted first, but does not work. Next, the adapter tries to apply "short-circuit" rules that in one step transform the proverb into a representation that may match an existing query. One such rule is applicable here: CAUSE->DIRECT-EXPLANATION, which the adapter uses to transform the initial representation of the proverb as a causal link into an explanation. This transformation commits the adapter to using the proverb in a particular way, namely, to explain a past illegal action.

```
[Attempting to integrate into a model of the planning
process]...Failed
[Attempting to operationalize using CAUSE->DIRECT
EXPLANATION] ...Succeeded!

Transformed representation of the proverb is as fol-
lows:
EXPLAIN AN ILLEGAL ACTION
    By * THERE EXISTS A VIOLATION OF A MAINTENANCE GOAL
       * THE VIOLATION OF THE MAINTENANCE GOAL
         --ENABLES-->
         THE ILLEGAL ACTION

*causal-explanation.290
   explained *illegal-action.289
               actor *agent.288
   causals    (*enables.285
               cause  *violates.286
                          goal  *maintenance-goal.287
                                    actor *agent.288
               caused *illegal-action.289)
```

After successfully transforming the proverb, the adapter retrieves queries that the transformed proverb may be able to answer. Brainstormer finds three candidate queries, labeled Q1, Q2, and Q3; it tries Q3 first because any answers to it subsume answers to Q1 and Q2. If Q3 didn't work, the adapter would back up and try the other two queries.

```
The following queries may be relevant:
    Q1: FIND AN EXPLANATION OF THE HOSTAGE-HOLDING
    Q2: FIND AN EXPLANATION OF THE KILLING
    Q3: FIND AN EXPLANATION OF THE TERRORIST ATTACK

    Applying pruning heuristic
        PREFER MORE GENERAL EXPLANATIONS
    Preferred queries are: Q3
```

Next, the adapter tries to match the transformed version of the proverb to this query. This is where problem reformulation takes place: To use the explanation of an illegal action to answer the query, the terrorist attack in the query must first be redescribed as an illegal action. Brainstormer has a very simple theory of illegality that it uses to implement redescription inference in this instance: An action is illegal if it is a standard kind of illegal action (e.g., murder) or if it results in what we call an "illegally caused state."

Reducing talk of illegal actions to talk of illegally caused states is not circular, because certain of Brainstormer's state representations are labeled as likely candidates for being illegally caused. The state of a person being dead is one such, because intentionally causing the death of someone is often illegal.[3] This theory of illegal actions is not intended to be taken very seriously: It should be thought of as an illustrative proxy for a better account. Given a more elaborate account of illegality, however, the same general kinds of inferential strategies would suffice for redescription.

```
[Attempting to match proverb to Q3
    [Redescribing THE TERRORIST ATTACK as
    AN ILLEGAL ACTION
        [Redescribing
            THE GROUP OF TERRORISTS FROM THE P.L.O.
            as AN AGENT]
```

---

[3]There are exceptions, of course: legally sanctioned executions, killings on the battlefield, and so forth.

```
     [Redescribing THE DEATH OF A PERSON
          as AN ILLEGALLY CAUSED STATE
          Hypothesizing that
          THE DEATH OF THE PERSON CAN BE DESCRIBED AS
          AN ILLEGALLY CAUSED STATE]]]
  ... succeeded
```

```
Transformed representation of the proverb is
  as follows:
  EXPLAIN A TERRORIST ATTACK CARRIED OUT BY A GROUP OF
  TERRORISTS FROM THE P.L.O.
     By * THE TERRORIST ATTACK CAN BE DESCRIBED AS
          AN ILLEGAL ACTION
        * THERE EXISTS A VIOLATION OF A MAINTENANCE
          GOAL OF THE GROUP OF TERRORISTS
        * THE VIOLATION OF THE MAINTENANCE GOAL
          --ENABLES-->
          THE ILLEGAL ACTION
```

```
*causal-explanation.330
   explained terrorist-attack.206<--VIEW-->illegal-ac-
tion.313
                    actor group.208<--VIEW-->agent.325
                              prototypical-member
                                   terrorist
                                   organization PLO
                         events (hold-hostages.209 kill.207)
      causals      (*enables.322
                         cause  *violates.323
                                   goal  *maintenance-goal.324
                                             actor
agent.325<--VIEW-->group.208
                         caused illegal-action.313
                                   actor
agent.325<--VIEW-->group.208)
```

```
illegal-action.313
     actor         agent.325<--VIEW-->group.208
     illegality
         illegally-caused-state.327<--VIEW-->dead.220
```

```
actor person.210
```

Brainstormer uses its theory of illegality to redescribe the terrorist attack as an illegal action. Redescription is predicated on the plausible assumption that the death in the terrorist attack was, in fact, illegally caused; this assumption becomes a premise of the emerging explanation of the terrorist attack, which the adapter will later attempt to verify.

The group of terrorists must also be redescribed as an agent for redescription to go through. Groups are not classified as agents, but groups of agents can be redescribed as agents.

Again the adapter prints out the transformed version of the proverb. The representation of the proverb has now been fleshed out with the information added by matching it to the query. In particular, referents for various pieces of the explanation have now been established in the planner's problematic situation. For example, the agent of the illegal action (now represented as agent.325) has been tentatively identified as coreferential with the terrorist group in the planner's original description of its problem (group.208). The <--VIEW--> relations graphically depict the results of redescription inference; they can also be read as asserting coreference of the linked representations.

The adapter now attempts to verify the plausibility of its proposed explanation of the terrorist attack, by trying to discover evidence for its unconfirmed premises. The adapter begins by trying to confirm the premise introduced to plausibly redescribe the terrorist attack as an illegal action. The system has three verification strategies at its disposal. The first is to retrieve a belief from memory that matches the premise; the second is to plausibly assume the final unconfirmed premise; the third is to give up and ask the user. In this case, the first two strategies fail, so the system asks the user.

```
Attempting to verify THE DEATH OF THE PERSON CAN BE
DESCRIBED AS AN
        ILLEGALLY-CAUSED STATE
        [Trying MEMORY SEARCH] ... Failed
        [Trying PLAUSIBLE INFERENCE (PROVERB SUPPORT)]
... Failed
        [Trying ASK THE USER]

CAN THE DEATH OF THE PERSON BE DESCRIBED AS AN
ILLEGALLY CAUSED STATE?    (yes/no)   ==> yes
            ...Succeeded!
```

Confirming the next premise illustrates memory retrieval at work. The adapter successfully retrieves evidence that supports the premise that the terrorists are suffering. Notice that memory retrieval itself can trigger further redescription inference: The system plausibly redescribes the terrorists as Palestinian refugees, based on their membership in the P.L.O.

```
Attempting to verify THERE EXISTS A VIOLATION OF A
MAINTENANCE
    GOAL OF A GROUP OF TERRORISTS FROM THE P.L.O.
    [Trying MEMORY SEARCH
        [Redescribing
            THE GROUP OF TERRORISTS FROM THE P.L.O. AS
            PALESTINIAN REFUGEES]]
    ... Succeeded!

Retrieved PALESTINIAN-REFUGEE-CAMPS-SITUATION:
    PALESTINIAN REFUGEES ARE CONFINED TO REFUGEE CAMPS
    --CAUSES-->
    A VIOLATION OF THE GOAL OF PALESTINIAN REFUGEES
    TO MAINTAIN GOOD LIVING CONDITIONS
```

One unconfirmed premise remains, which is that the suffering of the terrorists is causally linked to their carrying out the terrorist attack. The adapter uses its second verification strategy to simply assume this premise. This assumption amounts to "wishfully hypothesizing" that the proverb, in fact, applies: after all, the main point of the proverb is to assert the existence of a causal link of this kind.

```
[Attempting to verify A VIOLATION OF A GOAL OF
PALESTINIAN REFUGEES
        TO MAINTAIN GOOD LIVING CONDITIONS
        ENABLES AN ILLEGAL ACTION CARRIED OUT BY A
        GROUP OF TERRORISTS FROM THE P.L.O.
        [Trying MEMORY SEARCH] ... Failed
        [Trying PLAUSIBLE INFERENCE (PROVERB SUPPORT)]]
    ... Succeeded!

Final representation of the proverb is as follows:
EXPLAIN A TERRORIST ATTACK CARRIED OUT BY A
GROUP OF TERRORISTS FROM THE P.L.O.
        By * THE TERRORIST ATTACK CAN BE DESCRIBED
            AS AN ILLEGAL ACTION
          * THERE EXISTS A VIOLATION OF A GOAL OF
            PALESTINIAN REFUGEES TO MAINTAIN GOOD LIVING
            CONDITIONS
          * THE VIOLATION OF THE MAINTENANCE GOAL
            --ENABLES-->
            THE ILLEGAL ACTION
```

```
         * PALESTINIAN REFUGEES ARE CONFINED
           TO REFUGEE CAMPS
         * PALESTINIAN REFUGEES ARE CONFINED
           TO REFUGEE CAMPS
           --CAUSES-->
           THE VIOLATION OF THE GOAL OF PALESTINIAN
           REFUGEES TO MAINTAIN GOOD LIVING CONDITIONS
```

The adapter has now constructed a complete and adequately confirmed answer to the planner's original query for an explanation of the terrorist attack. (We omit its slot-filler representation from the transcript.) Control now returns to the planner, which proceeds to use this answer to further transform its goals and to retrieve a plan schema.

```
---Transforming goal
PREVENT FUTURE TERRORIST ATTACKS CARRIED OUT BY
    GROUPS OF TERRORISTS FROM THE P.L.O. THAT HAVE
    SIMILAR CAUSES
      into the new goal
    STOP A VIOLATION OF A GOAL OF PALESTINIAN REFUGEES
    TO MAINTAIN GOOD LIVING CONDITIONS
    ---Attempting to retrieve a standard plan ...
Failed.

---Transforming goal
STOP A VIOLATION OF A GOAL OF PALESTINIAN REFUGEES TO
    MAINTAIN GOOD LIVING CONDITIONS
      into the new goal
    ACHIEVE GOOD LIVING CONDITIONS FOR PALESTINIAN
    REFUGEES
---Attempting to retrieve a standard plan ...
Succeeded!
    Index     : A GOAL TO ACHIEVE GOOD LIVING
                CONDITIONS FOR PALESTINIAN REFUGEES
    Retrieved: A PLAN TO BUILD A HOUSING PROJECT

---Transforming goal
STOP A VIOLATION OF A GOAL OF PALESTINIAN REFUGEES
    TO MAINTAIN GOOD LIVING CONDITIONS
      into the new goal
STOP CONFINEMENT OF PALESTINIAN REFUGEES
---Attempting to retrieve a standard plan ... Failed.
```

Problem reformulation plays a crucial role in this example. The terrorist attack must be redescribed as an illegal action for

Brainstormer to successfully relate the proverb *He who has suffered more than is fitting will do more than is lawful* to its problem. Once this redescription has been carried out, the abstract causal knowledge in the proverb allows Brainstormer to generate suggestions that it would never have considered in the absence of the proverb. First, the adapter uses the proverb's abstract description of suffering as a goal violation to recall knowledge of the Palestinian refugee problem. Second, the planner uses the causal link between suffering and illegal actions to relate knowledge about the refugees to Brainstormer's goal of preventing future terrorist attacks.

9.8 Conclusion: Brainstormer as a Model of Reasoning from First Principles

When people are faced with novel problems for which none of their past experience seems immediately appropriate, they are often advised to "go back to first principles." Brainstormer can be thought of as a cognitively plausible model of reasoning from first principles. Brainstormer's approach contrasts sharply with that of another school of thought in artificial intelligence, typified by GPS (Newell, 1963) and SOAR (Laird et al., 1986). On the GPS view, a problem solver is initially equipped with "first principles" in the form of atomic operators or inference rules. Experience to guide problem solving is acquired gradually in the form of *macros* or frozen chains of inference or operator applications that proved useful in the past. Reasoning from first principles is thus conceived of as a knowledge-poor process of search and inference.

Even supposing for a moment that people fall back on GPS-like operators when they lack domain-specific expertise, it seems more than a little implausible that the process by which they bring this knowledge to bear is itself knowledge-poor. People frequently encounter problems that are, to some extent, novel, and consequently are experts at coping with the unfamiliar.

Therefore, in designing Brainstormer , we have taken a very different approach from that of GPS and SOAR. Whereas we agree that people often solve novel problems by falling back on abstract first principles (in Brainstormer first principles are encoded as culturally shared cases) we start from the assumption that the process by which this abstract knowledge is applied to novel problems is knowledge rich. For example, Brainstormer employs viewing schemas to guide problem reformulation. A considerable body of knowledge is also required to transform culturally-shared cases into operational planner representations (see Jones, 1992).

The overall picture that emerges is very different from GPS and SOAR: reasoning from first principles is not a knowledge-poor, search-intensive process, but is a memory-intensive process that relies on a variety of different kinds of knowledge organized appropriately in memory.

Part III
Sample Implementation

10. Micro SWALE

This chapter is intended for the reader who wants to gain a hands on understanding of the issues related to programming explanation-building systems. We present a miniature version of the SWALE program discussed in Part II. This miniature version contains modules that are, of course, much simpler than the modules of the original SWALE system, although the basic functionality is preserved. The user can learn a lot about what is involved in building such systems by studying and running the code listed at the end of the chapter. Those who really want to become intimately familiar with this kind of work will want to make their own modifications to the program. For those readers, we have included a set of suggested exercises.

10.1. How to Run Micro SWALE

Micro SWALE is written in standard Common Lisp, as described in *Common Lisp: The Language, Second Edition* (Steele 1990). You need a Common Lisp interpreter and the code that appears at the end of this chapter. The code has been divided into files, and each file represents one module. You can either use a text or Lisp editor to enter this code into the appropriate files, or contact the authors for information on how to download the files.

Once you have the files, start your Lisp, using the appropriate method for your particular implementation, and load the `swale` module. This should automatically load the other required files. If not, consult your Lisp manual for information on how the `require` and `provide` functions work in your implementation of Lisp. If all else fails here, change the

```
(require module)
```

forms at the beginning of each file to

```
(load  filename)
```

forms, where *filename* is the name you gave to *module*. Your files will no longer be portable, but at least they'll load. Now, just type

```
(explain-swale)
```

A log of the output you should expect to see appears at the end of this chapter, after the code. You can expect spacing and generated names (e.g., names like m-xp4) to vary slightly, but if there is a significant difference between what you see and what output log shows, then there is some bug in the code, due to either a transcription error or an unexpected difference in Common Lisp implementations. Please send us information and we'll see what we can do to resolve the problem.

10.2. Micro SWALE Module Organization

The code for Micro SWALE is distributed into about a dozen small modules. Figure 10.1 groups them together by functionality. The names inside of boxes (e.g., swale) are modules. The gray boxes group these modules into conceptual units. The top unit contains the code specific to the Swale example. The next unit contains the general explanation code. The bottom unit contains the code for representing memory structures.

The names outside the boxes (e.g., explain-swale) are the primary functions defined by the modules and exported to the modules "above." Lines connecting modules roughly indicate who depends on whom.

Each module is responsible for a different part of the Micro SWALE system:

- swale runs the Micro SWALE example. It's tiny, because all it really does is call the explainer with a pre-defined story.
- swale-mem defines the initial memory elements for the Micro SWALE example.
- explainer explains stories. It calls the retriever, accepter, and tweaker, roughly as described in earler chapters.
- retriever finds candidate explanations for a story. It finds XPs in memory and applies them to the story.
- accepter looks for problems with an explanation.
- tweaker tries to fix explanations that have problems. It modifies XPs and applies the modified versions to the story.
- applier applies an XP to a story. It's tiny.

- `mops` manages MOP memory, which consists of frames that are indexed by features.
- `frames` creates frames and manages their slots and abstractions.
- `index` handles the indexing of frames.
- `print-utils` contains utilities for printing messages and MOPs in a readable form.

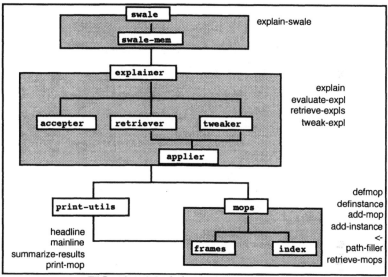

FIG. 10.1. Modules in Micro SWALE.

The remainder of this chapter discusses each module, focusing particularly on its primary functions, followed by suggested exercises for extending the Micro SWALE system.

10.3. The swale Module

This module defines one primary function, `explain-swale`.

```
(explain-swale)
```

resets memory to the memory structures contained in `swale-mem`, and calls the explainer on the Swale story.

10.4. The swale-mem Module

This module defines MOPs and instances for horses, horse races, jogging, the Jim Fixx XP, Swale, and the anomaly of Swale's death. For a description of MOPs, instances, and frames, see the later sections on the mops and frames modules. Here we discuss some of the particular MOPs and instances defined in swale-mem and why they are defined the way they are.

10.4.1. Simple objects

Many of the MOPs in swale-mem are straightforward. Some simply define primitive objects (e.g., animals, horses, hearts, etc.). For example,

```
(defmop m-animal (m-animate))
(defmop m-human (m-animal))
(defmop m-horse (m-animal))
```

says that humans and horses are animals. All concepts are given names beginning with "m-" (for MOP) to distinguish them from English words.

Primitive concepts, such as m-horse and m-human, provide distinguishable names. For example, even though the definitions of m-horse and m-human are identical, they generate separable concepts. That is, if Swale is defined to be a horse, and the jogging script is defined to take a human actor, then Swale can be identified as not a human and therefore rejected as an actor of jogging.

Many concept definitions include extra information. For example,

```
(defmop m-healthy-animal (m-animal)
  :health m-good)
```

defines a subclass of animals whose health is good. :health is called *role* of the MOP, and m-good is the *filler* of that role. The combination of a role and its filler is called a *slot*. We will usually identify a slot with its role, so we will say that m-good fills the :health slot of m-healthy-animal. All our roles are given names beginning with a colon (:), to distinguish them from fillers.

Slots allow us to give specific attributes of a concept. A concept can have any number of slots. A slot can have only one filler, but a filler might be a list of items, as we shall see. Certain roles, such as :actor, :events, and :outcome, are used for particular purposes, but there is no predefined set of possible roles.

10.4.2. Instances

M-horse and m-human are abstract concepts. Stories will be about particular individual instances of those concepts. For example, Swale and Jim Fixx are instances of a racehorse and a human, respectively.

In swale-mem, Swale is defined thus:

```
(definstance m-swale
      (m-racehorse m-healthy-animal
       m-young-animal))
```

This says that Swale is a healthy, young racehorse. m-racehorse, m-healthy-animal and m-young-animal are abstract concepts defined elsewhere in swale-mem. We could have defined Swale more directly like this:

```
(definstance m-swale (m-racehorse)
   :health m-good
   :age m-young)
```

This definition says the same thing. For Micro SWALE to be able to make use of this definition, however, you first have to do the exercise on nested constraints.

10.4.3. Simple events

Only slightly more complicated are the definitions for simple events. For example, here's the definition of the MOP for running events:

```
(defmop m-run-event (m-event)
   :actor m-animal
   :action m-move-body-part
   :object m-leg
   :speed m-fast)
```

This defines a generalization of all running events involving animals. There can be instances of events too. For example, `swale-mem` defines `m-swale-won-belmont`, which is an instance of a winning event.

10.4.4. Scripts

Scripts are more complex than simple events. A script has a set of roles, such as the actor of the script, a sequence of events, and a set of connections between the roles of the script and its events. For example, here is the MOP for the horse race script:

```
(defmop m-horserace-event (m-script-event)
  :owner m-human
  :jockey m-human
  :actor m-racehorse
  :events ((:enter m-enter-race-event)
   (:mount m-mount-event)
   (:run m-run-event))
  :constraints (((:owner)
    (:events :enter :actor))
   ((:jockey)
    (:events :mount :actor))
   ((:actor)
    (:events :enter :entry)
    (:events :mount :object)
    (:events :run :actor))))
```

`M-horserace-event` has three roles: an owner, a jockey, and a racehorse. There are three events: being entered in the race, mounting the horse, and the race itself. (We picked just a few events, for simplicity. We left representing the outcome of the race as an exercise for the reader.) Finally, there are the connections between the events. The connections are the tricky part.

For example, we have to represent the fact that the horse that's entered in the race is the one that the jockey mounts and the one that runs the race. To do this, we need to be able to refer unambiguously to the various events.

To do this, we use *labeled event lists*. In `m-horserace-event`, in the `:events` slot, we have a list of *(label event)* forms. They label the entering with `:enter`, the mounting with `:mount`, and the running with `:run`.

Then, in the `:constraints` slot, we connect the parts of various events together. The `:constraints` slot is filled with a list of constraints. Each constraint is a list of *paths*.

A *path* is a list of roles, such as (`:events   :enter :actor`). We apply a path to a concept by successively finding

the filler of each role in the path.   For example, if we apply
(:events :enter :actor) to m-horserace-event, the
first role, :events, returns the list of labeled events. A list of
labeled events is treated like an "anonymous" concept (see the
function slots-of in the frames module). The second role,
:enter, returns the event labeled with :enter in that list. The
third role, :actor, returns the actor of that entering event.

By definition, a constraint says that all its paths must resolve
to the same object.   Thus, the third constraint in
m-horserace-event that the actor of the script, the horse
entered, the horse mounted, and the horse that runs must all be
the same object.

10.4.5. Explanation patterns

Like scripts, XP's (explanation patterns) have events with
shared elements. The difference is that XP's specify causal
connections between the events. Labeled event lists help here, too.
Here's the XP for death due to illness:

```
(defmop m-die-from-illness-xp (m-xp)
  :events ((:illness m-bad-health-state)
           (:outcome m-dead-state))
  :causals ((:illness => :outcome))
  :constraints (((:events :illness :object)
                 (:events :outcome :object)))))
```

The :events and :constraints slots are treated the same as
with scripts. So the constraint in this XP says that the object of
the illness is the same as one who dies.

The :causals slots contains a list of causal forms. Each
causal is a list of event labels, followed by a =>, followed by more
event labels. The events before the => are the antecedent events,
and the events after the => are the consequent events. A causal
form represents the claim that the antecedent events combined
caused the consequent events. Thus, the previous XP says that
the illness state caused the death. The Jim Fixx XP (m-fixx-xp)
has a slightly more complex causality and will be discussed in
more detail later.

10.4.6. States

States are a major kludge in swale-mem. Here's an example:

```
(defmop m-bad-health-state (m-state)
  :object m-unhealthy-animal)
```

To understand this definition, we also need to see this one:

```
(defmop m-unhealthy-animal (m-animal)
  :health m-bad)
```

In other words, being in bad health is defined as whatever state an unhealthy animal is in. Although logical, why such a strangely roundabout definition?

The answer is that the states in Micro SWALE that we are interested in, such as health and age, are attributes of an object, and attributes in a frame-based system are normally specified in the slots of the object. In an XP, however, we need to refer to "the state where an object has a certain attribute." For example, the "death from illness XP" needs to link the state of being unhealthy to another state of being dead. Therefore, as needed, we construct states for attributes, defining them in terms of an appropriate abstraction of the object involved.

Many of these attributes change over time. For example, the story to be explained is Swale's death, so Swale must be dead. But in explaining this death, we have to make inferences based on when Swale was alive and healthy. Some other systems, such as CYC (Lenat & Guha, 1990) handles this by having frames represent "slices in time" of an object, (e.g., "Swale when he was 3," "Swale when he was sick," "Swale when he was dead") all of which are part of the whole Swale history.

For simplicity, we take a different approach in Micro SWALE. Code that matches states is careful not to match prior states with present states. Currently this only affects the Tweaker function `apply-constraint`.

10.5. The Explainer Module

This module defines the top-level function `explain`, and two subfunctions, `initialize-explainer` and `run-explainer`, as shown in Table 10.1.

Table 10.1. Main Forms in the `explainer` Module.

Form	Type
`(explain &optional story)`	[Function]
`(initialize-explainer story)`	[Function]
`(run-explainer)`	[Function]

`Explain` takes one optional argument. If given, it should be the name of an instance of a story. The only story currently defined is `m-swale-story`. Fig. 10.2 shows a graphical view of `explain`.

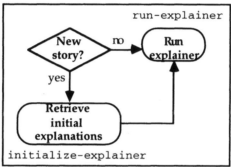

FIG. 10.2. The `explain` function.

`(Explain 'm-swale-story)` will find an acceptable explanation for Swale's death, if possible. `explain` keeps a queue of candidate explanations. After it returns one explanation, it's possible that there are others yet to try. `(explain)` with no arguments will look for another acceptable explanation for the same story.

`Initialize-explainer` just calls the retriever function `retrieve-expls` to get an initial set of possible explanations. `Run-explainer` calls the Accepter function `evaluate-expl` to evaluate the first explanation on the queue. `Evaluate-expl` returns a (possibly empty) list of problems. `Run-explainer` then calls the Accepter function `explanation-status` to determine the seriousness of these problems. If the explanation is acceptable, it will be returned. If the explanation is tweakable, the explainer calls the Tweaker function `tweak-expl` to construct a set of new explanations. Then the explainer calls the Retriever function `retrieve-expls` to see if features in the problems found by the Accepter retrieve other possible explanations from memory. Fig. 10.3 shows a graphical view of `run-explainer`.

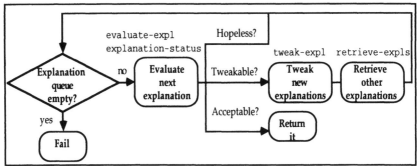

FIG. 10.3. The `run-explainer` function.

Both `retrieve-expls` and `tweak-expl` return candidate explanations, which are added to the explanation queue. `run-explainer` continues in a loop until either an acceptable explanation is found, or the explanation queue is exhausted.

10.6. The Retriever Module

This module defines the main function for retrieving explanations from memory, given a story and, optionally, a list of problems with a previous explanation of the story. The main functions are shown in Table 10.2.

Table 10.2. Main Forms in the `retriever` Module.

Form	Type
`(story->cues story)`	[Function]
`(problems->cues problems)`	[Function]
`(retrieve-xps story problems)`	[Function]
`(already-tried-xp-p xp story)`	[Function]

This module is pretty simple. Components of the story and problems are extracted to be cues for retrieving XPs from memory. Each XP retrieved is applied to the story to create a candidate explanation, unless there's already an explanation with the same story and XP in memory. Fig. 10.4. gives a graphical view of the flow of control in the `retriever` module.

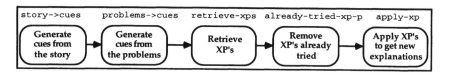

FIG. 10.4. Flow of control in the `retriever` module.

10.7. The Accepter Module

This module defines the main function for evaluating explanations. Table 10.3 shows the main forms, each of which corresponds to one of three classes of problems:
- relevance problems—does the explanation actually explain the anomaly?
- believability problems—are the components of the explanation believable?
- usefulness problems—does the explanation satisfy the specified purpose (e.g., predicting when the anomaly might occur again)?

Table 10.3. Main Forms in the `accepter` Module.

Form	Type
(relevance-problems *xp*)	[Function]
(believability-problems *xp*)	[Function]
(usefulness-problems *xp purpose*)	[Function]

Figure 10.5 shows the flow of control in this module; basically, problems are collected from each of the functions.

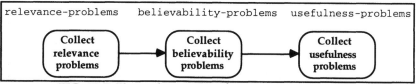

FIG. 10.5. Flow of control in the `accepter` module.

`Relevance-problems` collects relevance problems. An explanation has relevance problems if the anomaly to be explained doesn't match the outcome of the associated explanation pattern (XP). Fig. 10.6 shows the flow of control for this function.

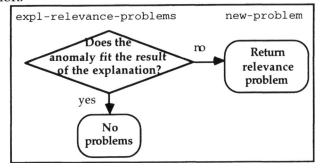

FIG. 10.6. Flow of control in `relevance-problems`.

`Usefulness-problems` collects usefulness-problems. An explanation has usefulness problems if it doesn't satisfy the needs of the purpose for which the explanation was constructed. Figure 10.7 shows the flow of control for this function.

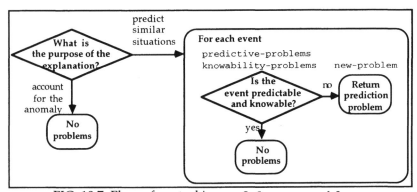

FIG. 10.7. Flow of control in `usefulness-problems`.

Currently, there are two possible purposes for an explanation: simply account for what happened, or predict when it may happen again. If the purpose is to account for what happened, then any explanation that is relevant is OK. If the purpose is to predict, however, then only explanations whose components are predictable and knowable will work. For example, explaining

Swale's death by presuming a heart defect is a possible account, but having a bad heart is a hidden state and not normally knowable, so the explanation is not useful for prediction.

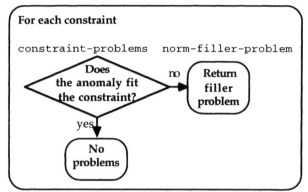

FIG. 10.8. Flow of control in `believability-problems`.

`Believability-problems` collects believability problems. The code for testing for believability is one of the more complicated sections of code in Micro SWALE. The top-level flow of control isn't bad, though, as shown in Fig. 10.8.

The complexity arises in applying constraints. To explain how it works, we'll trace how the constraints in the Jim Fixx XP are applied to the death of Swale.

First, here is the Jim Fixx XP:

```
(defmop m-fixx-xp (m-xp)
  :observed m-healthy-animal
  :expected m-unhealthy-animal
  :events ((:jog m-jog-event)
    (:run m-run-event)
    (:exert m-exert-event)
    (:defect m-heart-defect-state)
    (:outcome m-dead-state))
  :causals ((:jog => :run)
    (:run => :exert)
    (:defect :exert => :outcome))
  :constraints (((:events :jog :actor)
    (:events :run :actor)
    (:events :exert :actor)
    (:events :defect :owner)
    (:events :outcome :object)))))
```

This XP has five events/states: jogging, running, exertion, heart defect, and death. The jogging caused the running, the running caused exertion, and the heart defect plus the exertion caused the death.

When the Accepter evaluates this XP with respect to Swale's death, `relevance-problems` finds it relevant, because Swale's death (`m-swale-dead-state`) fits the outcome (`m-dead-state`).

When `usefulness-problems` looks at each event, it will complain that `m-heart-defect-state` is not knowable, because that state is marked in `swale-mem` as a hidden state. This means that the XP is not good for predicting future deaths, but it still may be able to account for what happened.

`Believability-problems` looks at each constraint. In this case, there's just one:

```
((:events :jog :actor)
 (:events :run :actor)
 (:events :exert :actor)
 (:events :defect :owner)
 (:events :outcome :object))
```

This says that the actor of the jogging, the actor of the running, the actor of the exertion, the owner of the defective heart, and the object that dies, are one and the same.

First, we have to find all the paths that refer to the outcome event. If there are no such paths, then we can ignore the constraint, because it doesn't affect whether the XP applies to a particular anomaly.

Paths referring to the outcome will have the form (`:events :outcome ...`) (See `outcome-path-p`). In this case, there is one such path:

```
(:events :outcome :object)
```

Because the outcome is supposed to be `m-swale-dead-state`, we apply the remainder of the path following `:outcome`, that is, (`:object`), to `m-swale-dead-state`, to find the component of `m-swale-dead-state` being constrained. This yields `m-swale`.

We now apply the other paths in the constraint to the events in the XP, to see what `m-swale` is supposed to match.

```
(:events :jog :actor)           =>    m-human
(:events :run :actor)           =>    m-animal
(:events :exert :actor)         =>    m-animal
(:events :defect :owner)        =>    m-animal
```

Because Swale is an animal, three of the paths are satisfied, but the first one fails. `believability-problems` therefore creates an instance of a problem MOP. In particular, it creates an instance of a "nonnormative filler" problem. A nonnormative filler problem is one where applying an XP to the story causes some event in the XP to have a slot with an non-standard filler.

```
m-non-normative-filler-problem
   :explanation name of the explanation with the
problem
   :path (:events :jog :actor)
   :expected-value m-human
   :observed-value m-swale
```

This instance says "Using this explanation would make Swale the actor of the jogging event, but that path should have a human." This instance holds the information that the Tweaker will need to try and fix the problem.

10.8. The Tweaker Module

This module defines the main function for tweaking an explanation. Fig. 10.9 shows the flow of control.

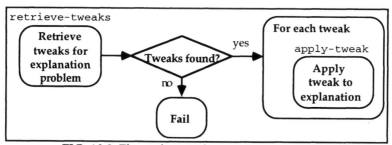

FIG. 10.9. Flow of control in `tweaker` module.

Given an explanation and a list of problems with it, the Tweaker looks for possible tweaks for the XP underlying the explanation, applies the tweaks to generate new XPs, and applies the XPs to the original story to generate new explanations.

Tweaks are retrieved by the type of problem they resolve. Three tweaks for the nonstandard filler problem are defined in `swale-mem`, corresponding to three important tweaks in the original SWALE system. Only one tweak, however, actually does anything.

The `m-replace-action-use-stereotypes-tweak` looks like this:

```
(defmop m-replace-action-use-stereotypes-tweak
  (m-tweak)
  :function replace-action-search-through-stereotypes
  :problem m-non-normative-filler-problem)
```

This says that to fix a problem with a nonstandard filler, call `replace-action-search-through-stereotypes`. Figure 10.10 shows the flow of control for this tweak.

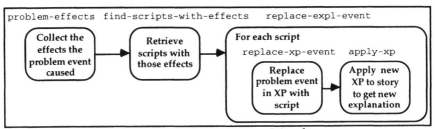

FIG. 10.10. Flow of control for the
`replace-action-search-through-stereotypes` tweaking
function.

Basically, if the Accepter has rejected an actor doing an action in an XP, this function looks for other events typical of that actor that would have the same effect as the problematic event. Each one that is found can replace the problematic event in the XP to generate a new XP without that problem.

In this case, the actor is Swale and the problematic event is jogging. The steps followed in fixing this problem are:

- Find out what effects jogging had in the XP. In the Jim Fixx XP, jogging caused running.
- Find scripts for Swale that have running in them. There are no scripts specifically for Swale, but there is one for

racehorses, namely the horse race script, and it includes running.

- Make a copy of the Jim Fixx XP, with jogging replaced by horse racing.
- Apply this new XP to the original Swale story, to get a new explanation: Swale ran in a horse race, and the exertion, combined with a hidden heart defect, led to his death.

As with the constraint checking code in the Accepter, most of the code complexity comes from dealing with the labeled events.

10.9. The Applier Module

This is a very small module. It just defines the function `apply-xp`, which connects an XP with a story. The module exists as a separate unit so that it can be easily shared by the Tweaker and Retriever.

10.10. The MOPs Module

The modules defines the functions needed to create and retrieve MOPs and instances of MOPs.

10.10.1. Creating MOPs

For creating MOPs, there are two pairs of functions. First, we have `defmop` and `definstance`:

- (`defmop` *name abstractions slot slot* ...) creates a MOP with the given name, abstractions, and slots.
- (`definstance` *name abstractions slot slot* ...) creates an instance with the given name, abstractions, and slots.

A MOP is an abstract concept (e.g., the concept of all horses or all horse races). We've already seen a number of examples of `defmop` and `definstance` in the discussion of the `swale-mem` module. They are useful for "memory files" that predefine an initial set of MOPs and instances.

Being special forms, analogous to `defun` or `defstruct`, they are not appropriate when a program needs to create a new MOP or instance dynamically. For example, when the Accepter finds a problem with an explanation, it needs to dynamically create an instance of a problem. When the Tweaker creates a new XP, it needs to dynamically create a new XP MOP. To do this, they call the functions add-mop and add-instance:

(add-mop *name abstractions slots...*) creates a MOP with the given name, abstractions, and slots.

(add-instance *name abstractions slots...*) creates an instance with the given name, abstractions, and slots.

To see example calls of add-instance, look at new-evaluation and new-problem in the Accepter. To see an example call of add-mop, look at new-xp in the Tweaker.

Not surprisingly, defmop and definstance are defined in terms of add-mop and add-instance, which are, in turn, defined in terms of frames. Frames are discussed in the section on the frames module.

Creating a MOP or instance has three simple steps:

- remove any existing MOP or instance of the same name in memory,
- construct a new MOP or instance frame,
- index the new structure.

Indexing is described in the section on the index module.

10.10.2. Retrieving MOPs

A memory would be pretty useless if you couldn't get anything out of it. There are two ways to get MOPs and instances from memory:

- by name
- by index cues

The first method is provided by the underlying frame system. If you have the name of the MOP or instance, you have access to its slots, abstractions, and so on. This is just what we need when we have a MOP that has MOPs as components. For example, the horse race script contains the names of various event MOPs. With those names, we have access to the components of each event.

The second method is what we need when we know something about the MOP, but not the name of the MOP itself. For example, Micro SWALE needs to find explanations for death. Given some instance of m-dead-state (e.g., m-swale-dead-state) it needs the name of some explanation MOPs that might explain the death.

The function to retrieve MOPs given some cues is `retrieve-mops`:

> (`retrieve-mops` *cues abstraction*), given a list of cues and some abstraction, returns all MOPs and instances of the abstraction whose labels match the given cues.

Cues are normally the names of other MOPs. How indexing works is discussed later in the section on the `index` module. Here's an example call:

```
(retrieve-mops '(m-dead-state) 'm-xp)
```

This will return any XP indexed with `m-dead-state`. For other example calls of `retrieve-mops` in Micro SWALE, see `retrieve-xps` in the Retriever, and `retrieve-tweaks` and `retrieve-scripts` in the Tweaker.

10.11. The Frames Module

A frame is a very general data structure, useful for representing different kinds of knowledge, including concepts, abstractions, indices, and so on. The functions in the `frames` module provide the basic functionality of frames, for use and extension by other modules. For example, the `mops` module is built on top of the `frames` module.

10.11.1. Creating frames

There's one function for creating frames:

> (`add-frame` `&key` `:name` `:absts` `:slots` `:props`) adds a new frame to memory with the given name, abstractions, slots, and properties. If a frame of that name already exists, it is redefined.

Normally, you won't call `add-frame` directly. Instead, you'll use one of the MOP creation functions. For example calls to `add-frame`, see the `mops` module.

The code for `add-frame` is straightforward. It creates a frame structure, where `:name`, `:absts`, `:slots`, and `:props` specify the name, abstractions, slots, and frame properties, respectively.

- :name can be any symbol (e.g., m-swale).
- :absts should be either the name of a MOP or a (possibly empty) list of MOP names (e.g., (m-racehorse m-healthy-animal)).
- :slots should be a list of the form (*role filler role filler* ...) (e.g., (:actor   m-swale   :action   m-ingest :object m-hay)). A role should be a symbol. A filler can be anything. By convention, we preface all role names with a colon (:).
- :props should be a list of the form (*key value key value* ...) (e.g., (:type   instance)).

The frame system knows about abstractions and slots and how they interact. It does not know anything about :props. It simply stores the :props list with the frame, but otherwise ignores it. Systems built on top of the frames system can use properties to store additional information. For example, the MOPs system uses a :type property to distinguish instances from abstract concepts.

10.11.2. The abstraction hierarchy

One common question that a reasoning system such as Micro SWALE asks is "What kind of thing is X?" In particular, it asks questions like "Is this a running event?" "Is Swale a human being?" "Is this a physical object?"

To answer this kind of question, the frame system provides the function abstp.

(abstp *name₁ name₂*) returns true if *name₁* is an abstraction of *name₂,* where *name₁* and *name₂* are the names of frames.

For example, to ask if Swale is a human, we would type:

```
(abstp 'm-human 'm-swale)
```

The abstractions listed in the definition of a MOP or instance are called the *immediate* abstractions of the frame, because they are exactly one step away from the frame. These immediate abstractions can be chained together to form an *abstraction hierarchy*. Such hierarchies are drawn as graphs, with the more abstract concepts above the more specific concepts, and lines linking each concept to its immediate abstractions.

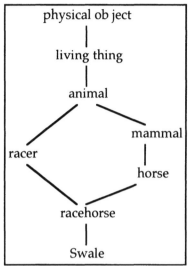

FIG. 10.11. Example abstraction hierarchy.

For example, in a marginally more sophisticated memory than that in `swale-mem`, we might have defined the hierarchy shown in Fig. 10.11.

Abstraction links only "go up". You can get from horse to mammal to animal, but you can't go down from animal to racer.

One concept is defined to be an abstraction of another if there is a (possibly empty) chain of immediate abstraction links from the second concept to the first. Thus, all of the concepts in Fig. 10.11, including Swale himself, are abstractions of Swale. On the other hand, there is no abstraction relationship between racer and horse; neither is above the other.

If one concept is an abstraction of another, then we can also say that the second concept is a *specialization* of the first.

The abstraction hierarchy is important for two reasons. First, we use it to see if something is of the right type for some purpose. In Micro SWALE,

- The Accepter function `expl-relevance-problems` uses `abstp` to see if the anomaly to be explained matches the outcome of XP being applied.
- The Accepter function `norm-filler-problems` uses `abstp` to see if a potential filler for an event or state in an XP matches the normal filler for that concept.

- The Accepter function `knowable-p` uses `abstp` to see if a state is under the abstraction "hidden state."
- The Tweaker function `script-includes-effect-p` uses `abstp` to see if a script includes event of a particular type.
- The Mops function `retrieve-mops` uses abstp to see if a retrieved item is of the type requested.

Second, the abstraction hierarchy is important because a concept "inherits" the slots of its abstractions. This means that the Swale concept in Fig. 10.11 will behave as if it had the slots of racehorses, horses, racers, and so on.

10.11.3. The slots of a frame

The other major question a reasoning system wants to know about a frame is "What is the value of attribute X?" For example, "What color is this thing?","When did this event happen?", "Who was the actor of this event?", "How old is this person?"

Such information is stored in the slots of a frame. To find out about the filler of some slot in a frame, the frame system provides the function `<-`:

(`<-` *name role*) returns the filler of role in the frame named. Read this as "the *role* of *name*."

For example, to get the age of Swale, if known, we would type:

```
(<- 'm-swale :age)
```

The `<-` function handles inherited fillers. That means that if `m-swale` doesn't have an age slot, `<-` will search all the abstractions of `m-swale` for an age slot. Thus, even though `swale-mem` doesn't give an explicit :age slot for `m-swale`, the foregoing call will return `m-young`, because `<-` will find that filler in `m-young-animal`, one of the abstractions of `m-swale`.

The function for inheriting fillers is `inherit-filler`. It looks at every abstraction of the given frame, keeping track of the most specific filler for the given role found so far. This allows `inherit-filler` to handle inheritance from multiple abstractions in a reasonable fashion. `inherit-filler` will complain if it finds two fillers and neither is more specific than the others.

For example, if one abstraction had the filler `m-young` and another had the filler `m-old`, neither is more specific than the other, and there is a conflict.

`<-` actually has a slightly more general syntax:

(`<-` *name role₁ role₂ role₃* ...)

This follows the path of roles, starting at name. (Paths were described in the subsection on scripts in the section on the `swale-mem` module.) For example, we could get the age of the actor of `m-event.1` with

```
(<- 'm-event.1 :actor :age)
```

First, `<-` gets the actor of the event, then it gets the age of the actor. A related function, handy if the roles are in some list in a variable, is this:

(`path-filler` *name path*) returns the filler found by following the roles in the path, starting with the frame named.

10.11.4. Frame memory

The frame system maintains a table linking a frame with its name. Two other functions besides `add-frame` are handy for managing this table are:

(`frame-of` *name*) returns the frame in memory with the given name, if any.

(`clear-frame-memory`) removes all frame from memory.

Normally, you shouldn't need to worry about these functions. In particular, you should use `clear-mop-memory`, not `clear-frame-memory`, because the former clears both the table of names and frames and the table of indices.

10.12. The Index Module

This module defines the internal functions necessary to support `retrieve-mops` and the indexing functions in the `mops` module. The primary functions are:

(`index-fetch` *cues index*), which retrieves items, given a set of cues (`index-store` *labels item index*), which stores an item under a set of labels

(`index-remove` *labels item index*), which removes an item under a set of labels

(`clear-index` *index*), which simply clears the index of all items

The function `index-remove` is called by the `mops` module when MOPs are redefined.

Cues and *labels* are both lists of symbols, usually the names of MOPs. The two terms are used to distinguish their function:

- Cues are used for retrieval.
- Labels are used for storage.

Given a set of cues, we want to retrieve items with matching labels.

`Index-store` is straightforward. For each list of labels, we just keep a list of the items stored under it. When storing a new item under a set of labels, we look for an existing entry with the same set of labels. If there is one, we add the new item to it. If not, we make a new entry with the given set of labels and item. A set of labels is the same as another if it has the elements, possibly in a different order.

`Index-fetch` retrieves items, given a set of cues, by looking through the list of entries for "matching" sets of labels. The rule for matching is this: A set of labels matches a set of cues if every label is an abstraction of some cue.

For example, suppose we had entries for the following sets of labels (it doesn't matter what items are stored in those entries; all are returned):

Entry	Labels
1	horse
2	death
3	animal, death
4	jogger, death

Here are the entries that would be retrieved for a given set of cues:

Cues	Retrieves
horse	1
Swale	1
Swale, death	1, 2, 3
Fixx, death	2, 3, 4
Swale, death, cars	1, 2, 3

A set of cues will retrieve an entry only if the cues contain at least as much information, if not more, than the labels. Why? Because in order to match, for every label, either that label or something strictly more specific than it must be in the set of cues.

This rule for matching cues and labels is intended to reflect a common sense view of how human memory works. The more cues we are given, the better we are at recalling things. Note that in this model, extraneous cues have no effect.

This matching rule allows the indexer (whether it be a human or an automatic indexing process) a fair amount of control over when a MOP or instance will be retrieved.

- To have an item be easily recalled, index it with a small set of general labels.
- To have an item be recalled only in very specific circumstances, index it with a set of very specific labels.
- To have an item be recalled in several distinct situations, index it under multiple sets of specific labels.

10.12.1. Indexing MOPs

Although the functions described here are part of the mops module, we had to defer describing them until indexing and inheritance had been discussed.

MOPs and instances are indexed automatically by add-mop, and add-instance, which call index-mop and unindex-mop:

(index-mop *name*) indexes *name* for later retrieval.

(unindex-mop *name*) removes *name* from the internal index. unindex-mop is called when MOPs and instances are redefined to remove any old versions.

Index-mop looks for a (possibly inherited) slot of the MOP called :indices. The filler of this slot should be a list of lists of roles or paths. The fillers of those roles or paths, when applied to the MOP being indexed, become the features under which to index the MOP.

For example, here is a MOP for "an explanation":

```
(defmop m-explanation ()
   :story m-story
   :xp m-xp
   :indices ((:story :xp)))
```

This says two things. First, it says that an explanation is a combination of a story and an XP. Second, it gives a list of roles for indexing explanations. Thus,

```
(definstance m-swale-explanation (m-explanation)
   :story m-swale-story
   :xp m-fixx-xp)
```

would be indexed[1] by the set of labels (m-swale-story m-fixx-xp).

10.13. The print-utils Module

This module is just a collection of handy functions for printing messages. All printing goes through these functions. If you want to change how the output of Micro SWALE looks, try to localize your changes to this module.

There are five main forms for printing. These are summarized in Table 10.4.

Table 10.4. Main Forms for Printing Messages.

Form	Type
(headline *string*)	[Function]
(mainline *format arg arg* ...)	[Function]
(summarize-results *result null-msg* *non-null-msg*)	[Function]
(print-mop *name*)	[Function]
(print-index *index*)	[Function]

(headline *string*) prints the string in a highly emphasized manner on the user's terminal. The particular definition given here uses vertical spacing and underlining. We use it to announce when

---

[1]Don't confuse this simple model of automatic index generation with the *indexing problem*. As discussed in chapter 4, the indexing problem means "finding good abstract labels for concepts" (e.g., labeling a particular event as a case of revenge).

the main reasoning modules are called. `Headline` is a simple function to use.

```
(headline "Micro Accepter")
```

will print "`Micro Accepter`" underlined, with vertical spacing around it.

`Mainline` is used like `format`, except that you don't specify an output stream. For example, if the variable `item` was `m-swale`, then

```
(mainline "Looking for ~S" item)
```

would print "`Looking for M-SWALE.`" `Mainline` makes sure that the output appears on a new line by itself.

(`summarize-results` result *null-msg non-null-msg*) prints either *null-msg* or *non-null-msg*, depending on whether or not *result* is `nil`, and returns *result*. `summarize-results` is handy for telling the user what happened without interrupting the flow of control. Both *null-msg* and *non-null-msg* are optional. Here's a simple call to `summarize-results`:

```
(summarize-results (retrieve-tweaks  story)
  "...  none found.")
```

If `retrieve-tweaks` returns `nil`, then the "`...    none found`" message will be printed. If `retrieve-tweaks` returns a non-`nil` value, then nothing will be printed. In either case, the value returned by `retrieve-tweaks` will be returned by `summarize-results`.

```
(summarize-results (retrieve-tweaks story)
  "... none found."
  "... found ~S.")
```

will print "`...    none found.`" if `retrieve-tweaks` returns `nil`. If it returns, say,

```
(m-replace-actor-tweak
 m-replace-action-tweak)
```

then `summarize-results` will print

```
... found (m-replace-actor-tweak
          m-replace-action-tweak)
```

`Print-mop` prints a MOP's name, its type (instance or MOP), abstractions, and slots, indented in a readable fashion. `Print-index` does the same for an index; it prints the index in a readable fashion, with labels and entries separated and indented.

10.14. Exercises

We made Micro SWALE as small as possible for comprehensibility and portability. Obviously, we had to sacrifice many features in the shrinking process. Below, we suggest some exercises that may give you a better feeling for how case-based explanation works, and make the system more realistic. Many people in the past have found these micro systems to be useful not only for pedagogical purposes, but for prototyping new projects.

10.14.1. Indexing Explanations

If you call (`explain 'm-swale-story`) after running the SWALE example, without resetting memory to its initial state, it does something stupid. Not only does it not find the explanations it has already built, but it fails to be able to build them again! In particular, the Retriever fails to find any XPs.

The problem is that when an XP is used to generate an explanation, that explanation is indexed in memory by the story and XP involved. When the Retriever finds an explanation which already exists for a particular XP and story, it doesn't return the XP. This makes sense for all the explanations that are generated that aren't acceptable. We want to retrieve them to avoid making the same mistake twice.

What's missing is that acceptable explanations are not being indexed in such a way that the Explainer can find them again later, given a story to explain.

Change Micro SWALE so that
- when an acceptable explanation is found, it is indexed so that it can be retrieved with just the story, and
- when a story is to be explained, the Explainer first looks to see if it has already explained it.

10.14.2. The Janis Joplin XP

Implement the Janis Joplin explanation for Swale's death. You need to define a number of new MOPs. A major one, obviously, is a Janis Joplin XP, similar to the Jim Fixx XP. Its events should include fame leading to taking drugs leading to death. When applied to Swale's death, the Accepter should accept Swale as famous, but reject Swale as an actor capable of taking drugs, just as it rejected Swale as a jogger.

You need a Tweaker function to look for someone to give Swale drugs. Redefine `replace-actor-search-through-stereotypes`, which is currently a dummy function in the `tweaker` module, to do this. Just as `replace-action-search-through-stereotypes` looked for "a script where Swale runs," `replace-actor-search-through-stereo-types` should look for "a script where Swale is given drugs." You also need to define the script for it to find, which is the script of someone giving drugs to an athlete to help the athlete perform better.

You should expect to make a number of other, minor changes to memory, such as defining racehorses to be famous athletes, defining a drug-taking event, and so on.

10.14.3. Handling XP Causals

The Tweaker function `problem-effects` calls `find-consequences` to find out what effects an event has in an explanation. For example, if `m-expl4` is an explanation based on `m-fixx-xp`, then

```
(find-consequences 'm-expl4 ':jog)
```

will return a list of the events in `m-fixx-xp` that the event labeled `:jog` caused. If you look at `find-consequences`, however, you'll discover that it cheats! It gets the next event in the labeled events list, and doesn't look at the list of causals at all.

Change `find-consequences` to look through the list of causals in the XP of the explanation to get the effects of a particular event. Each causal is a list of antecedent event labels, followed by a =>, followed by consequent event labels. Use the rule "if the event label appears in the antecedents of the causal, then collect all the consequents of that causal." Make sure that you collect all the consequents if the event appears in the antecedents of several causals.

10.14.4. Nested Constraints

In the section on the `swale-mem` module, we described several nonobvious representations. In particular, the definition of `m-swale` and the definition of `m-bad-health-state` were both unintuitive. More natural definitions might be

```
(definstance m-swale (m-racehorse)
  :health m-healthy
  :age m-young)

(defmop m-bad-health-state (m-state)
  :object m-animal
  :constraints (((:object :health) m-sick)))
```

To see what needs to be changed, consider why these definitions don't work currently. The problems arise when we try to apply the death from illness XP to the Swale story. Here's that XP again:

```
(defmop m-die-from-illness-xp (m-xp)
  :events ((:illness m-bad-health-state)
           (:outcome m-dead-state))
  :causals ((:illness => :outcome))
  :constraints (((:events :illness :object)
                 (:events :outcome :object))))
```

The first problem is noticing nested constraints. Consider the fillers of the paths of the aforementioned constraints when the XP applied to `m-swale-dead-state`, listed in Table 10.5.

Because Swale is an animal, there appears to be no problem. It's only if we look at the constraints inside `m-bad-health-state` that we see that `m-swale` should be constrained to have `m-sick` in its `:health` slot. This is a nested constraint, and the constraint application functions need to look for them.

The next problem is that the constraint application functions don't know how to handle the constraint given in m-bad-health-state. The constraint has a specific value `m-sick`, and the functions only handle paths. What such a constraint says should be clear: the filler of the `:health` slot of the `:object` should be `m-sick` (or some specialization of `m-sick`).

Table 10.5. Example of Nested Constraints.

Constraint path	:object of	Filler
`(:events :illness` `:object)`	`m-bad-health-state`	`m-animal`
`(:events :outcome` `:object)`	`m-swale-dead-state`	`m-swale`

Furthermore, when a nested constraint fails, as it is supposed to in this case, the constraint path, (e.g. (`:events` `:illness` `:object`)) needs to be extended to include the nested constraint path. In particular, the Accepter should produce a problem instance like this:

```
m-non-normative-filler-problem
    :explanation name of the explanation with the
problem
    :path (:events :illness :object :health)
    :expected-value m-bad
    :observed-value m-good
```

One other problem that is fairly easy to fix is that the foregoing problem instance will generate the cues (`m-sick m-healthy`), so the Jim Fixx XP needs to be redefined in `swale-mem` to have those indices. These actually seem like better indices than the ones it currently has.

Fix these problems in the constraint application functions in the `accepter` module (`apply-constraint`, `norm-filler-problems`, etc.). Try to keep the functions short, and the flow of control as clear as possible. You should probably define several new subfunctions to handle constraint nesting.

10.15. The Code for Micro SWALE

Here are the modules for the Micro SWALE system. Each module uses require and provide to link it with the other modules it depends on. Each module should appear in a separate file. Exactly what you call each file, and where you put it, depends on your particular Common Lisp. Commonly, the file names will have the form *module-name*.`lisp` or *module-name*.`lsp` or possibly *module-name*.`l`.

If you have all these files and load the `swale` module, then all the modules should load automatically, in the right order.

10.15.1. Code for the `swale` Module

```
;;; ------------------------------------------------------------
;;; SWALE Demo
;;; ------------------------------------------------------------
;;; Programmer: Chris Riesbeck


(require "explainer")


;;; Run the Swale story with fresh memory.
;;; ------------------------------------------------------------

(defun explain-swale ()
  (reset-swale-memory)
  (explain 'm-swale-story))


(defun reset-swale-memory ()
  (clear-mop-memory)
  (load-swale-memory))

(defun load-swale-memory ()
  (unprovide "swale-mem")
  (require "swale-mem"))

;;; Warning: in some implementations, the following doesn't seem
;;; to be enough to "unprovide" a module so that require will
;;; load it again. Check your manual for information about
;;; require and provide if reset-swale-memory fails to reload
;;; swale-mem. Replace the require in load-swale-memory with an
;;; explicit load if you have to.


(defun unprovide (module)
  (setq *modules*
        (remove module *modules* :test #'string-equal)))



;;; End of module
;;; ------------------------------------------------------------


(provide "swale")
```

10.15.2. Code for the `swale-mem` Module

The following is the code for the `swale-mem` module.

```
;;;----------------------------------------------------------------
;;; MOPs for SWALE Demo
;;; ----------------------------------------------------------------
;;; Programmer: Chris Riesbeck


(require "mops")


;;; Abstract values
;;; ----------------------------------------------------------------

(defmop m-value)
(defmop m-sick (m-value))
(defmop m-healthy (m-value))


;;; Things
;;; ----------------------------------------------------------------

(defmop m-thing)
(defmop m-animate (m-thing))
(defmop m-animal (m-animate))
(defmop m-human (m-animal))
(defmop m-horse (m-animal))
(defmop m-racehorse (m-horse))

(defmop m-healthy-animal (m-animal)
  :health m-healthy)

(defmop m-unhealthy-animal (m-animal)
  :health m-sick)

(defmop m-alive-animal (m-animal)
  :health m-alive)

(defmop m-dead-animal (m-animal)
  :health m-dead)

(defmop m-young-animal (m-animal)
  :age m-young)

(defmop m-old-animal (m-animal)
  :age m-old)

(defmop m-body-part)
(defmop m-heart (m-body-part))
(defmop m-leg (m-body-part))
```

```
(defmop m-bad-heart (m-heart)
  :health m-sick)

(defmop m-bad-heart-animal (m-animal)
  :heart m-bad-heart)



;;; Events
;;; --------------------------------------------------------------

(defmop m-fact)

(defmop m-event (m-fact))

(defmop m-run-event (m-event)
  :actor m-animal
  :action m-move-body-part
  :object m-leg
  :speed m-fast)

(defmop m-exert-event (m-event)
  :actor m-animal)

(defmop m-warm-up-event (m-event)
  :actor m-animal)

(defmop m-cool-off-event (m-event)
  :actor m-animal)

(defmop m-enter-race-event (m-event)
  :actor m-human
  :object m-race
  :entry m-horse)

(defmop m-mount-event (m-event)
  :actor m-human
  :object m-animal)

(defmop m-win-event (m-event)
  :actor m-animal
  :object m-race)


;;; States
;;; --------------------------------------------------------------

(defmop m-state (m-fact)
  :object m-thing :value m-value :time m-time)
```

```
(defmop m-hidden-state (m-state))

(defmop m-present (m-time))
(defmop m-past (m-time))
(defmop m-future (m-time))

(defmop m-alive-state (m-state)
  :object m-alive-animal)

(defmop m-dead-state (m-state)
  :object m-dead-animal)

(defmop m-bad-health-state (m-state)
  :object m-unhealthy-animal)

(defmop m-old-age-state (m-state)
  :object m-old-animal)

(defmop m-heart-defect-state (m-state m-hidden-state)
  :object m-bad-heart-animal)


;;; Abstract explanation MOPs
;;; -------------------------------------------------------------

(defmop m-anomaly)
(defmop m-event-sequence-conflict (m-anomaly))

(defmop m-story ()
  :anomaly m-anomaly
  :background (m-fact))


(defmop m-explanation ()
  :story m-story
  :xp m-xp
  :indices ((:story :xp)))


(defmop m-explanation-problem)

(defmop m-relevance-problem (m-explanation-problem)
  :status hopeless)

(defmop m-believability-problem (m-explanation-problem)
  :status tweakable)

(defmop m-detail-problem (m-explanation-problem)
  :status acceptable)

(defmop m-irrelevant-to-surprising-feature-problem
```

```
    (m-relevance-problem))

(defmop m-non-normative-filler-problem
    (m-believability-problem))
(defmop m-contradictory-filler-problem
    (m-believability-problem))

(defmop m-non-knowable-antecedent-problem (m-detail-problem))

(defmop m-explanation-evaluation ()
  :explanation m-explanation
  :problems (m-problem))


;;; The SWALE story
;;; ------------------------------------------------------------


;;; The anomaly of SWALE's death
;;; ------------------------------------------------------------

(definstance m-SWALE
    (m-racehorse m-healthy-animal m-young-animal))

(definstance m-expectation-1 (m-dead-state)
  :object m-SWALE
  :time m-future)

(definstance m-SWALE-dead-state (m-dead-state)
  :object m-SWALE
  :time m-present)

(definstance m-SWALE-anomaly (m-event-sequence-conflict)
  :event-sequence m-racehorse-life
  :expectation m-expectation-1
  :surprising-fact m-SWALE-dead-state)

(definstance m-belmont-race (m-race))

(definstance m-SWALE-won-belmont (m-win-event)
  :actor m-SWALE
  :action m-win
  :object m-belmont-race)

(definstance m-SWALE-story (m-story)
    :anomaly m-SWALE-anomaly
    :background m-SWALE-won-belmont)

;;; Scripts
... ------------------------------------------------------------
```

```
(defmop m-script-event (m-event)
  :indices (((:actor))))


(defmop m-horserace-event (m-script-event)
  :owner m-human
  :jockey m-human
  :actor m-racehorse
  :events ((:enter m-enter-race-event)
           (:mount m-mount-event)
           (:run m-run-event))
  :constraints ((((:owner)
                  (:events :enter :actor))
                 ((:jockey)
                  (:events :mount :actor))
                 ((:actor)
                  (:events :enter :entry)
                  (:events :mount :object)
                  (:events :run :actor)))))

(defmop m-jog-event (m-script-event)
  :actor m-human
  :events ((:warm-up m-warm-up-event)
           (:run m-run-event)
           (:cool-off m-cool-off-event))
  :constraints ((((:actor)
                  (:events :warm-up :actor)
                  (:events :run :actor)
                  (:events :cool-off :actor)))))


;;; XPs and explanations
;;; ------------------------------------------------------------

(defmop m-xp ()
    :indices (((:observed (:events :outcome)))))


(defmop m-die-from-old-age-xp (m-xp)
  :events ((:old-age m-old-age-state)
           (:outcome m-dead-state))
  :causals ((:old-age => :outcome))
  :constraints ((((:events :old-age :object)
                  (:events :outcome :object)))))

(defmop m-die-from-illness-xp (m-xp)
  :events ((:illness m-bad-health-state)
           (:outcome m-dead-state))
  :causals ((:illness => :outcome))
  :constraints ((((:events :illness :object)
                  (:events :outcome :object)))))
```

```
(defmop m-fixx-xp (m-xp)
  :observed m-healthy-animal
  :expected m-unhealthy-animal
  :events ((:jog m-jog-event)
           (:run m-run-event)
           (:exert m-exert-event)
           (:defect m-heart-defect-state)
           (:outcome m-dead-state))
  :causals ((:jog => :run)
            (:run => :exert)
            (:defect :exert => :outcome))
  :constraints ((((:events :jog :actor)
                  (:events :run :actor)
                  (:events :exert :actor)
                  (:events :defect :owner)
                  (:events :outcome :object)))))


;;; Tweaks
;;; -------------------------------------------------------------

(defmop m-tweak ()
  :problem m-problem
  :indices ((:problem)))


(defmop m-replace-action-use-stereotypes-tweak (m-tweak)
  :function replace-action-search-through-stereotypes
  :problem m-non-normative-filler-problem)

(defmop m-replace-actor-use-stereotypes-tweak (m-tweak)
  :function replace-actor-search-through-stereotypes
  :problem m-non-normative-filler-problem)

(defmop m-replace-action-use-causals-tweak (m-tweak)
  :function replace-action-search-through-causal-rules
  :problem m-non-normative-filler-problem)


;;; End of data
;;; -------------------------------------------------------------

(provide "swale-mem")
```

10.15.3. Code for the Explainer Module

The following is the code for the Explainer module.

```
;;; -------------------------------------------------------------
;;; Micro-EXPLAINER
```

```
;;; Programmer: Chris Riesbeck

;;; Top-level controller for Micro Explainer


(require "mops")
(require "print-utils")
(require "retriever")
(require "accepter")
(require "tweaker")


;;; The Explainer
;;; --------------------------------------------------------------


;;; (EXPLAIN &optional story) => explanation
;;;    Returns an explanation for the story, if any.
;;;
;;; If called again with no arguments, gets another explanation,
;;; if any.
;;;
;;; Ex.  (EXPLAIN 'M-SWALE-STORY) => first explanation
;;;      (EXPLAIN) => second explanation


(defun explain (&optional story)
  (when story
    (initialize-explainer story))
  (run-explainer))


;;; Initialize the explainer for a new story
;;; --------------------------------------------------------------

(defvar *story*)

(defun initialize-explainer (story)

  (headline "Micro Explainer")
  (mainline "Trying to explain ~S" story)
  (mainline "which has the anomaly:")
  (print-mop (<- story :anomaly))

  (setq *story* story)
  (initialize-explanation-queue (retrieve-expls story)))
```

```
;;; Run the explainer on the current story
;;; --------------------------------------------------------------

(defun run-explainer ()
  (loop until (null (explanation-queue))
        thereis (acceptable-explanation (next-explanation))))

(defun acceptable-explanation (expl)
  (let ((problems (evaluate-expl expl 'prediction)))
    (case (explanation-status expl problems)
      (acceptable expl)
      (tweakable
       (add-explanations (tweak-expl expl problems))
       (add-explanations (retrieve-expls *story* problems))
       nil)
      (t nil))))


;;; The internal explanation queue
;;; --------------------------------------------------------------


(defvar *expls*)

(defun initialize-explanation-queue (expls)
  (setq *expls* expls))

(defun explanation-queue () *expls*)

(defun next-explanation () (pop *expls*))

(defun add-explanations (expls)
  (setq *expls*
        (append *expls* expls)))


;;; End of module
;;; --------------------------------------------------------------

(provide "explainer")
```

10.15.4. Code for the Retriever Module

The following is the code for the Retriever module.

```
;;; --------------------------------------------------------------
;;; Micro RETRIEVER
;;; --------------------------------------------------------------
;;; Programmer: Alex Kass, Chris Riesbeck


(require "mops")
```

```
(require "applier")
(require "print-utils")


;;; Explanation retriever
;;; ------------------------------------------------------------

;;; (RETRIEVE-EXPLS story) => list of explanations
;;;    Finds candidate XP's for story that haven't been tried yet
;;;    and returns the explanations each generates.

(defun retrieve-expls (story &optional problems)

  (headline "Micro XP Retriever")
  (mainline "Searching for XP's.")

  (loop for xp in (retrieve-untried-xps story problems)
        collect (apply-xp xp story)))


;;; XP retriever
;;; ------------------------------------------------------------

(defun retrieve-untried-xps (story problems)
  (summarize-results
    (loop for xp in (retrieve-xps story problems)
        unless (already-tried-xp-p xp story)
          collect xp)
    "... no XP's found."
    "... found ~{~S~^, ~}."))


(defun retrieve-xps (story problems)
  (retrieve-mops (append (story->cues story)
                         (problems->cues problems))
                 'm-xp))

(defun already-tried-xp-p (xp story)
  (retrieve-mops (list xp story) 'm-explanation))


;;; Generate retrieval cues from story or explanation problems
;;; ------------------------------------------------------------

(defun story->cues (story)
  (list (<- story :anomaly :surprising-fact)))
```

```
(defun problems->cues (problems)
  (unless (null problems)
    (summarize-results
     (loop for problem in problems
           append (problem->cues problem))
     "... no cues found.")))

(defun problem->cues (problem)

  (mainline "Looking for retrieval cues in ~S." problem)

  (let ((expected (<- problem :expected-value))
        (observed (<- problem :observed-value)))

    (unless (null expected)

      (mainline "... Cue: observed ~S, rather than ~S."
         observed expected)

      (list observed))))


;;; End of module
;;; -----------------------------------------------------------

(provide "retriever")
```

10.15.5. Code for the Accepter Module

The following is the code for the Accepter module.

```
;;; -----------------------------------------------------------
;;; Micro ACCEPTER
;;; -----------------------------------------------------------
;;; Programmer: David Leake, Alex Kass, Chris Riesbeck


(require "mops")
(require "print-utils")


;;; Explanation evaluation
;;; -----------------------------------------------------------
;;;
;;; (EVALUATE-EXPL explanation) => problems
;;;    Collects problems with the explanation.

(defun evaluate-expl (expl purpose)
  (headline "Micro-Accepter")
  (mainline "Evaluating ~S for the purpose ~S." expl purpose)
  (mainline "The underling XP is")
  (print-mop (<- expl :xp)))
```

```
   (summarize-results
    (collect-problems expl purpose)
    "Explanation has no problems.")))


(defun collect-problems (expl purpose)
  (append (relevance-problems expl)
          (believability-problems expl)
          (usefulness-problems expl purpose)))


;;; Problem evaluation
;;; -----------------------------------------------------------
;;;
;;; Classifies a list of problems as acceptable, tweakable, or
;;; hopeless.

(defun explanation-status (expl problems)
  (cond ((null problems) 'acceptable)
        (t

          (mainline "Checking seriousness of problems.")

          (summarize-results
           (reduce #'worse-problem-status problems
                   :initial-value 'acceptable)
           "Couldn't determine status!"
           (format nil "... ~S is ~~S." expl)))))


(defun worse-problem-status (status problem)
  (let ((problem-status (<- problem :status)))
    (cond ((worse-status-p problem-status status)
           problem-status)
          (t status))))

(defun worse-status-p (status1 status2)
  (and status1
       (let ((status-scale '(hopeless tweakable acceptable)))
         (< (position status1 status-scale)
            (position status2 status-scale)))))


;;; Relevance
;;; -----------------------------------------------------------

(defun relevance-problems (expl)
  (let ((fact (<- expl :story :anomaly :surprising-fact)))

    (mainline "Checking if explanation accounts for ~S."
```

```
              fact)

    (summarize-results
      (expl-relevance-problems expl fact)
     "... appears relevant.")))

(defun expl-relevance-problems (expl fact)
  (cond ((abstp (<- expl :xp :events :outcome) fact)
         '())
        (t
         (list
           (new-problem
                'm-irrelevant-to-surprising-feature-problem
                  :explanation expl
                  :feature-unaccounted-for fact)))))



;;; Explanation believability
;;; ------------------------------------------------------------

(defun believability-problems (expl)

  (mainline "Checking believability.")

  (summarize-results (expl-constraints-problems expl)
     "... no problems."
     "... explanation is not believable."))


;;; Apply XP constraints to the known outcome
;;; ------------------------------------------------------------

(defun expl-constraints-problems (expl)
  (let ((fact (<- expl :story :anomaly :surprising-fact)))
    (loop for constraint in (<- expl :xp :constraints)
          append (constraint-problems constraint fact expl))))


(defun constraint-problems (constraint fact expl)
  (loop for path in constraint
        when (outcome-path-p path)
          append (apply-constraint constraint fact expl
                                     (outcome-path-path path))))


;;; Collect the constraint paths referring to the outcome
;;; ------------------------------------------------------------

(defun outcome-paths (constraint)
  (loop for path in constraint
```

```
              when (outcome-path-p path)
                collect (outcome-path-path path))))

(defun outcome-path-p (path)
  (and (consp path)
       (eql (first path) :events)
       (eql (second path) :outcome)))

(defun outcome-path-path (path)
  (rest (rest path)))


;;; Apply the constraint to a particular component of fact
;;; -----------------------------------------------------------

;;; Note: since the fact(s) refer to what was true, and the
;;; outcome refers to what has become true, don't use outcome
;;; related paths as constraints.

(defun apply-constraint (constraint fact expl path)
  (loop for constrainer in constraint
        unless (outcome-path-p constrainer)
          append (norm-filler-problems (expl-norm expl
                                          constrainer)
                                        (fact-filler fact path)
                                        constrainer
                                        expl)))

(defun expl-norm (expl constrainer)
  (path-filler (<- expl :xp) constrainer))

(defun fact-filler (fact path)
  (path-filler fact path))

(defun norm-filler-problems (expected observed constrainer expl)
  (unless (or (null expected)
              (abstp expected observed))
    (list (new-problem 'm-non-normative-filler-problem
                       :explanation expl
                       :path constrainer
                       :expected-value expected
                       :observed-value observed))))
```

```
;;; Usefulness check
;;; -----------------------------------------------------------


(defun usefulness-problems (expl purpose)

  (mainline
     "Checking if explanation is useful for the purpose ~S."
     purpose)

  (summarize-results
   (case purpose
     ((accounting-for-event)
      (mainline "... Already tested by relevance check.")
      '())
     ((prediction) (usefulness-for-prediction-problems expl)))
    (format nil "... Explanation is adequate for ~S." purpose)
    (format nil "... Explanation is not adequate for ~S."
       purpose)))


;;; Check usefulness for prediction
;;; -----------------------------------------------------------

(defun usefulness-for-prediction-problems (expl)

  (mainline "Is the explanation predictive?")

  (loop for (label fact) in (<- expl :xp :events)
        append (knowability-problems expl label fact)))


(defun knowability-problems (expl label fact)
  (unless (knowable-p fact)
    (list (new-problem 'm-non-knowable-antecedent-problem
                       :explanation expl
                       :fact fact
                       :event-label label))))


;;; Knowable?
;;; -----------------------------------------------------------

(defun knowable-p (fact)
  (not (abstp 'm-hidden-state fact)))



;;; Evaluation construction
```

```
(defun new-evaluation (&rest args)
  (add-instance (gentemp "M-EXPL-EVAL")
                'm-explanation-evaluation
                args))


;;; Problem construction
;;; -------------------------------------------------------------


(defun new-problem (type &rest args)
  (mainline "Problem found!")
  (print-mop (add-instance (gentemp "M-PROB")
                           type
                           args)))


;;; End of module
;;; -------------------------------------------------------------

(provide "accepter")
```

10.15.6. Code for the Tweaker Module

The following is the code for the Tweaker module.

```
;;; -------------------------------------------------------------
;;; Micro TWEAKER
;;; -------------------------------------------------------------
;;; Programmer: Alex Kass, Chris Riesbeck


(require "mops")
(require "applier")
(require "print-utils")


;;; Tweak explanation
;;; -------------------------------------------------------------

;;; Deficiency: Can't solve more than one problem per tweak.

(defun tweak-expl (expl problems)
  (headline "Micro Tweaker")
  (loop for problem in problems
        append (tweak-problem expl problem)))

(defun tweak-problem (expl problem)
  (loop for tweak in (retrieve-tweaks problem)
        append (apply-tweak tweak expl problem)))
```

```
;;; Retrieving tweaks
;;; --------------------------------------------------------------


;;; (RETRIEVE-TWEAKS problem) => list of tweaks
;;;    Returns a list of tweaks appropriate to a problem.

(defun retrieve-tweaks (problem)

  (mainline "Looking for candidate tweaks in memory for ~S."
    problem)

  (summarize-results (retrieve-mops (list problem) 'm-tweak)
   "... no tweaks found."
   "... found ~{~S~^, ~}."))


;;; Apply a tweak to an explanation to resolve a problem
;;; --------------------------------------------------------------


(defun apply-tweak (tweak expl problem)
  (let ((fn (<- tweak :function)))

    (mainline "Trying tweak ~S on ~S." (<- tweak :function) expl)

    (summarize-results (funcall fn expl problem)
                       "... tweak failed."
                       "... tweak generated ~{~S~^, ~}.")))


;;; Tweakers
;;; --------------------------------------------------------------

;;; A tweaker takes an explanation and a problem and returns a
;;; (possibly empty) list of tweaked explanations.


;;; Tweaker: Replace an actor with a more appropriate one
;;; --------------------------------------------------------------

;;; This is a dummy tweak, left as an exercise for the reader

(defun replace-actor-search-through-stereotypes (expl problem)
  nil)


;;; Tweaker: Replace an event with a causal equivalent
... --------------------------------------------------------------
```

```
;;; This is a dummy tweak, left as an exercise for the reader

(defun replace-action-search-through-causal-rules (expl problem)
  nil)


;;; Tweaker: Replace an event with a scriptal equivalent
;;;-----------------------------------------------------------

;;; Algorithm: Given an action that the Accepter says the actor
;;; doesn't do, find the effects of that action in the XP, then
;;; find a script for the actor that includes the same effects.
;;;
;;; Example: The XP says "SWALE jogged," but the accepter rejects
;;; this action for SWALE.  The effect of jogging in the XP was
;;; that SWALE ran.  REPLACE-ACTION-SEARCH-THROUGH-STEREOTYPES
;;; looks for a stereotypical script for SWALE that includes
;;; running. It finds the horseracing script, so horseracing
;;; replaces jogging in the tweaked XP and associated explanation.


(defun replace-action-search-through-stereotypes (expl problem)
  (let ((actor (<- problem :observed-value))
        (label (problem-label problem))
        (effects (problem-effects expl problem)))
    (unless (null effects)
      (loop for script in
            (find-scripts-with-effects actor effects)
            collect (replace-expl-event expl label script)))))


(defun problem-label (problem)
  (second (<- problem :path)))


;;; Find the effects an event had in an explanation
;;; -----------------------------------------------------------


(defun problem-effects (expl problem)

  (mainline "Looking for effects to be accounted for.")

  (summarize-results
    (find-consequences expl (problem-label problem))
    "... no effects found."
    "... found ~{~S~^, ~}."))


(defun find-consequences (expl label)
```

```
  (let ((labelled-events (label-member (<- expl :xp) label)))
    (unless (null (rest labelled-events))
      (list (labelled-event-event (second labelled-events)))))))))
```

```
;;; Find scripts for actor with desired effects
;;; -----------------------------------------------------------------
```

```
(defun find-scripts-with-effects (actor effects)

  (mainline "Looking for scripts for ~S that include ~{~S~^, ~}."
            actor effects)

  (summarize-results
    (loop for script in (retrieve-scripts actor)
          when (script-includes-effects-p script effects)
          collect script)
    "... no scripts found."
    "... found ~{~S~^, ~}."))
```

```
(defun retrieve-scripts (actor)
  (retrieve-mops (list actor) 'm-script-event))
```

```
(defun script-includes-effects-p (script effects)
  (loop for effect in effects
        always (script-includes-effect-p script effect)))
```

```
(defun script-includes-effect-p (script effect)
  (loop for (nil event) in (<- script :events)
        thereis (abstp effect event)))
```

```
;;; Generate explanation by replacing labelled event in its XP
;;; -----------------------------------------------------------------
```

```
(defun replace-expl-event (expl label event)
  (apply-xp (replace-xp-event (<- expl :xp) label event)
            (<- expl :story)))
```

```
(defun replace-xp-event (xp label new-event)
  (let* ((old-event (label-event xp label))
         (new-events (replace-labelled-event (<- xp :events)
                                             label
                                             new-event))
         (new-xp (new-xp :events new-events
```

```
                              :causals (<- xp :causals)
                              :observed (<- xp :observed)
                              :expected (<- xp :expected))))

    (mainline "Creating a new XP ~S with ~S instead of ~S"
              new-xp new-event old-event)

    new-xp))


;;; Functions to handle labelled event lists
;;; ------------------------------------------------------------


(defstruct (labelled-event (:type list)) label event)

(defun label-event (name label)
  (<- name :events label))

(defun label-member (name label)
  (member label (<- name :events)
          :key #'labelled-event-label))

(defun replace-labelled-event (labelled-events label new-event)
  (substitute (make-labelled-event :label label :event new-event)
              (assoc label labelled-events)
              labelled-events))


;;; XP maker
;;; ------------------------------------------------------------

(defun new-xp (&rest args)
  (add-mop (gentemp "M-XP") 'm-xp args))


;;; End of module
;;; ------------------------------------------------------------

(provide "tweaker")
```

10.15.7. Code for the Applier Module

The following is the code for the Applier module.

```
;;; ------------------------------------------------------------
;;; Micro APPLIER
;;; ------------------------------------------------------------
;;; Programmer: Chris Riesbeck


(require "mops")
```

```
;;; Apply an XP to a story
;;; -----------------------------------------------------------

(defun apply-xp (xp story)

  (mainline "Applying ~S." xp)

  (summarize-results (new-explanation :story story :xp xp)
     "... didn't work."
     "... generated ~S."))



;;; Explanation maker
;;; -----------------------------------------------------------

(defun new-explanation (&rest args)
  (add-instance (gentemp "M-EXPL")
                'm-explanation
                args))



;;; End of module
;;; -----------------------------------------------------------

(provide "applier")
```

10.15.8. Code for the MOPs Module

The following is the code for the MOPs module.

```
;;; -----------------------------------------------------------
;;; Memory Organization Packages (MOPs)
;;; -----------------------------------------------------------
;;; Programmer: Chris Riesbeck


(require "frames")
(require "index")


;;; DEFMOP and DEFINSTANCE
;;; -----------------------------------------------------------


(defmacro defmop (name &optional absts &rest args)
  `(add-mop ',name ',absts ',args))

(defmacro definstance (name &optional absts &rest args)
  `(add-instance ',name ',absts ',args))
```

```
(defun add-mop (name absts slots)
  (add-mop-frame name absts slots :type ':mop))

(defun add-instance (name absts slots)
  (add-mop-frame name absts slots :type ':instance))

(defun add-mop-frame (name absts slots &rest props)
  (unindex-mop name)
  (index-mop
   (add-frame :name name
              :absts absts
              :slots slots
              :props props)))


;;; The MOP index
;;; -------------------------------------------------------------


(defvar *memory-index*)

(setq *memory-index* (make-index))

(defun mop-index-fetch (cues)
  (index-fetch cues *memory-index*))

(defun mop-index-store (labels name)
  (index-store labels name *memory-index*)
  name)

(defun mop-index-remove (labels name)
  (index-remove labels name *memory-index*)
  name)


;;; Automatic MOP indexing
;;; -------------------------------------------------------------


(defun index-mop (name)
  (indexer-map #'mop-index-store name))

(defun unindex-mop (name)
  (indexer-map #'mop-index-remove name))

(defun indexer-map (fn name)
  (loop for abst in (absts-of name)
        do (loop for index in (<- abst :indices)
                 do (funcall fn (instantiate-index index name)
```

```
                              name)))
    name)

(defun instantiate-index (index name)
  (loop for path in index
        for value = (instantiate-index-path path name)
        unless (null value)
          collect value))

(defun instantiate-index-path (path name)
  (path-filler name (if (listp path) path (list path))))


;;; Retrieving mops
;;; -----------------------------------------------------------


(defun retrieve-mops (cues abst)
  (loop for mop in (mop-index-fetch cues)
        when (abstp abst mop)
          collect mop))


;;; Clearing MOP memory
;;; -----------------------------------------------------------

(defun clear-mop-memory ()
  (clear-frame-memory)
  (clear-index *memory-index*))


;;; End of module
;;; -----------------------------------------------------------

(provide "mops")
```

10.15.9. Code for the Frame Module

The following is the code for the Frame module.

```
;;; -----------------------------------------------------------
;;; Micro Frame System
;;; -----------------------------------------------------------
;;; Programmer: Chris Riesbeck



;;; Frame and slot structures
... -----------------------------------------------------------
```

```
(defstruct frame name slots absts props)

;;; We implement slots as simple lists to simplify handling
;;; fillers that are labelled lists.

(defstruct (slot (:type list)) role filler)


;;; Creating frames
;;; --------------------------------------------------------------

(defvar *frames* (make-hash-table))

(defun clear-frame-memory ()
  (clrhash *frames*))

(defun frame-of (name) (gethash name *frames*))

(defun add-frame (&key name absts slots props)
  (setf (gethash name *frames*)
        (make-frame :name name
                    :absts (collect-absts absts)
                    :slots (collect-slots slots)
                    :props props))
  name)


;;; Auxiliary functions:
;;;
;;; (COLLECT-ABSTS abst-spec) => list of names
;;;    Given either a single abstraction or a list of
;;;    abstractions, returns a list of abstractions, with any
;;;    redundancies removed.

(defun collect-absts (abst-spec)
  (remove-redundant-absts
    (if (listp abst-spec) abst-spec (list abst-spec))))


;;; (COLLECT-SLOTS slots-spec) => list of slots
;;;    Given a list of the form (role filler role filler ...)
;;;    returns a list of slots, one for each role-filler pair.

(defun collect-slots (slots-spec)
  (loop for (role filler) on slots-spec by #'cddr
        collect (make-slot :role role :filler filler)))


;;; Getting frame components
;;; --------------------------------------------------------------
```

```
(defun slots-of (source)
  (if (consp source)
      source
      (let ((frame (frame-of source)))
        (and (not (null frame))
             (frame-slots frame)))))

(defun absts-of (name &aux (frame (frame-of name)))
  (and (not (null frame))
       (frame-absts frame)))

(defun props-of (name &aux (frame (frame-of name)))
  (and (not (null frame))
       (frame-props frame)))
```

```
;;; Using the abstraction hierarchy
;;; -------------------------------------------------------------

;;; (ABSTP abst spec) => true or false
;;;    Return true if abst is spec or an abstraction of spec.
;;; (STRICT-ABSTP abst spec) => true or false
;;;    Return true if abst is an abstraction of spec, but not spec
;;;    itself.
;;; (REMOVE-REDUNDANT-ABSTS absts) => list of absts
;;;    Returns absts, minus duplicates and items which are known
;;;    abstractions of other items in the list.
```

```
(defun abstp (abst spec)
 (or (eql abst spec)
     (strict-abstp abst spec)))
```

```
(defun strict-abstp (abst spec)
  (loop for spec-abst in (absts-of spec)
        thereis (abstp abst spec-abst)))
```

```
(defun remove-redundant-absts (absts)
  (let ((l (remove-duplicates absts)))
    (set-difference l l :test #'strict-abstp)))
```

```
;;; Getting the filler of a slot in a frame
;;; -------------------------------------------------------------

;;; (<- name role role ...) => filler
;;;    Return the filler found by tracing the roles from the frame
;;;    named through its subcomponents. Fillers may be inherited.
```

```
(defun <- (name &rest roles)
  (path-filler name roles))

(defun path-filler (name roles)
  (loop for role in roles
        until (null name)
        do (setq name (inherit-filler name role))
        finally (return name)))


;;; Inheriting slots
;;; ------------------------------------------------------------


;;; (INHERIT-FILLER name role) => filler
;;;    Return either the explicit filler of role in the frame
;;;    named, or the most specific filler of role in the frame's
;;;    abstractions.

(defun inherit-filler (name role)
  (or (role-filler name role)
      (most-specific-inherited-filler name role)))

(defun most-specific-inherited-filler (name role)
  (let ((filler nil))
    (dolist (abst (absts-of name))
      (setq filler (more-specific-filler name role filler abst)))
    filler))

(defun more-specific-filler (name role filler abst)
  (let ((abst-filler (inherit-filler abst role)))
    (cond ((more-specific-p abst-filler filler) abst-filler)
          ((more-specific-p filler abst-filler) filler)
          (t (error
                "~S in ~S has incompatible fillers: ~S and ~S"
                role name filler abst-filler)))))

(defun more-specific-p (filler1 filler2)
  (or (null filler2)
      (abstp filler2 filler1)))


;;; Explicit slots
;;; ------------------------------------------------------------


(defun role-filler (name role)
  (let ((slot (role-slot name role)))
    (and slot (slot-filler slot))))
```

```
(defun role-slot (source role)
  (find role (slots-of source) :key #'slot-role))



;;; Frame properties
;;; ----------------------------------------------------------------

(defun frame-prop (name prop)
  (getf (props-of name) prop))

(defun set-frame-prop (name prop val)
  (setf (getf (frame-props (frame-of name)) prop) val))

(defsetf frame-prop set-frame-prop)


;;; End of module
;;; ----------------------------------------------------------------

(provide "frames")
```

10.15.10. Code for the Index Module

The following is the code for the Index module.

```
;;; ----------------------------------------------------------------
;;; Index Manager
;;; ----------------------------------------------------------------
;;; Programmer: Chris Riesbeck


(defstruct index entries)

(defstruct (index-entry (:type list)) labels items)


;;; Primary indexing functions
;;; ----------------------------------------------------------------

(defun clear-index (index)
  (setf (index-entries index) nil))

(defun index-fetch (cues index)
  (loop for (labels items) in (index-entries index)
        when (subsetp labels cues :test #'abstp)
          append items))

(defun index-store (labels item index)
  (unless (null labels)
    (let ((entry (index-entry labels index)))
```

```
            (cond ((null entry)
                  (add-index-entry labels item index))
                 (t (add-index-item item entry)))
          item)))

(defun index-remove (labels item index)
  (let ((entry (index-entry labels index)))
    (cond ((null entry) nil)
          ((not (member item (index-entry-items entry))) nil)
          (t (remove-index-item item entry) t))))


;;; Getting the entry for a set of labels (not cues!)
;;; ------------------------------------------------------------

(defun index-entry (labels index)
  (find labels (index-entries index)
        :test #'set-equalp
        :key #'index-entry-labels))

(defun set-equalp (x y)
  (and (subsetp x y) (subsetp y x)))


;;; Adding and removing items
;;; ------------------------------------------------------------

(defun add-index-entry (labels item index)
  (push (make-index-entry :labels labels
                          :items (list item))
        (index-entries index)))

(defun add-index-item (item entry)
  (pushnew item (index-entry-items entry)))

(defun remove-index-item (item entry)
  (setf (index-entry-items entry)
        (remove item (index-entry-items entry))))


;;; End of module
;;; ------------------------------------------------------------

(provide "index")
```

10.15.11. Code for the `print-utils` Module

The following is the code for the `print-utils` module.

```
;;; ------------------------------------------------------------
;;; Print utilities for Micro EXPLAINER
... ------------------------------------------------------------
```

```
;;; Programmer: Chris Riesbeck


(require "mops")
(require "index")


;;; Printing headings
;;; ------------------------------------------------------------


;;; (HEADLINE string) => undefined
;;;
;;; Print the string in a highly visible way. Currently, adds
;;; surrounding vertical space and underlining.

(defun headline (str)
  (format t "~2%~A~%~V,,,'-<~>~&" str (length str)))


;;; Printing messages
;;; ------------------------------------------------------------

;;; (MAINLINE format-string arg arg ...) => undefined
;;;
;;; Print the arguments, on a separate line.

(defun mainline (format-string &rest args)
  (unless (null format-string)
    (apply #'format t "~&~@?~&" format-string args)))


;;; Summarizing results
;;; ------------------------------------------------------------

;;; (SUMMARIZE-RESULTS arg format1 format2) => value of arg
;;;
;;; If the value of arg is NIL, (format t format1) else
;;; (format t format2 value-of-arg).

(defun summarize-results (results
                          &optional msg-if-null msg-if-non-null)
  (if (null results)
      (unless (null msg-if-null)
        (mainline msg-if-null))
      (unless (null msg-if-non-null)
        (mainline msg-if-non-null results)))
  results)
```

```
;;; Printing MOPs
;;; ----------------------------------------------------------------


;;; (PRINT-MOP name) => name
;;;    Prints the type, abstractions, slots, and other properties
;;;    of a frame.

(defun print-mop (name)
  (print-mop-type (frame-prop name :type))
  (print-mop-absts (absts-of name))
  (print-mop-slots (slots-of name))
  (format t "~%")
  name)

(defun print-mop-type (type)
  (unless (null type)
    (format t "~&  ~S" type)))

(defun print-mop-absts (absts)
  (unless (null absts)
    (format t " isa ~{~S~^, ~}" absts)))

(defun print-mop-slots (slots)
  (loop for (role filler) in slots
        do (format t "~&  ~S: ~S" role filler)))


;;; Print the index in a readable fashion
;;; ----------------------------------------------------------------

(defun print-index (index)
  (loop for (labels items) in (index-entries index)
        do (format t "~{~S~^ + ~}~%  => ~S~%"
                labels (first items))
           (format t "~{~5T~S~%~}" (rest items))))


;;; End of module
;;; ----------------------------------------------------------------

(provide "print-utils")
```

10.16. Micro SWALE Output

Here is the output produced by (explain-SWALE).

```
> (explain-SWALE)
```

```
Micro Explainer
---------------
Trying to explain M-SWALE-STORY
which has the anomaly:
  :INSTANCE isa M-EVENT-SEQUENCE-CONFLICT
  :EVENT-SEQUENCE: M-RACEHORSE-LIFE
  :EXPECTATION: M-EXPECTATION-1
  :SURPRISING-FACT: M-SWALE-DEAD-STATE


Micro XP Retriever
------------------
Searching for XP's.
... found M-DIE-FROM-ILLNESS-XP, M-DIE-FROM-OLD-AGE-XP.
Applying M-DIE-FROM-ILLNESS-XP.
... generated M-EXPL1.
Applying M-DIE-FROM-OLD-AGE-XP.
... generated M-EXPL2.


Micro-Accepter
--------------
Evaluating M-EXPL1 for the purpose PREDICTION.
The underling XP is
  :MOP isa M-XP
  :EVENTS: ((:ILLNESS M-BAD-HEALTH-STATE)
            (:OUTCOME M-DEAD-STATE))
  :CAUSALS: ((:ILLNESS => :OUTCOME))
  :CONSTRAINTS: ((((:EVENTS :ILLNESS :OBJECT)
                  (:EVENTS :OUTCOME :OBJECT)))
Checking if explanation accounts for M-SWALE-DEAD-STATE.
... appears relevant.
Checking believability.
Problem found!
  :INSTANCE isa M-NON-NORMATIVE-FILLER-PROBLEM
  :EXPLANATION: M-EXPL1
  :PATH: (:EVENTS :ILLNESS :OBJECT)
  :EXPECTED-VALUE: M-UNHEALTHY-ANIMAL
  :OBSERVED-VALUE: M-SWALE
... explanation is not believable.
Checking if explanation is useful for the purpose PREDICTION.
Is the explanation predictive?
... Explanation is adequate for PREDICTION.
Checking seriousness of problems.
... M-EXPL1 is TWEAKABLE.


Micro Tweaker
-------------
Looking for candidate tweaks in memory for M-PROB3.
```

```
... found M-REPLACE-ACTION-USE-CAUSALS-TWEAK,
M-REPLACE-ACTOR-USE-STEREOTYPES-TWEAK,
M-REPLACE-ACTION-USE-STEREOTYPES-TWEAK.
Trying tweak REPLACE-ACTION-SEARCH-THROUGH-CAUSAL-RULES on
  M-EXPL1.
... tweak failed.
Trying tweak REPLACE-ACTOR-SEARCH-THROUGH-STEREOTYPES on
  M-EXPL1.
... tweak failed.
Trying tweak REPLACE-ACTION-SEARCH-THROUGH-STEREOTYPES on
  M-EXPL1.
Looking for effects to be accounted for.
... found M-DEAD-STATE.
Looking for scripts for M-SWALE that include M-DEAD-STATE.
... no scripts found.
... tweak failed.


Micro XP Retriever
------------------
Searching for XP's.
Looking for retrieval cues in M-PROB3.
... Cue: observed M-SWALE, rather than M-UNHEALTHY-ANIMAL.
... found M-FIXX-XP.
Applying M-FIXX-XP.
... generated M-EXPL4.


Micro-Accepter
--------------
Evaluating M-EXPL2 for the purpose PREDICTION.
The underling XP is
  :MOP isa M-XP
  :EVENTS: ((:OLD-AGE M-OLD-AGE-STATE) (:OUTCOME M-DEAD-STATE))
  :CAUSALS: ((:OLD-AGE => :OUTCOME))
  :CONSTRAINTS: (((:EVENTS :OLD-AGE :OBJECT)
                  (:EVENTS :OUTCOME :OBJECT)))
Checking if explanation accounts for M-SWALE-DEAD-STATE.
... appears relevant.
Checking believability.
Problem found!
  :INSTANCE isa M-NON-NORMATIVE-FILLER-PROBLEM
  :EXPLANATION: M-EXPL2
  :PATH: (:EVENTS :OLD-AGE :OBJECT)
  :EXPECTED-VALUE: M-OLD-ANIMAL
  :OBSERVED-VALUE: M-SWALE
... explanation is not believable.
Checking if explanation is useful for the purpose PREDICTION.
Is the explanation predictive?
... Explanation is adequate for PREDICTION.
Checking seriousness of problems.
```

```
... M-EXPL2 is TWEAKABLE.
```

Micro Tweaker

```
Looking for candidate tweaks in memory for M-PROB5.
... found M-REPLACE-ACTION-USE-CAUSALS-TWEAK,
M-REPLACE-ACTOR-USE-STEREOTYPES-TWEAK,
M-REPLACE-ACTION-USE-STEREOTYPES-TWEAK.
Trying tweak REPLACE-ACTION-SEARCH-THROUGH-CAUSAL-RULES on
  M-EXPL2.
... tweak failed.
Trying tweak REPLACE-ACTOR-SEARCH-THROUGH-STEREOTYPES on
  M-EXPL2.
... tweak failed.
Trying tweak REPLACE-ACTION-SEARCH-THROUGH-STEREOTYPES on
  M-EXPL2.
Looking for effects to be accounted for.
... found M-DEAD-STATE.
Looking for scripts for M-SWALE that include M-DEAD-STATE.
... no scripts found.
... tweak failed.
```

Micro XP Retriever

```
Searching for XP's.
Looking for retrieval cues in M-PROB5.
... Cue: observed M-SWALE, rather than M-OLD-ANIMAL.
... no XP's found.
```

Micro-Accepter

```
Evaluating M-EXPL4 for the purpose PREDICTION.
The underling XP is
  :MOP isa M-XP
  :OBSERVED: M-HEALTHY-ANIMAL
  :EXPECTED: M-UNHEALTHY-ANIMAL
  :EVENTS: ((:JOG M-JOG-EVENT) (:RUN M-RUN-EVENT)
            (:EXERT M-EXERT-EVENT) (:DEFECT M-HEART-DEFECT-STATE)
            (:OUTCOME M-DEAD-STATE))
  :CAUSALS: ((:JOG => :RUN) (:RUN => :EXERT)
            (:DEFECT :EXERT => :OUTCOME))
  :CONSTRAINTS: (((:EVENTS :JOG :ACTOR) (:EVENTS :RUN :ACTOR)
                  (:EVENTS :EXERT :ACTOR)
                  (:EVENTS :DEFECT :OWNER)
                  (:EVENTS :OUTCOME :OBJECT)))
Checking if explanation accounts for M-SWALE-DEAD-STATE.
... appears relevant.
Checking believability.
```

```
Problem found!
  :INSTANCE isa M-NON-NORMATIVE-FILLER-PROBLEM
  :EXPLANATION: M-EXPL4
  :PATH: (:EVENTS :JOG :ACTOR)
  :EXPECTED-VALUE: M-HUMAN
  :OBSERVED-VALUE: M-SWALE
... explanation is not believable.
Checking if explanation is useful for the purpose PREDICTION.
Is the explanation predictive?
Problem found!
  :INSTANCE isa M-NON-KNOWABLE-ANTECEDENT-PROBLEM
  :EXPLANATION: M-EXPL4
  :FACT: M-HEART-DEFECT-STATE
  :EVENT-LABEL: :DEFECT
... Explanation is not adequate for PREDICTION.
Checking seriousness of problems.
... M-EXPL4 is TWEAKABLE.


Micro Tweaker
-------------
Looking for candidate tweaks in memory for M-PROB6.
... found M-REPLACE-ACTION-USE-CAUSALS-TWEAK,
M-REPLACE-ACTOR-USE-STEREOTYPES-TWEAK,
M-REPLACE-ACTION-USE-STEREOTYPES-TWEAK.
Trying tweak REPLACE-ACTION-SEARCH-THROUGH-CAUSAL-RULES on
  M-EXPL4.
... tweak failed.
Trying tweak REPLACE-ACTOR-SEARCH-THROUGH-STEREOTYPES on
  M-EXPL4.
... tweak failed.
Trying tweak REPLACE-ACTION-SEARCH-THROUGH-STEREOTYPES on
  M-EXPL4.
Looking for effects to be accounted for.
... found M-RUN-EVENT.
Looking for scripts for M-SWALE that include M-RUN-EVENT.
... found M-HORSERACE-EVENT.
Creating a new XP M-XP8 with M-HORSERACE-EVENT instead of
  M-JOG-EVENT
Applying M-XP8.
... generated M-EXPL9.
... tweak generated M-EXPL9.
Looking for candidate tweaks in memory for M-PROB7.
... no tweaks found.


Micro XP Retriever
------------------
Searching for XP's.
Looking for retrieval cues in M-PROB6.
... Cue: observed M-SWALE, rather than M-HUMAN.
```

```
Looking for retrieval cues in M-PROB7.
... no XP's found.


Micro-Accepter
--------------
Evaluating M-EXPL9 for the purpose PREDICTION.
The underling XP is
  :MOP isa M-XP
  :EVENTS: ((:JOG M-HORSERACE-EVENT) (:RUN M-RUN-EVENT)
            (:EXERT M-EXERT-EVENT) (:DEFECT M-HEART-DEFECT-STATE)
            (:OUTCOME M-DEAD-STATE))
  :CAUSALS: ((:JOG => :RUN) (:RUN => :EXERT)
            (:DEFECT :EXERT => :OUTCOME))
  :OBSERVED: M-HEALTHY-ANIMAL
  :EXPECTED: M-UNHEALTHY-ANIMAL
Checking if explanation accounts for M-SWALE-DEAD-STATE.
... appears relevant.
Checking believability.
... no problems.
Checking if explanation is useful for the purpose PREDICTION.
Is the explanation predictive?
Problem found!
  :INSTANCE isa M-NON-KNOWABLE-ANTECEDENT-PROBLEM
  :EXPLANATION: M-EXPL9
  :FACT: M-HEART-DEFECT-STATE
  :EVENT-LABEL: :DEFECT
... Explanation is not adequate for PREDICTION.
Checking seriousness of problems.
... M-EXPL9 is ACCEPTABLE.
M-EXPL9
```

References

Alterman, R. (1986). An adaptive planner. In *Proceedings of AAAI-86* (pp. 65-69), American Association for Artificial Intelligence, San Mateo, CA: Morgan Kaufmann.

Ashley, K. D. (1988) *Modelling legal argument: Reasoning with cases and hypotheticals.* Unpublished doctoral dissertation, Department of Computer and Information Science, University of Massachussetts, Amherst.

Bareiss, R. (1989). *Exemplar-Based Knowledge Acquisition.* San Diego, CA: Academic Press.

Barletta, R., & Mark, W. (1988). Explanation-based indexing of cases. In J. Kolodner (Ed.), *Proceedings of a Workshop on Case-Based Reasoning,* (pp. 50-60). San Mateo, CA: Morgan Kaufmann.

Barsalou, L. W. (1991). Deriving categories to achieve goals. In G. H. Bower (Eds.), *The Psychology of Learning and Motivation: Advances in Research and Theory* (Vol. 27). New York: Academic Press.

Birnbaum, L. A. (1986). *Integrated processing in planning and understanding.* Unpublished doctoral dissertation, Yale University.

Carbonell, J. G. (1979) *Subjective understanding: Computer models of belief systems.* Unpublished doctoral dissertation, Yale University.

Carbonell, J. G. (1983). Learning by analogy: Formulating and generalizing plans from past experience. In R. S. Michalski, J. G. Carbonell, & T. M. Mitchell (Eds.), *Machine Learning: An Artificial Intelligence Approach.* San Mateo, CA: Morgan Kaufmann.

Carbonell, J. G. (1986). Derivational analogy: A theory of reconstructive problem solving and expertise acquisition. In R. S. Michalski, J. G. Carbonell, & T. M. Mitchell (Eds.), *Machine Learning: An Artificial Intelligence Approach* (Vol. 2). San Mateo, CA: Morgan Kaufmann.

Charniak, E. (1981). A commonsense representation for problem solving and language comprehension information. *Artificial Intelligence, 16,* 225-255.

Charniak, E. (1986). A neat theory of marker passing. In *Proceedings of AAAI-86* (pp. 584-588), American Association for Artificial Intelligence. San Mateo, CA: Morgan Kaufmann.

Cheeseman, P., Kelly, J., Self, M., Stutz, J., Taylor, W., & Freeman, D. (1988). AutoClass: A Bayesian classification system. In *Proceedings of the Fifth International Workshop on Machine Learning.* San Mateo, CA: Morgan Kaufman.

Colby, K. M. (1973). The structure of belief systems. In R. C. Schank & K. M. Colby (Eds.), *Computer Models of Thought and Language* (pp. 251-286). San Francisco: W.H. Freeman and Company.

Cullingford, R. (1978). *Script application: Computer understanding of newspaper stories.* Unpublished doctoral dissertation, Yale University.

Dehn, N. J. (1989). *The role of reconstructive and dynamic memory.* Unpublished doctoral dissertation, Yale University.

DeJong, G. F. (1979). *Skimming stories in real time: an experiment in integrated understanding.* Unpublished doctoral dissertation, Yale University.

DeJong, G. F. (1983). An approach to learning from observation. In *Proceedings of the International Machine Learning Workshop,* (pp. 171-176). San Mateo, CA: Morgan Kaufmann.

DeJong, G. F., & Mooney, R. (1986). Explanation-Based Learning: An alternative view. *Machine Learning, 1*(1), 145-176.

Dreyfuss, H.L. (1972). *What Computers Can't Do: A Critique of Artificial Reason.* New York: Harper & Row.

Domeshek, E. A. (1992) *Do the right thing: A component theory for indexing stories as social advice.* Unpublished doctoral dissertation, Yale University.

Feigenbaum, E. A. (1963). The simulation of verbal learning behavior. In E.A. Feigenbaum and J. Feldman (Eds.), *Computers and Thought,* (pp. 297–309). New York: McGraw-Hill.

Fikes, R. E., Nilsson, N. (1971). Strips: A new approach to the application of theorem proving to problem solving. *Artificial Intelligence 2,* 189-208.

Fisher, D. H. (1987). Knowledge acquisition via incremental conceptual clustering. *Machine Learning, 2,* 139-172.

Goel, A., & Chandra, B. (1989). Use of device models in adaptation of design cases. In K. Hammond (Ed.), *Proceedings of a Workshop on Case-Based Reasoning.* San Mateo, CA: Morgan Kaufmann.

Granger, R. (1980) *Adaptive understanding: Correcting erroneous inferences.* Unpublished doctoral dissertation, Yale University.

Graesser, A.C., Person, N., & Huber, J. (1992). Mechanisms that generate questions. In T.W. Lauer, E. Peacock, & A.C. Graesser (Eds.), *Questions and Information Systems,* (pp. 167-187). Hillsdale, NJ: Lawrence Erlbaum Associates.

Hammond, K. J. (1986). *Case-based planning: An integrated theory of planning, learning and memory.* Unpublished doctoral dissertation, Yale University.

Hammond, K. J. (1988). Opportunistic memory: Storing and recalling suspended goals. In *Proceedings of a Workshop on Case-Based Reasoning,* (pp. 154-168). San Mateo, CA: Morgan Kaufmann.

Hammond, K. J. (1989). *Case-Based Planning: Viewing Planning as a Memory Task.* Boston, MA: Academic Press.

Hillis, W. D. (1985). *The Connection Machine.* Cambridge, MA: MIT Press.

Hinrichs, T. (1988). Towards an architecture for open world problem solving. In J. Kolodner (Ed.), *Proceedings of a Workshop on Case-Based Reasoning.* San Mateo, CA: Morgan Kaufmann.

Hobbs, J. R., Stickel, M., Appelt, D., & Martin, P. (1990). *Interpretation as abduction,* Technical Note No. 499. Stanford, CA: SRI International.

Hunter, L. E. (1989). *Knowledge acquisition planning: Gaining expertise through experience.* Unpublished doctoral dissertation, Yale University.

Hunter, L. E. (1990). Planning to learn. In *Proceedings of the Twelfth Annual Conference of the Cognitive Science Society,* (pp. 261-268). Hillsdale, NJ: Lawrence Erlbaum Associates

Jacobs, P. S. (1987). Knowledge-intensive natural language generation. *Artificial Intelligence 33,* 325-378.

Jones, E. K. (1992). *The Flexible Use of Abstract Knowledge in Planning.* Unpublished doctoral dissertation, Yale University.

Kahneman, D., Slovic, P., & Tversky, A. (1982). *Judgement Under Uncertainty: Heuristics And Biases.* Cambridge, England: Cambridge University Press.

Kass, A. (1986). Modifying explanations to understand stories. In *Proceedings of the Eighth Annual Conference of the Cognitive Science Society.* Hillsdale, NJ: Lawrence Erlbaum Associates.

Kass, A. (1990a). Adaptation-based explanation: Extending script/frame theory to handle novel input. In *Proceedings of the Eleventh International Joint Conference on Artificial Intelligence,* (pp. 143-147). San Mateo, CA: Morgan Kaufmann.

Kass, A. M. (1990b) *Developing creative hypotheses by adapting explanations.* Unpublished doctoral dissertation, Yale University.

Kass, A., & Leake, D. B. (1987). *Types of explanations.* Technical Report No. 523. Yale University Department of Computer Science.

Kass, A., Leake, D. B., & Owens, C. C. (1986). SWALE: A program that explains. In *Explanation Patterns: Understanding Mechanically and Creatively* (pp. 232-254). Hillsdale, NJ: Lawrence Erlbaum Associates.

Kautz, H., & Allen, J. (1986). Generalized plan recognition. In *Proceedings of AAAI-86* (pp. 32-37), American Association for Artificial Intelligence. San Mateo, CA: Morgan Kaufmann.

Keller, R. (1988a). Defining operationality for explanation-based learning. *Artificial Intelligence, 35*(2), 227-241.

Keller, R. (1988b). Operationality and generality in explanation-based learning: separate dimensions or opposite endpoints? In *Proceedings of the 1988 AAAI Spring Symposium on Explanation-based Learning.* San Mateo, CA: Morgan Kaufmann.

Kolodner, J.L. (1984). *Retrieval and Organizational Strategies in Conceptual Memory.* Hillsdale, NJ: Lawrence Erlbaum Associates.

Kolodner, J. L. (1987). Extending problem solver capabilities through case-based inference. In *Proceedings of the Fourth International Workshop on Machine Learning,* (pp. 167-178). San Mateo, CA: Morgan Kaufmann.

Kolodner, J. L. (1989). Selecting the best case for a case-based reasoner. In *Proceedings of the Eleventh Annual Conference of the Cognitive Science Society,* (pp. 155–162). Hillsdale, NJ: Lawrence Erlbaum Associates.

Kolodner, J. L., Simpson, R. L., & Sycra-Cyranski, K. (1985). A process model of case-based reasoning in problem-solving. In *Proceedings of the Ninth International Joint Conference on Artificial Intelligence.* Los Altos, CA: Morgan Kaufman.

Kolodner, J. L., & Thau, R. (1988). *Design and implementation of a case memory.* (Technical Report No. GIT-ICS-88/34). Atlanta, GA: Georgia Institute of Technology.

Konolige, K. (1990). A general theory of abduction. In *Proceedings of the AAAI Spring Symposium on Automated Abduction*. San Mateo, CA: Morgan Kaufmann.

Koton, P. (1988). Reasoning about evidence in causal explanations. In J. Kolodner (Ed.), *Proceedings of a Workshop on Case-Based Reasoning* (pp. 260-270). San Mateo, CA: Morgan Kaufmann.

Laird, J., Rosenbloom P. S., and Newell, A. (1986). *Universal Subgoaling and Chunking: The Automatic Generation and Learning of Goal Hierarchies*. Hingham, MA: Kluwer Academic Publishers.

Leake, D. B. (1989). Anomaly detection strategies for schema-based story understanding. In *Proceedings of the Eleventh Annual Conference of the Cognitive Science Society*, (pp. 490-497). Hillsdale, NJ: Lawrence Erlbaum Associates.

Leake, D. B. (1990) *Evaluating explanations*. Unpublished doctoral dissertation, Yale University.

Leake, D. B. (1991). An indexing vocabulary for case-based explanation. In *Proceedings of the Ninth National Conference on Artificial Intelligence*, (pp. 10-15). San Mateo, CA: Morgan Kaufmann.

Leake, D. B. (1992). *Evaluating Explanations: A Content Theory*. Hillsdale, NJ: Lawrence Erlbaum Associates.

Leake, D. B., & Owens, C. C. (1986). Organizing memory for explanation. In *Proceedings of the Eighth Annual Conference of the Cognitive Science Society*. Hillsdale, NJ: Lawrence Erlbaum Associates.

Leake, D. B., & Ram, A. (1993). *Goal-driven learning: Fundamental issues and symposium report* (Technical Report No. 85). Bloomington, IN: Cognitive Science Program, Indiana University.

Lebowitz, M. (1980) *Generalization and memory in an integrated understanding system*. Unpublished doctoral dissertation, Yale University.

Lenat, D. B. (1980) A.M.: An artificial intelligence approach to discovery in mathematics as heuristic search. In R. Davis & D. B. Leanat, (Eds.), *Knowledge-based Systems in Artificial Intelligence*. New York: McGraw-Hill.

Lenat, D. B., & Brown, J. S. (1984). Why AM and EURISKO appear to work. *Artificial Intelligence, 23*(3) 269–294.

Lenat, D. B., & Guha, R. V. (1990). *Building Large Knowledge-Based Systems: Representation and Inference in the Cyc Project.* Reading, MA: Addison-Wesley.

Lytinen, S. (1984) *The organization of knowledge in a multi-lingual, integrated parser.* Unpublished doctoral disseration, Yale University.

Mark, W. (1989). Case-based reasoning for autoclave management. In *Proceedings of the Second Workshop on Case-Based Reasoning.* San Mateo, CA: Morgan Kaufmann.

Martin, C. E. (1990) *Direct memory access parsing.* Unpublished doctoral dissertation: Yale University.

McDermott, D. V., & Sussman, G. J. (1973). *The CONNIVER reference manual* (AI Memo No. 259). Cambridge, MA: MIT AI Laboratory.

Minsky, M. (1961). Steps toward artificial intelligence. *Proceedings of the Institute of Radio Engineers, 49,* 8-30.

Minsky, M. (1975). A framework for representing knowledge. In P. Winston (Eds.), *The Psychology of Computer Vision* (pp. 211-277). New York: McGraw-Hill.

Mitchell, T. M., Keller, R. M., & Kedar-Cabelli, S. T. (1986). Explanation-based generalization: A unifying view. *Machine Learning, 1*(1), 47-80.

Mooney, R. (1990). *A General Explanation-based Learning Mechanism and its Application to Narrative Understanding.* San Mateo, CA: Morgan Kaufmann.

Mooney, R., & DeJong, G. (1985). Learning schemata for natural language processing. In *Proceedings of the Ninth International Joint Conference on Artificial Intelligence,* (pp. 681-687). San Mateo, CA: Morgan Kaufmann.

Moore, J., &. Newell, A. (1973). How can Merlin understand? In *Knowledge and Cognition.* Hillsdale, NJ: Lawrence Erlbaum Associates.

Morris, S., & O'Rorke, P. (1990). An approach to theory revision using abduction. In *Proceedings of the AAAI Spring Symposium on Automated Abduction.* San Mateo, CA: Morgan Kaufmann.

Mostow, D. J. (1983). Machine transformation of advice into a heuristic search procedure. In R. S. Michalski, J. G. Carbonell, & T. M. Mitchell (Eds.), *Machine Learning: An Artificial Intelligence Approach.* Cambridge, MA: Tioga Publishing Company.

Newell, A., &. Simon, H.A. (1963). GPS, a program that simulates human thought. In E.A. Feigenbaum and J. Feldman (Eds.),

Computers and Thought (pp. 279–293). New York:McGraw-Hill.

Ng, E., & Bereiter, C. (1991). Three levels of goal orientation in learning. *The Journal of the Learning Sciences, 1*(3), 243-271.

Ng, H., & Mooney, R. (1990). On the role of coherence in abductive explanation. In *Proceedings of the Eighth National Conference on Artificial Intelligence,* (pp. 337-342). San Mateo, CA: Morgan Kaufmann.

Owens, C. C. (1988). *Domain-independent prototype cases for planning. Proceedings of a Workshop on Case-Based Reasoning.* San Mateo, CA: Morgan Kaufmann.

Owens, C. C. (1989). Integrating feature extraction and memory search. In *Proceedings of the Eleventh Annual Conference of the Cognitive Science Society.* Hillsdale, NJ: Lawrence Erlbaum Associates

Owens, C. C. (1990) *Indexing and retrieving abstract planning knowledge.* Unpublished doctoral dissertation: Yale University.

Owens, C. C. (1993). Integrating feature extraction and memory search. *Machine Learning, 10,* 311-339.

Pearl, J. (1988). *Probabilistic Reasoning In Intelligent Systems: Networks of Plausible Inference.* San Mateo, CA: Morgan Kaufmann.

Quinlan, J. R. (1983). Induction of decision trees. *Machine Learning, 1*(1).

Ram, A. (1984). *Modelling characters and their decisions: A theory of compliance decisions* (Technical Report T-145). Urbana, IL: University of Illinois at Urbana-Champaign.

Ram, A. (1989). *Question-driven understanding: An integrated theory of story understanding, memory and learning.* Unpublished doctoral dissertation: Yale University.

Ram, A. (1990a). Decision models: A theory of volitional explanation. In *Proceedings of the Twelfth Annual Conference of the Cognitive Science Society.* (pp. 198--205). Hillsdale, NJ: Lawrence Erlbaum Associates.

Ram, A. (1990b). Knowledge goals: A theory of interestingness. In *Proceedings of the Twelfth Annual Conference of the Cognitive Science Society.* (pp. 206-214). Hillsdale, NJ: Lawrence Erlbaum Associates.

Ram, A. (1991). A theory of questions and question asking. *The Journal of the Learning Sciences, 1*(3), 273-318.

Ram, A. (1992). Natural language understanding for information-filtering systems. *Communications of the ACM, 35,* 80-81.

Ram, A. (1993). Indexing, elaboration and refinement: Incremental learning of explanatory cases. *Machine Learning, 10,* 201-248.

Ram, A., & Cox, M. T. (1993). Introspective reasoning using meta-explanations for multistrategy learning. In R. S. Michalski & G. Tecuci (Eds.), *Machine Learning: A Multistrategy Approach, Volume IV.* San Mateo, CA: Morgan Kaufmann.

Ram, A., & Hunter, L. (1992). The use of explicit goals for knowledge to guide inference and learning. *Applied Intelligence, 2,* 47-73.

Ram, A., & Leake, D. (1991). Evaluation of explanatory hypotheses. In *Proceedings of the Thirteenth Annual Conference of the Cognitive Science Society.* (pp. 867-871). Hillsdale, NJ: Lawrence Erlbaum Associates.

Ram, A., & Santamaria, J. C. (1993b). Learning continuous perception-action models through experience. In W. Shen (Ed.), *Proceedings of the AAAI Workshop on Learning Action Models.* San Mateo, CA: Morgan Kaufmann.

Restak, R. M. (1979). *The Brain: The Last Frontier.* Garden City, NY: Doubleday.

Rieger, C. (1975). Conceptual memory and inference. In R. C. Schank (Ed.), *Conceptual Information Processing.* Amsterdam: North-Holland/Elsevier.

Rissland, E., & Skalak, D. (1989). Combining case-based and rule-based reasoning: A heuristic approach. In *Proceedings of IJCAI-89.* San Mateo, CA: Morgan Kaufmann.

Scardamalia, M., & Bereiter, C. (1991). Higher levels of agency for children in knowledge building: A challenge for the design of new knowledge media. *The Journal of the Learning Sciences, 1(1),* 37-68.

Schank, R. C. (1972). Conceptual dependency: A theory of natural language understanding. *Cognitive Psychology, 3(4),* 552-631.

Schank, R. C. (1975). *Conceptual Information Processing.* Amsterdam: North-Holland/Elsevier.

Schank, R. C. (1982). *Dynamic Memory: A Theory of Learning in Computers and People.* Cambridge, England: Cambridge University Press.

Schank, R. C. (1986). *Explanation Patterns: Understanding Mechanically and Creatively.* Hillsdale, NJ: Lawrence Erlbaum.

Schank, R. C., & Abelson, R. (1977). *Scripts, Plans, Goals and Understanding.* Hillsdale, NJ: Lawrence Erlbaum Associates.

Schank, R. C., Collins, G. C., & Hunter, L. E. (1986). Transcending inductive category formation in learning. *Behavioral and Brain Sciences, 9*, 639-686.

Schank, R. C., & Leake, D. B. (1986). Computer understanding and creativity. *Information Processing 86.* Amsterdam: North-Holland, Elsevier Science Publishers B. V.

Schank, R. C., & Leake, D. B. (1989). Creativity and learning in a case-based explainer. *Artificial Intelligence, 40*, 353-385.

Schank, R. C. & Ram, A. (1988). Question-driving parsing: A new approach to natural language understanding. *Journal of Japanese Society for Artificial Intelligence, 3*(3), 260–270.

Schank, R. C., & Riesbeck, C. (1981). *Inside Computer Understanding: Five Programs with Miniatures.* Hillsdale, NJ: Lawrence Erlbaum Associates.

Segre, A. (1988). *Machine Learning of Robot Assembly Plans.* Boston: Kluwer Academic Publishers.

Seifert, C. M. (1988). A retrieval model for case-based memory. In E. Rissland & J. King (Ed.), *Proceedings of a Case-Based Reasoning Workshop,* (pp. 120-125). San Mateo, CA: Morgan Kaufmann.

Seifert, C. M. (1987). Planning principles specific to mutual goals. In *The Ninth Annual Conference of the Cognitive Science Society.* (pp. 990-995). Hillsdale, NJ: Lawrence Erlbaum Associates

Shortliffe, E. H., Axline, S. G., Buchanan, B. G., Merigan, T. C., & Cohen, N. S. (1973). An artificial intelligence program to advise physicians regarding antimicobial therapy. *Computers and Biomedical Research, 6*, 544-560.

Simmons, R. G. (1988) *Combining Associational and Causal Reasoning to Solve Interpretation and Planning Problems.* Unpublished doctoral dissertation: Massachusetts Institute of Technology.

Simoudis, E. (1990). CASCADE. In *Proceedings of the Third Workshop on Case-Based Reasoning.* San Mateo, CA: Morgan Kaufmann.

Sowa, J. F. (1984). *Conceptual Structures: Information Processing in Mind and Machines.* Reading, MA, Addison-Wesley.

Stanfill, C., & Kahle, B. (1986). Parallel free-text search on the connection machine system. *Communications of the ACM, 29*(12), 1213-1228.

Stanfill, C., & Waltz, D. (1986). Toward memory-based reasoning. *Communications of the ACM, 29*(12), 1213-1228.

Steele, G. L. (1990). *Common Lisp: The Language* (2nd ed.). Bedford, MA: Digital Press.

Stepp, R. E., & Michalski, R. S. (1986). Conceptual clustering: Inventing goal-oriented classifications of structured objects. In R. S. Michalski, J. G. Carbonell, & T. M. Mitchell (Eds.), *Machine Learning* (Vol. 2, pp. 471-498). San Mateo, CA: Morgan Kaufmann.

Stickel, M. E. (1990). A method for abductive reasoning in natural-language interpretation. In *Proceedings Of The AAAI Spring Symposium On Automated Abduction*. San Mateo, CA: Morgan Kaufmann.

Sussman, G. J. (1975). *A Computer Model of Skill Acquisition*, Vol. 1 of *Artificial Intelligence Series*. American New York: Elsevier.

Thagard, P. (1989). Explanatory coherence. *The Behavioral and Brain Sciences, 12*(3), 435-502.

Thagard, P., & Holyoak, K. (1989). Why indexing is the wrong way to think about analog retrieval. In *Proceedings of a workshop on Case-Based Reasoning*. San Mateo, CA: Morgan Kaufmann.

Turing, A. M. (1963). Computing machinery and intelligence, In E. A. Feigenbaum & J. Feldman (Eds.), *Computers and Thought*. New York: McGraw-Hill.

Weizenbaum, J. (1976). *Computer Power and Human Reason: From Judgement to Calculation*. San Francisco: W.H. Freeman.

White, G. M. (1987). Proverbs and cultural models. In *Cultural Models in Language and Thought* (pp. 151-172.). New York, Cambridge University Press.

Wilensky, R. (1978) *Understanding goal-based stories*. Unpublished doctoral dissertation. Yale University.

Wilensky, R. (1981). Meta-planning: Representing and using knowledge about planning in problem solving and natural language understanding. *Cognitive Science, 5*, 197-233.

Wilensky, R. (1983). *Planning and Understanding*. Reading, MA: Addison-Wesley.

Wilensky, R. (1986). Knowledge representation—a critique and a proposal. In J. L. Kolodner & C. K. Riesbeck (Eds.), *Experience, Memory, and Reasoning* (pp. 15-28). Hillsdale, NJ: Lawrence Erlbaum Associates

Winograd, T. (1972). *Understanding Natural Language*. New York: Academic Press.

Wisniewski, E. J., & Medin, D. L. (1991). Harpoons and long sticks: The interaction of theory and similarity in rule induction. In D. Fisher & M. J. Pazzani (Eds.), *Concept Formation: Knowledge and Experience in Unsupervised Learning.* San Mateo, CA: Morgan Kaufmann.

Zukier, H. (1986). The paradigmatic and narrative modes in goal-guided inference. In R. Sorrentino & E. Higgins (Eds.), *Handbook of Motivation and Cognition: Foundations of Social Behavior* (pp. 465-502). Guilford, CT: Guilford Press.

Author Index

Subject Index

as a spectrum 8-14
as explanation 26
People vs. computers 7

viewing schemas 315

XP (See Explanation
  patterns)